PATENT GAMES IN THE GLOBAL SOUTH

In this thought-provoking analysis, the author takes three examples of emerging markets (Brazil, India, and Nigeria) and tells their stories of pharmaceutical patent law-making.

Adopting historiographical and socio-legal approaches, focus is drawn to the role of history, social networks and how relationships between a variety of actors shape the framing of, and subsequently the responses to, national implementation of international patent law. In doing so, the book reveals why the experience of Nigeria – a country active in opposing the inclusion of IP to the WTO framework during the Uruguay Rounds – is so different from that of Brazil and India.

This book makes an original and useful contribution to the further understanding of how both state and non-state actors conceptualise, establish and interpret pharmaceutical patents law, and its domestic implications on medicines access, public health and development. *Patent Games in the Global South* was awarded the 2018 SIEL–Hart Prize in International Economic Law.

Studies in International Trade and Investment Law: Volume 21

Winner of the 2018 SIEL–Hart Prize in International Economic Law.

siel | Society of International Economic Law

Studies in International Trade and Investment Law

Series Editors
Gabrielle Marceau
Krista Nadakavukaren Schefer
Federico Ortino
Gregory Shaffer

This series offers a forum for publication of original and scholarly analyses of emerging and significant issues in international trade and investment law – broadly understood to include the whole of the law of the WTO, the public international law of foreign investment, the law of the EU common commercial policy and other regional trade regimes, and any legal or regulatory topic that interacts with global trade and foreign investment. The aim of the series is to produce works which will be readily accessible to trade and investment law scholars and practitioners alike.

Recent titles in this series:

The Right to Development and International Economic Law: Legal and Moral Dimensions
Isabella Bunn

Free Trade and Cultural Diversity in International Law
Jingxia Shi

Tied Aid and Development Aid Policies in the Framework of EU and WTO Law: The Imperative for Change
Annamaria La Chimia

Balancing Human Rights, Environmental Protection and International Trade: Lessons from the EU Experience
Emily Reid

Public Procurement and Labour Rights: Towards Coherence in International Instruments of Procurement Regulation
Maria Anna Corvaglia

The China-Australia Free Trade Agreement: A 21st-Century Model
Edited by Colin Picker, Heng Wang and Weihuan Zhou

Regional Economic Integration and Dispute Settlement in East Asia: The Evolving Legal Framework
Anna G Tevini

The EU, World Trade Law and the Right to Food: Rethinking Free Trade Agreements with Developing Countries
Giovanni Gruni

Patent Games in the Global South: Pharmaceutical Patent Law Making in Brazil, India and Nigeria
Amaka Vanni

Patent Games in the Global South

Pharmaceutical Patent Law Making in Brazil, India and Nigeria

Amaka Vanni

•HART•

OXFORD • LONDON • NEW YORK • NEW DELHI • SYDNEY

HART PUBLISHING

Bloomsbury Publishing Plc

Kemp House, Chawley Park, Cumnor Hill, Oxford, OX2 9PH, UK

1385 Broadway, New York, NY 10018, USA

HART PUBLISHING, the Hart/Stag logo, BLOOMSBURY and the Diana logo are trademarks of Bloomsbury Publishing Plc

First published in Great Britain 2019

A catalogue record for this book is available from the British Library.

Library of Congress Cataloging-in-Publication data

Names: Vanni, Amaka, author.

Title: Patent games in the global south : pharmaceutical patent law making in Brazil, India and Nigeria / Amaka Vanni.

Description: Oxford ; New York : Hart, 2019. | Series: Studies in international trade and investment law; volume 21 | Based on author's thesis (doctoral - University of Warwick, 2016) issued under title: Narratives and counter-narratives in pharmaceutical patent law making : experiences from 3 developing countries. | Includes bibliographical references and index.

Identifiers: LCCN 2019039846 (print) | LCCN 2019039847 (ebook) | ISBN 9781509927395 (hardback) | ISBN 9781509927418 (Epub)

Subjects: LCSH: Drugs—Brazil—Patents. | Drugs—Nigeria—Patents. | Drugs—India—Patents.

Classification: LCC K1519.D78 V36 2019 (print) | LCC K1519.D78 (ebook) | DDC 346.04/86—dc23

LC record available at https://lccn.loc.gov/2019039846

LC ebook record available at https://lccn.loc.gov/2019039847

ISBN: HB: 978-1-50992-739-5
ePDF: 978-1-50992-740-1
ePub: 978-1-50992-741-8

Typeset by Compuscript Ltd, Shannon
Printed and bound in Great Britain by CPI Group (UK) Ltd, Croydon CR0 4YY

FSC www.fsc.org MIX Paper from responsible sources FSC® C013604

To find out more about our authors and books visit www.hartpublishing.co.uk. Here you will find extracts, author information, details of forthcoming events and the option to sign up for our newsletters.

For my mum, Mrs Paula Chinwe Okafor

Acknowledgements

Most earnest thanks to God for making this possible in every way.

This project would not have been possible without the guidance and support of many people. I would like to thank Professor Fiona Smith for her guidance and support during my doctoral thesis that culminated in this book.

For the various organisations and individuals that supported me during my doctoral fieldwork in Brazil, India and Nigeria. In these countries, I spoke and interacted with many people – from politicians and government officials to pharmaceutical company executives and non-governmental organisation representatives. Without their kindness in sharing some time from their busy schedules, this research would not have been possible. In Brazil, a special thanks goes to the Brazilian Interdisciplinary AIDS Association (ABIA) and the Working Group on Intellectual Property (GTPI/REBRIP). GTPI's institutional support was essential in carrying out my field research in Brazil by providing insight into Brazilian civil society activism that no textbook could provide. Specifically, I would like to thank Pedro Villardi, Marcela Viera and Felipe Carvalho for taking me under their wings and introducing me to their contacts both in Rio and Brasilia.

My time in India and Nigeria were equally pleasant and memorable. In both countries I was fortunate to be able to count on the support of various people and institutions. In India, I have to thank the Centre for Study of Law and Governance (CSLG) at Jawaharlal Nehru University, New Delhi. I want to give special mention to my host supervisors Professor Amit Prakash and Dr Praktisha Braxi. I also want to thank Leena Menghaney at MSF in Delhi and KM Gopakumar at Third World Network in Delhi for introducing me to their contacts and giving access to valuable documents. I also spent many afternoons at the Human Rights Law Network (HRLN) in Delhi going through archive materials and legal documents on access to medicines. For this I say a big thank you to Colins Gonsalves and everyone at HRLN for this valuable access. Many thanks also to my friends in Delhi – Latika Vashist, Amit Bindal and Nishi Kohli and her wonderful family. In Nigeria, I would like to thank the Ministry of Trade and Investment for providing institutional support and office space to carry out my research in Nigeria. I want to especially thank Mrs Uju Hassan-Baba and the Director of Trade, Dr Felix Asikpata, for their guidance and support against bureaucracies.

Many institutions provided financial support and space for this work. The School of Law at the University of Warwick partially funded my fieldwork, thereby reducing the financial burden of conducting a three-country field research. My thanks also to the Institute for Global Law and Policy (IGLP) at Harvard Law School, University of Milan (Italy), the Centre for Socio-Legal

Studies (CSLS) at University of Oxford, and the Society for Latin American Studies for the postgraduate travel grant to conduct my fieldwork in Brazil.

I am grateful to all the staff and my colleagues at the School of Law at the University of Warwick for their support and assistance. I would like to thank Jayan Nayar, George Meszros, Sharifa Sekalala, Andrew Williams, Celine Tan and Upendra Baxi for feedback and helpful advice at different stages of this research. Many thanks to Professor David Nelken (King's College London), Octavio Ferraz (King's College London), Professor Adebambo Adewope SAN (Nigerian Institute of Legal Research at the Supreme Court of Nigeria), Professor Uzoamaka Emilia Anagbogu-Ezenwa (Centre for International Legal Studies, Austria), Swaraj Barowoah (Spicy IP), Barrister Booyamen Lawal, and May Ann Rosales for contributing to this research in one way or another.

Finally, there is little I can say which would be sufficient to thank my family and friends who have supported me in this. I do not think there is anything I can do to reward them for years of demand, both financial and otherwise. To my parents and my siblings – thank you. To my ever-supportive partner and my darling son – thank you for bearing with me and for being understanding.

Table of Contents

List of Abbreviations

A2M	Access to Medicines
ABIA	*Associação Brasileira Interdisciplinar de AIDS*
ABIFINA	*Associação Brasileira das Indústrias de Química Fina, Biotecnologia e Suas Especialidades*
ACTN	Advisory Committee for Trade Negotiations
AIDS	Acquired Immune Deficiency Syndrome
AMTC	Affordable Medicines and Treatment Campaign
APIs	Active pharmaceutical ingredients
ASUU	Academic Staff Union of Universities
ARV	Anti-retroviral
ANVISA	*Agência Nacional de Vigilância Sanitária*
AZT	Azidothymidine
BRICS	Brazil, Russia, India, China and South Africa
CEME	*Central de Medicamentos*
CL	Compulsory licence
CLS	Critical Legal Studies
CLT	Critical Legal Theory
CPTPP	Comprehensive and Progressive Agreement for Trans-Pacific Partnership
DCs	Developing countries
DFID	Department for International Development
DNP+	Delhi Network of Positive People
DPCO	Drugs Control of Prices Order
DSP	Dispute settlement procedures
ECOWAS	Economic Community of West African States

EDL	Essential drug list
EFV	Efavirenz
EU	European Union
FDI	Foreign direct investment
FMOH	Federal Ministry of Health (Nigeria)
FTC	Emtricitabine
FYP	Five-Year Plan
GAPA	*Grupo de Apoio à Prevenção à AIDS*
GATTS	General Agreement on Tariffs and Trade
GDP	Gross domestic product
GIPI	Inter-ministerial Group on Intellectual Property
GTPI/REBRIP	Working Group of Intellectual Property of the Brazilian Network for the Integration of Peoples
HIV	Human immunodeficiency virus
IDMA	Indian Drug Manufacturers' Association
IMF	International Monetary Fund
INPI	*Instituto Nacional da Propriedade Industrial*
INR	Indian rupees
IP	Intellectual property
IPA	Indian Patent Act 1972
IPAA	Indian Patent (Amendment) Act
IPAB	Intellectual Property Appellate Board
IPC	Intellectual Property Committee
IPLB	Industrial Property Law of Brazil
IPR	Intellectual property rights
ISI	Import substitution industrialisation
LDCs	Least developed countries
LGBT	Lesbian, gay, bisexual and transgender
MFN	Most favoured nation

MNC	Multi-national companies
MSF	*Médecins Sans Frontières*
M&As	Mergers and acquisitions
NACA	National Agency for the Control of AIDS
NAP	*Programa Nacional de Doenças Sexualmente Transmissíveis e AIDS*
NAFDAC	National Agency for Food, Drugs, Administration and Control
NAIL	New Approaches to International Law
NANS	National Association of Nigerian Students
NCE	New chemical entity
NDP	National drug policy
NDLEA	National Drug Law Enforcement Agency
NGOs	Non-governmental organisations
NIEO	New international economic order
NME	New medical entity
NOTAP	National Office for Technology Acquisition and Promotion
NPPA	National Pharmaceutical Pricing Authority
NWGPL	National Working Group on Patent Laws
OECD	Organisation for Economic Co-operation and Development
OI	Opportunistic infections
OPPI	Organisation of Pharmaceutical Producers in India
PCT	Patent Cooperation Treaty
PDA	Patent and Design Act
PhRMA	Pharmaceutical Research and Manufacturers of America
PLWHA	People living with HIV/AIDS
PMG-MAN	Pharmaceutical Manufacturers Group of Manufacturers Association of Nigeria
PPP	Public–private partnership
PSDB	*Partido da Social Democracia Brasileira*

RENAME	*Relação Nacional de Medicamentos Essenciais*
R&D	Research and development
SAP	Structural adjustment program
SPLT	Substantive Patent Law Treaty
SUS	*Sistema Unico de Saude*
TB	Tuberculosis
TDF	Tenofivir disoproxil fumarate
TRIPS	Agreement on Trade-Related Aspects of Intellectual Property Rights
TWAIL	Third World Approaches to International Law
TWN	Third World Network
UK	United Kingdom
UNAIDS	Joint United Nations Programme on HIV/AIDS
UNGA	United Nations General Assembly
UNDP	United Nations Development Programme
UNCTAD	United Nations Conference on Trade and Development*
UNHRC	United Nations Human Rights Commission
US	United States
USTR	US Trade Representative
VL	Voluntary licence
WAHO	West African Health Organization
WHO	World Health Organization
WIPO	World Intellectual Property Organization
WTO	World Trade Organization

1

General Overview

I. INTRODUCTION

THIS BOOK CHRONICLES the complex relationship of pharmaceutical patents and access to medicines within the limiting space of the World Trade Organization (WTO) Agreement on Trade-Related Aspects of Intellectual Property Rights (TRIPS Agreement).[1] It does so by suggesting that to obtain a fuller understanding of this complex relationship, one should factor in three phenomena. First, the history and origins of patent law, bearing in mind various theories and understanding of patents that have emerged and developed through specific historical conjunctures, and how these affect the way a country understands the utility and importance of patents in achieving overall nationalistic goals. Second, the role of local politics (including the presence of state and non-state actors) in influencing and shaping pharmaceutical patent law-making and processes. Third, the power of international politics and political actors to exert pressure on the other to influence patent law and policy outcomes. The third point is truer for the developing country context than for developed or advanced economies.

Patent Games in the Global South explores the contours of that complex relationship by taking as examples Brazil, India, and Nigeria, and tells the story of patent law-making within each of them. In doing so, this book puts forward the hypothesis that for countries in the Global South keen on building a human-focused patent regime, the presence and participation of a strong indigenous pharmaceutical manufacturing sector and even stronger civil society activism are imperative. This is because the presence of these actors is paramount in the mobilisation of knowledge, cognitive-shaping of public discourse, creation of expertise, and participation in the politics and games required in building a pharmaceutical patent regulatory framework. Regrettably, as we shall see in these chapters, the contestation, presence and participation of these actors are asymmetrical.

At a fundamental level, this book attempts to explore pharmaceutical patent law-making in Nigeria. Specifically, how do patents affect, if at all, access to essential medicines in Nigeria? How is patent conceptualised into law and

[1] 'Agreement on Trade-Related Aspects Of Intellectual Property Rights' (World Trade Organization, 1995), available at www.wto.org/english/docs_e/legal_e/27-trips.pdf.

policy vis-à-vis the TRIPS Agreement among policy-making circles in Nigeria? How do ideas regarding patents circulate? That is, what influences the way in which particular policy options are constructed – and, by extension, how do others get extinguished with regard to patent law and policy in Nigeria? How do non-state actors – private sector and civil society groups – challenge and/or influence this understanding and conceptualisation of patents into Nigerian law and policy? I focus on Nigeria because aside from it being my home country, it is also the largest economy in Africa with a growing population and an expanding industrial sector. The choice of Nigeria as a case study on the intersection between patent law, development, and access to medicine discourse is informed by two factors. First, the prominent position of the country within the continent affords it the power to influence and set policy agenda on norms governing patent law and public policy discourse in sub-Saharan Africa. Second, the country has always been a significant interlocutor for Africa and the Global South at various international forums. At the onset and in the course of the Uruguay Round negotiations that established the WTO, especially during the TRIPS Agreement negotiations, Nigeria was outspoken in its objection to the inclusion of an intellectual property (IP) regime within the multilateral trade framework. Nevertheless, there is a sharp disconnect between government rhetoric at international forums and government actions at the local level. This is in stark contrast to the prevailing situation in traditional 'TRIPS opponent' countries such as Brazil and India, whose stance at international forums is usually reflective of their IP policies at home.

But in the course of undertaking this research, it became urgent to widen the discourse to include Brazil and India – countries different from Nigeria and yet similar in many ways. Both countries are the focus of attention when it comes to balancing a patent regime with each respective country's needs and aspirations, even as they continue to face so many hurdles as they seek to balance protecting the IP of inventors, on one hand, and fulfilling the social contract needs of their citizens on the other. Still, their inclusion in this book provides a toolbox, and not a fixed roadmap, for Nigeria in assessing the value to be promoted or protected as the country designs and develops its IP rules in fulfilment of its TRIPS Agreement obligations.[2] Further, the experiences of Brazil and India, as the chapters in this book show, are relevant in raising awareness and increasing the knowledge of Nigerian law-makers on legal norms, debates, and cases in other jurisdictions to make better informed decisions on laws to adopt and discard based on the distinct circumstance(s) and needs of Nigeria.

At a more general level, this book investigates the growing Third World resistance against hegemonic IP rules. It is an exercise in the quest for legal

[2] See generally Irene Calboli, 'The Role Of Comparative Legal Analysis In Intellectual Property Law: From Good To Great?' in G Dinwoodie (ed), *Methods and Perspectives in Intellectual Property* (Cheltenham, Edward Elgar, 2013) on the importance of comparative legal analysis with particular emphasis on the role that this methodology could play for intellectual property scholarship.

re-ordering of patent law in the Third World – a sort of unmasking of alternative approaches to patent law-making and un-making. Such approaches are alternative in the sense that the IP law-making engaged in this book moves away from the dominant European–US models to a development-oriented IP regime. Through an empirical study of the Brazilian and Indian patent regimes, this book maps out the broad interpretations and domestication of international law in the Third World, and the ways these interpretations widen the aperture on international norms and rules governing IP whilst also being 'TRIPS compliant' in that challenges at the WTO have failed to materialise.

Consequently, this book pays particular attention to how the local politics between the subaltern state, non-state actors, and transnational capital, as well as the factions within subaltern states – often ignored in debates surrounding intellectual property rights (IPRs) and their relation to access to health – are involved in the game of recalibration of global IP norms and discourses. This book also exposes some of the contradictions involved in this emerging subaltern jurisprudence on IP law. These contradictions are not surprising. While both Brazil and India are making huge strides in designing patent regime systems that best meet their needs, their respective regimes are still flawed as certain policies and actors inadvertently promote IP practices that impede development and public health management. As analyses in this book show, protectionist interests are fighting back. These actions do not mean a failure of these regimes. Instead, they show that the IP ecosystem is complex, does not exist in isolation, and the presence of various actors means it will continue to calibrate and recalibrate the global IP regime.

Thirdly, this work also highlights the changes in ways postcolonial states engage and interact with international law in general and IP in particular, which can no longer be analysed within the statist paradigm alone. The presence of transnational civil society groups, mobilising across state boundaries and operating in forums previously thought as the exclusive turf of nation-states, is rapidly expanding and shaping laws and practices in the field of international IP law. In this regard, the discoveries and overall findings provided in this book form part of emergent discourse on new constitutionalism in the Global South.

Over the years, subaltern jurisdictions have become the battleground for the promotion of global ideals of human, social, economic, and environmental development. The struggles on access to medicines (A2M) have somewhat shifted from WTO forum disputes to local or national courts in the Global South. This is due to a prevailing perception in contemporary international legal discourse where the developing world has often been seen as the 'other'. In this view, Third World countries are usually the importer of international regulations, from the European civilising missions, International Monetary Fund (IMF) fiscal conditionalities and the World Bank development programmes, to many other such stipulations by donor states and organisations usually located in the Global North.

Within this narrative, international law discourses have the tendency to reduce the Global South to what Upendra Baxi calls the 'geographies of injustice'.[3] That is, the use of international law – be it in human rights, investment, trade, or others – as an instrument for social change, with its applications based on Euro-centric ideals to provide solutions to the needs and concerns of the Third World. One of the consequences of this is a reproduction of patterns of silence and the erasure of significant legal, institutional, and socio-political development and law-making in the Third World. This book, however, shows emerging critical legal trends from the Global South, particularly the anti-evergreening provisions in Indian patent law such as sections 3(d)(e) and (i). These laws, as this book shows, are visibly altering 'received geographies of core-and-periphery, relocating southward some of the most innovative and energetic modes of producing value'.[4]

At a theoretical level, this book builds heavily on critical legal theory (CLT), although it touches on insight by postcolonial theory and critical development theory. CLT challenges and overturns accepted norms and standards in legal theory and practice.[5] According to this school of thought, the failings in the international law project are not marginal or exceptional, but are endemic, consistent and structural.[6] As a result, this school of thought uses a broad array of techniques to address separate but interrelated failings perceived in the international legal project to show the cruelty of the current systems of law.[7] Though CLT constitutes various strands, its unifying stance is the need to rethink the foundations of international law and create space for an emancipatory and inclusive international legal project.[8] It is this rationale and its philosophical assumptions that underlie this research project.

Within CLT, this book builds on critical Third World scholarship, specifically Third World Approaches to International Law (TWAIL). TWAIL is

[3] Upendra Baxi, 'Geographies of Injustice: Human Rights at the Altar of Convenience' in C Scott (ed), *Torture as Tort: Comparative Perspectives on the Development of Transnational Human Rights Litigation* (Oxford, Hart Publishing, 2001) 197.

[4] Jean Comaroff and John L Comaroff, 'Theory From The South: Or, How Euro-America Is Evolving Toward Africa' (2012) 22 *Anthropological Forum* 117.

[5] The critical international legal theory (CLT) is sometimes known as critical legal studies (CLS) or new approaches to international law (NAIL). CLS draws from different philosophical traditions such as Marxism, the critical theory of the Frankfurt School, and Post-Structuralism. See Roberto Mangabeira Unger, 'The Critical Legal Studies Movement' (1983) 96 *Harvard Law Review* 561; Nigel Purvis, 'Critical Legal Studies in Public International Law' (1991) 32 *Harvard International Law Journal* 81; Mark Tushnet, 'Critical Legal Studies: A Political History' (1991) 100 *The Yale Law Journal* 1515; Anthony Carty, 'Critical International Law: Recent Trends in the Theory of International Law' (1991) 2 *European Journal of International Law* 66; Matthew Stone, Illan rua Wall and Costas Douzinas, *New Critical Legal Thinking* (New York, Birkbeck Law Press–Routledge, 2012); Alan Hunt, 'The Theory of Critical Legal Studies' (1986) 6 *Oxford Journal of Legal Studies* 1; Jason Beckett, 'Critical International Legal Theory', Oxford Bibliographies Online Datasets (2012).

[6] Hunt (ibid) 30–32.

[7] Beckett, 'Critical' (2012).

[8] Hunt, 'Theory' (1986) 43; Beckett (n 5).

an intellectual movement devoted to providing an alternative narrative of international law that has developed to perpetuate the domination and subordination of the Third World. Within this oppositional space, TWAIL performs both deconstructive and reformative functions.[9]

As a deconstructive tool, TWAIL identifies, unpacks and challenges the history, oppressive structures and processes of international law.[10] As a reformative tool, it reconstructs international law to be cognisant and responsive to the needs and aspirations of peoples of the Third World.[11] It is this particular understanding of *twailian* theory – the gradual unpacking, deconstruction and inclusion of legal projects operating at the margins of the mainstream discipline – that underpins the critical engagement of this research with the pharmaceutical patent regime.[12] By focusing on domestic jurisprudential experiences in detail, this research examines the ways international law 'unfolds on the mundane and quotidian plane through sites and objects which appear unrelated to the international'.[13] By focusing on domestic phenomenon that is not ostensibly international but in actuality is, the research expands *twailian* materiality by delving into 'the everyday life of international [IP] law'[14] through the examination of practices that occur, not only through typical international legal IP practices, but also through many other sites and objects in which international law operates today.

In order to explore this issue, I engaged in multi-sited ethnography from 2014 to 2015, conducting over 50 interviews with actors in access to medicines and patent discourses in Brazil, India and Nigeria, and again in July 2016 to interview pharmaceutical companies in Nigeria. These actors include government officials, pharmaceutical manufacturing companies or their representatives, civil society groups, legal scholars, lawyers and judges. The reason for multi-sited ethnography is that it allows for the objective study of social phenomena that cannot be accounted for by focusing on a single site. This is important as this method aims to give voice to marginalised groups, in the sense of following people, connections, associations and relationships across space.

[9] James Thuo Gathii, 'TWAIL: A Brief History of its Origins, its Decentralized Network, and a Tentative Bibliography' (2011) 26 *Trade, Law and Development* 39.

[10] ibid.

[11] ibid.

[12] BS Chimni, 'Third World Approaches to International Law: A Manifesto' (2006) 8 *International Community Law Review* 5; Makau Mutua, 'What Is TWAIL?' (2000) 94 *The American Society of International Law Proceedings* 31, 35.

[13] Luis Eslava and Sundhuha Pahuja, 'Between Resistance and Reform: TWAIL and the Universality of International Law' (2011) 3 *Trade, Law and Development* 103. Eslava and Puhuja suggest that TWAIL needs to expand its emphasis on materiality to think of international law as not only an ideological project that has material consequences but also as a material project itself. To contest international law's shortcoming, Eslava and Pahuja contend paying attention to the ways in which international law constantly constitutes and reconstitutes what people think of as places, subjects and modalities of administration. This can be achieved by exploring the way that international law operates, including its daily functioning on the mundane, quotidian, and material plane.

[14] ibid.

While seeking to be inclusive as much as possible by presenting varying perspectives, I am also mindful that some of the views may make some of the interviewees susceptible to attack, retaliation, or possibly government sanctions. Therefore, in cases in which the opinions expressed by respondents have the potential to draw such attacks or inflame existing tensions among different groups with an interest in patent law, I do not reveal the speakers' identities unless the views concerned are already a matter of public record. In 2014, I accessed the archives of the Working Group of Intellectual Property of the Brazilian Network for the Integration of Peoples (GTPI/REBRIP) in Brazil for historical records while in 2015, I observed meetings on trade policy organised by the WTO Desk at the Ministry of Trade and Investment to gauge the views on and awareness of patents as a development policy tool among government officials. Finally, I drew on secondary data, including legislation and policy documents, for theoretical and contextual analysis.

In excavating patent law-making and governance within the countries under focus in this book, the following key points are underscored. First, the innovative interpretation of global patent rules in the local forums of the countries under study was inspired by and made possible as a result of disappointment and disillusionment with the assertions of benefit and progress attached to instituting a *particular* form of patent regime. Second, the possibility of using patents to effect the twin goals of development and public health management is likely when patent law is implemented in combination with checks such as trained patent officers to enforce stringent requirements for patent applications and to effectively scrutinise patent application to prevent evergreening, and balances in the form of complementary policies such as public good protection strategies, enhancing local capacity in research and development (R&D) and healthy market competition. Third, in the specific case of Nigeria, patent regime (including the TRIPS Agreement) is *not* the reason for lack of access to medicines. Rather, as the chapter on Nigeria reveals, the issue of lack of access to essential medicines and development can be attributed to corruption, incompetence, and market and government failure. Any solution to improve access must start from these issues.

II. TERMINOLOGY

For purposes of this book, it is necessary to clarify the meaning of certain terms and explain the context for their use in this book.

A. Developed Countries

There are no definitions of 'developed' countries within the WTO. However, there are large and easily discernible differences in the size and state of economies, and the standard of living enjoyed by citizens of different countries. It is generally assumed that countries within the Organization for Economic Co-operation and Development (OECD) are considered to be developed countries. This is because each of these countries has completed the development process. In this book, the term is used to apply to certain countries possessing strong pharmaceutical industries such as the United States of America (US), Japan, Canada, Switzerland, Germany, France, Sweden and others. Other terms such as 'the West', 'First World' and 'the Global North' are also used interchangeably to mean developed countries.

B. Global South/Third World

Admittedly, the term 'Third World' has become controversial in recent times. Certain scholars posit that it is defunct due to the collapse of the former Soviet Union and the Cold War politics that demanded that international systems be divided into categories.[15] However, this is not the view in this book. As BS Chimni aptly points out, too much is often made of numbers, variations and differences in the presence of structures and the process of global capitalism that continue to bind and unite.[16] He continues that even international law recognises the diverse set of countries with differences in the patterns of their economies, despite its practice of prescribing uniform global standards. This therefore validates the existence of the category 'Third World'.[17]

For this book, 'Third World' refers to the previously colonised 'socio-political geography that, during the mid-twentieth century, came to be seen as "non-aligned" – belonging neither to the "free" nor to the "communist" world'.[18] Of course, certain scholars such as Balakrishnan Rajagopal have argued that the term should be liberated from its geographical 'national' mooring to mean instead 'actual terrain that power operates on, rather than some predetermined given one such as the "nation"'.[19] This enables us, according to Rajagopal, to focus on issues of class, gender, sexuality, region, language, and so on, which have been submerged by the totalising power of the 'national allegory'.[20] Due to the postcolonial lens adopted in the critical inquiry this book seeks to undertake, distinguishing between 'Third World' and 'First World' captures the oppositional dialectic between the European and the non-European, and identifies the

[15] See RBJ Walker, 'Space/Time/Sovereignty' in M Denham and MO Lombardi (eds), *Perspectives on Third World Sovereignty: The Postmodern Paradox* (New York, St Martin's Press, 1996) 15.
[16] Chimni, 'Third World Approaches' (2006).
[17] ibid.
[18] Luis Eslava, 'TWAIL Coordinates' [2019] *Groningen Journal of International Law*, available at https://grojil.org/2019/04/01/twail-coordinates.
[19] Balakrishnan Rajagopal, 'Locating The Third World In Cultural Geography' (1999) 15 *Third World Legal Studies* 19.
[20] ibid.

plunder of the latter by the former.[21] This aligns with the definition put forward by Karin Mickelson who posits Third World to mean 'a chorus of distinctive voices that blend, though not harmoniously, in attempting to make heard a common set of concerns'.[22] In this book, the terms 'Third World', 'Global South' and 'subaltern' are used interchangeably.

C. Local Pharmaceutical Industry

In this book, the term 'local pharmaceutical industry' refers to indigenous pharmaceutical manufacturing companies in developing countries. These companies are able to meet a certain percentage of the local demand for drugs within each country and contribute to the local economy to a certain extent. These companies usually focus their activities on the production and distribution of generic drugs.

D. Multinational Pharmaceutical Companies

The term 'multinational pharmaceutical companies' refers to pharmaceutical manufacturing companies in developed countries. These companies have strong research capacities and engage in the advanced development of innovative medicines.

E. Non-state Actors

These are individuals and organisations that are not states and participate in governance and law-making at the global, regional, sub-regional and local levels. They include individuals, private firms, civil society groups, social movements, trade associations, terrorist groups and transnational corporations.

III. WHY BRAZIL AND INDIA?

Although Nigeria is ultimately the central focus of this study, Brazil and India play a very important role. These countries were chosen as case studies for many reasons. First, like Nigeria, both countries were involved in pressing for a new international economic order (NIEO) based on economic nationalism and the rejection of global liberalism during the 1970s and 1980s, and were also active

[21] See Mutua, 'TWAIL' (2000).

[22] See Karin Mickelson, 'Rhetoric and Rage: Third World Voices in International Legal Discourse' (1998) 18 *Wisconsin International Law Journal* 360.

in opposing the inclusion of IP as part of global trade rules. In this regard, these countries have always sought changes to prevailing notions of the IP regime towards a more development-oriented IP framework, access to medicines, and South–South collaboration.

Second, these countries are important regional powers with the ability to influence the legal, political and social cultures within their regional bloc. Their emerging market status gives them the economic clout 'capable of striking new and imaginative balances between proprietary and access interests'.[23] As Rochelle C Dreyfuss has shown, these countries straddle the problems of both the North, eg emerging creative industries which require the protection of creative works, and the South, eg large swathes of the population who are poor with profound access needs. As such, they are forced to acquire not only the political will needed to accommodate the demands of all kinds of IP producers and users, but also to contribute to the reforms that are the cornerstone of the global administrative law agenda.[24] Importantly, the size of the economies of these countries means they can protect themselves from easy economic bullying from key advanced economies such as the US.

Third, Brazil and India are also hothouses of social movements. This is apparent in the grassroots mobilisation for acquired immune deficiency syndrome (AIDS) and treatment access movements. For socio-legal purposes, these countries provide useful fodder for competing theoretical ideas about social movements – identities, concerns and emotional underpinnings. As will be seen in coming chapters, both the Brazilian AIDS programme and the Indian patent regime are testaments to the strategic effort and coalition of social movements in these countries, especially in funnelling information and in producing knowledge.

IV. BOOK OUTLINE

Patent Games is divided into seven chapters. Chapter one is introductory and gives a broad overview of the issues covered. Chapter two performs the critical function of explaining basic concepts such as patents, and explores the development of patent law from the national phase to the global phase.

Chapter three maps out the theoretical framework that underpins the work in this book, and is divided into two parts. Part 1 focuses on TWAIL theory and uses it as a resource to uncover the historical origins of international IP law and its continuities in the postcolonial. Thus, this section begins by identifying TWAIL as a theoretical position seeking to build a genealogy of the

[23] Rochelle C Dreyfuss, 'The Role Of India, China, Brazil And Other Emerging Economies in Establishing Access Norms For Intellectual Property And Intellectual Property Lawmaking' [2009] *SSRN Electronic Journal* 3.

[24] ibid, 21.

present through a careful analysis of the ways international IP law reproduces a renewed colonial order in the twentieth century. It then goes on to situate TWAIL within patent regime discourse. Here, the legal structure of global patent rules is examined, interrogating twailian understanding that is key in both the Paris Convention and the TRIPS Agreement. Particular attention is paid to the TRIPS Agreement – the political context in which it was created, the goals it sought to advance, and the manner and effects of its operation, as well as to key text within the TRIPS Agreement, especially its complicity in the economic exploitation of the subaltern. Gaps within the twailian approach to patent regime is discussed by exploring the methodological limit of TWAIL as it pertains to this study. Part 2 focuses on nodal governance and provides the lens for understanding and exploring local actor participation in patent law-making and governance. Establishing the theoretical frame of reference for this book, this chapter employs a critical reading of the global IP framework and examines how the TRIPS framework has been inserted into the postcolonial development agenda and its continued use as a hegemonic political tool.

Chapter four begins the series of case study analyses. Focusing on Brazil, the chapter specifically centres on the intersection of Brazil's HIV/AIDS programme and its patent law and policies. It sets out how patent law and policies have been applied at the domestic level and how the A2M discourse has evolved in the wake of the TRIPS Agreement implementation. The focus, then, is how local political dynamics and actors play into issues related to IPRs and medicine access. Though Brazil's overall application of IP standards has been comparatively mixed and uneven, the book argues that the prosaic implementation of pro-right to health policies even after the country phased fully into the TRIPS Agreement is a hermeneutic expression of resistance and reform of international law norms on patent law and medicine access discourse(s). Chapter five continues with the series of case study analyses by critically investigating the Indian patent regime. India is often cited as an example of an 'innovative developing country' with a robust pharmaceutical sector and the capacity to carry out health innovations. This chapter analyses the government intervention policies that made these structural changes possible and examines how the growth of the sector is strongly linked to a wide range of factors which propelled Indian pharmaceutical firms on a path that spurred the growth of highly sophisticated generic drugs.

Chapter six focuses on Nigeria and maps the historical evolution of patent law in the country. After a schematic representation of the excruciating health burdens in Nigeria to help understand the critical situation and urgent actions required to tackle these multiple health emergencies, the chapter proceeds to examine the current patent law in Nigeria vis-à-vis the TRIPS Agreement to show how the latter interacts with laws, institutions and actors at the domestic level. This chapter seeks to understand how issues of access to medicine are framed locally and the cognisance of policy-makers of patent law as a development tool.

Chapter seven concludes the book and focuses on the insights derived from the case studies. The individual and collective significance of the findings of the case studies are summarised and their benefits to the book are restated. The hope of this work is that the reader will understand that adroitly marketing the TRIPS Agreement as a trade tool inherently makes it unsuitable for development objectives, despite the inclusion of certain flexibilities. This necessitates the need for a conceptual recasting of the TRIPS-harmonised regime not based on the dominant European–US models but on a development-oriented IP regime embraced by both India and Brazil.

Finally, two limitations must be noted. First, this book does not chart all the relevant social movements and legal cases or judgments that have ever had an impact on pharmaceutical patent jurisprudence and medicines access movement within the countries under discussion. The organisations and cases discussed herein either reflect jurisprudential rigour and/or legal lucidity (in terms of cases) or the organisation provided access to key documents/archival materials to back up analyses. The chapter on Brazil, for instance, benefits greatly from access provided by the GTPI/REBRIP during my doctoral fieldwork, which culminated in the work in this book. The same is true for working at the WTO office in Nigeria's Federal Ministry of Trade, Industry and Commerce, and being a research fellow at India's Centre for Study of Law and Governance at Jawaharlal Nehru University, Delhi. Second, the book does not claim that the actors and organisations highlighted herein self-identify as part of TWAIL legal scholarships. Rather, their actions not only echo Twailian ethical commitment but speaks strongly of TWAIL's ongoing relevance even beyond the ivory towers of academia and within Third World grassroot politics and activism.

2

Understanding Patents

I. INTRODUCTION

A PATENT IS a temporary exclusive right granted to the inventor of a product or process which is 'new' (or 'novel'), involves an 'inventive step' (or is 'non-obvious'), and is capable of industrial application (or 'useful').[1] In its contemporary context, a patent is defined as

> a document, issued, upon application, by a government office which describes an invention and creates a legal situation in which the patented invention can normally only be exploited (manufactured, used, sold, or imported) with the authorisation of the owner of the patent.[2]

Patents are designed to reward inventors, encourage technical progress and foster dissemination of information.[3] According to May and Sell, a patent is an institutionalised bargain between the state and the inventor, where the

> State agrees to establish the legal mechanisms that ensure that the inventor can extract payment for their idea when others use it while the inventor allow the State to lodge the idea in its public records where it can be accessed by interested parties.[4]

The development of a patent system can be grouped into three phases: national, multinational and global. These phases are discussed briefly below.

II. THE NATIONAL PHASE

In their initial stages in fifteenth-century Europe, where they originated, economic factors influenced patent customs with links to national development objectives and economic advancement goals such as assisting in the growth

[1] Frederick M Abbott, 'Intellectual Property, International Protection' (2009) Florida State University College of Law Public Law Research Paper No 601, 2.

[2] *WIPO Intellectual Property Handbook*, 2nd edn (Geneva, WIPO, 2004).

[3] Carlos M Correa, 'Pharmaceutical Innovation, Incremental Patenting and Compulsory Licensing' (2011) 1, available at http://apps.who.int/medicinedocs/documents/s21395en/s21395en.pdf; Abbott, 'Intellectual Property' (2009).

[4] Christopher May and Susan K Sell, *Intellectual Property Rights* (Boulder, Lynne Rienner Publishers, 2006) 8.

of new industries by importation or through native invention.[5] They were developed out of the realisation that there was a societal need to both recognise and protect invention to encourage local manufacturing and attain economic development. In commenting on the origins of patents, legal historian Edward Walterscheid notes that the patent customs that originated from Venice (1421)[6] and spread to England (1449), Germany (1484), France (1551) and Austria (1794) arose out of the desire of European rulers to encourage the development of new industries within their realms.[7] To achieve these economic plans, patent customs then took two forms: importation of knowledge into the realm, which involved local artisans travelling abroad to learn a new trade (apprenticeship); or through invention within the realm.[8] However, due to the reluctance of artisans to teach foreigners the secrets of their trade, the latter became the preferred method of encouraging local manufacturing. In this regard, patents were introduced to promote economic development rather than private property rights that prioritised trade and are seen as a trade tool, as they are today.[9]

Of course, in addition to patents, many incentives were put in place to encourage local manufacturing. These include financial grants, favourable tax treatment, sovereign protection and bans on the emigration of skilled labour.[10] In England, however, the grant of monopolies by the Crown became a popular practice known as *literae parentes*. This practice bestowed monopoly rights and privileges upon individuals for a limited period in furtherance of royal policies and was put in place because the English Crown recognised the costs and risks associated with the introduction of a new trade or industry.[11] As such, patents were introduced in England as a form of incentive to attract new trade and manufacturing practices based on the premise of the potential for substantial economic return to those taking such risks and incurring such expenses.

[5] Edward C Walterscheid, 'The Early Evolution of the United States Patent Law: Antecedents (Part 2)' (1994) 76 *Journal of the Patent and Trademark Office Society* 850.

[6] Walterscheid suggests that the earliest patentee of record is Filippo Brunelleschi, who received a monopoly patent from the city-state of Florence in 1421, after which 11 patents were granted 75 years prior to the official patent law enactment in 1474, and approximately 100 patents have been found in the Venetian archives, which were issued in the following 75 years.

[7] ibid. Many of the other European countries established their patent laws in the other half of the 19th century – Russia (1812), Prussia (1815), Belgium and the Netherlands (1817), Spain (1820), Bavaria (1825), Sardinia (1826), the Vatican State (1833) and Sweden (1834). The US introduced patents in 1793.

[8] Walterscheid, 'Antecedents (Part 2)' (1994); Ha-Joon Chang, 'Intellectual Property Rights and Economic Development: Historical Lessons and Emerging Issues' (2001) 2 *Journal of Human Development* 288.

[9] Edward C Walterscheid, 'The Early Evolution of the United States Patent Law: Antecedents (Part 1)' (1994) 76 *Journal of the Patent and Trademark Office Society* 669; Srividhya Ragavan, *Patent and Trade Disparities in Developing Countries* (Oxford, Oxford University Press, 2012) 16.

[10] Walterscheid, 'Antecedents (Part 1)' (ibid); Chang, 'Historical Lessons and Emerging Issues' (2001) 289.

[11] Ragavan, *Patent and Trade Disparities* (2012) 3.

In a similar vein, early patent custom introduced in the United States in 1641 aimed at national economic benefits. In fact, American founding fathers believed patents had an end role to serve the society – the American society – and not the larger international society.[12] As a result, they made policies that allowed everyone, including emigrants, to benefit from monopoly policies. This presents a significant departure from the present-day debate, which as subsequent sections show, is different from the patent narrative currently pursued by the US.

However, it could be argued that Jefferson's claim is quite rhetorical and that this welfarist concern is actually more parochial and nationalist and not for the loftier global circulation of ideas. In other words, the patent system reflected significant differential treatment between nationals and non-nationals as a way to privilege the former. This difference is even more apparent in terms of US copyright statutes. Even European nations at that time also adopted differential treatment between nationals and non-nationals.[13] For example, patenting of *imported inventions* by nationals was often explicitly allowed in Britain, Austria and France, while patents were granted without any proof of originality in the US.[14]

Socio-economic realities also shaped the narratives on early patent laws. History has shown that during adverse economic conditions, private rights tend to give way to government interventions to improve public rights and access to protected materials. So, while early patent customs were engineered to be of benefit to the state, these monopolies were rescinded once perceived to not be of value to the realm.[15] Put differently, patents proliferated 'only when the economic climate remained conducive for research in order to appropriately channelize the early development and address public welfare concerns'.[16] Conversely, patents were abolished where economic conditions become unfavourable, especially in times of economic hardship. In those hard times, monopoly grant becomes limited and restrictions are placed on already granted monopolies. For instance, during the industrial depression in England and during the Great Depression in the US, patent grants were suspended.[17] The various European capitals also abolished patents during periods of socio-economic upheavals. The Netherlands abolished its patent system in 1869 after the rise of the free trade movement, which viewed patents as a form of protectionism and rejected them as a restriction on trade.[18] Germany followed in 1817, while Switzerland had no formal patent system until 1907.[19] According to Srividhya Ragavan, this is due to the

[12] ibid, 11.
[13] Chang (n 8) 290.
[14] ibid, 291.
[15] ibid.
[16] Ragavan (n 9) 33.
[17] ibid, 19.
[18] Cicero Gontijo, 'Changing the Patent System from the Paris Convention to the TRIPS Agreement: The Position of Brazil' (2005) 26 *Global Issues Paper* 5; Chang (n 8) 291.
[19] Petra Moser, 'Patents And Innovation: Evidence From Economic History' (2013) 27 *Journal of Economic Perspectives* 26.

'disconnect between such times and the patent system and its objectives of social benefits as patented products become less accessible to even fewer people during the abnormal economic times'.[20]

III. THE MULTILATERAL PHASE – THE PARIS CONVENTION

Harmonisation of patent law intensified as many countries started introducing individual local patent laws and international commerce increased. Harmonisation was couched on the need to guarantee uniform protection and recognition across territorial borders. In 1883, the first international IP treaty, the Paris Convention on the Protection of Industrial Property ('Paris Convention'), was signed. It provides protection based on national treatment, where a member country must treat the citizens of another country as its own. The Paris Convention was also non-specific, allowing countries to interpret or apply the law the way they deem fit and based on individual needs. This allowed for individuality in rules. In this regard, the Paris Convention did not harmonise the patent rules of its members. The Paris Convention was signed by 11 countries – Belgium, Brazil, Ecuador, El Salvador, France, Great Britain, Guatemala, Italy, The Netherlands, Portugal, Serbia, Spain, Switzerland, Tunisia and the US. Through colonisation, the patent rules of the Paris Convention were transplanted directly from the metropolitan states to the colonial territories, even though these territories had not signed the Paris Convention.[21] Such extension to the colonies, according to Ruth Okediji, was for purposes generally associated with the overarching colonial strategies of assimilation, incorporation and control.[22]

Misgivings towards the Paris Convention abound. Many formal colonies that signed onto the agreement did not need to. This is because many of the technological sectors were still nascent with no real breakthroughs. If anything, the Paris Convention served the monopolistic interest of patent-holders usually located in the West.[23] These misgivings were also voiced by Brazil, as we shall see in chapter four, over a century later. In spite of its numerous revisions (1900, 1911, 1925, 1934, 1958 and 1967), the Paris Convention remained 'a rich man's club' that further strengthened the monopolistic rights of the patent-holder.[24]

[20] ibid, 19.

[21] Ulf Anderfelt, *International Patent-Legislation and Developing Countries* (The Hague, Martinus Nijhoff, 1971) 119; see also GHC Bodenhausen, *Guide to the Application of the Paris Convention for the Protection of Industrial Property, as Revised at Stockholm in 1967* (Geneva, United International Bureaux for the Protection of Intellectual Property, 1968).

[22] Ruth L Okediji, 'The International Relations of Intellectual Property: Narratives of Developing Country Participation in the Global Intellectual Property System' (2003) 7 *Singapore Journal of International and Comparative Law* 225.

[23] Surendra J Patel, 'Intellectual Property Rights in the Uruguay Round: A Disaster for the South?' (1989) 24 *Economic and Political Weekly* 981.

[24] ibid.

In a similar vein, Ruth Okediji notes that the patent law under the Paris Convention was merely for securing national economic interests against other European countries in colonial territories.[25] It was also engineered by the industrialised countries in order to secure import monopolies for the producer nations of the West so as to satisfy the needs of expanding capitalism.[26] This is because Article 5^{quater} under the Paris Convention prohibits countries from revoking patents on the ground that the patented articles are being imported rather than locally manufactured.[27] As a result, a foreigner could obtain a patent monopoly with absolutely no associated obligation to produce the patented article or ensure its supply in the patent-granting country; this issue was raised many decades later in India (chapter five). This practice of importing technology had the effect of retarding the industrial development of the importing county, since foreign monopoly grant blocks domestic producers.[28]

In fact, this issue of patent monopoly was the main point of contention between developing and developed countries. This simmering discontent also explains why developing countries have sought the adjustment of the global patent regime at various international and local forums. As we shall see in coming chapters, there was a push in Brazil for a revision of the Paris Convention to reduce incidents of patent monopoly abuse of pharmaceutical patents by foreign multinational companies operating in the country at that time. A similar narrative also circulated in India as many such foreign pharmaceutical companies did not locally manufacture their patented invention or work their patent locally, but relied instead on the importation of the patented article while blocking indigenous companies that would normally manufacture locally. Early data from the Nigerian Patent Office also revealed that majority of the patents granted in the country at that time were owned by foreigners who did not locally work on the patented article. This shows that developing countries have always been cognisant of the asymmetrical effect of global patent rules and their tendency to favour the more economically powerful nations. It is

[25] Okediji, 'International Relations' (2003) 224–25.

[26] Rajeev Dhavan, Lindsay Harris and Gopal Jain, 'Conquest by Patent: The Paris Convention Revisited' (1990) 32 *Journal of Indian Law Institute* 131.

[27] Article 5^{quater} states: 'When a product is imported into a country of the Union where there exists a patent protecting a process of manufacture of the said product, the patentee shall have all the rights, with regard to the imported product, that are accorded to him by the legislation of the country of importation, on the basis of the process patent, with respect to products manufactured in that country.'

[28] Dhavan, Harris and Jain, 'Conquest by Patent' (1990) 132. See also Edith Penrose, 'International Patenting and the Less-Developed Countries' (1973) 83 *The Economic Journal* 768; Constantine Vaitsos, 'Patents Revisited: Their Function in Developing Countries' (1972) 9 *The Journal of Development Studies* 71; Owen T Adikibi, 'The Multinational Corporation And Monopoly Of Patents in Nigeria' (1988) 16 *World Development* 511; AK Menescal, 'Changing WIPO's Ways? The 2004 Development Agenda in Historical Perspective' (2005) *Journal of World Intellectual Property* 761; Peter K Yu, 'A Tale of Two Development Agendas' (2009) 35 *Ohio Northern University Law Review* 465.

this reservation about the impact on economic development that continues to animate contemporary discussion on pharmaceutical patents.

Furthermore, the Paris Convention was still regarded by certain developed countries, such as the US, as insufficient. Corporate interests in the US regarded the Paris Convention as 'toothless' due to the lack of enforcement mechanisms that led to, among other things, the frequent 'disregard for the protection of non-nationals' intellectual property outside most of developed countries and sometimes even between them'.[29] Moreover, the fact that the Paris Convention allowed countries to implement patent rules specific to them and created a patchwork system of disparate norms, rules and levels of protection was also seen as problematic.[30] As a result, those who considered the Paris Convention unsuitable expended considerable resources in establishing patent rules at another point in time.

The 1960s to the 1970s is known as the decolonisation period for many former colonies located in Asia, Africa and the Caribbean. As these countries gained their independence, they 'became more assertive of their rights and aware of their international obligations'.[31] Peter Yu writes that they were torn between affirming and denouncing international obligations into which their former colonial rulers had entered on their behalf.[32] Significantly, those willing to affirm their international obligations considered the extant standards to be too high and did not take into account specific economic conditions and technological gaps. For example, they found that the issue of patent monopoly under the Paris Convention hampered efforts to catch up with other developed countries.[33] As a result, many of these countries set about joining different multilateral organisations to suit their interests and which allowed them to influence international standards in their favour. According to Drahos, this process of forum-shifting – of joining various multilateral agreements and international organisations – was adopted by many developing countries after mostly unsuccessful attempts in changing the rules against abuses of patent monopolies with the Paris Convention.[34]

Many newly independent countries shifted the discussion of IP-related issues to other international forums like the World Intellectual Property

[29] May and Sell, *Intellectual Property Rights* (2006) 4; Peter Drahos, 'Developing Countries and International Intellectual Property Standard-Setting' (2002) 5 *The Journal of World Intellectual Property* 768.

[30] Okediji (n 22) 316.

[31] Yu, 'Two Development Agendas' (2009) 470.

[32] ibid.

[33] P Roffe and G Vea, 'The WIPO Development Agenda in an Historical and Political Context' in NW Netanel (ed), The Development Agenda: Global Intellectual Property and Developing Countries (Oxford, Oxford University Press, 2008) 92.

[34] Drahos, 'Developing Countries' (2002); see also Menescal, 'Changing WIPO's Ways?' (2005); Laurence R Helfer, 'Regime Shifting: The TRIPS Agreement and New Dynamics of International Intellectual Property Lawmaking' (2004) 29 *Yale Journal of International Law* 1.

Organization (WIPO), the United Nations (UN) and the UN Conference on Trade and Development (UNCTAD). Developing countries found these forums neutral due to the large presence of new decolonised countries and also because of the bloc voting and one-country-one-vote rule employed for consensus rule-making.[35] By shifting to these forums, these countries actively sought to recalibrate, revise or reinterpret the Paris Convention to satisfy their needs.[36] According to Andrea Menescal, an intense and critical debate concerning abuses of patent monopolies by the Paris Union system and the prevalence of right-holders' interests in the Paris Convention was tabled at the UN.[37] As a result, Brazil (co-sponsored by Bolivia) submitted to the UN General Assembly (UNGA) in October 1961 a resolution entitled 'The Role of Patents in the Transfer of Technology to Under-Developed Countries'.[38] The resolution highlighted, among other things, abuses and misuses of patent monopolies, the importance of co-operation in the field of applied science and technology for promoting the exchange of knowledge via transfer of technology from developed to developing countries, and the need for a Development Agenda in the international patent system.[39] Though the final resolution presented to and adopted by the UNGA in December 1961 differed 'considerably from the original Draft submitted', as the initial resolution was vehemently opposed by developed countries,[40] it nonetheless showed emergent reformist narratives adopted by developing countries to change the multilateral architecture and to remedy colonial inequities.[41]

Certain scholars have linked the countermovement towards an equitable global IP regime and the demands made by Third World countries in the form of a New International Economic Order (NIEO) that also emerged around that time.[42] The NIEO was spearheaded through UNCTAD and highlighted efforts by developing countries to assert greater control over technology transfer, multinational enterprises and other economic activities related to economic development goals.[43] Menescal, for example, writes that the policy demands

[35] Helfer (ibid) 565–67.

[36] ibid, 564.

[37] Menescal (n 28) 765.

[38] ibid; see also Roffe and Vea, 'WIPO Development Agenda' (2008) 95.

[39] ibid 767.

[40] Menescal (n 28) 765; Dhavan, Harris and Jain (n 26) 162.

[41] Roffe and Vea (n 33) 92.

[42] Ruth L Okediji, 'History Lessons for the WIPO Development Agenda' in in N Netanel (ed), *The Development Agenda: Global Intellectual Property and Developing Countries*, 1st edn (Oxford, Oxford University Press, 2008); Yu (n 28); Susan K Sell, 'Intellectual Property Protection and Antitrust in the Developing World: Crisis, Coercion, and Choice' (1995) 49 *International Organization* 315; Susan K Sell, 'The Quest for Global Governance in Intellectual Property and Public Health: Structural, Discursive, and Institutional Dimensions' (2004) 77 *Temple Law Review* 363.

[43] 'Declaration On The Establishment Of A New International Economic Order' (1974), available at www.un-documents.net/s6r3201.htm; Dianne Otto, 'Subalternity And International Law: The Problems Of Global Community And The Incommensurability Of Difference' (1996) 5 *Social and Legal Studies* 337; Nils Gilman, 'The New International Economic Order: A Reintroduction' (2015) 6 *Humanity: An International Journal of Human Rights, Humanitarianism, and Development* 1; Okediji, 'History Lessons' (2008).

made by less developed countries, especially with regard to transfer of technology, are reminiscent of the draft resolution Brazil introduced before the UNGA.[44] Likewise, Susan Sell notes that the Development Agenda raised by developing countries animated the NIEO approach to patents.[45] Similarly, Okediji observes that the political similarities between the NIEO and the Development Agenda are powerful reflections of a deeply pathological process in the construction of IP relations between developed and developing countries.[46] Yet, decades later, the issue of an inequitable international patent regime still contours discussions on patents and their impact on development. As subsequent chapters will show, this countermovement and the reformist ideas have continued even within the new IP regime – the TRIPS Agreement – that replaced the Paris Convention.[47]

IV. THE GLOBAL PHASE – TRIPS AGREEMENT

As developing countries shifted to other forums outside the Paris Convention in order to recalibrate the agreement, the US employed the same method to increase global IP rules and norms. For the US, bilateral agreements seemed to be the preferred approach in achieving high IP norms and standards outside of the WIPO and the Paris Convention. Furthermore, the US moved the issue of IP negotiations to the General Agreement on Tariffs and Trade (GATT)[48] – a forum in which it was the single most influential player – and it was this move that annihilated the dominance and reformist aspirations of developing countries.

Unlike the WIPO, the GATT was a negotiating forum where trade deals were not openly and freely negotiated.[49] This allowed some countries to drive a hard bargain in areas where they stood to benefit. Developed countries with their vast expertise had an unfair advantage over many developing countries that were dealing with substantial IP law-making for the first time. Drahos points out that most developing countries did not have prior knowledge of IP or proposals to the TRIPS Agreement and were ill-prepared for the negotiations,[50] demonstrating

[44] Menescal (n 28) 773.

[45] Sell, 'The Quest for Global Governance' (2004) 372.

[46] Okediji (n 42) 152.

[47] Even though it is beyond the ambit of this thesis, it is worth mentioning that other international agreements dealing with IP were also signed during the 20th century. These include the Madrid Agreement on trademarks and indication of source (1891), the Hague Agreement on designs (1925), the Rome Convention on performance (1961), the International Convention for the Protection of New Varieties of Plants, Acts of 1961 and 1991, the Patent Co-operation Treaty (1970) and the Treaty on Intellectual Property in Respect of Integrated Circuits (1989).

[48] Sell (n 42) 385.

[49] Drahos (n 29) 769.

[50] Peter Drahos, *Trade-Offs and Trade Linkages: TRIPS in a Negotiating Context* (Quaker United Nations, 2000), available at www.anu.edu.au/fellows/pdrahos/reports/pdfs/2001tradeoffstradelinkages.pdf.

'a high degree of ignorance amongst technology-importing countries as to the costs of increasing intellectual property protection'.[51] This view is supported by Chakravarthi Raghavan, who writes that the reason the US chose the GATT as the location for introducing new issue areas to international trade is because Third World countries are at their weakest, in terms of collective organisation and bargaining, inside the GATT.[52] Sell, on the other hand, writes that the US 'favoured GATT because it would permit them to link intellectual property protection to trade'.[53] The US negotiators anticipated better results owing to the large and attractive US market that could be used as negotiating leverage.[54] At GATT, the US was able to push forward a higher IP standard than those contained in the Paris Convention.

The TRIPS Agreement is among the foremost international law frameworks that deal specifically with the aegis and utilisation of IPRs. It provides for a high global minimum standard for the protection of IPRs. According to May and Sell, even though the TRIPS Agreement does not determine national legislation, WTO members should ensure that their national IP legislation adheres to the minimum level of protection for IPRs laid out in the TRIPS Agreement, thanks to the surveillance of adherence to various mechanisms and provisions such as the Trade Policy Review process.[55] With the aim of reducing distortions and impediments to international trade, the TRIPS Agreement was anticipated to not only promote effective and adequate protection of IPRs, but to also engender positive development goals through the transfer of technology from developed to developing countries, spurring local industrialisation in the latter.[56] Contracting developing country members also hoped that the TRIPS Agreement would increase much-needed foreign direct investment (FDI) due to harmonised IP laws. Further, it was believed that a stronger global IP regime would not only ensure certainty and predictability, but would also stimulate more local research and development devoted to the special needs of developing countries that are not felt in technology exporting countries.[57]

The TRIPS Agreement is currently the most comprehensive international agreement on IP matters as it introduced a strong compliance mechanism by judicialising dispute settlement among members[58] as well as the concept of

[51] ibid.

[52] Chakravarthi Raghavan, *Recolonization: General Agreement On Tariffs and Trade, The Uruguay Round And The Third World* (Penang, Third World Network, 1990) 60.

[53] Sell (n 42) 385.

[54] ibid.

[55] May and Sell (n 4) 4.

[56] United Nations Conference on Trade and Development, 'Report On The TRIPS Agreement And Developing Countries' (United Nations, 1996).

[57] ibid, 32.

[58] TRIPS Agreement, Art 64.

non-discrimination in all fields of technology for patent application.[59] In order to limit abuse and monopoly, it codified certain exceptions[60] and incorporated a set of procedural rules for issuing compulsory licences (CLs) for patents.[61] To ensure that countries with different levels of IP effectively comply with the new regime and to support developing countries, the TRIPS Agreement allowed for tiered transition periods for its gradual implementation,[62] and promised technical assistance[63] and technology transfer for least developed countries.[64] The TRIPS Agreement also allowed the use of CLs in many instances including public interest, abuse or anti-competitive conduct, or for non-commercial government use,[65] among others.

However, by limiting the use of CLs 'predominantly for the supply of the domestic market of the Member authorising such use'[66] in Article 31(f), the TRIPS Agreement has come under considerable criticism. Compulsory licensing refers to the granting of patent without the consent of the patent owner for a fee.[67] Article 31(f) of the TRIPS Agreement is seen as problematic because it created situations of ambiguity and confusion. Certain countries could face difficulties when trying to utilise CLs as they do not have the local manufacturing capability, thereby creating significant restrictions on the quantities of drugs that can be exported.[68] This poses huge problems for developing or least developed countries that have little or no manufacturing capability, and severely limits access to medicines for the majority in poor countries.[69]

This situation would be further exacerbated by the HIV/AIDS epidemic that significantly affected many developing and least developed countries. To rectify this issue, WTO Member States adopted the Declaration on TRIPS

[59] Pedro Roffe, Christoph Spennemann and Johanna von Braun, 'From Paris to Doha: The WTO Doha Declaration on the TRIPS Agreement and Public Health' in P Roffe, G Tansey and D Vivas Egui (eds), *Negotiating Health: Intellectual Property and Access to Medicines* (London, Earthscan Publications, 2006) 9.

[60] TRIPS Agreement, Arts 13, 17, 26.2, 30, and 41–61.

[61] ibid, Art 31.

[62] ibid, Art 65.

[63] ibid, Art 67.

[64] ibid, Art 66.2.

[65] ibid, Art 31(a)–(l); see also Jerome H Reichman, 'Comment: Compulsory Licensing Of Patented Pharmaceutical Inventions: Evaluating The Options' (2009) 37 *The Journal of Law, Medicine and Ethics*; Duncan Mathews, 'Is History Repeating Itself? The Outcome of Negotiations on Access to Medicines, The HIV/AIDS Pandemic and Intellectual Property Rights in the World Trade Organisation' (2004) 1 *Law, Social Justice and Global Development Journal*, available at https://warwick.ac.uk/fac/soc/law/elj/lgd/2004_1/matthews/matthews.rtf.

[66] TRIPS Agreement, Art 31(f).

[67] ibid, Art 31; see also Jayashree Watal, 'Developing Countries And The Protection Of Intellectual Property Rights: Current Issues In The WTO' in G Bermann and P Mavroidis (eds), *WTO Law and Developing Countries* (Cambridge, Cambridge University Press, 2007) 134.

[68] Frederick M Abbott, 'The TRIPS Agreement, Access To Medicines, And The WTO Doha Ministerial Conference' (2005) 5 *The Journal of World Intellectual Property* 15. See also Mathews, 'Is History Repeating Itself?' (2004).

[69] FM Scherer and Jayashree Watal, 'Post-TRIPS Options for Access to Patented Medicines in Developing Nations' (2002) 5 *Journal of International Economic Law* 925.

and Public Health (Doha Declaration) in 2001.[70] The Doha Declaration reaffirmed the rights of developing countries to protect the health of their populations as well as the right to interpret the TRIPS Agreement in a manner supportive to access to medicines for all.[71] Significantly, the Doha Declaration states that 'IP protection, as mandated by TRIPS, can be temporarily overridden to address public health issues and concerns as defined by States' government'.[72] The Doha Declaration also recognised the gravity of health issues facing many developing and least developed countries, especially those resulting in HIV/AIDS, malaria and tuberculosis, and reaffirmed that the TRIPS Agreement does not (and should not) prevent members from taking measures to protect public health and promote access to medicines.

Considering that many developing Member States with insufficient or no manufacturing capacities in the pharmaceutical sector could face difficulties in effectively using compulsory licensing, the WTO General Council adopted Article 31(bis)[73] which allowed export of generic drug medication from one country to poorer countries that lack manufacturing facilities. This allowed any Member country, either acting individually or as a regional group, to grant compulsory licences to export pharmaceutical products to countries with insufficient or no manufacturing capacities.

Despite these flexibility clauses, the implementation of the TRIPS Agreement, especially in Third World countries, has been contentious. This is because, as aptly pointed out by Joseph Stiglitz[74] and Thomas Pogge,[75] the protection of IPRs as required by the TRIPS Agreement does not take into account the differences in the development levels and socioeconomic needs of developed and developing countries, and are usually implemented with no form of social security in place. This severely unjust agreement, they contend, imposes human rights violations on account of the avoidable mortality and morbidity it foreseeably produces. The resultant effects on developing countries currently confronted with numerous health issues such as HIV/AIDS, malaria and

[70] 'Declaration on the TRIPS agreement and public health' (2001), available at www.wto.org/english/thewto_e/minist_e/min01_e/mindecl_trips_e.htm ('Doha Declaration'); see also Duncan Matthews, 'From The August 30, 2003 WTO Decision To The December 6, 2005 Agreement On An Amendment To TRIPS Improving Access To Medicines In Developing Countries' (2006) 2 *Intellectual Property Quarterly* 91.

[71] Doha Declaration, para 4.

[72] Valbona Muzaka, 'Developing Countries And The Struggle On The Access To Medicines Front: Victories Won And Lost' (2009) 30 *Third World Quarterly* 1344.

[73] 'Implementation of paragraph 6 of the Doha Declaration on the TRIPS Agreement and public health' (2001), available at /www.wto.org/english/tratop_e/trips_e/implem_para6_e.htm.

[74] Giovanni Dosi and Joseph E Stiglitz, 'The Role of Intellectual Property in the Development Process, with some Lessons from Developed Countries: An Introduction' in M Cimoli, G Dosi, K Maskus, R Okediji, J Reichman and J Stiglitz (eds), *Intellectual Property Rights: Legal and Economic Challenges for Development*, 1st edn (Oxford, Oxford University Press, 2014) 5; Joseph E Stiglitz, 'Economic Foundations of Intellectual Property Rights' (2008) 57 *Duke Law Journal* 1694.

[75] Thomas W Pogge, 'Human Rights and Global Health: A Research Program' (2005) 36 *Metaphilosophy* 182.

tuberculosis include but are not limited to the unaffordability and unavailability of basic essential medicines for the majority who need it, as well as premature deaths and extreme poverty.

Apart from criticism from commentators located in the Global North, many developing countries have often criticised the TRIPS Agreement even during the negotiating phase for many reasons. First, before the creation of the WTO, many developing countries in Africa, Asia, Latin America and the Caribbean did not recognise patents on pharmaceutical products. This is to ensure domestic accessibility and affordability of drugs. As will be seen in coming chapters, this welfare and developmental reason particularly orients the Indian and Brazilian patent regimes post-independence. Further, many of the countries in the Global South saw IP rules as a form of re-colonisation or economic imperialism,[76] especially as the IP regime under the TRIPS Agreement ignores the ownership system already in place in these societies. Many of these countries have a history of owning knowledge collectively, and the idea of profiting from an idea or invention to the exclusion of others for a specified period of time disregard their indigenous system. For these countries and the diverse cultures within them, the standard mandated by the TRIPS system impairs their development by not only failing to give them access to knowledge but also by failing to protect *their* IPRs, especially in traditional knowledge and biodiversity.[77] This leads to asymmetric rent payments whereby developing countries pay IP rents to Western firms for their IP, but not receiving in return rents from Western firms on IPRs developing countries view as theirs.

V. CONCLUSION

Recent years have seen the pendulum on access to medicine issue swing from developing countries to developed countries. Against the background of soaring drug prices in the US, Canada and the EU, questions on the utility of patent vis-à-vis its impact on innovation and societal well-being continue to frame debates in public media and government institutions. It is this need to find solutions to the incoherencies between patent rights, human rights and international trade that led the United Nations Secretary-General to convene a High-Level Panel on Access to Medicines (HLP) to advise on ways of improving access to medicines so that everyone can benefit from medical advancement in treatment, diagnostics and preventives (eg vaccines). In particular, the HLP sought

[76] Raghavan, *Recolonization* (1990).

[77] Dosi and Stiglitz, 'The Role of Intellectual Property' (2014) 2. See also Ikechi Mgbeoji, *Global Biopiracy: Patents, Plants And Indigenous Knowledge* (Vancouver, UBC Press, 2014); Chidi Oguamanam, *International Law And Indigenous Knowledge* (Toronto, University of Toronto Press, 2008).

to propose solutions for addressing the incoherencies between international human rights, trade, IPRs and public health objectives.[78]

The Report produced by the Panel (HLP Report) makes a number of important recommendations. These are as follows:

- governments should make use of TRIPS Agreement flexibilities to promote access by taking advantage of compulsory licensing;[79]
- governments should require manufacturers and distributors of health technologies to disclose to drug regulatory and other authorities information on cost of research and development (R&D), production and distribution as well as any public funding received in the development of new medical technologies;[80]
- governments and the private sector should refrain from explicit or implicit threats or tactics that undermine the right of WTO members to use TRIPS flexibilities;[81]
- new models of innovation delinking R&D costs from the price of medicines should be pursued[82],
- governments should implement IP laws, including patent laws, in a manner that guards against the grant of exclusive rights where not warranted by substantial inventive contribution;[83] and
- new models for innovation should be pursued, including new mechanisms for financing.[84]

The HLP Report also emphasised the importance of civil society advocacy in achieving access to medications. As the coming chapters will show, strong advocacy remains essential in medicine access debates in the countries discussed herein.

The overarching aim of this chapter was to sketch a background on the evolution of patents from the national to the global. Unlike their counterparts in the Global North, where patents were introduced to achieve specific national objectives, for Brazil, India and Nigeria, patent law came as a result of colonial conquest and sustained as a consequence of the influence of international agreements. However, as we examine the development, politics and the making of patent law, we will see the ways in which both Brazil and India developed and continue to recalibrate their patent regimes as a tool for development. The failure of Nigeria becomes all the more glaring in light of this.

[78] United National Development Program, 'The United Nations Secretary-General's High-Level Panel on Access To Medicines Report' (United Nations Development Program, 2016) 7.
[79] ibid.
[80] ibid, 28.
[81] ibid, 27.
[82] ibid, 29.
[83] ibid, 27–28.
[84] ibid, 30–31.

3

Views from the South: Critical Approaches to the Global Patent Regime

I. INTRODUCTION

THIS CHAPTER PROVIDES the theoretical/methodological framework that underpins the arguments in the book. It adopts a critical approach to analysing and unpacking global pharmaceutical patent law and, to a larger extent, international law – particularly who it recognises, how it circulates, who benefits from it, and who is erased. Examining the evolution of the global patent regime through a historiographical mapping of the broader international law framework provides an opportunity to look into its colonial legacies. This is important as it helps us understand the contradictions and injustices inherent in international law processes from the perspective of Third World states, and how these contradictions and injustices permeate into the patent regime framework. Importantly, it highlights the absenting of Third World legal rules and norms on ways of rewarding innovation and creativity, and how this absenting continues to hurt in the present liberal capitalist modernity.

Theories are imagined and executed in a definite cultural and social environment. Positivist international law, which emerged after the Peace of Westphalia in 1648, was/is built on the domination and imperialistic expansion of the European empires.[1] International law – the economic structures, politics, knowledge production and relations underpinning it – became Eurocentric, the 'preserve of the civilised, Christian states, into which overseas and foreign nations could enter only with the consent of and on the conditions laid down by the Western powers'.[2] It assumed European states – their behaviours and legal rules – as the foundations and determinants of international law (or law of nations). As a

[1] Jan Hendrik Willem Verzijl, *International Law In Historical Perspective* (Leyden, AW Sijthoff, 1970). See Antony Anghie, *Imperialism, Sovereignty And The Making of International Law* (Cambridge, Cambridge University Press, 2005) on the relationship between positivism and colonialism, especially the way in which positivism managed the colonial confrontation.

[2] Malcolm N Shaw, *International Law*, 5th edn (Cambridge, Cambridge University Press, 2003) 27.

result, much of the scholarship in this genre, the language and the world order it purports to describe or explain, is couched in Eurocentric thinking that not only glosses over, but also distances it from, the cruelties and brutalities of colonialism and imperialism from which international law emerged.[3]

There is the tendency for international law scholars and lawyers to equate the decolonisation process with the end of imperialism.[4] For example, in his classic statement, Malcolm Shaw asserts that as a result of the decolonisation process, Western supremacy over international law has been eroded.[5] Conflating the decolonisation process with the idea that colonialism and imperialistic exploitations are of no relevance to current international economic governance ignores, according to Ann Orford, not only the ability of concepts to move across space and time, but also how 'legal concepts and practices that were developed in the age of formal empire continue to shape international law in the post-colonial era'.[6] The continued influence of colonialism even in the postcolonial era, though not overt, is still very much present as the process of decolonisation occurred within the Eurocentric notion of statehood – a concept on which the very regime of international law is built upon.[7] Even upon independence, former colonies had no choice but to be 'states' in the Western tradition in order to become part of the existing international system. Today, international law's key concepts such as development, political economy, sovereignty, and nationhood, which were formed in the imperial project, are continually reiterated and redeployed in the contexts and languages of contemporary international legal and investment agreements.[8] Indeed, international law in the twenty-first century has found its way home in a universal teleology of progressive humanitarianism[9] and reflects the continuity of colonial law in the postcolonial. Put differently, key concepts developed and used to perpetuate colonial expansion have been assimilated in international state relations such that even decolonisation could not dismantle them.

[3] See ibid; see also Michael W Doyle, *Ways Of War And Peace* (New York, Norton, 1998); Brad R Roth, *Governmental Illegitimacy In International Law* (Oxford, Oxford University Press, 1996); Jack L Goldsmith and Eric A Posner, *The Limits Of International Law* (Oxford, Oxford University Press, 2007).

[4] Shaw, *International Law* (2003) 40.

[5] ibid. Certain Third World scholars are also guilty of the sin of conflating the decolonisation period with the end of Western imperialism and colonialism. See for instance Mohammed Bedjaoui, *International Law* (Dordrecht, Martinus Nijhoff, 1992), who viewed the decolonisation processes of the 1950s and 1960s as representing a 'historical rupture' that allowed the colonised to gain 'freedom' from the hold of colonial politics and exploitation.

[6] Anne Orford, 'The Past As Law Or History? The Relevance Of Imperialism For Modern International Law' (2012) 2 IILJ Working Paper 2.

[7] James T Gathii, 'International Law And Eurocentricity' (1998) 9 *European Journal of International Law* 189; see also James Thuo Gathii and Brad R Roth, 'Neoliberalism, Colonialism and International Governance: Decentering the International Law of Governmental Legitimacy' (2000) 98 *Michigan Law Review* 1996, 2040–43.

[8] Gathii (ibid) 189; Gathii and Roth (ibid) 2041.

[9] Martti Koskenmiemi, 'Histories of International Law: Dealing with Eurocentrism' (Utrecht, Utrecht University, 2011).

Seen this way, studying the colonial encounter that shaped (and continues to shape) the very foundation of international law is a practical and necessary exercise since international law now plays a role that extends beyond adjudicating relations between states to adjudicating in local jurisdictions the global ideals of human, economic, political and environmental development. Therefore, a well-rounded study that investigates and deconstructs not only the workings and foundations of the international law system but also questions its equitability and neutrality while fully incorporating the lived experiences of marginalised, oppressed and excluded communities is imperative to make international law project a 'terrain of transformative struggle'.[10] These reasonings underscore the employment of critical approaches to international (patent) law, specifically TWAIL, in this book.

This chapter is divided into two parts. Part I focuses on TWAIL theory. Here, TWAIL is used to uncover the historical origins of international patent law and its continuities in the postcolonial. It also performs the role of a vigilant critic in the quest to reform and reorient international law. This Part begins by tracing the objectives and tenets of this particular school of thought. It considers the global patent regime through a Twailian lens, paying particular attention to the Paris Convention and the TRIPS Agreement – the political context in which it was created, the goals it sought to advance, and the manner and effects of its operation. A Twailian examination of global patent broadens the argument of law as a 'site not only for the creation of new obligations but also for the transmission of inherited obligations'.[11] It illustrates how the expansion and globalisation of patent rules was part of the civilising mission[12] – the project of governing and exploiting non-European peoples and resources. It also sets the stage for understanding that the counter-hegemonic patent reforms in Brazil and India, as shall be seen in succeeding chapters, are part of a wider effort of resistance against and reform of hegemonic international [patent] law. Next, it provides an analysis of the patent provisions of the TRIPS Agreement through a Twailian lens. It highlights how the language used in the TRIPS Agreement resumes the social hierarchies honed during the colonial era, and masks relationships of power and control, as well as the continued domination and exploitation of the countries in the Global South. Part I concludes by exploring the methodological limit of TWAIL as it pertains to this research. The relevance of TWAIL to this book lies in its provision of not only a lens for understanding the historical position and experience(s) of Third World countries in international law in general and patent law in particular. It also provides a tool in recognising the ways patent law-making in the local forums of the Global South

[10] Usha Natarajan, John Reynolds, Amar Bhatia and Sujith Xavier, 'Introduction: TWAIL – On Praxis And The Intellectual' (2016) 37 *Third World Quarterly* 1947.

[11] Orford, 'Law or History' (2012) 9.

[12] Anghie, *The Making of International Law* (2005).

are contributing to and expanding the aperture on norms governing global patent law and medicine access discourses.

Part II focuses on nodal governance theory, which performs the function of a supplementary theory to fill in the gaps of TWAIL. Here, nodal governance is used to generate insight into the dynamic power and influence of certain non-state actors to relentlessly expand global IP systems by exerting influence on the state structure to achieve their objectives. Part II begins by unpacking the meaning of nodal theory – how nodes work, their principal categories, and the ways in which they influence changes in governance. In this respect, nodal governance is seen as a form of governance in which nodal networks are constantly reconstituting themselves to bring changes to a power relationship, either with the state or a fellow nodal network.

PART I: TWAIL THEORY

II. UNDERSTANDING TWAIL

TWAIL argues that the current international legal framework is an imperial project[13] created to legitimise the further subordination of the Third World by the West.

TWAIL arose as a legal scholarship that furthers and includes the interests of the Global South (or the colonised) in international law discourse. It aspires to 'address the material and ethical concerns of Third World peoples'[14] by generating debate around questions of colonial history, power, identity and the extent of the inclusion of Third World peoples in international law. For instance, in Brazil, India, and Nigeria – countries under study in this book – patent law was introduced during the colonial period for the benefit of the colonial government without regard to the socio-economic or cultural needs or practices of those countries. And even though the postcolonial state governments of the aforementioned countries have reformed certain parts of their patent systems, it is important to question and deconstruct the system in order to understand why it was created in the first place and who it sought to benefit. It is in this exercise that TWAIL provides the structure for such mapping and analyses in this book.

In locating Global South engagement within the global patent regime, TWAIL also provides a useful framework for challenging the construction and

[13] Antony Anghie (n 1). See also Antony Anghie, 'The Evolution Of International Law: Colonial And Postcolonial Realities' (2006) 27 *Third World Quarterly* 739; BS Chimni, 'The Past, Present and Future of International Law: A Critical Third World Approach' (2007) 8 *Melbourne Journal of International Law* 1; BS Chimni, 'Third World Approaches to International Law: A Manifesto' (2006) 8 *International Community Law Review* 3; James Thuo Gathii, 'TWAIL: A Brief History of its Origins, its Decentralized Network, and a Tentative Bibliography' (2011) 26 *Trade, Law and Development* 37; and Makau Mutua and Antony Anghie, 'What Is TWAIL' (2000) 94 *Proceedings of the Annual Meeting (American Society of International Law)* 31.

[14] Chimni, 'A Manifesto' (2006) 4.

history of the international patent regime. It argues that colonialism and the imperial expansionist project, from which the current global patent was borne out of, continues to impinge upon and structure the global patent regime. In other words, the colonial mission, which birthed international law, subordinated non-European people and societies and continues to influence and configure the current international law project. As such, international regimes such as the TRIPS Agreement are thus nothing but a modern-day extension of this colonial engagement. This is not a completely new concept. Certain IP scholars have analysed the continued influence of colonial law on the IP regime. For instance, Ikechi Mgbeoji has shown how powerful states and their corporations in the Global North use the language of patent to continue the appropriation of indigenous people's knowledge and prey on the genetic resources developed by countries and cultures in the Third World.[15] Similarly, Chidi Oguamanam examines the ways global IP converges with histories of subjugation along lines of nation and race to create a rift between Western and non-Western knowledge systems.[16] The point here is this: patent regime spread to the Third World in concert with colonial expansionism for the efficient subjugation and exploitation of colonies.

TWAIL scholarship is far from uniform and has in no way followed a single line of enquiry.[17] Some TWAIL scholars are more oppositional, such as Joel Ngugi[18] and Makau Mutua,[19] than reconstructive, such as BS Chimni[20] and Obiora Okafor.[21] However, these scholars are united by the mission to question, unearth and reform the rules of international law that are unjust to the Third World.[22] In so doing, they are unpacking the hypocrisies inherent in the international legal system, challenging its selective application, and offering crucial clues for its democratic reshaping.[23]

The TWAIL movement is reinforced by rich analyses of issues which can be divided into three distinct phases. TWAIL I, for instance, focused on the decolonisation process, statehood, colonialism as a 'system of totalizing degradation',[24]

[15] See Ikechi Mgbeoji, *Global Biopiracy: Patents, Plants And Indigenous Knowledge* (Vancouver, UBC Press, 2014).

[16] Chidi Oguamanam, *International Law And Indigenous Knowledge* (Toronto, University of Toronto Press, 2008).

[17] See Richard Falk, Balakrishnan Rajagopal and Jacqueline Stevens, *International Law and the Third World: Reshaping Justice* (London, Routledge, 2008).

[18] See Joel Ngugi, 'Making New Wine for Old Wineskins: Can the Reform of International Law Emancipate the Third World in the Age of Globalization' (2002) 8 *UC Davis Journal of International Law and Policy* 73.

[19] Mutua and Anghie, 'What Is TWAIL' (2000).

[20] Chimni, 'Past, Present and Future' (2007).

[21] Obiora Chinedu Okafor, 'Enacting Twailian Praxis In Nonacademic Habitats: Toward A Conceptual Framework' '(2016) 110 *AJIL Unbound* 20.

[22] Chimni (n 13) 468.

[23] Gathii, 'TWAIL: A Brief History of its Origins' (2011) 37.

[24] David Scott, *Conscripts Of Modernity* (Durham, Duke University Press, 2004) 95. See also David Scott, *Refashioning Futures: Criticism after Postcoloniality* (Princeton, Princeton University Press, 1999).

and the role of powerful nations to use international law as a hegemonic force. This phase was also closely aligned with the decolonisation movement, the diplomatic initiatives undertaken by the newly independent Third World states and placed immense faith in the United Nations to cause the changes necessary to usher in a just world order.[25] TWAIL II, on the other, focuses on the roles and powers of international organisations in perpetuating Third World domination and marginalisation.[26] Thus, the distinct feature of TWAIL II lies in the examination of the global political economy by looking into the extent to which colonial relations continue to shape the fundamentals of international law.[27] In this group, works by Upendra Baxi, Antony Anghie, BS Chimni, M Sonarajah, James Gathii, Obiora Okafor, Makau Mutua, to mention a few, comes to mind. TWAIL III continues the tradition of the network in applying its commitment to democratic concerns and transformative action in addressing multiple issues related to society, politics, identity and economics. As a result, it has not only garnered a level of sophistication and complexity since its emergence in the decolonisation discourse, but it is also cognisant of contemporary concerns and contexts. The result is a rich and varied scholarship on concepts such as statehood,[28] international criminal law,[29] taxation,[30] international criminal court,[31] the role of social movement,[32] food sovereignty,[33] human rights,[34] the war on terror,[35] feminism,[36] international humanitarian law,[37] urban law,[38] ethics,[39]

[25] Antony Anghie and BS Chimni, 'Third World Approaches To International Law And Individual Responsibility In Internal Conflicts' (2003) 2 *Chinese Journal of International Law* 77.

[26] Madhav Khosla, 'The TWAIL Discourse: The Emergence Of A New Phase' (2007) 9 *International Community Law Review* 292.

[27] Anghie (n 1) 81–84.

[28] Makau Mutua, 'Why Redraw The Map Of Africa: A Moral And Legal Inquiry' (1995) 16 *Michigan Journal of International Law* 1113.

[29] Asad G Kiyani, 'Third World Approaches to International Criminal Law' (2016) 109 *AJIL Unbound* 255.

[30] Jalia Kangave, '"Taxing" TWAIL: A Preliminary Inquiry into TWAIL's Application to the Taxation of Foreign Direct Investment' (2008) 10 *International Community Law Review* 389.

[31] Parvathi Menon, 'Self-Referring To The International Criminal Court: A Continuation Of War By Other Means' (2016) 109 *AJIL Unbound* 260.

[32] Balakrishnan Rajagopal, *International Law from Below: Development, Social Movements and Third World Resistance* (Cambridge, Cambridge University Press, 2003).

[33] Michael Fakhri, 'Third World Sovereignty, Indigenous Sovereignty, And Food Sovereignty: Living With Sovereignty Despite The Map' (2018) 9 *Transnational Legal Theory* 218.

[34] Makau Mutua, 'Savages, Victims, And Saviors: The Metaphor Of Human Rights' (2001) 42 *Harvard International Law Journal*; Balakrishnan Rajagopal, 'Counter-Hegemonic International Law: Rethinking Human Rights And Development As A Third World Strategy' (2006) 27 *Third World Quarterly* 971.

[35] Khosla, 'The TWAIL Discourse' (2007) 291.

[36] Vasuki Nesiah, 'The Ground Beneath Her Feet: Third World Feminisms' (2003) 4 *Journal of International Women's Studies* 30; Mosope Fagbongbe, 'The Future Of Women's Rights From A TWAIL Perspective' (2008) 10 *International Community Law Review* 401.

[37] Ntina Tzouvala, 'TWAIL And The "Unwilling or Unable" Doctrine, Continuities, and Ruptures' (2016) 109 *AJIL Unbound* 266.

[38] Luis Eslava, *Local Space, Global Life* (Cambridge, Cambridge University Press, 2015).

[39] Kwadwo Appiagyei-Atua, 'Ethical Dimensions Of Third-World Approaches To International Law (TWAIL): A Critical Review' (2015) 8 *African Journal of Legal Studies* 209.

environment,[40] plant varieties,[41] Islamic contributions to the shared history of public international law,[42] and on praxis and the intellectual.[43]

In spite of this assortment of voices within, TWAIL scholarship remains committed to a reading of international laws that historicises the 'structure of modern colonial power' as well as its reformation that incorporates the views and experiences of the often-ignored subaltern to recreate a just world order.[44] Importantly, in giving voice and advocating for wider inclusion of those on the peripheries of the international system, TWAIL has achieved the inclusion of the margins as part of the centre, urging the world to recognise and engage with evolving scholarly movements and legal reforms happening outside European/western/occidental legal systems.

A. Key Themes within TWAIL Discourse

According to TWAIL's vision statement, the scholarship is particularly interested in 'the challenges and opportunities facing "third world" peoples in the new world order'.[45] It also recognises the role the dominant narrative in international law plays in perpetuating the domination and marginalisation of the people of the Third World. As such, TWAIL is concerned with:

> (a) the need to contextualize international law's privileging of European and North American voices by providing institutional and imaginative opportunities for participation from the third world; and (b) to formulate a substantive critique of the politics and scholarship of mainstream international law insofar as it has helped reproduce structures that marginalize and dominate third world peoples.[46]

TWAIL is therefore interested in formulating and disseminating critical approaches to the relationships of power that constitute, and are constituted

[40] Antonius Rickson Hippolyte, 'Negative Environmental Sovereignty In The Third World: A Twail Analysis Of ICSID's Disregard For Environmental Justice In The South' (2012) SSRN Electronic Journal; Usha Natarajan, 'Third World Approaches To International Law (TWAIL) And The Environment' in A Philippopoulos-Mihalopoulos and V Brooks (eds), *Research Methods in Environmental Law*, 1st edn (Cheltenham, Edward Elgar Publishing, 2017).

[41] Titilayo Adebola, 'The Regime Complex for Plant Variety Protection: Revisiting TRIPS Implementation in Nigeria', PhD thesis (University of Warwick, 2017).

[42] Corri Zoli, 'Islamic Contributions to International Humanitarian Law: Recalibrating TWAIL Approaches for Existing Contributions and Legacies' (2016) 109 *AJIL Unbound* 271.

[43] See Sujith Xavier, Amar Bhatia, Usha Natarajan and John Reynolds, 'Conspiring In Cairo & Canada: Placing TWAIL Scholarship And Praxis' (2017) 33 *Windsor Yearbook of Access to Justice* i, a special issue on TWAIL from the Cairo Conference in 2015, which focuses on different aspects of the intellectual as a political actor.

[44] Gathii (n 13) 40.

[45] TWAIL vision statement found in Karin Mickelson, 'Taking Stock Of TWAIL Histories' (2008) 10 *International Community Law Review* 357.

[46] ibid.

by, the current world order.[47] Reading TWAIL's vision statement makes one cognisant of its central tenets.

(a) *Contesting Eurocentricity in International Law:* The TWAIL movement understands and acknowledges that international law privileges Europe, European knowledge and ideals.[48] It also recognises the trajectory of international law – from its colonial usage and extension over time to the non-European world, which existed outside the realm of European law, as well as the exclusion of the rich body of doctrine and principle that originated from Third World legal systems from the larger body of international law.[49] Fundamentally, these European experiences and influences continue to set and inform the contemporary international law. If, at all, countries in the Global South are included, they are usually mentioned as an aside, not as a focus, original contributor, or active participant to international law-making, and 'often only to confirm the "universal" or "global" norms, ideas, rights, and concepts evinced in US and European constitutional systems and law'.[50] This has created, according to James Gathii, a hierarchy of power and structural relationship especially within the colonial and neo-colonial imperial and economic relationship between former European colonial powers and the colonised.[51]

Another added effect of the supremacy of European experiences and ideals in international law is the erasure of the rich contribution from other parts of the world to this particular body of law. Corri Zoli, for example, provides a persuasive argument regarding the role and contribution of Islam in the making of international law, especially the contributions of Islamic norms to international humanitarian law and the role of Muslim states in the early Geneva and Hague diplomatic conferences.[52] Thus, for TWAIL, dismantling the one-sided hegemonic Eurocentric narratives of international law involves teasing out encounters of difference along many axes – race, religion, class, gender, ethnicity, and economics, among others – and in interdisciplinary ways – social, theoretical, epistemological and ontological – from the geopolitical Third World.[53]

[47] ibid.

[48] Ibironke Odumosu, 'Challenges For The (Present/) Future Of Third World Approaches To International Law' (2008) 10 *International Community Law Review* 468.

[49] Dianne Otto, 'Subalternity And International Law: The Problems Of Global Community And The Incommensurability of Difference' (1996) 5 *Social and Legal Studies* 337; see also Obiora C Okafor, 'Newness, Imperialism And International Legal Reform In Our Time: A TWAIL Perspective' (2005) 43 *Osgoode Hall Law Journal* 171.

[50] Vidya Kumar, 'Towards A Constitutionalism Of The Wretched', *Völkerrechtsblog* (2017), available at https://voelkerrechtsblog.org/towards-a-constitutionalism-of-the-wretched.

[51] Gathii, 'Eurocentricity' (1998) 184.

[52] Zoli, 'Islamic Contributions' (2016); see also Upendra Baxi, 'New Approaches to the History of International Law' (2006) 19 *Leiden Journal of International Law* 555.

[53] Gathii (n 13) 27–32.

The agenda of this critical scholarship, therefore, is in bringing in the subaltern, particularly retelling and rewriting via the inclusion of subaltern experiences. In other words, a more inclusive international law that would overcome its Eurocentric origins and considers non-European history and ideals in the international legal framework to reflect the rich diverse experience within the general international system. This is very crucial as the inclusion of Third World voices, knowledge production and experiences within the Eurocentric/Western discourses of international law assists in dismantling and challenging the hegemony of this dominant narrative of international law. Dismantling the strong structures of Eurocentricity and its legacy from international law allows for a democratic and fair international law reflective of the needs of and sensitive to the concerns of and aware of the legal happenings in the Third World. The result is a body of international legal scholarship that takes international legal history seriously, particularly in the relations between formerly colonial countries and their colonial metropole.[54]

(b) *Contesting the Universality Paradox*: International law contains a paradox: while being a product of European legal culture and thought – and therefore a narrowly regional body of law – it has been conceived, thanks to imperial and colonialist expansionism, as an abstract, neutral, and universally valid set of norms applicable to all states, whatever their legal cultures or indigenous ways of understanding law. This universality, according to Sundhya Pahuja, is not the neutral inclusion of all peoples, but 'rather a process by which a particular form of sociopolitical organization was universalized'.[55] This was achieved by completely recasting non-Western political entities into the mould of modern European states, which in turn required the irreparable destruction of all traditional forms of polity in existence.[56] This recasting required not only classifying groups of people along binaries of civilised (Europe) and uncivilised (non-European) in need of 'civilising' and 'saving' via colonial rule, but also elevating European laws, structures and institutions as superior and denigrating 'others' as inferior.

If anything, this language of universality helped conceal, as Emmanuelle Jouannet states, the 'ambitions of Western states in terms of empire and domination, and the submission of the world to their own conceptions of economic and legal order'.[57] It was through this production of ideology of the superiority of European legal rules and norms that classical international law crystallised its universalist appeal and, in the process,

[54] ibid, 40.
[55] Sundhya Pahuja, *Decolonising International Law: Development, Economic Growth, and the Politics of Universality* (Cambridge, Cambridge University Press, 2011) 46.
[56] Emmanuelle Jouannet, 'Universalism And Imperialism: The True-False Paradox Of International Law?' (2007) 18 *European Journal of International Law* 382.
[57] ibid.

perpetuated its social dominance over the Global South. But as critical legal scholars, including TWAIL, have shown, international law is neither neutral nor egalitarian even as the promise of universality has inspired many attempts by Third World states to use international law as a site of political struggle. Many such attempts, however, have had the unintended consequence of further perpetuating Third World domination and marginalisation. It is this particular form of universality that Twailian scholarship is critical of and disavows, especially when it is given a sanction of legality within the international legal order and therefore a requirement for Third World states.

Instead, TWAIL scholarship gestures towards a promise of universality as such.[58] That is, a universality that is quasi-transcendent – it recognises the impossibility of genuine singular universality, but is not fearful of plurality. In other words, a universality which 'is not one but that recognizes the multiple identities, heterogeneity, and rejection of universalist modes of reasoning'.[59] In a similar vein, Makau Mutua has argued that international law must adopt 'a moral equivalency of cultures and people'[60] in the process, reinforcing Ricoeur's assertion that international law must, on the one hand, accept the universal claim attached to a few values and on the other hand, recognise that other potential universals are contained in so-called exotic [non-European, subaltern] cultures.[61]

It is important to note at this point that TWAIL acknowledges that Third World states are not merely passive objects in international law and it would be simplistic to argue so. Some Third World states have mastered the art of 'playing' international law to their advantage in the capricious game of politics, both at local and international levels. For example, Shalini Randeria has shown how certain Third World states, usually seen as weak against the forces of globalisation and international law, transpose the processes of globalisation into the national arena by capitalising on their perceived weakness.[62] The Third World state is not merely a victim of neo-liberal economic structures and the constituting international legal framework, but an active participant, manoeuvring itself internationally and locally. Thus, in playing 'cunning' politics, they render themselves unaccountable both to their citizens and to international institutions.[63] In a similar vein, Parvathi Menon has shown how African states use international law

[58] ibid.

[59] James Thuo Gathii, 'Rejoinder: Twailing International Law' (2000) 98 *Michigan Law Review* 2071.

[60] Mutua, 'Savages, Victims, And Saviors (2001) 36.

[61] P Ricoeur, *Oneself As Another* (trans K Blamey) (Chicago, University of Chicago Press, 1992) 289.

[62] Shalini Randeria, 'Cunning States And Unaccountable International Institutions: Legal Plurality, Social Movements And Rights Of Local Communities To Common Property Resources' (2003) 44 *European Journal of Sociology* 27.

[63] ibid 28.

and institutions to legitimise their actions and delegitimise internal political 'others' (political opposition and rebel groups, in particular).[64] By employing the rhetoric of international humanitarian law, these states elevate internal issues to the status of 'international crisis', thereby opening up such issues to investigation and/or prosecution by the Office of the Prosecutor of the International Criminal Court.[65] Thus, these states do not only exploit international criminal law for their own political games: the law itself provides a legal cover for such exploitation.[66]

(c) *Importance of History*: For TWAIL, history matters, and the historical dimensions of international law even more so. Paying attention to past events and processes, according to TWAIL, helps us understand its present form. It helps us understand our present place in international law and map the consequences of this placement. For TWAIL, telling this story also involves the inclusion of the brutal and bloody colonial beginnings of international law and the devastation it wrought on the lives, bodies, histories and systems of geographically located Third World countries. Therefore, to transform the present and future of international law from a state of subjection to emancipation, one must first understand the 'problem-space' in which the system occupies.[67] The term 'problem-space' is borrowed from David Scott who explains it to mean a language, an ensemble of questions and answers around which a horizon of identifiable stakes (conceptual as well as ideological-political) hangs. In this respect, the context is not only the particular problems posed as such but also the particular questions that seem worth asking and the kind of answers that seem worth having.

Understanding this problem-space involves engaging in an honest mapping of the origins and influences of the international legal system by delving into the past only because otherwise it would be impossible to understand how the present came into being and what the trend portends for the future. Doing this not only broadens our perspective, but also has the potential to stimulate informed curiosity about the future of international law, thereby allowing for an animation of its democratic emancipatory potentials.[68] In essence, TWAIL seeks a kind of international legal scholarship that takes legal historiography seriously, particularly in the relations between former colonies and the European metropolis by shining light on its colonialist underpinnings and pretences, developing in the process new ways of thinking about international law, as well as its reconstruction, that are responsive to the needs and aspirations of peoples of the Third World.

[64] Menon, 'Self-Referring To The International Criminal Court' (2016).
[65] ibid, 260.
[66] Menon (n 31) 261.
[67] See Scott, *Conscripts of Modernity* (2004) 4.
[68] Pahuja, *Decolonising International Law* (2011).

Furthermore, for TWAIL, the importance of history is not static and located in the past. The colonial influence of international law continues to manifest even in the present. This is especially pertinent as international law cannot be neglected at a time when it is slowly becoming domestic law, manifesting itself in debates on health, access to knowledge, food security, environment, services and socio-economic development issues. Therefore, the ultimate goal of the dialectic interaction between TWAIL and international law is the inclusion of non-European history and ideals in the international legal framework to reflect the rich, diverse experience within the general international system, as well as to transform international law to be more sensitive to the concerns of the Third World.

(d) *A Commitment to Reforming International Law*: Another key TWAIL tenet is the reform of international legal discourse through the reform of international rules and structures that are unjust for the Third World. This can be achieved through alternative reconceptualisation of international legal ordering and governance. That is, the engagement of alternative counter-hegemonic ideas that expose and gently reform the deficiencies in the international legal system. In this regard, TWAIL argues that the recognition of the various ongoing reform projects in the local jurisdictions of the Third World is part of a Twailian project to eradicate conditions of underdevelopment in the Global South and reform the international. For instance, Balakrishnan Rajagopal notes the role of social movement in the Global South in reshaping and contributing to international law.[69] This *materialist approach* argues that the various reform projects happening in the local forums of the Third World should be seen as the everyday life of international law.[70] Championed by Sundhya Pahuja and Luis Eslava, this particular strand of TWAIL emphasis on materiality thinks of international law as 'not only an ideological project located in a particular material context, and with material consequences but also as material'.[71] Looking into the way international law operates, including its daily functioning on the mundane quotidian level, they argue, reveals that these domestic legal reforms may not ostensibly appear as part of the international, but in actuality are.[72] Focusing on the prosaic life of international law in domestic spaces and the way these daily occurrences reverberate in the 'international' illustrates that TWAIL is neither nihilistic with no positive

[69] Rajagopal, *International Law From Below* (2003).

[70] Luis Eslava and Sundhya Pahuja, 'Between Resistance And Reform: TWAIL And The Universality of International Law' (2011) 3 *Trade, Law and Development* 104; Luis Eslava and Sundhya Pahuja, 'Beyond the (Post)Colonial: TWAIL And The Everyday Life Of International Law' (2012) 45 *Journal of Law and Politics in Africa, Asia and Latin America – Verfassung und Recht in Übersee (VRÜ)* 195.

[71] ibid.

[72] Eslava and Pahuja, 'Between Resistance and Reform' (2011) 103.

agenda for action or reform of international law and relations,[73] nor privileges the West, Western dialect and dialectic modalities.[74] It shows, instead, that TWAIL provides a praxis of (the new) universality by mapping the numerous forms of resistance already at play in the struggle against the (post)colonial normative order now being institutionalised and administered across the Third World. It is only when the everyday engagement of international law in domestic forums of the Global South is placed in a historical context that these everyday actions are instilled with meaning and function. This new praxis, therefore, allows us to look at daily engagement and contestation of patent regimes in the local forums of Brazil and India to see how global patent law as it relates to medicine access is conceptualised, resisted and reformed in legal and policy discourse within the confines of the TRIPS Agreement. And for this current inquiry, it is through this materialist approach, the looking beyond the international to map the change happening outside normative international law framework, that TWAIL further benefits this book.

In sum, it is the call for a historiographical engagement with international law, the acknowledgement of legal heterogeneity, the rejection of universalist modes of reasoning and the recognition of counter-hegemonic reforms and ideas that TWAIL becomes a useful methodological tool for contextualising, historicising, mapping and analysing patent law regime and reforms in the countries under study, allowing us, in the process, to locate a particular kind of narrative which gave birth to patent discourses in these countries. This location helps in not only identifying what constitutes the conditions of possibility of the present, but provides a starting point from which to begin the process of revolutionary *re*imagination and *re*ordering.

III. SITUATING TWAIL WITHIN THE GLOBAL PATENT REGIME

In this section, I broadly examine the legal structure of global patent rules, paying particular attention to the TRIPS Agreement – the political context in which it was created, the goals it sought to advance, and the manner and effects of its operation. A Twailian analysis of global patent rules places international IP law in the context of law as a 'site not only for the creation of new obligations

[73] DP Fidler, 'Revolt Against Or From Within The West? TWAIL, The Developing World, And The Future Direction Of International Law' (2003) 2 *Chinese Journal of International Law* 29. See also Jayan Nayar, 'Between Hope And Despair: The Iraq War And International Law Futures?' in P Shiner and A Williams (eds), *The Iraq War and International Law*, 1st edn (Oxford, Hart Publishing, 2008).

[74] SG Sreejith, 'An Auto-Critique Of TWAIL's Historical Fallacy: Sketching An Alternative Manifesto' (2016) 38 *Third World Quarterly* 1516.

but also for the transmission of inherited obligations'.[75] Such analysis illustrates the evolution and globalisation of patent rules within the concept of North–South divide. It also shows the ways countries in the Global South, as shall be seen in succeeding chapters, have sought to reconfigure the global patent regime through the development of counter-hegemonic patent laws that reflect their needs, telling, in the process, a story of a multifaceted and complex engagement of international law. As a consequence, it reveals the recurrent tension within the international legal system as a site of contestation for the subaltern.[76]

If we trace the origins of protection and monopolisation of property right from the perspective of the Third World, it is clear IP law spread from the key European monarchies to the colonial territories in Africa, Caribbean, Asia, Latin America and the Pacific. This spread in the form of the Paris Convention as a result of increase in commerce among imperial European states that wanted to protect and maintain their competitive advantage with other European monarchies, but also to safeguard the interests and exploits in the colonial territories regardless of distinct cultural practices and political organisation. In spite of its numerous revisions (1900, 1911, 1925, 1934, 1958 and 1967), the Paris Convention remained an agreement that spread and deepened a Eurocentric understanding of property rights protection, justified and enforced the monopolistic rights of a patent-holder. In the colonial territories, these rights helped in the conquest of non-European peoples for both economic and political purposes.

This move in global IP universalisation demonstrates Western-centric universalism – a canopy application of rules and norms from the core to the periphery, irrespective of fit, level of development, or needs – at work. Via the Paris Convention, the colonies were swept into the then nascent global IP regime, exemplifying how the politically imagined space of the Third World became and continues to be a repository of the Western ideals of how law should work in subjugated spaces.[77] Seen in this way, the Paris Convention firmly secured a Eurocentric notion and definition of property rights, which came to be regarded as the acceptable, legitimate and relevant standard of protection. This legitimacy and relevance were then applied as 'universal' and extended to the Third World, ignoring the inappropriateness of the privatisation of property, especially in Third World societies, where common-pool and community sharing of resources are valued and practised.

By instituting private monopolies and the notion of private property in those parts, the Paris Convention underscores the continued use of international law as a hegemonic political and exploitative tool even as such laws are inimical to the economic development of the colonies. For instance, Article 5^{quater} under the Paris Convention prohibits countries from revoking patents on the ground

[75] Orford (n 6) 9.
[76] Anghie (n 1).
[77] Angie (n 1).

that the patented articles are being imported rather than locally manufactured,[78] while, as shall be shown in coming chapters, colonial patent-owners neither worked nor produced the patented article locally in the colonies. As a result, a foreigner could obtain a patent monopoly with absolutely no associated obligation to produce the patented article or ensure its supply in the patent-granting country, especially in the colonies. This practice has the effect of retarding the industrial development of the importing country, since a foreign monopoly grant blocks domestic production.[79] This shows that though the Paris Convention was engineered by the Western countries as an international legal instrument, it is a significantly and aggressively imperialist tool used to secure import monopolies for the producer nations of the West so as to satisfy the needs of expanding capitalism.[80] In this vein, the Paris Convention not only serves 'the legal and political imagination of people committed to imperial administration and colonial practice',[81] but also their monopolistic economic interest by ensuring the transfer of wealth from the colonies to the metropolis.

As analyses in this book will show, the issue of patent monopoly was (and continues to be) a point of contention between developed and developing countries, as was evident when Brazil pushed for a revision of the Paris Convention at the UNGA in 1961 to reduce incidents of patent monopoly abuse of pharmaceutical patents by foreign multinational companies operating in the country at that time (chapter four). The push for patent reform in India was also borne out of the fact that many foreign pharmaceutical companies operating in the country at that time did not locally manufacture their patented invention or work their patent locally, but relied instead on the importation of the patented article whilst blocking indigenous companies that would normally manufacture locally (chapter five). Analyses of the patent regime in Nigeria also revealed that majority of the patents in the country were owned by foreigners who did not locally work the patented article, as well as the colonial patent law in effect at that time was unfavourable to national needs of the country (chapter six).

78 Article 5^{quater} states: 'When a product is imported into a country of the Union where there exists a patent protecting a process of manufacture of the said product, the patentee shall have all the rights, with regard to the imported product, that are accorded to him by the legislation of the country of importation, on the basis of the process patent, with respect to products manufactured in that country.'

79 Rajeev Dhavan, Lindsay Harris and Gopal Jain, 'Conquest By Patent: The Paris Convention Revisited' (1990) 32 *Journal of Indian Law Institute* 132. See also Edith Penrose, 'International Patenting And The Less-Developed Countries' (1973) 83 *The Economic Journal* 768; Constantine Vaitsos, 'Patents Revisited: Their Function In Developing Countries' (1972) 9 *The Journal of Development Studies* 71; Owen T Adikibi, 'The Multinational Corporation And Monopoly Of Patents In Nigeria' (1988) 16 *World Development* 511; AK Menescal, 'Changing WIPO's Ways? The 2004 Development Agenda In Historical Perspective' (2005) *Journal of World Intellectual Property* 761; Peter K Yu, 'A Tale Of Two Development Agendas' (2009) 35 *Ohio Northern University Law Review* 465.

80 Dhavan, Harris and Jain (ibid) 131.

81 Michael Fakhri, 'Third World Sovereignty, Indigenous Sovereignty, And Food Sovereignty: Living With Sovereignty Despite The Map' (2018) 9 *Transnational Legal Theory* 3.

Even in contemporary times, the issue of patent monopoly continues to be a thorny issue between the developing and developed countries, as well as between various interests within the Global South.

Further, the fact that the global patent protection framework historically came from the Global North, with minimal contributions from, or recognition of the centuries-old ownership system already in place, in the Third World, also accentuates the Twailian cynicism and scepticism of global IP rules.[82] It foregrounds a fundamental issue – the imposition on different contexts and realities of Eurocentric 'ideals'.[83] That is, the imposition of Eurocentric property right ideals and the forced inclusion of the Third World into the global IP framework, continuing the blanket application of hegemonic European normative values and ownership of property on non-European people. This is especially true in the realm of patent law where Western legal rules and cultural-intellectual values were foisted on the states outside Europe via colonial edicts and represented as universally valid regardless of fit and relevance to local realities, and in so doing, denied, erased or suppressed non-European subjectivity. The resultant effect is the further entrenchment of economic inequality, which benefited the more economically advanced nations (the colonisers) to the detriment of the colonised. It is this detrimental impact on socioeconomic development of Third World states that has animated (and continues to animate) contemporary discussion about IP in general and patents in particular. In this mode, TWAIL scholars cannot divorce the colonial exploitative origins of global patent rules from their current mutation since colonialism, like any mode of production, is a total system which includes an ideological aspect that continues to be operationalised even in the present.

In modern times, one can see how these colonial characteristics continue to shape global IP governance systems, especially the TRIPS Agreement and, correspondingly, how these systems continue to retard the development of postcolonial states. The adoption and ratification of the TRIPS Agreement signalled a seismic shift in global IP governance. This is especially so for many postcolonial states that excluded many areas as beyond the ambit of IP, as well as the presence of the dispute settlement enforcement mechanism within the WTO. However, tracing the history of the inclusion of IP as part of the Uruguay Round of multilateral trade negotiations emphasises the influence of industries, especially pharmaceutical companies, on the scope and wide-reaching tentacles

[82] Peter Drahos, 'Developing Countries And International Intellectual Property Standard-Setting' (2002) 5 *The Journal of World Intellectual Property* 765; Ruth L Okediji, 'The International Relations Of Intellectual Property: Narratives Of Developing Country Participation In The Global Intellectual Property System' (2003) 7 *Singapore Journal of International and Comparative Law* 225; Yu, 'Two Development Agendas' (2009); Peris S Jones, 'When "Development" Devastates: Donor Discourses, Access To HIV/AIDS Treatment in Africa and Rethinking the Landscape of Development' (2004) 25 *Third World Quarterly* 387.

[83] Koskenniemi, 'Histories of International Law' (2011).

of the TRIPS Agreement. It shows how our current understanding and knowledge regarding the concept and scope of patentable subject matter was shaped and dictated by industry and the national interests of Western states.[84] This influence explains why the TRIPS Agreement has induced such confidence crises from many in the Global South, including civil society groups, patient groups and human rights activists.

This influence also explains why for TWAIL, the TRIPS Agreement is seen as an ideological project. Ideological in the sense that it consists of a set of '*complexes of ideas* which tend to generate activities toward *maintenance of ideas of the existing order*' (emphasis added).[85] In this view, the complex ideas become the various components of IPR such as patents, trade secrets, geographical indications, industrial designs, copyrights and layout designs, while the maintenance of ideas of the existing order becomes prescription of 'minimum uniform global standards'[86] of IP protection in which every member of the WTO has to abide by. In other words, the concept of IPRs becomes an ideology coined to justify access to and control of Third World property rights, while the TRIPS Agreement *is* the legal conduit in which this particular idea of IP is restructured, protected, sustained and operationalised.

The insidious aspect of the operationalisation of this 'ideology' lies in its neutered language that masks the patterns of power inherent in the TRIPS Agreement. This is especially so with words such as 'universal' or 'scientific', which can be claimed to be applicable across the board but in actuality is not because only 'western-frames of knowledge is deemed scientific while centuries-old efforts in indigenous and traditional medicines is diminished as "unorthodox" or "lacking scientific grounding"'.[87] This is further masked when languages such as 'development paradigm' or 'transfer of technology'[88] are used in the TRIPS Agreement, which might seem benign but instead disguise the real motive of maintaining an existing order slanted in favour of the West. It is safe to say that in the TRIPS Agreement, the holy triad of language, cognition and development not only concretised the Euro-American concept of property ownership but also brought about change in the form and substance of property rights through the

[84] Mgbeoji, *Global Biopiracy* (2014), on how the sophisticated legal system powerful states prey on the genetic resources developed by countries and cultures in the Third World.

[85] Joel M Ngugi, 'The World Bank and the Ideology of Reform and Development in International Economic Development Discourse' (2006) 14 *Cardozo Journal of International and Comparative Law* 12.

[86] BS Chimni, 'A Just World Under Law: A View From The South' (2007) 22 *American University International Law Review* 205; Chimni (n 13) 5.

[87] Mgbeoji (n 15) 121.

[88] Article 7 of the TRIPS Agreement states 'the protection and enforcement of intellectual property rights should contribute to the *promotion of technological innovation and to the transfer and dissemination of technology*, to the mutual advantage of producers and users of technological knowledge and *in a manner conducive to social and economic welfare, and to a balance of rights and obligations*' (emphasis added).

intervention of international law. Unsurprisingly, these uniform standards and language are now included in bilateral, plurilateral and investment agreements leading to worldwide convergence on IP standards that broadens this *existing order*. For example, the bilateral agreement between the US and Jordan conforms to a higher level of patent protection than in the TRIPS Agreement.[89] Free trade agreements with many Arab countries have also continued with this trend. The IP chapter in the Comprehensive and Progressive Agreement for Trans-Pacific Partnership (CPTPP), which was one of the contentious issues during the negotiation, have also continued with the TRIP-Plus trend. The point here is this: the neutered language of the TRIPS Agreement is being replicated in future agreements that demand even higher standards, with serious negative implications for the economies of its Third World signatories.

The unilateral pressure of the US via the threat of Section 301 and loss of market access in the build-up to the Uruguay Round, which proved effective in forcing many developing countries to accept the unfavourable terms of the TRIPS Agreement, also lends impetus to the Twalian criticism of the TRIPS Agreement. The Special 301 Report, prepared annually by the Office of the US Trade Representative (USTR), classifies specific countries based on the appropriateness of their IP laws vis-à-vis the US standard.[90] The Report is used as a trade policy tool by the US to monitor IP regimes in different countries and to initiate unilateral trade sanctions against countries it deems to not have sufficient IPR protection.[91] Consequently, Section 301 allows the US to withdraw trade benefits or impose duties on goods from foreign countries with IP laws deemed insufficient by the US or countries that refused to amend their IP laws to reflect the US's domestic legal standards. Countries found to have 'insufficient' laws are put on the Priority Watch List and are possible targets of US trade and investment sanctions. Third World countries such as Brazil, Argentina, Thailand, South Africa and India have featured on the list.[92] India, for instance, has been on the list since 1974 because of its Patent Act of 1970 and recently because of its Section 3(d).[93] Trade sanctions were initiated against Brazil over its informatics policy in 1985.[94] According to Drahos, the US's use of Section 301 contributed

[89] Hamed El-Said and Mohammed El-Said, 'TRIPS, Bilateralism, Multilateralism & Implications For Developing Countries: Jordan's Drug Sector' (2005) 2 *Manchester Journal of International Economic Law* 59; Mohammed El-Said, 'The Road From TRIPS-Minus, To TRIPS, To TRIPS-Plus' (2005) 8 *The Journal of World Intellectual Property* 53.

[90] See generally Office of the United States Trade Representative, 'The Special 301 Report' (2016), available at https://ustr.gov/sites/default/files/USTR-2016-Special-301-Report.pdf.

[91] Chakravarthi Raghavan, *Recolonization: General Agreement On Tariffs And Trade, The Uruguay Round And The Third World* (Penang, Third World Network, 1990) 83–85.

[92] ibid, 84; BS Chimni, 'Political Economy Of The Uruguay Round Of Negotiations: A Perspective' (1992) 29 *International Studies* 143.

[93] Raghavan, *Recolonization* (1990) 83–84.

[94] ibid.

to the insertion of IP matters into the GATT talks.[95] By placing countries on the Special 301 Report, the US creates pressure on these countries to accept and implement higher IP protection.

This narrative is further magnified if we study TRIPS negotiating history, which shows how the West – the US, European Union (EU), Canada and Japan (known as the Quadrilateral Group, or the Quad) – dominated the negotiations.[96] This is not surprising as the US specifically moved IP issues to GATT because it had a stronger bargaining position there. Many developing countries were excluded through the use of enclave committees such as the Quad – the committee of the most powerful states – where the impetus for particular decisions and the negotiating position of these states were developed.[97] This is not to say that some developing countries did not win some concessions in return for signing the TRIPS Agreement.[98] They did; however, the issue here is the unilateral pressure of the US that squelched the priorities and interests of Third World states. These negotiating tactics is the reason why Euromerican-engineered IP rules prevailed in the language and modalities of the TRIPS Agreement. Consequently, a Euromerican legal narrative – reflecting the desires of multinational corporations in Europe and the US for a higher global IP standard – came to shape the IP norms at the Uruguay Round. In this context, the TRIPS Agreement therefore represents, as Ikechi Mgbeoji observes, 'an instrumentalist goal of states, especially powerful multinational corporations capable of influencing and using the machinery of their parent state to influence domestic patent regimes of other states'.[99] Correspondingly, this sentiment reinforces the argument that the GATT/WTO rules are designed to serve mercantilist purposes that sustain the linkage between colonialism and international trade rules.[100] By virtue of this, international economic governance regimes and corresponding institutions represent the coloniser while ostensibly claiming the virtues of neutrality, objectivity and working towards the development of the Third World.[101]

TWAIL also highlights the perceived hypocrisy and double standard apparent not only within the TRIPS Agreement but also in the politico-economic pressure that bears on Third World countries in the way they interpret their

[95] Peter Drahos, 'Global Intellectual Property Rights In Information: The Story Of TRIPS At The GATT' (1995) 13 *Prometheus* 11.

[96] Raghavan (n 91) 61; See also Drahos, 'The Story of TRIPS at the GATT' (1995); Susan Sell and Christopher May, 'Moments In Law: Contestation And Settlement In The History Of Intellectual Property' (2001) 8 *Review of International Political Economy* 468.

[97] Peter Drahos, 'Trade-Offs And Trade Linkages: TRIPS In A Negotiating Context' (Quaker United Nations, 2000), available at www.anu.edu.au/fellows/pdrahos/reports/pdfs/2001tradeoffstradelinkages.pdf, 14.

[98] See Raghavan (n 91) 69–80.

[99] Mgbeoji (n 15) 2.

[100] See generally Surendra Raj Bhandari, 'From The Era Of Colonialism To Globalization: Making Rules In The GATT/WTO' in JH Paik, SW Lee and KYL Tan (eds), *Asian Approaches to International Law and the Legacy of Colonialism: The Law of the Sea, Territorial Disputes and International Dispute Settlement*, 1st edn (London, Routledge, 2013).

[101] Anghie (n 1) 140.

TRIPS Agreement obligations locally.[102] The fact that many of today's advanced economies did not allow patents on chemical and pharmaceutical substances afforded them the opportunity to develop their pharmaceutical industries via imitation or otherwise.[103] For example, chemical substances remained un-patentable until 1967 in West Germany, 1968 in the Nordic countries, 1976 in Japan, 1978 in Switzerland, and 1992 in Spain.[104] Pharmaceutical products remained un-patentable until 1967 in West Germany and France, 1979 in Italy, and 1992 in Spain,[105] while pharmaceutical products were also un-patentable in Canada into the 1990s.[106] It was only when these countries began to achieve technological breakthroughs that their preference for weak IP laws changed[107] and fuelled the calls for a stronger global patent system. In other words, it was only when owners and manufacturers of innovations saw the considerable advantages in IP monopolistic potentials that states increased support for stronger international protection.[108] In this sense, the TRIPS Agreement was drafted and ratified to maintain the interests of Western powers, particularly the US. Thus, IP became an 'instrument of power and, once captured, the basis of further accumulation of power'.[109] For this reason, the TWAIL movement believes that the global IP regime of protection and enforcement is a Western construct created to gain competitive advantage over emerging rival manufacturing centres in newly developing economies of the developing world.[110] This transplanting of Western legal regimes into countries in the Global South not only robbed Third World states of opportunities which Western countries had, but also hampered access to the information, knowledge and technology needed for competitiveness, internal growth and development.

In addition, the TRIPS Agreement is seen as a neo-colonising tool for the continued perpetuation of economic and political power imbalances by promoting foreign-owned IP rights, further deepening the wealth difference

[102] Ha-Joon Chang, *Kicking Away The Ladder: The "Real" History Of Free Trade – FPIF* (Foreign Policy in Focus 2003), available at http://fpif.org/kicking_away_the_ladder_the_real_history_of_free_trade; Giovanni Dosi and Joseph E Stiglitz, 'The Role Of Intellectual Property In The Development Process, With Some Lessons From Developed Countries: An Introduction' in M Cimoli, G Dosi, K Maskus, R Okediji, J Reichman and J Stiglitz (eds), *Intellectual Property Rights: Legal and Economic Challenges for Development*, 1st edn (Oxford, Oxford University Press 2014); see also Sell and May, 'Moments In Law' (2001).

[103] Chang (ibid); see also Srividhya Ragavan, *Patent and Trade Disparities in Developing Countries* (Oxford, Oxford University Press, 2012); Srividhya Ragavan, 'Of The Inequals Of Uruguay Rounds' (2006) 10 *Marquette Intellectual Property Law Review* 273.

[104] Surendra J Patel, 'Intellectual Property Rights In The Uruguay Round: A Disaster For The South?' (1989) 24 *Economic and Political Weekly* 980.

[105] ibid.

[106] ibid.

[107] Chimni, 'Political Economy of the Uruguay Round of Negotiations' (1992).

[108] Sell and May (n 96) 486.

[109] ibid.

[110] Ruth L Okediji, 'Back To Bilateralism? Pendulum Swings In International Intellectual Property Protection' (2004) 1 *University of Ottawa Law and Technology Journal* 128.

between the Global North and South. According to Anghie, an essential component in the process of neo-colonialisation by economic means is the establishment of an international legal instrument, which confers legally enforceable rights that support and safeguard economic penetration and control.[111] The TRIPS Agreement does this by establishing economic, social and political dependence through the licensing and enforcement of IPR. In doing so, contemporary international law continues to maintain and deepen the North–South divide using extraordinarily flexible and continuously new techniques.[112]

Pertinent to this narrative is the argument that the overall legal and institutional rules of WTO are, in essence, a process of freeing transnational capital from spatial and temporal constraints and obligations through an effective system of cross-retaliation.[113] In other words, the continued displacement and replacement of the state with market governance tethers on international economic governance, especially those relating to strong property like the TRIPS Agreement. For example, the *Brazil – Measures Affecting Patent Protection*[114] case where the US argued that Brazil violates the TRIPS Agreement because it authorises compulsory licensing on the ground of the patentee's failure to work locally underscores this argument. Although the US eventually withdrew the case, it still highlights attempts by a developed country to send a signal to developing countries not to adopt measures which are not in line with the US strategy. Another example is the South African pharmaceutical patent lawsuit in which 40 Western pharmaceutical companies, together with the South African Pharmaceutical Manufacturers Association, filed a lawsuit against the South African Government for the Medicines and Related Substances Act Amendment of 1997. The Amendment Act aimed at designing a new drug policy and making more affordable HIV/AIDS medicines available to the masses. Specifically, Section 15C provides for CLs[115] and empowers the Minister of Health to set conditions for parallel imports of medicines in general, and generic drugs in particular, even if the drugs are still protected under the South African patent

[111] Antony Anghie, 'Time Present And Time Past: Globalization, International Financial Institutions, And The Third World' (2000) 32 *New York University Journal International Law & Politics* 243; See also Anghie (n 1), ch 5; See Andreas Rahmatian, 'Neo-Colonial Aspects Of Global Intellectual Property Protection' (2009) 12 *The Journal of World Intellectual Property* 40; Mgbeoji (n 15); Antony Anghie, *Colonialism, Sovereignty, And The Making Of International Law* (Cambridge, Cambridge University Press, 2004); Chimni (n 92).

[112] Anghie, 'Time Present and Time Past' (2000) 243.

[113] Chimni (n 92) 147.

[114] *Brazil – Measures Affecting Patent Protection* [2001] WTO Dispute Settlement Body, WT/DS199 (WTO Dispute Settlement Body). See also Daya Shanker, 'Brazil, The Pharmaceutical Industry And The WTO' (2002) 5 *The Journal of World Intellectual Property* 53.

[115] Section 15C of the 1997 Amendment Act provides 'The Minister may prescribe conditions for the supply of more affordable medicines in certain circumstances so as to protect the health of the public and in particular may, notwithstanding anything to the contrary contained in the Patents Act 1978 (Act No. 57 of 1978), determine that the rights with regard to any medicine under a patent granted in the Republic shall not extend to acts in respect of such medicine which has been put onto the market by the owner of the medicine or with his or her consent.'

law.[116] The complainants argued that various aspects of the Amendment Act, especially Section 15C, which they stated granted the health minister 'ill-defined authority to issue compulsory licenses, authorize parallel imports and potentially otherwise abrogate patent rights'.[117] In addition, they also argued that Section 22F discriminates against patented drugs, skewing the competition between patented and generic drugs in favour of the latter.[118] However, due to public outcry and the publicity it generated, the pharmaceutical companies withdrew their lawsuit, thus allowing the Act to go through Parliament. Again, this reflects the extent Western states (and Western-backed corporations) can go in order to ensure enforcement in Third World countries of IPR that originate in the West or are owned by enterprises of industrialised nations. Importantly, for TWAIL scholars, it demonstrates how international law, in this case, the TRIPS Agreement, continues to provide 'legitimacy and authority to claims that third world states should adopt market-based reforms, even when they are inconsistent with the needs of the these countries'.[119]

Examining TRIPS Agreement negotiations and the circumstances surrounding it, it is clear why TWAIL scholarship view the TRIPS Agreement (and indeed, the WTO) as a neo-colonialist institution that has continued to reproduce technologies that embody the enduring inequalities and exploitation inherent in the colonial encounter. The pressure exerted upon the Global South during the Uruguay Round to adopt legal rules fashioned by powerful states can be intimately linked to 'the pressure exerted upon peripheral states during the nineteenth century to introduce reforms that would render them "civilised" and, hence, equal to Western state'.[120] Specifically, the unilateral and retaliatory measure by the US is reminiscent of the racism and cultural superiority that accompanied colonial conquests.[121] It demonstrates the way powerful countries continue to deny the agency and legal innovations of non-Europeans, through a totalising discourse such as 'best IPR practices' – a term used by the US in the Special 301 Report to applaud several countries whose IP policies and laws are acceptable to its interests. In employing this term to describe domestic IP

[116] Section 15C(b) of the 1997 Amendment Act provides 'the conditions on which any medicine, which is identical in composition, meets the same quality standard and is intended to have 55 the same proprietary name as that of another medicine already registered in the Republic. but which is imported by a person other than the person who is the holder of the registration certificate of the medicine already registered and which originates from any site of manufacture of the original manufacturer as approved by the council in the prescribed manner, may be imported.'

[117] See Tshimanga Kongolo, 'Public Interest Versus The Pharmaceutical Industry's Monopoly In South Africa' (2005) 4 *The Journal of World Intellectual Property* 619–21.

[118] ibid, 621.

[119] James Gathii, 'The Agenda of Third World Approaches to International Law (TWAIL)' in J Dunoff and M Pollack (eds), International Legal Theory: Foundations and Frontiers (Cambridge University Press, 2019) 15.

[120] Tzouvala, 'TWAIL' (2016) 3.

[121] Makau Mutua, 'Why Redraw The Map Of Africa: A Moral And Legal Inquiry' (1995) 16 *Michigan Journal of International Law* 1127.

policies, the US seeks not only the total economic, political and social transformation of 'the other' but also ignores the insights or advancement of 'the other'. In most instances, the 'best practices' are ill-fitted to their domestic needs. Hence, TWAIL scholars are convinced that the TRIPS Agreement is a continuation and a renewal of colonial order in the postcolonial, and curbs the right of governments to intervene in the economy for the benefit of their people while expanding the 'space' for multi-national companies (MNCs) and governments of the Global North.[122]

For TWAIL scholars, the TRIPS Agreement presents two important and interconnected narratives: the globalisation of US-engineered IP rules and the forced inclusion of the subaltern into this US-led IP expansionism. It is this narrative that informs the Twailian critical interrogation and problematisation of the TRIPS Agreement in many ways. The reality of the Uruguay Round negotiation is that it was dominated by coercion. States coerced other states, mainly developing countries, with the aggressive unilateralism of the US being the dominant mechanism for standard-setting. This coercion, though economic in nature, forced many developing countries to be subsumed into an unfavourable global IP regime with pronounced effects on development, as the HIV/AIDS crisis has proven. Connected to this is the very inclusion of areas traditionally thought to be beyond the ambit of trade and is akin to the recolonisation of the economic independence of the Global South by Western international institutions.[123] Importantly, this capitulation of sovereign economic power by Third World countries, irrespective of how minor, drastically reduces the possibilities of undertaking an independent path to development.

This in turn reduces the ability of Third World states to make autonomous policy choices regarding appropriate levels of IP protection within their jurisdictions, with tremendous consequences.[124] This is because the proposals ensconced within the TRIPS Agreement legitimise the invasion of the national economic space of the developing countries, deny any serious choice to the people of the developing world to shape their future, further cementing their subaltern status.[125] In fact, the HIV/AIDS crisis and other public health pandemics that have ravaged many Third World countries continue to show the debilitating effect of global patent regime on national policies. Situations when a developing country has managed to carve out space within the confines of the TRIPS Agreement to issue CLs have been met with economic backlash from developed countries like the US. The consequence, according to Anghie, is a reproduction of power, an intensification of inequalities,[126] and the institutionalisation of 'technological protectionism that raises enormous barriers for the entry of

[122] Raghavan (n 91) 40.
[123] Chimni, 'The Past, Present and Future of International Law' (n 13), p 36.
[124] Raghavan (n 91). See also Chimni (n 13) 148. See also Mutua (n 34) 38.
[125] ibid, 137.
[126] Anghie, 'Time Present and Time Past' (n 111) 243.

newcomers into the scientific and technological process'.[127] The corresponding result is an unfolding complex regime interaction 'where forces of globalisation and global governance reflect negative distributional outcomes and distributional disequilibrium regarding access to knowledge and public goods'.[128]

IV. READING TRIPS TEXT THROUGH TWAILIAN LENS

For TWAIL scholars, the TRIPS Agreement embodies all that is wrong with international law, especially its complicity in the economic exploitation of the subaltern. The Twailian objections to the TRIPS Agreement run along the main lines of what the movement is against: Eurocentric universalism, disregard for the needs and views of the Third World, and the implicit marginalisation of these countries inherent in contemporary international legal framework.

A. Principal Objection: Universality of IP

The TRIPS Agreement promotes a particular universality in IPR protection. That is, it provides a high global minimum standard for the protection of IPRs.[129] The resultant effect is, according to Sell and May, 'certain behaviour that was once legal in some jurisdiction is now illegal in all and is subject to criminal penalties when national legislation is brought into line with TRIPS commitment'.[130] This is the principal Twailian objection to the TRIPS Agreement.

As stated earlier, before the creation of the WTO, many developing countries did not recognise patents on pharmaceutical products to ensure domestic accessibility and affordability of drugs, and therefore had little incentive to implement highly protective IP rules. For instance, the Indian Patent Act[131] allowed Indian manufacturers to legally produce generic versions of medicines patented in other countries. The philosophy behind this law was to encourage and ensure access to foreign technologies to Indian society that otherwise might be unavailable to its people due to cost and pricing structures under a proprietary intellectual property protection system. However, by signing the TRIPS Agreement, India as well as other developing countries had to tighten their IP laws to the higher standards stipulated in the TRIPS Agreement.

[127] Chimni (n 13) 148.

[128] Chidi Oguamanam, 'IP In Global Governance: A Venture In Critical Reflection' (2011) 2 *World Intellectual Property Organization Journal* 196.

[129] 'Agreement On Trade-Related Aspects Of Intellectual Property Rights' (Geneva, World Trade Organization, 1995), available at www.wto.org/english/docs_e/legal_e/27-trips.pdf, Art 1. See also George A Bermann and Petros C Mavroidis, *WTO Law and Developing Countries* (Cambridge, Cambridge University Press, 2007) 129.

[130] Sell and May (n 96) 493.

[131] See ch 5.

The consequential effect is that many developing countries are permanently locked in a state of technological dependence. This, many TWAIL scholars believe, undermines opportunities for growth for developing countries who are now on the receiving end of importing technology. The solution to this jurisprudential mess, TWAIL scholars argue, is a reconfiguration of the TRIPS Agreement that recognises and is sensitive to the development needs of various countries in the Global South, and which allows room for flexible application of IP protection in their various jurisdictions.

B. Stricter and Stronger Patents Protection: Articles 27, 30 and 31

Articles 27 to 34 of the TRIPS Agreement deal with the protection of patents in all fields of technology. Of great importance is Article 27, which establishes patent protection for any invention, 'whether products or processes, in all fields of technology';[132] Article 30, which provides limited exceptions to the exclusive rights conferred by a patent,[133] and Article 31 which allows compulsory licensing,[134] which is a legal mechanism that allows a government to grant to itself or a third party the right to produce or import a patented product without authorisation of the patent-holder[135] (though subject to certain conditions). These conditions are mainly contained in Article 31(a)–(j). Finally, Article 33 gives a 20-year patent protection counted from the filing date.

For TWAIL scholars, health advocates and many developing countries, Article 31(f) has been the focus of simmering discontent. The discontent stems from the non-recognition of asymmetric development levels and production capacities among WTO Member States by restricting the use of CL for domestic markets of members authorising such use.[136] The consequence of this rule is that it acts as a disincentive for local research and development that would encourage local production and stimulate importation of technology. In addition, the type of patent involved and the added protection of 20 years denies many developing countries the freedom to determine the patent duration period according to individual needs and policy requirements. The concomitant effect of this patent monopoly is a spike in the cost of patented drugs, which in turn makes them inaccessible to the many impoverished people in the Third World desperately in need of these drugs.[137]

[132] TRIPS Agreement, Art 27.
[133] TRIPS Agreement, Art 30.
[134] TRIPS Agreement, Art 31.
[135] Duncan Matthews, 'From the August 30, 2003 WTO Decision To The December 6, 2005 Agreement On An Amendment To TRIPS Improving Access To Medicines In Developing Countries' (2006) 21 *Intellectual Property Quarterly* 2.
[136] TRIPS Agreement, Art 31(f).
[137] James Thuo Gathii, 'Approaches To Accessing Essential Medicines And The TRIPS Agreement' in P K Yu (ed), *Intellectual Property and Information Wealth* (Santa Barbara, Greenwood Publishing Group, 2006).

Echoing the Twailian discontent, the United Nations Human Rights Commission (UNHRC) has put forward the claims of apparent conflicts between the IPRs contained in the TRIPS Agreement, on one hand, and international human rights law, on the other.[138] According to the Report, the TRIPS Agreement does not adequately reflect 'the fundamental nature and indivisibility of all human rights, including the right of everyone to enjoy the benefits of scientific progress and its applications, the right to health, the right to food, and the right to self-determination'.[139] Other scholars such as Joseph Stiglitz and Thomas Pogge contend that the ensuing high prices of essential medicines caused by patent monopoly is responsible for avoidable deaths and diseases on a massive scale. Therefore, Pogge continues, pharmaceutical patents as globalised through the TRIPS Agreement 'cannot be defended nor justified in terms of mutual benefits or usefulness because the global poor are deprived of their freedom to buy medicines yet often cannot benefit from the enhanced arsenal of advanced medicines'.[140]

Accompanied by the worldwide campaign against the HIV/AIDS epidemic, the TRIPS Agreement suffered adverse criticisms regarding public health issues. With severe irk directed towards this particular article, the WTO General Council adopted the Doha Declaration on the TRIPS Agreement and Public Health ('the Declaration' hereafter).[141] The value of the Declaration lies in its clarification of the flexibilities and public health safeguards within the TRIPS Agreement. Indeed, the Declaration has yielded a number of firsts and established important precedents. First, it recognises the gravity of health issues facing many developing and least developed countries (LDCs), especially those resulting in HIV/AIDS, malaria and tuberculosis. Second, the Declaration reaffirmed that the TRIPS Agreement does not (and should not) prevent members from taking measures to protect public health and promote access to medicines. Third, considering that many developing members with insufficient or no manufacturing capacities in the pharmaceutical sector could face difficulties in making effective use of compulsory licensing, Ministers to the conference 'instruct[ed] the Council for TRIPS to find an expeditious solution to this problem and report to the General Council by the end of 2002'.[142]

[138] United Nations Human Rights Commission, 'Intellectual Property and Human Rights' (2000), available at www.unhchr.ch/Huridocda/Huridoca.nsf/0/c462b62cf8a07b13c12569700046704e?Opendocument, E/CN/.4/Sub.2/ 2000/7, para 2.

[139] ibid.

[140] Thomas Pogge, 'The Health Impact Fund: Better Pharmaceutical Innovations at Much Lower Prices' in T Pogge, M Rimmer and K Rubenstein (eds), *Incentives for Global Public Health: Patent Law and Access to Essential Medicines* (Cambridge, Cambridge University Press 2010).

[141] 'Declaration on the TRIPS Agreement and Public Health' (2001), available at www.wto.org/english/thewto_e/minist_e/min01_e/mindecl_trips_e.htm.

[142] ibid.

The solution later came in the August 2003 Article 31 (bis), which waives the TRIPS provision that requires predominantly all of the product made under compulsory licence to be for the domestic market of the producer.

V. MIND THE GAP: ON LIMITATIONS OF TWAIL

For all its usefulness in interpreting patent law-making and reform in the Global South, TWAIL provides only a partial engagement and is thus methodologically and analytically insufficient for this book in two important dimensions. First, the erroneous assumption that Third World states have local actors to participate in the reform and resistance of international legal scholarship. In this context, 'actor' refers to participants in local forums other than the state. This includes private sector interests such as pharmaceutical companies (transnational and indigenous firms), civil society groups, social movements and donor organisations. By not exploring actor presence and agency, TWAIL ignores the impetus of actor politics and the politics of knowledge production that govern actor involvement *within* and *between* Third World states. That is, *who* participates in this reform of and resistance against international (patent) law in the local forums of the Global South; *what* informs this participation; and *how* the knowledge about participation is produced. In fact, as shall be seen in the analyses of patent law-making as part of the TRIPS Agreement implementation in the local forums of Brazil, India and Nigeria, there exists a vast difference in actor presence and participation among and within Third World states. This is important as actor network as well as the various roles played by or contestation between these local networks and the mechanics of knowledge production are what structure the engagement in the resistance and reform of international law as preached by the TWAIL movement.

The second limitation is that the Twailian scholarship suffers from the notion that Third World states are automatically endowed with emancipatory capabilities because of their postcolonial status.[143] That is, due to the 'problem space' they occupy – in this case, postcolonialism – TWAIL assumes that Third World states have the competency to engage in counter-hegemonic international law-making. In other words, in calling for the refocus of attention to the local levels, TWAIL scholarship assumes the competency of such actors, where they exist, to participate in local counter-hegemonic international law-making. 'Competency' here means the ability of actors to enrol support simultaneously at a number of different sites of law-making and law enforcement (national, international and transnational), and their ability to mobilise leading sources of expertise to reform, reconstruct or dismantle hegemonic patent regimes.

[143] Antonius R Hippolyte, 'Correcting TWAIL's Blind Spots' (2016) 18 *International Community Law Review* 34; Naya, 'Between Hope And Despair' (2008) 320.

An example of this is the ability of generic pharmaceutical companies in India to mobilise the Government on patent issues and to collaborate with civil society groups to generate and produce expertise on key IP issues. As will be seen in the chapter on Nigeria, not only is competency imperative in ensuring effective engagement, the willingness of such actors to engage in the long and arduous task of reforming and resisting international law is equally essential. As analyses in this book will show, Brazilian and Indian actors are willing and competent to engage in the reform of local patent law, whereas their Nigerian counterparts are generally unwilling to engage, and this is due to lack of capacity and knowledge. In failing to acknowledge that not all developing countries are participating in the same way in international law-making, TWAIL overlooks the asymmetries between and within the Third World.

Thus, by overlooking these important dimensions (actor presence, competency and willingness), TWAIL ignores not only local histories and identities *between* and *within* the Third World, but also how these asymmetries define which Third World state engages in reform and resistance vis-à-vis international law and scholarship, and who is excluded. In not addressing the local ecosystem of actor participation, which includes looking into local presence, willingness, competence and the politics of knowledge governance which frames this participation, TWAIL weakens its critical scholarship premise to connect to 'the concrete experiences and claims found in local spaces' that is central to its mission.[144] In as much as TWAIL scholarship suggests focusing on the reform of and resistance against international law at the local forums, attention should also be paid to the presence and competence of local actors, their willingness to engage and the mechanics of knowledge production that informs such participation to bring about the desired change.[145] In focusing in the ecosystem of non-state actor involvement, what is uncovered is not only the way such internal dynamics unfold, but also how it informs which Third World country participates in counter-hegemonic law-making in local forums, as well as who is excluded.

Finally, understanding Third World engagement should also include exploring the local actor participation ecosystem. It is in doing so that the manner in how knowledge is captured and repurposed by actors as they attempt to reform, reconstruct or dismantle the patent regime is uncovered and understood. In addition, it reveals how actors co-ordinate actions in a variety of different sites at different levels of the global regime and mobilise forms of counter-expertise from within and without the established legal regimes. This is important because it illuminates how and why actors mobilise in a particular locality and not in others. The next section addresses this lacuna, drawing from the nodal governance theory to supplement the Twailian contribution and address the actor/knowledge gap.

[144] Kiyani, 'Third World Approaches' (2016).

[145] Scott Burris, Peter Drahos and Clifford Shearing, 'Nodal Governance' (2005) 30 *Australian Journal of Legal Philosophy* 31.

PART II: NODAL GOVERNANCE

VI. UNDERSTANDING NODAL GOVERNANCE

The theory of nodal governance explains how a variety of actors operating within social systems interact along networks to govern the systems they inhabit.[146] It posits that governance in such systems is instituted 'in nodes that mobilise the knowledge and capacity of members to manage the course of events'.[147] In this respect, nodal governance is a theory that focuses on the role of nodes in governance, especially the way such nodal links create concentrations of power for the purposes of exercising and/or influencing governance.

The idea of nodal governance was initially developed by Clifford Shearing and Jennifer Wood by building on the work of Friedrich von Hayek to explain multiple modes of governance in the changing governance landscape, wherein state governments constitute but one set of nodes.[148] According to Shearing and Wood, nodal governance theory recognises the interaction between state and non-state actors (node) as well as between nodes, and how these interactions extend 'the existing activities of non-state agencies as well as the emergence of new forms of governmental activity outside of the State'.[149] In other words, the nodal framework provides an account of how a governing order emerges from the operation of highly complex systems.

A node can either be an actor within a network or a combination of one or two networks united for a common goal. Nodes take a variety of forms, from formalised institutional expressions (business corporations), voluntary groupings (non-governmental organisations or NGOs), to super-structures, eg combinations of representatives from different nodal organisations such as the Pharmaceutical Research and Manufacturers of America (PhRMA) or the Indian Drug Manufacturers' Association (IDMA).[150] A super-structural node, in other words, brings together one or more networks for the purpose of producing various kinds of action, such as lobbying the state for a favourable law or policy. Other examples of such super-structural nodes include the Brazilian Association of Fine Chemical Industry (*Associação Brasileira das Indústrias de Química Fina, Biotecnologia e Suas Especialidades*, or ABIFINA) and the Pharmaceutical Manufacturers Group of Manufacturers Association of Nigeria (PMG-MAN).

[146] ibid 31–33.

[147] ibid 33.

[148] Clifford Shearing and Jennifer Wood, 'Nodal Governance, Democracy, And The New 'Denizens' (2003) 30 *Journal of Law and Society* 400; Jennifer Wood and Clifford D Shearing, *Imagining Security* (Cullompton, Willan, 2007).

[149] Shearing and Wood, 'Nodal Governance' (2003) 403.

[150] Burris, Drahos and Shearing, 'Nodal Governance' (n 149) 13. Burris, Drahos and Shearing recognise a fourth group – an informal sector made up of people who operate outside of the first and second, such as criminal gangs.

Regardless of type, a node has four essential characteristics: first, it should have a way of thinking (mentalities) that cognitively shapes how individuals and organisations see the world and act accordingly.[151] It is in these mentalities and purposes that nodes differ greatly from each other in terms of goals and legal conduct. Second, it should have a set of processes (technologies) for applying and exercising influence over the course of events at issue.[152] Third, it should also have resources to support and mobilise the operation of the node and fuel its influence.[153] Fourth, there should be a system (institutions) that enables the directed mobilisation of resources, mentalities, and technologies over time.[154]

Thus, to be a governing node, according to this theory, a node should have some institutional form, even if temporary. It need not be a formally constituted or legally recognised entity, but it should have sufficient stability and structure to enable the mobilisation of resources, mentalities and technologies over time. The lobbying tactics of the IDMA in India in the wake of the amendment of the Indian Patent Act provides an example of a successful governing node, as the group had the stability and structure to mobilise its mentalities, resources and technologies over time to achieve a tempered patent regime for India. Conversely, in Brazil and Nigeria, the super-structural nodes of ABIFINA and PMG-MAN were not able to participate in patent law-making because both groups, though formally recognised by the state, did not have sufficient stability and structure to enable the mobilisation of resources, mentalities and technologies over patent-related matters due to various domestic economic factors.

All nodes are not created equal, and the grouping and structure of each node affect its arrangement or interface with the state.[155] For example, the relation of the state with big corporations, voluntary groups or a super-structural node, though non-linear in nature, is often one of co-operative arrangement and sometimes contestation. For example, IDMA's lobby of the Indian Parliament, urging the government to oppose an IP dimension to GATT in order to protect public health and the pharmaceutical sector, highlights a corporative nodal relationship. On the other hand, the civil society protests in Brazil on access to HIV medicines are an example of contested nodal engagement with the state.

Notwithstanding which side of the interface prevails, the capacity of a node to exert influence and the potency of its influence depends on the resources available for exerting influence, technologies in use, as well as the institutional structure.[156] In other words, the ability of the nodal network to enrol such resources and governing technologies at a number of different sites to mobilise

[151] Burris, Drahos and Shearing, 'Nodal Governance' (n 149) 12.
[152] ibid.
[153] ibid.
[154] ibid.
[155] Shearing and Wood, 'Nodal Governance' (n 152) 415.
[156] Peter Drahos, 'Intellectual Property and Pharmaceutical Markets: A Nodal Governance Approach' (2004) 77 *Temple Law Review* 409.

the state and others to comply with its direction also affects the effectiveness of its influence. For example, a small NGO can mobilise resources to exert influence at one site such as the local, municipal or national levels of governance. The ability of social movements in India to petition government by writing *amicus curiae* briefs is an example. However, because these groups are usually limited by financial capacity, they are unable to exact influence simultaneously and at multiple sites.

A business corporation could simultaneously exert influence at a national and local level. For example, 12 US corporations, according to Susan Sell, were primarily responsible for the lobbying that brought the TRIPS Agreement into being.[157] It was intense lobbying activity from these companies, particularly in the US, that laid the foundations of linking IP protection to trade in the multilateral context.[158]

Super-structural nodes, on the other hand, can channel their resources to exert simultaneous influence at the local, national and international levels. An example of this is the role of the PhRMA in influencing the USTR to include IP as part of the US foreign policy as well as its presence during the Uruguay Round negotiations.[159] It is this ability of the super-structural node to engage simultaneously at multiple sites that makes it powerful compared to the NGO or business corporation.

While the relationship between the state and a node differ, relationships between and among nodes also differ. This intra-node relationship takes different forms such as dialogue, democratic bargaining, or contestation of ideas.[160] As a result, nodes are constantly reconstituting themselves by regulating other nodes that are accessible to them through networks.[161] According to Burris, Drahos and Shearing, the pervasiveness of nodes not only influences the way knowledge is produced and diffused in a given system, but also informs how resources relevant to regulation are focused to bring about social action.[162] In other words, nodal governance facilitates understanding of how nodal networks produce the results they have by providing insight into who is able to participate and who is excluded, how knowledge is produced and disseminated, as well as the resources available for mobilisation purposes.[163] In the next section, a case study of the TRIPS

[157] Susan K Sell, *Private Power, Public Law: The Globalization Of Intellectual Property Rights* (Cambridge, Cambridge University Press, 2003) 1. These companies include Pfizer, IBM, Merck, General Electric, DuPont, Warner Communications, Hewlett-Packard, Bristol-Meyers, FMC Corporation, General Motors, Johnson & Johnson, Monsanto and Rockwell International.

[158] Sell, *Private Power, Public Law* (ibid) 137.

[159] Drahos, 'Intellectual Property and Pharmaceutical Markets' (2004) 411.

[160] Peter Drahos and Ruth Mayne, *Global Intellectual Property Rights: Knowledge, Access And Development* (Hampshire, Palgrave Macmillan, 2002) 164.

[161] Burris, Drahos and Shearing (n 149) 15.

[162] ibid.

[163] Burris, Drahos and Shearing (n 149) 15.

Agreement is presented to show how the nodal governance theory helps explain how a nodal network played a larger role in the formation of US trade policy and led to the globalisation of the private interests of its member corporations.

VII. NODAL GOVERNANCE AND THE PHARMACEUTICAL PATENT REGIME

The inclusion of IPRs in the Uruguay Round of multilateral trade negotiations did not happen by chance. It involved the dynamic influence and participation of American MNCs, especially pharmaceutical and biotechnology companies, that first actively shaped the national legislation on IP and, by corollary, the foreign trade policy of the US Government.[164] This raises the question of how and why did a group of private sector actors succeed in establishing, locally and internationally, a maximalist IP agenda. Nodal governance theory proffers insight on how these private companies were able to secure US government compliance with emerging global IPR standards that, in turn, constitute today's international patent law regime.

Having developed a large portfolio of R&D for innovation in the chemical, power machinery, electrical, petroleum and rubber industries, thanks to massive corporate research laboratories, these companies needed IPRs and licences to protect their investment.[165] This is because the owners and manufacturers of innovations saw the considerable advantages in IP monopolistic potentials of patents such as exclusive foreign market access, sustained competitive advantages and economic rents from patents.[166] These companies sought to institute locally as well as within all significant markets a regulatory agenda for a largely uniform patent rules that made it cheap to obtain patents, maximise the scope of patentable subject matter, and minimise state control over the use of patented technology.[167]

In fact, the need for IP protection was especially important in the pharmaceutical sector as these companies saw countries like India and

[164] Drahos (n 160); Sell (n 161); Drahos and Mayne, *Global Intellectual Property Rights* (2002); Susan K Sell and Aseem Prakash, 'Using Ideas Strategically: The Contest Between Business and NGO Networks in Intellectual Property Rights' (2004) 48 *International Studies Quarterly* 143; see also Duncan Matthews, *Trade-Related Aspects of Intellectual Property Rights: Will the Uruguay Round Consensus Hold?*, 1st edn (Coventry, Centre for the Study of Globalisation and Regionalisation (CSGR), University of Warwick, 2002), available at www2.warwick.ac.uk/fac/soc/pais/research/researchcentres/csgr/research/workingpapers-copy2/2002/wp9902.pdf; Peter Drahos and John Braithwaite, 'Intellectual Property, Corporate Strategy, Globalisation: TRIPS In Context' (2002) 20 *Wisconsin International Law Journal* 451.

[165] Peter Drahos and John Braithwaite, *Information Feudalism: Who Owns The Knowledge Economy?* (Oxford, Oxford University Press 2003) 49.

[166] ibid 47.

[167] Peter Drahos, '"IP World" – Made By TNC Inc.' in G Krikorian and A Kapczynski (eds), *Access To Knowledge In The Age Of Intellectual Property*, 1st edn (New York, Zone Books, 2010).

Brazil – with 'weak' IP laws but budding pharmaceutical sectors – as threats to their revenue and market access. Understandably, these companies saw the considerable advantages in IP monopolistic potentials of patents such as exclusive foreign market access and sustained competitive advantages as a way to protect their R&D investment. The very nature of IP, specifically patents and its ensuing monopoly, gives its owner strong protection over the exploitation of a patented invention. This temporary monopoly allows the inventor to set the terms of use and the price for access to the invented product. Thus, with the increase in the value of knowledge relative to other assets, companies are bound to protect not only this asset but also laws that may impact the value of and access to this asset.[168] With this goal in mind, new tactics were needed to develop a global network of universal patent standards while solving the problem of free riding – a situation where those who benefit from a good or service do not pay for them.

The process of linking IP with trade policy was spearheaded by Pfizer, a global pharmaceutical company with interest and investments in Third World countries such as India.[169] Pfizer's investment in many developing countries had 'sensitized it to the threat to international markets that generics posed for the pharmaceutical research-and-development industry'.[170] According to Drahos, Pfizer cognitively shaped and influenced fellow pharmaceutical manufacturers regarding the value of trade-based IP through lobbying, giving talks and delivering white paper presentations at business forums like the National Foreign Trade Council and the Business Round Table.[171] In these processes, Ed Pratt – CEO of Pfizer at that time – was able to delineate the links between trade, IP and investment as well as the importance of linking the IP regime to the GATT and making it enforceable under the GATT dispute resolution procedures.[172]

In this context, Pfizer plays the role of a quintessential node with a foreknowledge and particular mindset of thinking of IP (mentalities); it employed a set of technologies in the form of giving speeches and white paper presentations to apply and exert influence over the course of events at issue. All these were possible due to the resources and institutional structure of the company, which allowed it to mobilise support in the media and industry and resulted in policy from the Government. In other words, Pfizer was able to extract support within the nodal network of fellow pharmaceutical companies

[168] Peter Drahos and John Braithwaite, 'Who Owns The Knowledge Economy? Political Organising Behind TRIPS' (The Corner House, 2004) 3, available at www.thecornerhouse.org.uk/resource/who-owns-knowledge-economy.

[169] ibid 5.

[170] Drahos, '"IP World' (2010) 206.

[171] Burris, Drahos and Shearing (n 149) 42; Sell (n 161) 48.

[172] Burris, Drahos and Shearing (n 149).

and influence other networks of biochemical and technology companies to create ever-widening circles of influence that brought more networks (software, film and music sectors) into the cause of exporting the US IP standard to the wider world.[173] The combined influence of these nodes developed governmental support for strengthening the global protection of IP.[174]

Furthermore, Pfizer was able to achieve compliance from the US through the creation of the Advisory Committee for Trade Negotiations (ACTN).[175] The ACTN was set up by the US Congress in 1974 as a unique public–private forum to ensure that the private sector was represented in US trade policies.[176] Simply put, the ACTN was structured to allow direct engagement of the US business sector during trade negotiations. The ACTN was not only an open access interaction between business and the bureaucratic centre of trade policy; it also played a strategic role in the design of US policy on IP issues.[177] In 1972, Pfizer's CEO Ed Pratt became the chairman of the ACTN.[178] With Pratt as chairman, the ACTN began constructing a new trade and investment agenda.[179] He also represented the private sector and was an adviser to the US official delegation at the Uruguay Round trade talks in his capacity as chairman of the ACTN.[180] By bringing foreknowledge on IP to the table, Pratt was able to frame the contours of national IP legislation as well as add it into the pre-existing US foreign trade template.[181] As far as the ACTN was concerned, folding IP standards into US foreign trade policy, first in bilateral agreements and then in multilateral agreements like the GATT, was the single best way in which to spread those standards.[182]

During this period, the ACTN worked closely with the USTR to shape the services, investment and IP trade agenda of the US.[183] Crucially, the ACTN established a Task Force on Intellectual Property whose recommendation formed the backbone of the US strategy for IP. It advised the US to have a long-term objective of placing IP into the GATT as well as in unilateral and bilateral agreements.[184] In doing this, the ACTN signified it would pull every lever at its disposal in order

[173] Matthews, *Will the Uruguay Round Consensus Hold?* (2002) 5; Drahos and Braithwaite, *Information Feudalism* (2003) 65–71.

[174] Sell (n 161) 1.

[175] Drahos and Braithwaite (n 169) 72.

[176] ibid.

[177] Drahos (n 95); John Braithwaite and Peter Drahos, *Global Business Regulation* (Cambridge, Cambridge University Press, 2000) 62.

[178] Drahos and Braithwaite (n 169) 67.

[179] ibid 72; Drahos and Braithwaite, 'Who Owns the Knowledge Economy' (2004) 15.

[180] Sell (n 161) 50.

[181] Drahos and Braithwaite (n 169) 72.

[182] Drahos and Braithwaite (n 172) 15.

[183] Drahos and Braithwaite (n 169) 91.

[184] Drahos (n 95).

to obtain the right result for the US on IP.[185] Consequently, the US amended its trade laws to reflect this new IP universalisation goal. Particularly, it revised Section 301 of the Trade Act of 1974 to address unfair practices on IPRs in various countries.[186] This provision allowed the US to withdraw trade benefits or impose duties on goods from foreign countries with poor IP laws or countries that refused to amend their IP laws to standards that are acceptable to the US.[187] For example, the USTR initiated Section 301 of the Trade Act against Brazil in 1988.[188] This imposed a 100 per cent tariff on imports of Brazilian products such as paper, consumer electronics and agricultural products.[189] In fact, the effective use of Section 301 gave the US the needed leverage in dealing with the problem of poor IP laws and could be credited for the successful inclusion of IP rules at the GATT.[190] In another example, the US included the protection of IP as an investment activity in the Bilateral Investment Treaty programme that it signed with many developing countries in the 1980s.[191] If anything, the significance of including IP as part of the US foreign policy and successfully pushing forward legislative changes show how a node (Pfizer) mobilised the Government to achieve its goal. The levers of a very personal self-interest thus shaped a macro outcome.[192]

To successfully include IP into the multilateral framework of the GATT, the ACTN had to move beyond the perimeters of US governance to bring in other possible like-minded stakeholders into its mentality of a trade-related IP regime. To do this, the USTR set up the Quad consisting of the US, EU, Japan,and Canada with the purpose of developing a consensus for the Uruguay Round of multilateral trade negotiations.[193] In the nodal governance context, the Quad is a super-structural node of like-minded countries which sought to promote their interests in IP at the global forum. Pertinently, it summoned combined resources of the Quad countries and nodal network access of business organisations within each to pressure their governments to include IP in the next round of trade negotiations.[194] During the Uruguay Round, the Quad developed the impetus for particular decisions and the negotiating positions of developed states.

[185] Drahos and Braithwaite (n 169) 116.
[186] Braithwaite and Drahos, *Global Business Regulation* (2000) 62.
[187] Drahos, 'Trade-Offs and Trade Linkages' (2000).
[188] Drahos and Braithwaite (n 169) 104.
[189] ibid.
[190] Drahos (n 95); Braithwaite and Drahos (n 181) 62; Raghavan (n 91) 84; Chimni (n 92) 143.
[191] Drahos (n 171) 207.
[192] Drahos and Braithwaite (n 169) 113.
[193] Ibid, 118–20.
[194] Drahos (n 97) 14.

In addition to setting up the Quad, Pratt – together with John Opel, the then Chairman of IBM – also created the Intellectual Property Committee (IPC). Like the Quad, the IPC was another super-structural node and consisted of a coalition of 13 major US corporations, namely Bristol-Myers, DuPont, FMC Corporation, General Electric, General Motors, Hewlett-Packard, IBM, Johnson & Johnson, Merck, Monsanto, Pfizer, Rockwell International and Warner Communications.[195] According to Burris, Drahos and Shearing, the IPC was dedicated to the inclusion of a comprehensive agreement on IP in the GATT negotiations with the stated objective of activating its nodal networks in Europe in order to achieve a European buy-in of a trade-linked globally enforceable IP regime.[196] These objectives were achieved in 1988 when the Quad released a suggested draft text of an agreement on IP, which eventually formed the backbone of the TRIPS Agreement.[197]

The above analysis illustrates how and why IP language was conceptualised and included in the US trade policy discourse. The technical design of American IP strategy also underscores the power of nodal governance (pharmaceutical companies and big corporations) in reforming the global IP regime to suit collective objectives. In cognitive terms, by bringing foreknowledge on IP to the table, mobilising resources at multiple sites, and utilising institutional networks, these companies became a super-structural node that no government could ignore. They conceived the idea of linking the IP regime to the trade regime and successfully marshalled government support to bring it to pass, consequently enrolling and activating a strong global IP regime in the TRIPS Agreement.

VIII. APPLICATION OF NODAL GOVERNANCE TO THIS STUDY

The story of global IP law, which was formalised in the TRIPS Agreement, shows how owners of large IP portfolios achieved the goal of IP globalisation by deploying and enrolling multiple nodal networks to produce action. The TRIPS Agreement case study and the empirical findings underpin the critical observations of nodal governance and its relevance for this book.

First, nodal governance brings insight to the inner workings of local law-making and governance – the actors, governance, knowledge capacity and resource availability. Explicitly, it shows the 'circuitry of power in societies where information networks have become a dominant organisational form'.[198]

[195] Burris, Drahos and Shearing (n 149) 45.
[196] ibid, 46.
[197] Drahos and Braithwaite (n 169) 115–17.
[198] Burris, Drahos, and Shearing (n 149) 46.

This is shown in the role and activities of Pfizer in mobilising support among like-minded organisations (nodal network). It was the concentration of power from these networks that successfully gave rise to the ACTN and the IPC – super-nodes that 'give their constituent nodes highly effective regulatory access to the people and governmental nodes that had to be regulated'.[199] Those super-structural nodes in turn activated other private and public assemblages in the US, Europe, Canada and Japan at the Uruguay Round negotiations. This shows not only the *presence of actors*, but also the power dynamics between actors to channel available resources and bring about the desired outcome.[200] Thus, all actor(s) should first be present for such actors to be able to access people and governmental nodes that had to be regulated. If actors were not present, there would not have been a nodal network to activate and access. As will be seen in coming chapters, the presence of actor networks in the form of pharmaceutical manufacturers and dynamic NGO networks has been key in advancing a particular agenda on patents in Brazil and India. Employing the nodal governance theory in analysing the actions of these non-state actors reveals how these groups embedded themselves in a spirit of resistance against a new global IP regime. In the process, they demanded and achieved a public interest and human rights-oriented IP regime in their respective jurisdictions.

Second, it shows the importance of decentred (ie between state and local governance) but competent performance in activating both private and public assemblages within the state structure. Pratt, as head of the ACTN, was able to bring in and activate other nodal networks.[201] In doing so, he was able to enlist not only the influence of CEOs of fellow companies with large portfolios but more financial resources.[202] Knowledge, capacity and resources thus became focused and concentrated. While NGOs in Brazil and India lack the economic muscle of big corporations in the US, they have been able to adroitly market their activism by employing human rights principles (right to health in Brazil and right to life in India) to mobilise government action and contest transnational corporate power. Generic pharmaceutical companies were able to use similar tactics in the run up to India's Patent Act amendment to facilitate efforts with a similar result from the Indian Government.

Third, mentalities matter. Big corporations in the US were able to frame their way of thinking to cognitively shape how the US Government approached its foreign trade policy. According to Susan Sell, the big corporations displayed impressive framing skills in presenting their case to the Government and their

[199] ibid, 47.
[200] ibid.
[201] ibid.
[202] ibid.

foreign counterparts, not merely by making the link between IP and trade, but also by the very terms they used to describe their position.[203] As chapters four and five will demonstrate, ongoing contestations in Brazil and India over IP rights have been framed as 'right to health' and 'right to life', respectively. These have proved to be effective counter-framing to the highly protectionist IP maximalist agenda of western countries.

IX. CONCLUSION

The aim of this chapter was to show the conceptual theoretical framework that underpins this book. The assessment of the TRIPS Agreement illustrates the extent to which the international economic law framework has continued to ascribe universalism borne out of Western philosophical persuasions. Particularly, in using TWAIL, the book delved into and critique the Eurocentric foundations of modern international economic governance to show that the system has continued to perpetuate a world of deep injustice characterised by violence, exploitation and inequality.

In order to rectify international law injustices, TWAIL has suggested looking instead at the prosaic life of international law manifesting in the local forums. This is because processes of reform and resistance ongoing in these forums ostensibly might not look as being part of the international legal system, but in actuality are. In calling focus on the local as part of the international, TWAIL theory envisions a 'praxis' of (the new) universality by mapping the numerous forms of resistance already at play in the struggle against the (post)colonial normative order now being institutionalised and administered across the world.

However, the suggestion of focusing on the various forms of reform and resistance vis-à-vis international law at the local forums falls afoul of the assumption that Third World states automatically have the requisites needed. Particularly, TWAIL ignores the questions of who, why and how to participate in reform and resistance vis-à-vis international law and scholarship. To rectify this lacuna, this book drew from the nodal governance theory to show how non-state actors engage in governance through nodal networks to produce change. In highlighting how governance processes are facilitated, it shows how power and participation is constituted and who is excluded in the process. Thus, in combining TWAIL and nodal governance theory to illuminate the materialisation of the international in the local, the thesis shows the gamut of legal, historical, political and economic developments that demonstrate the internationalisation of pharmaceutical patent law in the local forums of Brazil, India and Nigeria.

[203] Sell (n 161) 51.

In the subsequent chapters, these theoretical frameworks will be put in context to show their practical relevance. Starting with Brazil, the next chapter examines the structure and implementation of patent law. This is important because it shows that the country is not strictly adhering to the patent regime of Western countries, but is instead adapting patent law to its own unique environment. Thus, it provides a real-life example of Third World resistance and reformation of global patent law. It also focuses on the actors involved in counter-hegemonic law-making, bringing attention to the nodal governance of civil society activism and the very nature of these networks themselves.

4

Brazil – The Juridical State

I. INTRODUCTION

BRAZIL REPRESENTS AN exemplary model in the implementation of a programme of universal and free access to antiretroviral (ARV) drugs. The country is often cited[1] as a model developing country that has successfully tackled and contained the HIV/AIDS epidemic. When global responses to HIV/AIDS were largely prevention-based, Brazil became the first developing country to adopt an official policy for the free access to and universal distribution of ARVs. The importance of Brazil's AIDS treatment programme extends far beyond the Brazilians that have received ARV treatment, which is estimated at around 550,000.[2] This has demonstrated that it is possible to offer free and universal access to ARV in a resource-limited country. In doing so, Brazil changed the narrative on health, human rights and access to medicines.

The success of the Brazilian Government's HIV/AIDS programme, as this chapter explains, did not happen in isolation. It was the result of domestic and international political processes that emerged from re-democratisation in the 1980s – a combination of both intentional leadership and the politics of that time and space. This re-democratisation process, which included the emergence of new political parties, the creation of a new Constitution, a freer press, active social movements, the ongoing Uruguay Round negotiations, and the explosion

[1] Jane Galvão, 'Brazil And Access To HIV/AIDS Drugs: A Question Of Human Rights And Public Health' (2005) 95 *American Journal of Public Health* 1110; Paulo R Teixeira, Marco Antônio Vitória and Jhoney Barcarolo, 'The Brazilian Experience In Providing Universal Access To Antiretroviral Therapy' in JP Moatti (ed), *Economics of Aids And Access To HIV/AIDS Care In Developing Countries; Issues And Challenges* (Paris, ANRS, 2003); Guillaume Loup, Andreia de Assis, Maria-Helena Costa-Couto, Sonia Fleury, Kenneth de Camargo Jr and Jean-Claude Thoenig, 'The Brazilian Experience Of "Scaling Up": A Public Policy Approach' in B Coriat (ed), *The Political Economy Of HIV/AIDS In Developing Countries: TRIPS, Public Health Systems, and Free Access* (London, Edward Elgar Publishing, 2008); Bill and Melinda Gates Foundation, '2003 Gates Award For Global Health – Brazilian National AIDS Program' (2003), available at www.gatesfoundation.org/Media-Center/Press-Releases/2003/05/Brazilian-National-AIDS-Program (accessed 28 May 2015).

[2] See UNAIDS: Brazil Factsheet, available at www.unaids.org/en/regionscountries/countries/brazil (accessed 18 May 2019). At the time of the fieldwork for this research in 2014, the number was estimated at about 350,000 according to the then Director of the National AIDS Programme, Dr Fabio Mesquita. Amaka Vanni, Interview with Fabio Mesquita (2014) (transcript on file with author).

of the HIV/AIDS epidemic at the time, provided the foundation for Brazil's contemporary AIDS treatment institutions.

This chapter focuses on the intersection between Brazil's HIV/AIDS programme and pharmaceutical patent regime. It traces the development and implementation of socially conscious patent law and pharmaceutical policies. It also maps the roles of various actors in the making of the AIDS programme – their motivations, challenges, and how they influenced these policies. That is, the way key actors – particularly civil society – captured and framed the state's understanding and application of patents for health and economic development purposes. In examining the Brazilian context, it finds that patents are not just perceived strictly as private rights, but also as legal rights with a social function that should be balanced with public interests. This stems from the constitutionalisation of a universal right to health and the subsequent institutionalisation of a universal public health system. In doing so, patents are jointly understood and conceptualised by both the state and non-state actors as not only an impediment to the legal commitment to universal healthcare, but also a tool for achieving this social function embedded within the constitutional framework. It is this understanding that shapes the interests of policy-makers, drives them to implement a socially-conscious patent regulatory system, and informs civil society activism and engagement with patent law. Likewise, the country also demonstrates that the significance of the active presence of domestic political actors and institutions is the most important determinant in the understanding, conceptualisation and direction of law and policy.

The analysis of Brazil epitomises TWAIL theory in two important ways. First, it helps to establish the links between the past and the present in the development of a patent regime to 'gain an understanding of how international norms and institutional practices have emerged and developed through specific historical conjunctures'.[3] In this way, it makes explicit the role of law in the history of the present. Second, in proceeding from the premise that international law should be understood as a field of practice that influences everyday life at very localised levels, it provides the analytics for recognising the materialisation of global patent law and attendant access to medicines litigation in the local jurisdictions of Brazil, an example of how international law constitutes and reconstitutes routines, spaces and objects. In this light, the postcolonial political behaviour is not only an ideological project located in a particular material context with material consequences, but also a material project itself.[4] In other words, the politics and activism surrounding the development of

[3] Luis Eslava, 'TWAIL Coordinates' (2019) *Groningen Journal of International Law*, available at https://grojil.org/2019/04/01/twail-coordinates (accessed 1 April 2019).

[4] Luis Eslava and Sundhya Pahuja, 'Between Resistance And Reform: TWAIL And The Universality Of International Law' (2011) 3 *Trade, Law and Development* 104; Luis Eslava and Sundhya Pahuja, 'Beyond The (Post)Colonial: TWAIL And The Everyday Life of International Law' (2012) 452 *Journal of Law and Politics in Africa, Asia and Latin America – Verfassung und Recht in Übersee (VRÜ)* 195.

the AIDS programme and subsequent reform in patent law is not an isolated incident happening in a local space. It is part of a larger network of resistance already at play in the struggle against the colonial normative order now being institutionalised and administered across the world.[5] In this regard, it shows the significance of international law – both its encompassing nature and ensuing contestations – in local spaces.[6]

As the chapter develops, the dynamic activism of social movement and civil society groups, which originated during the authoritarian military regime, becomes prominent. The success of the AIDS programme is largely due to the involvement of these social movement groups in producing expertise and knowledge regarding AIDS as well as in employing human rights principles in treatment campaigns. It was this human rights-based approach that produced cumulative and long-term effects on law and policy. Employing nodal governance insights, this chapter also shows how social movements, in collaboration with the Government, secured pharmaceutical autonomy for the Brazilian population. By strategically using ideas and networks, these groups were able to form strong domestic coalitions that exploited critical junctures in domestic politics to produce positive impacts on health, law and the economy. Thus, the nodal governance perspective shows how nodes (social movement) activate their nodal network to interpret their interests, recruit allies and convince the state of not only the justness of their cause but also of its constitutionality.

The remainder of this chapter is therefore structured as follows: section II looks at the development of the patent regime in Brazil from the colonial period to the present. Mapping the history of patent regime in Brazil provides a Twailian perspective of illuminating how colonial expansionism facilitated the enactment of Eurocentric patent rules under the guise of universality, thereby laying bare the exploitative nature of colonial patent rule. It also provides an understating of the ideas that informed patent law reforms in Brazil in order to make the patent regime work for the country's welfare and development needs. The section also examines Brazil's industrial property law and delineates the roles of – and sometimes dialectic relationship between – the Brazilian Patent Office (*Instituto Nacional da Propriedade Industrial* or INPI) and the Brazilian National Health Surveillance Agency (*Agência Nacional de Vigilância Sanitária* or ANVISA). This is important as it demonstrates that the creation of ANVISA is an attempt by the Brazilian state to recapture the discourse on patents from a strictly exclusive private right point of view, without regard to consumers and the public, to one that balances private rights with social responsibility. It is argued in this chapter that these everyday intimacies across spatial divides and scales of governance show how international law – in this case, Brazil's obligation under the TRIPS Agreement – not only can be reconceptualised beyond a 'restricted

[5] Eslava and Pahuja, 'Beyond the (Post)Colonial' (ibid).

[6] Karin Mickelson, 'Taking Stock Of TWAIL Histories' (2008) 10 *International Community Law Review* 358.

body of norms, or situated only in bureaucratic and institutional environments',[7] but also how international law transcends boundaries and becomes part of everyday realities of people as a result of this 'transcending'.[8]

Section IV of this chapter assesses three incidents which gave rise to the right to health law under the Brazilian Constitution, namely the generic drugs policy, the HIV/AIDS programme, and the CL for the ARV drug *Efavirenz*. Tracing these incidents help to cognitively map the local politics of the construction of particular policy options. Importantly, it exemplifies the tension faced by developing country governments as they seek to balance social justice with economic issues. Section V deals with local actors influencing law, policies and institutional agenda. Though some scholars contend that the confluence of various actors 'renders the Brazilian state weak on a fundamental level as it is captive to a wide array of distributional coalitions',[9] it is posited in this book that such confluence has played an important role in shaping public policy responses to the AIDS epidemic and in articulating a counter-hegemonic IP discourse. In other words, the activism of civil society groups in furthering a human rights approach to patent laws is an enactment of Twailian–materialist praxis as these actors have concomitantly influenced the Government in adopting alternative policy norms and IP rules that are advocacy-orientated and pro-human rights in their articulation. Section VI looks at Brazil's law-making and agenda-setting, from the local to the international level, by linking IP discourse with a development-related approach. Specifically, it looks at the shift in Brazil's stance in adopting international IP rules from being acquiescent and regulation-importing to a norm and law-making posture aimed at promoting development at home and abroad. In doing so, the country linked public interests, socio-economic needs, and changing realities at the local level to the international law-making framework, concomitantly providing an alternative to existing IP framework and unwittingly furthering a Twailian agenda in the reform of the global IP regime. The conclusion summarises the Brazilian context.

By and large, this chapter explores how Brazil developed a health-oriented patent examination system. Specifically, by predicating the engagement of the pharmaceutical patent regime to a right to health frame, the Brazilian state implemented a specific normative approach in which patent rights are balanced with socio-economic and technological development and the public interest. The participation of civil society enhanced the synergy between the drug sector and the patent system. This contributed to the development of a wider policy framework reflective of local, social and economic conditions and priorities. As such, it provides an example of how Nigeria can recalibrate its own patent

[7] Eslava and Pahuja, 'Between Resistance and Reform' (2011) 125.

[8] ibid.

[9] Bruno M Salama and Daniel Benoliel, 'Pharmaceutical Patent Bargains: The Brazilian Experience' (2010) 18 *Cardozo Journal of International and Comparative Law* 637.

policy in a manner that is compliant with the TRIPS Agreement while being responsive to its own socio-economic realities.

II. HISTORICAL EVOLUTION OF THE PATENT REGIME IN BRAZIL

A. Colonial Encounters

Brazil has always had an extensive engagement with the patent regime. The Portuguese Crown first introduced patent law in the country in 1809 through a royal decree by King Joao VI, thereby making Brazil the fourth country in the world to have a patent regime. It was also a founding member of the Paris Convention for the Protection of Industrial Property in 1883, which established the three pillars of the current patent system, ie independence of patents and trademarks, equal treatment of nationals and foreigners, and priority rights.[10] The imperial Constitution of 1824 provided inventors exclusive rights of ownership over their discoveries or products and guaranteed a temporary exclusive privilege or compensation for any loss from popularisation.[11] That is, it allowed for compensation of the inventor in case of proliferation without the inventor's permission.

Other laws such as the Law of 28 August 1830 provided for patents for only Brazilian nationals and allowed for the exhaustion of patents that had not yet been locally exploited after a period of two years.[12] The aim of these colonial IP laws was not to encourage innovation, as there was not only little to no local industrial activity ongoing at that time, but also little scientific progress in the fields of chemistry and physics.[13] Rather, these laws were based on the experiences of early-nineteenth-century Europe, which was dominated by the principle of territoriality or the belief that protection does not extend beyond the territory of the sovereign that granted the rights in the first place.[14] This principle is largely grounded on protecting colonial interests and territorial sovereignty.[15] Thus, patent law was not enacted to enhance indigenous innovation, as it was of little industrial importance. Rather, it was enacted to protect the interest of the

[10] Maria Auxiliadora Oliveira, Gabriela Costa Chaves and Ruth Epsztejn, 'Brazilian Intellectual Property Legislation' in J Bermudez and M Oliveira (eds), *Intellectual Property In The Context Of The WTO TRIPS Agreement: Challenges For Public Health*, 2nd edn (Rio de Janeiro, Oswaldo Cruz Foundation, 2004) 152.

[11] Cícero Gontijo, 'Changing The Patent System From The Paris Convention To The TRIPS Agreement: The Position Of Brazil' (2005) 26 *Global Issues Paper* 17–18.

[12] ibid.

[13] Oliveira, Chaves and Epsztejn, 'Brazilian Intellectual Property Legislation' (2004) 152.

[14] This principle was embedded in the Paris Convention. See Paris Convention for the Protection of Industrial Property, as amended (1979) 828 UNTS 305 ('Paris Convention'), art 4*bis*.

[15] Peter Drahos, 'The Universality Of Intellectual Property Rights: Origins And Developments' (1999), available at www.wipo.int/edocs/mdocs/tk/en/wipo_unhchr_ip_pnl_98/wipo_unhchr_ip_pnl_98_1.pdf (accessed 22 March 2014) 5.

Portuguese monarchy in exploiting Brazilian natural resources and to prevent any activity in the colony that might hinder or jeopardise such exploitation.[16] For TWAIL, this move to impose European patent rules on then colonised Brazil underscores how colonial patent laws entrench asymmetrical power relationships between the former colonies and former colonial powers. In projecting Eurocentric – in this case, Portuguese – patent law as universally applicable to Brazil, the Portuguese Crown was able to not only consolidate its expansion into Brazil but also achieve monopoly privileges that helped maintain a particular structure of technological and commercial control.

B. Post-colonial Interventions

In the beginning of the twentieth century, Brazil enacted various industrial property statutes, notably Decree 16.264/23 of 1923 Law, which created the Industrial Property Office and regulated both patents and trademarks.[17] However, socio-economic structural anomalies and the deepening economic crisis at the time shifted public sentiments regarding the utility of an IP system, and created local resistance against the international patent system. This 'wind of change' against the support for an IP system that secured the protection of patent-holders' rights can be attributed to the Brazilian dissatisfaction with the Paris Union, especially the monopoly by patent-holders, which has led to dependency on foreign-imported medicines as well as to the development ideas circulating among the Government and policy-makers at that time, such as the import substitution industrialisation (ISI) policy[18] – an economic and trade

[16] Edith Penrose, 'International Patenting And The Less-Developed Countries' (1973) 83 *The Economic Journal* 769; Jorge A Bermudez, Ruth Epsztejn, Maria Auxiliadora Oliveira and Lia Hasenclever, *The WTO TRIPS Agreement And Patent Protection In Brazil: Recent Changes And Implications For Local Production And Access To Medicines* (Rio de Janeiro, Oswaldo Cruz Foundation, 2002) 52. For the 'anti-developmental' nature of the IP regime during this period, see AK Menescal, 'Changing WIPO's Ways? The 2004 Development Agenda In Historical Perspective' (2005) 8 *Journal of World Intellectual Property* 761; Peter O'Brien, 'Developing Countries And The Patent System: An Economic Appraisal' (1974) 2 *World Development* 27.

[17] Graziela Ferrero Zucoloto, Patrick Alves and Dea Guerra Fioravante, Intellectual Property And Socio-Economic Development: Country Study Brazil, available at www.wipo.int/edocs/mdocs/mdocs/en/cdip_11/cdip_11_inf_3.pdf (accessed 11 May 2015); see also Bermudez et al, *The WTO TRIPS Agreement* (2002) 53.

[18] Import Substitution Industrialisation (ISI) is an economic policy adopted by economically less developed countries to stimulate local industrialisation by establishing domestic production facilities to manufacture goods which were formerly imported. ISI stems from the dependency theory, which viewed global economic structures as antithetical to Brazilian (and most areas of the less developed world) economic advancement aspirations. See Werner Baer, 'Import Substitution And Industrialization In Latin America: Experiences And Interpretations' (1972) 7 *Latin American Research Review* 95 on ISI policies in Brazil. See also Rex A Hudson, 'Import-Substitution Industrialization, 1945–64' in R Hudson (ed), *Brazil: A Country Study* (Washington DC, Library of Congress Federal Research Division, 1998).

policy that advocates the local manufacturing of goods to spur domestic industrialisation and reduce dependency on foreign imports.

To a certain degree, these discussions on the monopoly effect of the Paris Convention, especially on the country's access to pharmaceutical products, inventive activity, and technology transfer, exemplify the material practice of international law in the everyday operation and application of its rules and practices.[19] That is, the ways international law manifests on the ground by 'structuring our daily existence both in a physical sense, producing and reproducing the world in which we live'.[20] In this particular circumstance, the material effect was the exceptionally high price of pharmaceuticals, which was having real everyday impact on lives of ordinary Brazilians. The prohibitive cost of pharmaceutical medicines was due to the high incidence of patent monopoly abuse, especially by multinational pharmaceutical companies operating in Brazil on one hand, and the fact that foreigners dominated Brazilian applications without locally working any of the patent particles, on the other. For instance, in 1957, more than half (60 per cent) of the Brazilian pharmaceutical market was controlled by foreign capital, by 1959, the number was 75 per cent and by 1963, it was 90 per cent.[21] For many of these foreign companies, monopoly privileges derived from patents afforded opportunity to buy up and displace local companies.

To resolve the issue of patent abuse, the country set up a special 'inquiry commission' (*Comissao Parlamentar de Inquerito*) in 1961 to analyse domestic abuses of patent monopolies by foreign pharmaceutical corporations. The Commission found incidents of abuse in the form of 'restrictive practices in licensing agreements and the payment of high royalties including royalties for expired patents, which led to the high cost of medicines in Brazil'.[22] The culmination of the Brazilian frustration with the Paris Convention, the existing international patent system at that time, pushed the country to denounce at the United Nations General Assembly in October 1961 the 'imbalance between the national and the foreign sector of his country's economy due to patents and royalties'.[23] As a result, Brazil and Bolivia submitted a draft resolution on the need for a 'Development Agenda' for the international patent system. The resolution stated, inter alia, the importance of co-operation in the field of applied science and technology for promoting the exchange of knowledge,[24]

[19] Ann Orford, 'Constituting Order' cited in James Thuo Gathii, 'The Agenda Of Third World Approaches To International Law (TWAIL), forthcoming in *International Legal Theory: Foundations and Frontiers* (Cambridge, Cambridge University Press, 2019), available at https://ssrn.com/abstract=3304767 (accessed 18 May 2019).

[20] Luis Eslava, 'The Materiality Of International Law: Violence, History And Joe Sacco's The Great War' (2017) 5 *London Review of International Law* 50.

[21] Constantine Vaitsos, 'Patents Revisited: Their Function In Developing Countries' (1972) 9 *The Journal of Development Studies* 92.

[22] Menescal, 'Changing WIPO's Ways? (2005) 764.

[23] ibid.

[24] ibid.

the application of international patent rules in ways that are cognisant of the legitimate claims of patentees and the economic development needs and requirements of underdeveloped countries,[25] the effects of patents on the economies of underdeveloped countries, and the characteristics of the patent legislation of underdeveloped countries in light of economic development objectives.[26]

By presenting the issue of patent abuses at an international forum such as the UN, Brazil and other countries from the Global South were not only seeking to revise domestic law but were also seeking to forcibly change multilateral trade rules. Looking back at these events, Brazil's move to revise unfair global patent laws rules both locally and internationally can be recognised as instances of TWAIL in praxis. Here, praxis in the sense of inseparability of theory and practice, marriage of thought and action.[27] In pushing for a change in international trade rules that facilitate and maintain the domination and impoverishment of Third World peoples, Brazil was inadvertently enacting Twailian ethical commitment to challenging and reforming the features of the international legal system that helped reproduce structures that marginalise and dominate Third World peoples and contribute to an unjust global order.[28]

The fermentation of local discontent with the global IP regime circulating at that time provided the impetus for Brazil to enact Law Number 1.005/1971 in 1969 and Law Number 5.772/71 in 1971, both dealing with patents.[29] The former, which created the new Industrial Property Code, removed food, chemical and pharmaceutical substances, materials, products and medicines from the list of patentable materials, while the latter prohibited the patenting of processes for food, chemicals and medicines.[30]

According to some commentators, these new laws allowed local pharmaceutical companies to engage in large-scale reverse engineering of drugs without any legal restriction or repercussions, thus allowing a number of firms and laboratories to acquire synthetic capability formulae.[31] The ideas

[25] ibid.

[26] ibid.

[27] See Obiora Chinedu Okafor, 'Enacting Twailian Praxis In Nonacademic Habitats: Toward A Conceptual Framework' (2016) 110 *AJIL Unbound* 22.

[28] Mickelson, 'TWAIL Histories' (2008) 358. See also James Thuo Gathii, Henry J Richardson and Karen Knop, 'Introduction To Symposium On Theorizing TWAIL Activism' (2016) 110 *AJIL Unbound* 18 on essays demonstrating TWAIL, in addition to being a methodological and theoretical framework, also embraces practical work geared towards creating and constructing a just global order. In particular, Obiora Chinedu Okafor essay at n 27 provides practical guidelines for TWAIL scholars' interventions in environments such as international institutions and local activism.

[29] In 1945, Brazil implemented Law Number 7.903/1945, which included the novelty concept and removed product patent protection for medicines, food, and chemicals. See also Salama and Benoliel, 'Pharmaceutical Patent Bargains' (2010) 639; Srividhya Ragavan, *Patent and Trade Disparities in Developing Countries* (Oxford, Oxford University Press, 2012) 58; Christopher S Mayer, 'The Brazilian Pharmaceutical Industry Goes Walking from Ipanema to Prosperity: Will the New Intellectual Property Law Spur Domestic Investment?' (1998) 12 *Temple International and Comparative Law Journal* 37; Bermudez et al (n 16) 52.

[30] Bermudez et al (n 16) 52.

[31] Fabienne Orsi, Lia Hasenclever, Beatriz Fialho, Paulo Tigre and Benjamin Coriat, 'Intellectual Property Rights, Anti-AIDS Policy And Generic Drugs. Lessons From The Brazilian Public Health

underpinning these laws – similar to those underpinning the Indian Patent Act of 1970 (as will be seen in the next chapter) – would spur the development of the industrial sector, as the Government believed that the elimination of patent protection would create stronger domestic industries.[32] Reducing the high incidence of poverty and the high cost of medicines were some of the compelling reasons for implementing patent policies suitable for the country's needs at that time. Within a decade after the removal of patent products and processes, the 10 largest national pharmaceutical companies increased their market share by 10 per cent.[33] However, it is also arguable that the lack of patent protection discouraged foreign companies from further increasing their presence in the market.

In addition to legislative change, the military regime also created the Central Medicines Agency (*Central de Medicamentos* or CEME) under the Office of the President in 1971 to regulate the production and distribution of drugs by pharmaceutical laboratories subsumed or linked to various government ministries.[34] The CEME was tasked with the responsibility of developing policies for the sector and of leading the public procurement of medicines from public and private laboratories in order to develop the country's pharmaceutical and technology base. To complement the CEME mandate, the Government also enacted policies to attract investments so as to build up the fine chemical industry that produces specialised chemicals for active pharmaceutical ingredients (APIs) and their intermediates, as well as for fertilizers, in order to reduce dependency on imported APIs for pharmaceutical and chemical production.

This historical reflection of Brazil's engagement with the patent regime at the local and international level – leading the Global South in seeking to transform global IP rules – illustrates the country's comprehension of the patent system as a policy tool for the development of the state. This should also be viewed within the larger context of the development aspirations percolating at that time. While the reform in patent law did have a direct link to the pharmaceutical sector, the legislative change is indicative of a more general transformation of the development aspirations of postcolonial societies that lent to looking at things differently, some of which pertained to particular policy interventions for certain industrial sectors such as pharmaceuticals.

Program' (2003) in JP Moatti, T Barnett, B Coriat, Y Souteyrand, J Dumoulin and YA Flori (eds), *Economics of AIDS and Access to HIV/AIDS Care in Developing Countries* (Paris, Agence Nationale de Recherches sur le Sida, 2003) 122; see also Maurice Cassier and Marilena Correa, 'Patents, Innovation and Public Health: Brazilian Public-Sector Laboratories' Experience in Copying AIDS Drugs', available at www.lepublieur.com/anrs/ecoaids7.pdf (accessed 6 May 2015).

[32] Mayer, 'The Brazilian Pharmaceutical Industry' (1998) 379; Ragavan, *Patent and Trade Disparities* (2012) 59.

[33] Gary Gereffi, *The Pharmaceutical Industry And Dependency In The Third World* (Princeton, Princeton University Press, 1983) 229.

[34] Jorge AZ Bermudez, Maria Auxiliadora Oliveira and Egleubua Andrade de Oliveira, 'Expanding Access To Essential Medicines In Brazil: Recent Regulation And Public Policies' in J Bermudez and M Oliveira (eds), *Intellectual Property in the Context of the WTO TRIPS Agreement: Challenges for Public Health*, 2nd edn (Rio de Janeiro, Oswaldo Cruz Foundation, 2004) 129.

It is reasonable to read these events through a Twailian lens as efforts by the postcolonial Brazilian state to retrench and change the colonial legacies of patent law both at home and abroad that had a predominately negative effect towards a legal regime with an equitable outcome. It is this view – of balancing private rights and pursuing development goals – that underpinned Brazil's participation at the Uruguay Round, which was launched at that time. This explains why the country opposed the inclusion of IP in the global trade mechanism in the Group of 10. According to Piragibe dos Santos Tarragô, Brazil's chief TRIPS Agreement negotiator during the Uruguay Round from 1987 to 1993, the country considered the protection afforded by the Paris Convention sufficient and thus did not see the reason for a new agreement on IP.[35]

Crucially, Brazil (along with a number of developing countries including India and Nigeria) insisted on the inadequacy of the GATT to host negotiations on IPRs and maintained that the treaties on IP were fundamentally about the protection of rights, whereas the GATT essentially concerned trade in goods.[36] On patent, dos Santos Tarragô notes that Brazil was not only concerned about patent protection in the area of pharmaceuticals and biotechnology, but also cabout the ability 'to grant compulsory licences to acquire manufacturing capacity whenever the patent owner made use of its monopolistic rights to serve the market only by importation'.[37] This is because, for the country, the ability to develop structures and institutions in order to promote and foster technological and scientific development was of utmost importance.

Thus, during the Uruguay negotiations, the Brazilian delegation endeavoured to keep for the Government the maximum flexibility to apply CLs, should it be needed, to meet its requirements of public health, combat abusive practices and encourage local manufacturing. However, various factors (discussed in the next section), which included change in the domestic government, altered the Brazilian staunch opposition against the inclusion of IP to global trade rules. Brazil became more amenable to accepting patents for pharmaceuticals and adopted a tactical approach at the Uruguay Round.[38] Though the country did not succeed in opposing the inclusion of IP into the jurisdiction of the WTO, it succeeded in including considerable flexibilities to safeguard its national interest and give governments some latitude of policy space in implementing development policies and in defending the public interest. As will be seen in coming sections, it appears that this idea – of balancing patent right with development goals – still circulates among its policy circles.

[35] Piragibe dos Santos Tarragô, 'Negotiating For Brazil' in J Watal and A Taubman (eds), *The Making Of The TRIPS Agreement: Personal Insights From The Uruguay Round Negotiations*, 1st edn (Geneva, World Trade Organization, 2015) 241.

[36] ibid.

[37] ibid 247.

[38] Fieldwork interview with Pedro Paranagua (Brasilia, 2014) (transcript on file with author).

C. Global Experience

With its accession to the WTO in 1995 and the attendant implementation of the TRIPS Agreement, Brazil began – as part of its obligation to the TRIPS Agreement and the Single Undertaking – to recognise IP protection for all pharmaceutical products and processes. This period also coincided with the neoliberal efforts of the government at that time, which aimed at opening up the Brazilian economy, stem hyperinflation and jumpstart the country's sluggish economic growth. Thus, Law 9.279/96 (Industrial Property Law of Brazil or IPLB), which came into effect in 1996, not only changed key aspects of previous industrial property law but also implemented higher standards than those required by the TRIPS Agreement. However, even though the IPLB is protected by the Brazilian Constitution, it is secondary to Brazil's social interests and technological and economic development. Specifically, Article 5, XXIX of the Constitution, which reads:

> [T]he law shall ensure the authors of industrial inventions of a temporary privilege for their use, as well as protection of industrial creations, property of trademarks, names of companies and other distinctive signs, viewing the social interest and the technological and economic development of the country.[39]

The new industrial property law as it relates to the TRIPS Agreement and the politics surrounding its implementation is interesting in many ways as it points to, in the words of Chimni, the integral role played by the ruling elites in Third World states that 'seek to establish the global rule of transnational capital on the pretext of pursuing "national interests"'.[40] Though Brazil had the option of waiting until January 2005 to phase fully into the TRIPS Agreement regime, it did not use this transition period. Instead, it not only changed its industrial property code eight years earlier but also implemented some TRIPS-plus provisions. This raises important questions, chiefly: why did Brazil not utilise the full transition period like India and China? Further, why did it include TRIPS-plus provisions in its industrial property code? The answers hinge on the internal and external dynamics at play during this period.

Internally, various local compulsions were at play. Brazil was going through neoliberalisation policies under the leadership of Fernando Collor de Mello (1990–1992), which aimed at improving the Brazilian economy. Stressing the need for 'modernization', Collor de Mello rapidly liberalised the economy by drastically reducing tariffs, privatising public assets, removing price controls on medicines and abandoning industrial policies.[41] The implementation of these neoliberal reforms officially ended the ISI economic policy. As a result,

[39] Constitution of the Federal Republic of the Brazil (1988), Art 5, XXIX (Brazilian Constitution).

[40] BS Chimni, 'Third World Approaches To International Law: A Manifesto' (2006) 8 *International Community Law Review* 7.

[41] David Trubek, Diogo Coutinho and Mario Schapiro, 'Toward a New Law and Development: New State Activism in Brazil and the Challenge for Legal Institutions' (2012) World Bank Legal

tariffs on APIs and fine chemicals fell from 65 per cent to 20 per cent, while the privatisation of state petrochemical firms led to the closure of several upstream plants that had been established to produce APIs.[42]

The neoliberal structural reforms continued with the subsequent presidencies of Itamar Franco, who replaced Mello after the latter's impeachment, and Fernando Henrique Cardoso, who won by popular vote in 1995 and was a self-proclaimed advocate of the aforementioned development theory.[43] The period under the Cardoso government was also the period that the Brazilian Social Democracy Party (*Partido da Social Democracia Brasileira* or PSDB), centrist in its political and economic stance, was in power. Under a PSDB government, Brazil continued to move away from the *dirigiste* policies of the developmentalist period, embracing many of the neoliberal prescriptions favoured by the Washington Consensus.[44] Under the Cardoso Government, there was a shift in the consciousness of Brazil's ability to be a global player on one hand, and a general idea circulating among policy-makers that the implementation of the TRIPS Agreement earlier than planned would bring in FDI.[45] That is, a new thinking where Brazil positions as a regional leader, a respected spokesman for the developing world, and an increasingly important partner for the US and the EU, emerged. Thus, policy-makers believed that embracing IPR internally would not only be a positive step towards Brazil's economic liberalisation but would also improve the image of Brazil as a modern economy. This, it was hoped, would attract foreign companies to set up manufacturing plants in Brazil and reduce the country's dependence on technology imports.[46]

Another internal factor that allowed Brazil to phase into the TRIPS Agreement earlier was the weakened position of local generics at the time the IPLB was passed. With trade liberalisation and the removal of the ISI policy that protected local manufacturers, many petrochemical raw material firms were privatised while the local firms that remained could not compete with their foreign counterparts that flooded the market.[47] According to one commentator, over 1,500 production lines of local generic pharma-chemical companies were shut down due to the commercial opening of the Brazilian economy.[48] This view is reinforced by Orsi et al, who observed that the trade liberalisation of the 1990s

Review, Legal Studies Research Paper Series Paper No 1207, 283; Matthew Brian Flynn, 'Pharmaceutical Governance In Brazil: Globalization, Institutions And AIDS', PhD (University of Texas at Austin, 2010) 54.

[42] Fieldwork interview, Rio de Janeiro, June 2014. See also Flynn (ibid).

[43] In his memoir, Cardoso details how he combined principle and pragmatism to transform a harsh military dictatorship into a hopeful modern democracy, and how his background in sociology influenced his administration's major economic and social development achievements. See Fernando Henrique Cardoso and Brian Winter, *The Accidental President Of Brazil* (New York, Public Affairs, 2006).

[44] Trubek, Coutinho and Schapiro, 'Toward a New Law and Development' (2012) 283.

[45] Fieldwork interview (n 42).

[46] ibid.

[47] Cassier and Correa, 'Patents, Innovation and Public Health' 123.

[48] ibid.

negatively affected the Brazilian pharmaceutical sector as the 'privatisation of petrochemical raw material firms reinforced the phasing out of the production of synthetics intermediates in which the sector has competitive edge'.[49] The few drug manufacturers that remained in the market moved to less competitive areas, subsequently concentrating their production on low value-added commodities. In this environment, Brazilian firms could not compete in scale and technology with imported drugs distributed locally by specialised international traders.

The weakened position of local manufacturers meant that the sector could not mount any concerted sensitisation campaign against the possible adverse impact of the TRIPS Agreement on Brazil's indigenous generic pharmaceutical sector. The growth of neoliberal ideologies such as Thatcher and Reagan influenced Brazil in the 1990s as the country had a huge commercial opening without any kind of protection for (indigenous generic) pharmaceutical companies. It was difficult for these manufacturers because many closed down and laid off workers. The weakened status of these local manufacturers made them too weak to influence the Government on the TRIPS Agreement, as one of the representatives of the Brazilian generic pharmaceutical manufacturers explained.[50] In India, by contrast, trade liberalisation proceeded at a slower pace with policies in place to support local pharmaceutical sector. India also used the 10-year transition period, while within the two years of signing the TRIPS Agreement Brazil passed the Patent Law which simply ignored the domestic industrial policy and domestic companies. The impact of that decision can be seen even now. Today, India is a player in the international pharmaceutical market while Brazil is not.[51] This domestic economic configuration explains the muted role of Brazilian drug manufacturers in the lead-up to the country's harmonisation with the TRIPS Agreement regime.

In addition, the inaction of various civil society groups, particularly the health and AIDS activists, also explains why Brazil phased into the TRIPS Agreement regime quickly. Brazilian civil society groups were focused on internal political crisis and the re-democratisation process especially after the corruption scandal that led to the impeachment of President Collor. The crisis was that Collor, a conservative populist, implemented an incredibly corrupt government that carried out graft and embezzlement. In this crisis situation, it appeared that the young democracy (and the re-democratisation) process was going to come apart. This led to protests by civil society groups that were active in the democratic transition and had fought for the democratic process in previous years. According to one of the activists who was in Brazil at the time, the internal political crisis going on at the time was the main focus of many of the civil society actors who had played key roles in the re-democratisation process and felt that the corrupt government of President Collor threatened the polity.[52]

[49] ibid.
[50] Fieldwork interview (n 42).
[51] ibid.
[52] ibid.

And so everybody, including activists in the AIDS world such as Herbert D'Souza, who was the founder of ABIA and a major figure in the movement, were all preoccupied with the corruption of the Collor Government and specifically focused on creating a social movement and civil protest asking for the impeachment of Collor. These groups were totally focused on what needed to be done to try to save democracy and the re-democratisation process in Brazil, and in another time without that focus, they might have contested the TRIPS Agreement and early implementation by Brazil.[53]

This view is supported by Amy Nunn, who writes that IP regulations on access to AIDS medicines were largely unaddressed by the AIDS movement and treatment activists as they had not recognised the importance of the law for access to treatment because they were more focused on 'federal AIDS bureaucracies and moving trials through the judiciary rather than working with Congress'.[54] This preoccupation of both the civil society groups and the pharmaceutical sector explains why the new IP legislation – with very little TRIPS Agreement flexibilities designed to protect consumers and curtail industry abuses – was implemented.[55] As will be seen in the next sections, Brazilian civil society groups and AIDS activists have tried to rectify this by actively engaging with the law.

Externally, international politics brought to bear on Brazil. The country was under pressure from the US to change its IP laws since the early 1980s. Specifically, the US adopted trade restrictive measures towards Brazil, combining multilateral pressure in the GATT and Uruguay Round negotiations and bilateral actions.[56] In 1988, for example, the US initiated the Section 301 of the Trade Act – a unilateral action and contradictory to the ethics of the GATT/WTO – after the USTR found Brazil's pharmaceutical patent law 'unreasonable'.[57] In initiating this trade sanction, the US imposed a 100 per cent tariff on imports of Brazilian products such as paper, consumer electronics and agricultural products – about USD 40 million-worth of annual imports from Brazil at that time.[58]

[53] ibid.

[54] Amy Nunn, *The Politics And History Of AIDS Treatment In Brazil* (New York, Springer, 2008) 85.

[55] Cassandra M Sweet, 'The Political Economy Of Pharmaceutical Production In Brazil' in H Löfgren and O Williams (eds), *The New Political Economy Of Pharmaceutical: Production, Innovation And TRIPS in the Global South*, 1st edn (Hampshire, Palgrave Macmillan, 2013) 48; Flynn, 'Pharmaceutical Governance' (2010) 55.

[56] See Michelle Ratton Sanchez Badin, 'Developmental Responses To The International Trade Legal Game: Cases Of Intellectual Property And Export Credit Law Reforms in Brazil' in D Trubek, H Alviar Garcia, D Coutinho and A Santos (eds), *Law and the New Developmental State: The Brazilian Experience in Latin American Context*, 1st edn (Cambridge, Cambridge University Press, 2013) 260.

[57] Chakravarthi Raghavan, *Recolonization: General Agreement On Tariffs And Trade, The Uruguay Round And The Third World* (Penang, Third World Network, 1990) 84.

[58] ibid.

The use of Section 301 was indeed an extremely timely threat as the Brazilian economy was vulnerable and going through economic upheavals, such that the loss of millions of dollars' worth of export revenues hit home.[59] This is especially so as many of Brazil's political elite had interests in the agriculture export industry, and with the US being one of the main destination markets, Brazil was therefore particularly susceptible to US trade threats.[60] Consequently, many senators and deputies believed that implementing the TRIPS Agreement would not only improve trade with the US but would also ease trade sanctions. In fact, Piragibe dos Santos Tarragô notes that the threat to Brazil's agricultural exports was highly influential in breaking down Brazil's opposition to IP negotiations.[61]

Although these sanctions were suspended in 1990 after a visit from US President George Bush, the message was clear that the US would not tolerate any form of opposition to its foreign trade policy objectives. Importantly, the use of trade threats against Brazil explains the latter's capitulation at the Uruguay Round after leading the Global South resistance against the inclusion of IP rules in the global trade regime.

It was these externalities that prepared the ground for the full implementation of the TRIPS Agreement when it was finally introduced to the Brazilian Congress the following year.[62] Mapping the politics surrounding the implantation of the TRIPS Agreement has indeed shown how the interests of a transnational ruling elite influence the shaping of global policies and law on one hand, and the obvious dialectic between struggles in Third World countries and the external forces on the other hand.[63]

III. UNPACKING THE INDUSTRIAL PROPERTY LAW OF BRAZIL

The IPLB allows for patents on all pharmaceutical processes and products, consistent with Article 27 of the TRIPS Agreement. Section 1 of Chapter 2

[59] Matthew B Flynn, 'Corporate Power And State Resistance: Brazil's Use Of TRIPS Flexibilities For Its National AIDS Program' in K Shadlen, S Guennif, A Guzmán and N Lalitha (eds), *Intellectual Property, Pharmaceuticals and Public Health: Access to Drugs in Developing Countries* (Cheltenham, Edward Elgar Publishing, 2011) 154; see also Sweet, 'Pharmaceutical Production In Brazil' (2003) 49; see also Monica Steffen Guise Rosina, Daniel Wang and Thana Cristina De Campos, 'Access to Medicines: Pharmaceutical Patents and the Right to Health' in L Shaver (ed), *Access to Knowledge in Brazil: New Research on Intellectual Property, Innovation and Development*, 1st edn (Connecticut, Yale Law School, 2008) 183.

[60] Flynn (n 41) 55.

[61] dos Santos Tarragô, 'Negotiating' (2015) 245.

[62] In April 1991, the recently elected President Fernando Collor de Mello initiated the first attempt to change Brazil's industrial property law by sending Bill 824/1991 to Congress and requesting for its urgent appreciation, but the discussion was suspended due to the political moment, specifically the corruption scandal that led to the impeachment of President Collor.

[63] Chimni, 'A Manifesto' (2006) 7.

provides conditions for patentability and patentable objects in Brazil. Though the IPLB does not provide an explicit list of patentable matters, the INPI Guidelines for the Examination of Patent Filings in the areas of Biotechnology and Pharmaceuticals, as well as the ANVISA Subject Matter Guideline on what is held patentable in Brazil, provide the parameter for patentable objects.[64]

According to the INPI guidelines, the INPI authorises the following: synthetic processes of preparation of chemical compounds,[65] biological or enzymes processes,[66] natural biological processes,[67] new uses and subsequent pharmaceutical uses.[68] This means that the new law allows the patenting of chemical products (as processes were already patentable) and all sorts of food and pharmaceutical inventions. Article 8 stipulates that an object is patentable only when it meets 'the requirements of novelty, inventive activity and industrial application'.[69] INPI authorises applications that involve first use (ie new use of products already known outside the medical field as a medicine) and second use (ie claims involving a subsequent medical use for a product already known as a medicine). Specifically, novelty is determined by comparing the invention to be patented with the existing 'state of the art' that comprises material accessible to the public by means of written or oral description, use, or any other means in Brazil or abroad.[70] Article 10 lists non-patentable objects, which include but are not limited to discoveries, scientific theories, mathematical methods, abstract concepts, surgical methods, all or parts of living beings, and biological material found in nature, to mention a few.[71] These non-patentable items are generally in conformity with European standards and those in other developing countries such as India.

The IPLB includes certain flexibilities intended to mitigate the adverse effect of rights conferred to patent-holders with a view of restoring balance between private rights (IP) and social justice (economic and social rights.) These flexibilities include CLs, Bolar exceptions, experimental use, parallel imports and health sector participation in examining pharmaceutical patent applications. Specifically, Articles 68 to 74 allow for the issuance of a CL if the 'rights resulting are exercised in an abusive manner or if the patent is used in abuse of economic power'.[72] The abuse should be determined in a court or administrative court decision. The provisions further state instances for the grant of a CL, which

[64] Maristela Basso and Edson Beas Rodrigues Jr, *Intellectual Property Law in Brazil* (Alphen aan den Rijn, Kluwer Law International, 2010); see also Denis Barbosa, 'The New Brazilian Patent Law' (1997), available at http://denisbarbosa.addr.com/papers.htm (accessed 8 June 2014).
[65] Basso and Rodrigues (ibid) 60.
[66] ibid.
[67] ibid.
[68] ibid.
[69] IPLB, Art 8.
[70] IPLB, Art 11, para 1; Ragavan (n 29) 130.
[71] IPLB, Art 10, para 2.
[72] IPLB, Art 68, para 1(1).

include failure to exploit the patented product within Brazil (local working requirement),[73] failure to satisfy the needs of the local market,[74] dependent patents[75] and in situations of national emergency or public interest.[76] Compulsory licensing is also possible in case of dependent patents, that is, when a new invention that amounted to a substantial technical progress as compared to a prior one cannot be worked by reason of the prior patent's scope of claims.[77] In cases of national emergency or public interest, the President of Brazil may grant a CL via an Executive Order. Paragraphs 2 and 4 of Article 68 specify conditions for parallel importation, which allows for the importation of patented products by third parties provided it has been introduced in the market directly by the patent holder or with his consent.[78]

The IPLB also allows for the participation of the health sector in the examination of pharmaceutical patents. To interpret this rule, Law 10196/2001 was added as Article 299c to Brazil's IP legislation, which instituted the 'prior consent' (*Anuência Prévia*) mechanism.[79] The inclusion of the prior consent mechanism altered Brazil's IP regime; whereas INPI was previously solely responsible for patent examination and approval, the new law divided this competence between INPI and ANVISA.[80] To carry out this role, ANVISA – located at the Ministry of Health and responsible for the sanitary safety and quality assurance of pharmaceutical drugs – is empowered to grant patents for pharmaceutical products and processes on public health security grounds.[81] Under this arrangement, when an application for a pharmaceutical patent is filed, INPI first analyses whether it meets patentability and formal requirements, as determined by the IPLB. The application is then forwarded to ANVISA for a separate examination that the patent will not negatively affect public health. It is only after this rigorous examination that ANVISA grants its 'prior consent' for the issuance of a patent certificate.[82] Each examination is determined on a case-by-case basis, as ANVISA does not have a codified guideline on when to grant the prior consent.[83] However, ANVISA examiners refer to INPI regulatory guidelines to test whether the patent is new (novelty) and inventive in its applicability even though it is a lot stricter than INPI in its examinations. In this light, ANVISA aims to balance

[73] IPLB, para 1(2).
[74] IPLB, Art 68.
[75] IPLB, Art 70, para 1.
[76] IPLB, Art 71.
[77] Barbosa,'New Brazilian Patent Law' (1997).
[78] IPLB, Art 68, para 3.
[79] Rosina, Wang and De Campos, 'Access to Medicines' (2008) 191.
[80] Edson Beas Rodrigues Jr and Bryan Murphy, 'Brazil's Prior Consent Law: A Dialogue Between Brazil And The United States Over Where The TRIPS Agreement Currently Sets The Balance Between The Protection Of Pharmaceutical Patents And Access To Medicines' (2006) 16 *Albany Law Journal of Science and Technology* 427.
[81] Rosina, Wang and De Campos (n 59) 191; Rodrigues and Murphy (ibid).
[82] ANVISA Resolution 45, Art 1.
[83] Fieldwork interview with Monica Caetano (Rio de Janeiro, 2014) (transcript on file with author).

private rights (patent applications) with the state's social contract of ensuring security, well-being, development, and equality.[84]

In addition, ANVISA considers the decisions of various patent offices in the US, Europe, and developing countries on similar issues. But most importantly, each technical evaluation and final decision is based on how such patent application would affect the public health interest.[85] So while INPI is responsible for examining the legal sufficiency of patent applications, ANVISA is dedicated to protecting and promoting 'public health' in Brazil, similar to the US Food and Drug Agency.[86] Once an application is given the ANVISA consent, it is then sent to INPI for approval. On occasions when ANVISA does not grant its consent, the patent application is not authorised even with input from INPI.[87] This effectively means that ANVISA has veto power in the grant of pharmaceutical patents.[88]

Given the importance of medicine access, this particular role of ANVISA is a measure to protect patients as it prevents the grant of frivolous patent rights (evergreening). It has been suggested that the 'prior consent' prerogative of ANVISA provides the Ministry of Health with an instrument to influence patent examination, making it difficult to get private rights of exclusion over knowledge for pharmaceuticals.[89] In fact, according to Peter Drahos, the Brazilian model of double examination of pharmaceutical patents presents, from a social welfare point of view, one way in which developing countries can improve the quality of examination in a sector of vital national importance.[90] Therefore, by preventing patent abuse through the set-up of a rigorous process of examination, ANVISA becomes the 'gatekeeper' that not only serves to restrain term extension but also halts the grant of patent rights to inventions that are neither new nor inventive but are instead revised versions of known molecules. Importantly, the prior consent law reflects a novel use of its bureaucratic framework to roll back rights to the minimum required under the TRIPS Agreement and serves as a means for the Brazilian Government to take control of the sensitive field of pharmaceuticals.[91]

[84] ibid. See Carlos M Correa, 'Pharmaceutical Innovation, Incremental Patenting And Compulsory Licensing' (South Centre, 2011), available at http://apps.who.int/medicinedocs/documents/s21395en/s21395en.pdf (accessed 20 May 2015).

[85] Fieldwork interview with Caetano (n 83).

[86] Ruth L Okediji, 'Legal Innovation In International Intellectual Property Relations: Revisiting Twenty-One Years Of The TRIPS Agreement' (2014) 36 *University of Pennsylvania Journal of International Law* 241.

[87] ibid. See also Basso and Rodrigues, *Intellectual Property Law* (2010) 79.

[88] Rodrigues and Murphy, 'Brazil's Prior Consent Law' (2006) 427.

[89] Kenneth Shadlen, 'The Politics Of Patents And Drugs In Brazil And Mexico: The Industrial Bases Of Health Policies' (2009) 42 *Comparative Politics* 47; see also Renata Reis, Veriano Terto Jr and Maria Cristina Pimenta, *Intellectual Property Rights And Access To ARV Medicines* (São Paulo, ABIA, 2009) 25; see also Eduardo Da Gama Camara Jr, 'Prosecution Of Pharmaceutical Patents In Brazil: Tensions Between The Brazilian Patent Office And ANVISA – Intellectual Property – Brazil' (2013), available at www.mondaq.com/article.asp?articleid=253068 (accessed 20 May 2015).

[90] Peter Drahos, *The Global Governance Of Knowledge: Patent Offices And Their Clients* (Cambridge, Cambridge University Press 2010) 249.

[91] Da Gama Camara, 'Prosecution Of Pharmaceutical Patents In Brazil' (2013) 244.

There have been some controversies regarding ANVISA's competence to examine and approve patent applications, and this contestation of ANVISA's role is divided between health activists and academics on one hand and pharmaceutical companies on the other. From the point of view of the former, the participation of ANVISA in the examination of pharmaceutical patents is consistent with Article 8 of the TRIPS Agreement, which stipulates that states may formulate or amend laws or adopt regulations necessary to protect public health.[92] In this view, the interests of the public, usually ignored in IP decisions, are represented and protected. Further, it has also been argued that the role of ANVISA promotes the development of new technologies that will allow the national industry to also develop, thus benefiting Brazil's social needs.[93]

Many pharmaceutical patent-holding companies – usually led by foreign pharmaceutical firms – on the other hand, argue that ANVISA's role should be limited to evaluating the quality and safety of medicines. In 2004, for example, INPI rejected Roche's patent application for an ARV *Valcyte* (*valganciclovir hydrochloride*), citing ANVISA's prior consent refusal. Roche subsequently sued INPI on the ground that ANVISA is not competent to examine the requirement of inventive activity, novelty and industrial application due to lack of legal knowledge. In light of this, Roche averred the role of ANVISA is inconsistent with the TRIPS Agreement.[94] The court ruled that the second substantive examination by ANVISA is unconstitutional and violates Brazil's TRIPS Agreement obligation. The court agreed ANVISA was not competent to examine the requirements of inventive activity, novelty and industrial application on pharmaceutical patents due to lack of specific legal foresight on the matter.

Also, in *Aventis Pharma SA v INPI/ANVISA*, the French pharmaceutical company Aventis sued INPI after it rejected the former's patent application for its anti-cancer drug *Taxotere*, due to ANVISA's denial of prior consent.[95] In this case, the court ruled that patent rights are not absolute and should meet a certain set of social requirements in order to be granted. The court decided that access to medicines is a constitutionally recognised right in Brazil and as a result, sustained the prior consent mechanism.[96]

[92] Under Art 8(1) of the TRIPS Agreement, states may formulate or amend laws or adopt regulations necessary to protect public health and to promote the public interest in sectors of vital importance to their socio-economic and technological development. Article 8(2) allows for countries to take appropriate measures, provided that they are consistent with the provisions of the TRIPS Agreement, that may be needed to prevent the abuse of intellectual property rights by right holders or the resort to practices which unreasonably restrain trade or adversely affect the international transfer of technology.

[93] Reis, Terto Jr and Pimenta, *Access To ARV Medicines* (2009); Correa, *Pharmaceutical Innovation* (2011) 6.

[94] *F Hoffmann-La Roche AG v INPI/ANVISA* (2004) Vara Federal do Rio de Janeiro, Ordinary action 2004.5101506840-0 (Vara Federal do Rio de Janeiro); see also Basso and Rodrigues (n 64) 79.

[95] *Aventis Pharma SA v INPI/ANVISA* (2005) 38th Federal Court of Rio de Janeiro, 2004.51.01.513854-1 (38th Federal Court of Rio de Janeiro).

[96] ibid. A study by Carlos Correa found that found that six per cent of pharmaceutical patents were granted by INPI without being analysed by ANVISA. See Correa (n 84) 7.

In 2016, Novartis, the Swiss-based pharmaceutical company, sought a preliminary injunction against ANVISA, arguing that the agency was taking an unreasonable amount of time to issue a prior consent decision. The company also requested preventive measures against ANVISA to prevent it from examining the application for compliance with patentability requirements under Article 229-C of the Brazilian Patent Act. The judge granted a preliminary injunction against ANVISA and ordered the agency to analyse the prior approval of the patent application within 15 days, and to abstain from examining the application for compliance with any patentability requirements but instead focus only on aspects of public health.

To rectify this uncertainty regarding the role and prerogative of ANVISA regarding patent examination, ANVISA and INPI reached an agreement regarding the 'prior consent' provision. In a Joint Ordinance published in April 2017 and implemented the same year, the roles and responsibility of each organisation were explicitly delineated. Specifically, the Joint Ordinance established that 'ANVISA will analyse such requests in the light of public health'.[97] In other words, ANVISA's role is to analyse whether a patent application is a health risk. Here, a patent is considered a health risk when 'the product or the pharmaceutical process contained in it presents a health risk'[98] while the term 'health risk' is characterised as 'when the pharmaceutical product comprises or the pharmaceutical process results in a substance whose use has been prohibited in the country'.[99]

If a patent is considered a health risk, ANVISA can deny prior approval through a decision based on a technical opinion issued by the competent organisational unit within the Agency. ANVISA will then send the application back to INPI for final decision. ANVISA's technical opinion to INPI will be used as a third-party observation under Article 31 of the Patent Statute of 1996, which INPI can decide whether or not to agree with. In other words, ANVISA's opinion and decision is not binding.

In addition to the above, if a product or pharmaceutical process is considered to be of interest for the drug policies or pharmaceutical assistance under the Unified Health System (*Sistema Unico de Saude* or SUS), ANVISA may issue an opinion with a focus on patentability requirements.[100] Furthermore, the Joint Ordinance also allows the applicant a period of up to 60 days to file any document to support its application in the case of a negative decision by ANVISA, while there will be a period of 30 days to appeal the denial decision before ANVISA's Board of Directors. Finally, the Ordinance also established

[97] Article 4 of 'RESOLUÇÃO N° 168, DE 8 DE AGOSTO DE 2017' (2017), available at www.lex.com.br/legis_27485981_RESOLUCAO_N_168_DE_8_DE_AGOSTO_DE_2017.aspx (accessed 31 October 2018).

[98] ibid, para 1.

[99] ibid, para 2.

[100] ibid, Art 7.

the creation of an Interinstitutional Articulation Group comprising of both members of ANVISA and INPI.[101] The Interinstitutional Articulation Group seeks to share technical information and to harmonise understanding of patent issues in order to minimise 'discrepancies in the evaluation of pharmaceutical patent applications, which are of interest to the drug policies and pharmaceutical assistance under the Single System of Health – SUS'.[102]

A close reading of the Joint Ordinance reveals the ways in which the role of ANVISA as public health watchdog has been severely curtailed. In limiting ANVISA's recommendation regarding patent application vis-à-vis drug policies and implications for access to a mere recommendation that is not an essential requirement for approval, ANVISA has been stripped of the responsibility to protecting the Brazilian IP system from frivolous patenting and evergreening. Furthermore, the exclusion of civil society groups as members of the Interinstitutional Articulation Group eliminates the involvement of advocacy groups in meetings when necessary.

The Joint Ordinance has triggered polarised debates in the Brazilian public discourse. On one hand, government officials, private counsels and pharmaceutical companies claim the Joint Ordinance solves the issue of odious interpretation and alleviates the problem of bottleneck in patent applications.[103] In addition, the Joint Ordinance, it is believed, will reduce the pendency timeframe for patent application review, which is currently 95.4 months – one of the highest in the world.[104] However, civil society groups such as *Associação Brasileira Interdisciplinar de AIDS* (ABIA) point out that the Joint Ordinance is the maturation of the concerted action mounted by various forces within Brazil to narrow the discourse and understanding of the right to health. These forces, they argue, wants to limit ANVISA's contribution and powers to reject patents, making the agency merely an advisory body.[105]

IV. THE CONSTITUTIONAL RIGHT TO HEALTH

The new Brazilian Constitution of 1988 established health as a human right for all Brazilian citizens, one of the most important and significant structural reforms in the health sector. Specifically, Article 6 lists various rights, including

[101] Article 1, s 1 of 'PORTARIA CONJUNTA Nº 2, DE 20 DE OUTUBRO DE 2017' (2017), available at www.lex.com.br/legis_27542373_PORTARIA_CONJUNTA_N_2_DE_20_DE_OUTUBRO_DE_2017.aspx (accessed 31 October 2018).

[102] ibid, Art 1, s 2.

[103] Gabriel Di Blasi, 'Reaching A Milestone In Pharmaceutical Patenting In Brazil' (2019), available at www.future-science.com/doi/abs/10.4155/ppa-2018-0025 (accessed 8 February 2019).

[104] World Intellectual Property Organization, 'World Intellectual Property Indicators 2017' (WIPO, 2017) 18.

[105] Pedro Vallardi, 'Open Letter: Pharmaceuticals' Interests Must NOT Be Prioritized Over Public Health' (2017), available at http://deolhonaspatentes.org/wp-content/uploads/2017/06/Carta-aberta-Portaria-Conjunta.pdf (accessed 10 November 2018).

right to health, as social rights,[106] while Article 196 explicitly provides for the scope of the health rights, stating:

> The health is the right of all and the responsibility of the State, to be guaranteed by means of social and economic policies aimed at reducing the risk of illness and other hazards, and at the universal and equal access to actions and services for its promotion, protection and recovery.[107]

The right to health law as articulated in the Constitution has both tangible and intangible characteristics. Intangibly, it provides for individual and trans-collective rights. Individually, the right to health gives a person the right to demand a given provision (in this case, healthcare) from the state. The *Rosa Vieira v Municipality of Porto Alegre* case[108] established that the right to health is an individual entitlement which the state is mandated to satisfy, and not a mere declaration. It is not just a formal recognition from the Brazilian state or a consumer right as provided for in many Latin American Constitutions such as in Argentina. Rather, it is an essential right that should be integrally respected and fully guaranteed. Importantly, the case shows that the right to health is an inalienable consequence of the right to life, and the state should ensure that social and economic policies are implemented to guarantee universal and equal access to health services to its citizens.[109] This right therefore qualifies as a 'judicial prerogative that involves a citizen's power to demand that the State implement positive obligations imposed on it by the constitutional order'.[110]

[106] Brazilian Constitution, Art 6.

[107] Brazilian Constitution, Art 196.

[108] *Rosa Vieira v Municipality of Porto Alegre* (2000) Supreme Federal Tribunal, Rio Grande do Sol, No 271286 (Supreme Federal Tribunal, Rio Grande do Sol), available at www.globalhealthrights.org/health-topics/health-care-and-health-services/dina-rosa-vieira-v-municipality-of-porto-alegre (accessed 28 January 2019). In this case, Dina Rosa Vieira – HIV-positive, poor, destitute, and unable to afford the cost of ARV treatment – brought a case against the Municipality of Porto Alegre for failing to provide medication for the treatment of AIDS. The first instance court ruled in favour of Vieira on the grounds of right to health and life enshrined in the Constitution. The Municipality of Porto Alegre appealed the decision to the Supreme Court. The Supreme Court upheld the decision of the first instance court, specifically noting that 'the subjective right to health represents the undeniable judicial prerogative guaranteed to the general public by the Constitution, which not only translates as a constitutionally mandated right but also requires the Public Authority (or whomever constitutes such position) to provide and guarantee its citizens, including those carrying the HIV virus, universal and equal access to pharmaceutical assistance and medical-hospital access'.

[109] For broader discussion on right to health in Brazil, see also Teixeira, Vitória and Barcarolo, 'Antiretroviral Therapy' (2003) 69–88; Richard G Parker, 'Civil Society, Political Mobilization, And The Impact Of HIV Scale-Up On Health Systems In Brazil' (2009) 52 *Journal of Acquired Immune Deficiency Syndromes* S49; Octavio Luiz Motta Ferraz, 'The Right To Health In The Courts Of Brazil: Worsening Health Inequities?' (2013), available at www.hhrjournal.org/2013/08/29/the-right-to-health-in-the-courts-of-brazil-worsening-health-inequities (accessed 28 May 2015); / the-right-to-health-in-the-courts-of-brazil-worsening-health-inequities (accessed 28 May 2015); Alan Berkman, Jonathan Garcia, Miguel Munoz-Laboy, Vera SF Paiva and Richard Guy Parker, 'A Critical Analysis Of The Brazilian Response To HIV/AIDS: Lessons Learned For Controlling And Mitigating The Epidemic In Developing Countries' (2005) 95 *American Journal of Public Health* 1162; Kurt Weyland, *Democracy Without Equity* (Pittsburgh, University of Pittsburgh Press, 1996).

[110] *Rosa Vieira* (n 108).

Trans-individual right, on the other hand, can be either collective or diffusive in nature. It is a collective right, in the sense that members of a particular group with an established legal relationship can obtain protection on behalf of the entire group, such as when a group of HIV-positive soldiers obtain a legal ruling that prevents discrimination based on their HIV status. This collective right thus covers not only defendants in this particular case, but all individuals who may be HIV-positive in the future. In this way, there can be 'no satisfaction or loss in the group's representation except such as affects all members'.[111] On the other hand, the right to health is diffusive in nature when a group with undetermined membership but whose membership is derived from de facto circumstances shares benefits from said right.[112] For example, it can be argued that the *Rosa Vieira* case is diffusive in nature in the sense that other destitute HIV-positive individuals also benefit from free HIV treatment. This ruling therefore provides not just a singular protection but also a collective jurisdictional protection for other persons in similar circumstances.

Analysis of right to health cases by Rosina et al found that even though consequences of court decisions apply to all, most judges consider the right to health on a case-by-case basis and not collectively, and interpret the right to health and the principles of the SUS as the individual's right to any health-related expense.[113] This has led to tensions between universal access to healthcare and limited state resources. Octavio Ferraz contends that the right to health litigation is worsening Brazil's already pronounced health inequities and is thus detrimental to health equity. This is because 'the criterion for privileging litigants over the rest of the population is not based on any conception of need or justice but purely on their ability to access the judiciary, something that only a minority of citizens possess'.[114] Many health activists disagree with this view. Marcela Viera, for instance, argues that ensuring right to health is justice in itself because allowing people to die when there is a cure for an illness is unjust.[115] In a similar vein, Renata Reis points out that the idea behind the right to health is the bridging of income disparities in Brazilian society by extending preventive measures as well as basic services to the poor.[116] However, a recent study of court decisions has shown signs that judges are rethinking this approach, as the financial impact of high drug costs has become increasingly unsustainable. According to Rosina et al, there is a shift in judicial thinking, as the 'court started to deny some petitions for access, in light of public budgetary considerations'.[117]

[111] Roger Raupp Rios, 'Legal Responses To The HIV/AIDS Epidemic In Brazil' (2003), available at www.columbia.edu/itc/hs/pubhealth/p8725/all_week_8_articles.pdf (accessed 18 October 2018).

[112] ibid.

[113] Rosina, Wang and De Campos (n 59) 172.

[114] Ferraz, 'The Right to Health in the Courts of Brazil' (2013); see also Octavio Luiz Motta Ferraz, 'Between Usurpation And Abdication? The Right to Health in the Courts of Brazil and South Africa' (2009) 11 *Health and Human Rights Journal* 33.

[115] Fieldwork interview (Rio de Janeiro, 4 June 2014) (transcript on file with author).

[116] Fieldwork interview (Rio de Janeiro, 13 June 2014) (transcript on file with author).

[117] Rosina, Wang and De Campos (n 59) 191.

Tangibly, the right to health requires the state to provide free healthcare – medicines, medical technology and medical treatments – for all who need it. In response to this, Congress passed the Health Act of 1990, which created the SUS to offer free comprehensive, universal and preventive healthcare to the entire population, irrespective of employment, status or access to other forms of health insurance.[118] It is regulated by Laws 8080/90 and 8142/90.

The creation of the SUS is based on the three important principles of integrality, universality and equality.[119] *Universality* means that no citizen can be excluded from SUS coverage and each citizen is entitled to the satisfaction of one's health needs with the most advanced treatment available, irrespective of costs.[120] This principle of universality enables *equality* of access by ensuring that there is no discrimination in the provision of public health services and products to Brazilian citizens, while *integrality* provides for full healthcare coverage, from the most basic to the most complex needs. These three principles define the Brazilian state's promotion of health as a fundamental social right,[121] such that at least 80 per cent of the population depend solely on the public healthcare system.[122] It provides healthcare free of charge with universal access, based on the principle of equity and community participation, to 200 million inhabitants. There is no other country that provides free health care to that many users, and even in those countries where there is a universal health system, the population is smaller. In line with constitutional obligations, Ordinance 3.916/98 created the National Policy on Medicines and directed the Ministry of Health to issue a list of essential medicines – the *Relação Nacional de Medicamentos Essenciais* (RENAME). Importantly, the ordinance was aimed at guaranteeing access to affordable, safe and quality medicines.

The impact of the codification of the right to health is especially prominent in the Government's response to the HIV/AIDS epidemic. The first case of AIDS in Brazil was reported in 1982 and over time, São Paulo became the epicentre of the epidemic due to the concentration of key gay movements. As a result, São Paulo emerged as the key constituent that capably handled the AIDS epidemic, having set up the official response programme as early as 1984.[123] The initiative of

[118] Jane Galvão, 'Access To Antiretroviral Drugs In Brazil' (2002) 360 *The Lancet* 1862, 1863. See also Galvão, 'Brazil and Access to HIV/AIDS Drugs' (2005) 1112.

[119] Ferraz, 'Between Usurpation and Abdication' (2009) 34.

[120] ibid.

[121] A Nunn, E Da Fonseca and S Gruskin, 'Changing Global Essential Medicines Norms To Improve Access To AIDS Treatment: Lessons From Brazil' (2009) 4 *Global Public Health* 133.

[122] Jose Serra, 'The Political Economy Of The Brazilian Struggle Against AIDS' (2004), available at www.sss.ias.edu/files/papers/paper17.pdf (accessed 21 May 2015).

[123] See also Richard Parker, 'Building The Foundations For The Response To HIV/AIDS In Brazil: The Development Of HIV/AIDS Policy, 1982–1996' (2003) 147, available at www.columbia.edu/itc/hs/pubhealth/p8725/all_week_8_articles. For a fascinating and rich literature on AIDS activism from a variety of different angles, some of which come from the sociology of science/STS literature and illuminate interesting points about expertise, lay intervention, and the multiple roles of pharmaceutical companies and regulators, see Steven Epstein, *Impure Science: AIDS, Activism, And The Politics of Knowledge* (Oakland, University of California Press, 1996).

São Paulo in starting non-discriminatory universal access programmes not only convinced the Brazilian Government that AIDS can be treated and contained, but gave impetus to the demand of health activists for the national implementation of a similar programme. As a result, other state governments and even the federal Government borrowed heavily from the response to the epidemic developed in São Paulo. In fact, the first nationwide programme was established in 1986 in the form of the Brazilian National STD and AIDS Programme (*Programa Nacional de Doenças Sexualmente Transmissíveis e AIDS* or NAP) two years before the constitutionalisation of the right to health in 1988.

The NAP initially focused on epidemiological surveillance, medical assistance, release of non-discriminating and prevention messages to patients and to the general public, as well as limited dispensation of drugs to treat opportunistic infections.[124] It created awareness of the new infection whilst monitoring its spread among the population, but not treatment of the disease itself. This particular response by the Government – of monitoring and creating awareness instead of treatment and prevention – meant that the disease exploded especially in the urban areas and among vulnerable groups such as sex workers and injecting drug users. The proliferation of HIV/AIDS from a few cases in 1983 to a full-blown epidemic in 1993 triggered protests from civil society organisations (CSOs) made up of HIV/AIDS patients groups, academics, human right groups, health professionals, lesbian, gay, bisexual and transgender (LGBT) groups and religious organisations. Anchoring their agitation on anti-discrimination practices and the constitutional right to life and health, these protests pressured the Government to adopt progressive AIDS policies and provide free ARV to all those in need. AIDS activists groups such as *Grupo de Apoio à Prevenção à AIDS* (or GAPA) voiced their frustration by petitioning the judiciary, mobilising street campaigns and using mass media.[125] According to one of the activists involved in the early medicines access campaign in Brazil, these social movements played a critical role in producing knowledge and expertise by conceptualising AIDS-related policies such as treatment programmes, providing templates on how the state should manage AIDS treatments, using rights-based discourse to establish novel conceptions of citizenship and social solidarity, and pursuing legal action against insurance companies which refused to fund *azidothymidine* (AZT) treatment.[126] It was the ability of these diverse social groups – with very real differences in class and economic status – to develop a countervailing response to the stigma surrounding homosexuality and HIV that made the movement powerful and forced the Government to take notice.

Interpreting civil society activism for access to HIV medicines, including the production of knowledge regarding care and treatment, through a Twailian

[124] Galvão, 'Access to Antiretroviral Drugs in Brazil' (2002) 1862; Guido Carlos Levi and Marco Antonio A Vitória, 'Fighting Against AIDS: The Brazilian Experience' (2002) 16 *AIDS* 2372.

[125] Galvão (n 1) 1112.

[126] Fieldwork interview with Veriano Terto Jr (Rio de Janeiro, 2014) (transcript on file with author).

lens underscores how international legal transformation happens. In traditional international legal analysis, legal change is either 'internal', ie driven by the structure of norms, the function of institutions, and the interests of states, or 'external', ie compelled by changes in community values, interests or power.[127] In both instances, the West is not only predisposed as the maker of legal transformation while the Global South is erased as a site of legal knowledge production, it also elevates the elites as the producers of such knowledge, ignoring the importance of the role played by ordinary people.[128] However, we can discern from the early activism of HIV/AIDS patients groups, LGBT groups, etc how the complex interaction of these actors with the state framed and shaped legal norms vis-à-vis public health and health governance. Specifically, by hinging their activism on medicines access as a way of achieving countervailing treatment to the HIV epidemic while also fulfilling the right to health, which was then picked up by the state and international non-state actors such as the United Nations, these actors inadvertently challenged the 'traditional narratives of how international legal change has come about and how one might understand the place of law in progressive social praxis'.[129]

Importantly, it highlights patterns of Third World resistance to international law, which can no longer be analysed within statist terms alone. By this I mean that by showing the material interpretation of 'right to health and right to life' – tenets of the International Declaration of Human Rights – to also mean the dispensation of ARV medications by the state, the actors influenced not only the praxis (as shall be seen shortly) but also the politics of the Brazilian state regarding its responsibility to it its citizens. This praxis also undergirds the Brazilian state's activism in international fora as the country pursues a human rights-based approach to trade, development and IP rules.

The result of the above came in 1996 when the Government enacted Law 9313/96 – also known as the Sarney Law, named after the Congressman Jose Sarney who introduced the bill. Law 9313/96 guarantees free access to ARVs for treatment for all people in Brazil living with HIV/AIDS.[130] Specifically, Article 1 thereof stipulates that HIV-infected people and/or people living with AIDS are entitled to receive, at no cost, all medicines necessary for their treatment, from the SUS.[131]

The law therefore formalised and centralised ARV drug policy at the Ministry of Health. It also placed no restriction on the expenditure of the treatment

[127] Balakrishnan Rajagopal, 'International Law And Social Movement' (2003) 41 *Columbia Journal of Transnational Law* 397.

[128] Sujith Xavier, 'Learning From Below: Theorising Global Governance Through Ethnographies And Critical Reflections From The Global South' (2017) 33 *Windsor Yearbook of Access to Justice* 236.

[129] Balakrishnan Rajagopal, *International Law From Below* (Cambridge, Cambridge University Press, 2010) 1.

[130] Nunn, Da Fonseca and Gruskin, 'Lessons From Brazil' (2009) 134.

[131] Nunn, *AIDS Treatment In Brazil* (2008) 89.

to be borne by the Government.[132] The NAP is self-funded by the Brazilian Government as it gets its funds from the national, state and municipal budgets. According to Amy Nunn, by deliberately excluding means-test and regulatory clauses and including the words 'free of charge', the Congress via the Sarney Law signed a blank cheque for AIDS treatment.[133] The law also helped structure the purchase of ARV medicines for the NAP by decentralising the procurement and distribution of HIV and other essential medicines. This legislation has been suggested to be the most important health reform implemented for the NAP as it helped scale up generic production of pharmaceutical products in Brazil.[134]

The provision of free ARV turned the tide in favour of Brazil in the fight against HIV/AIDS.[135] For example, the free distribution of ARV led to a 50 per cent decline in AIDS mortality from 1996 to 2002.[136] There were also substantial reductions of around 80 per cent in hospitalisation and treatment associated with opportunistic infections within that timeframe.[137] This, according to estimates, resulted in cost savings close at that time to USD 1 billion for the Brazilian Government.[138] Other scholars note that the free distribution of ARV changed public perception of the disease as those who had not yet been diagnosed decided to get tested on the basis of information about the effectiveness of the drugs and their availability free of charge.[139] Thus, it can be argued that this particular policy of universal access led to the stabilisation of the number of new cases, and the enhancement in the quality of life of people living with AIDS.[140]

The approval of Law 9313/96 occurred at an interesting junction in Brazilian politics. Parallel to the enactment of the Sarney Law, the Congress approved Law 9.279/96, changing the industrial property law and allowing for patents on pharmaceutical processes and products. Thus, the Government approved a bill that mandated the national health system's provision of free ARV to HIV/AIDS patients on one hand, and implemented a new TRIPS-compliant industrial property law on the other. The introduction of the new industrial property law raised prices of the same drugs the Government was now obliged to purchase for

[132] Lei 9.313: Dispõe Sobre a Distribuição Gratuita de Medicamentos aos Portadores do Hiv e Doentes de AIDS 1996.

[133] Amy Nunn, Samuel Dickman, Nicoli Nattrass, Alexandra Cornwall and Sofia Gruskin, 'The Impacts Of AIDS Movements On The Policy Responses To HIV/AIDS In Brazil And South Africa: A Comparative Analysis' (2012) 7 *Global Public Health* 89.

[134] Fieldwork interview with Gabriela Chaves (Rio de Janeiro, 2014) (transcript on file with author).

[135] Galvão (n 118) 1863; Galvão (n 1) 1112; Nunn (n 54) 134.

[136] Serra, 'Political Economy' (2004).

[137] Nuria Homedes and Antonio Ugalde, 'Improving Access To Pharmaceuticals In Brazil And Argentina' (2006) 21 *Health Policy and Planning* 125.

[138] Serra (n 122); Galvão (n 118) 1862.

[139] Galvão (n 118) 1863.

[140] Carlos Andre F Passarelli and Veriano Terto Jr, 'Non-Governmental Organizations And Access To Anti-Retroviral Treatments in Brazil' (2003) 252, available at www.columbia.edu/itc/hs/pubhealth/p8725/all_week_8_articles.pdf (accessed 25 May 2015).

thousands of patients. Until 1996, these medicines were in the Brazilian public domain and could be reproduced by indigenous pharmaceutical companies without licences. The cumulative impact of these two laws profoundly changed the AIDS treatment programme. In addition, it brought the issue of availability of drugs to the HIV and medicine access discourse in Brazil.[141]

Many informants interviewed for this study contend that the ratification of two different and conflicting laws is emblematic of trying to implement international law in local spaces, thereby leading to insurmountable social fractions.[142] Importantly, this incident exemplifies and underscores the ethical and material concerns of TWAIL: how international law affect our immediate realities and the manner in which it shapes the most intimate aspects of everyday life of people in the Third World. It also demonstrates how a particular set of normative visions of the world – in this case, a globally harmonised patent rules – 'encapsulated in international law has translated into the effective transformation of realities on the ground.'[143] Within the context of this study, the combined effect of implementing a law that allows for free medicines for all and another law allowing for the legal protection of previously unprotected pharmaceutical products and inventions was an increase of government expenditure in the AIDS programme. For example, federal spending on AIDS increased from USD 330 million to USD 600 million from 1997 to 2002.[144] This increase in cost threatened the sustainability of the government's HIV/AIDS programme. The rise in cost, as suggested by some scholars, is due to three factors. First, the number of people on ARV treatment increased due to new infections. Second, because ARVs do not cure the HIV virus and due to the improved efficacy of ARVs, many HIV patients are living longer which means the treatment will be administered indefinitely. Third, patients need to change treatment to newer lines of ARV as immunities develop. These newer costs are expensive and under patent, meaning the patent owner has the sole right to sell and dictate the price of the drugs. These combined factors meant that the government was spending more on ARV provision and for longer periods – a threat to the sustainability and universality of the health programme. This would not be so had the Brazilian government not implemented patent protection for all products and processes as stipulated by TRIPS Agreement earlier than it should have.

In response to the rising costs and to mitigate the effect on the AIDS programme, the Brazilian Government passed Law 9787/99, known as the Law of Generic Medicines, in 1999. This law defines generic medicine as a product similar to the reference or innovator drug and is expected to be interchangeable

[141] Nunn (n 54) 93.

[142] Fieldwork interview with Paranagua (2014); fieldwork interview with Parker (Rio de Janeiro, 2014); fieldwork interview with Renata Reis (Rio de Janeiro, 2014); fieldwork interview with Chaves (2014).

[143] Luis Eslava, *Local Space, Global Life* (Cambridge, Cambridge University Press, 2015) 57.

[144] Serra (n 122).

with the latter.[145] With this definition, the law classified the Brazilian pharmaceutical markets into 'reference medicines' (brand or innovator medicines), 'generics' and 'similar medicines.'[146] It also dealt with various facets of licensing and inspection of pharmaceutical products and services as well as technical standards and norms for reference, innovative, generic and similar drugs.[147] Significantly, the law required that under the government system, all purchasing contracts are to be generic while all prescriptions are to be written using the generic name, essentially introducing generics into the Brazilian market.[148] This means that whereas private medical practices can prescribe any suitable drug, regardless of whether it is patented or generic, this law mandates all government prescriptions to exclusively refer to generic versions of drugs.

The Law of Generic Medicines also made the use of CLs more flexible and simpler, while regulatory reforms were introduced to accelerate the market entry of generics after the expiration of its on-patent version. In so doing, this law fundamentally helped promote competition between medicines and reduced the cost of medicines for chronic diseases such as HIV. For instance, ARV treatment expenditure for consumers was reduced from a yearly cost of USD 4,860 per person in 1997 to USD 1,000 per person in 2001.[149] This is because generics are 40 to 45 per cent cheaper than their on-patent counterpart.[150] Thanks to these price reductions, the Government managed to save approximately USD 1.2 billion on AIDS treatment costs.[151]

In addition, the law helped spur growth in the local pharmaceutical sector. A study by Cohen and Lybecker demonstrates that this law benefitted local producers and increased the market for generics by 40 per cent.[152] Other scholars such as Homedes and Ugalde point out that this law facilitated healthy competition among local manufacturers, spurring innovation and consolidation of the local pharmaceutical industry.[153] Former Brazilian Minister of Health Jose Serra contends that the incentive created by the Law of Generic Medicines helped build Brazil's capacity to internally produce eight of the 13 components of first line anti-AIDS drugs, thereby boosting local manufacturing capacity.[154] Brazil

[145] Bermudez et al (n 16) 136.

[146] Gabriela Chavez and Renata Reis, 'Health, Intellectual Property And Innovation: A Case Study Of Brazil' in C Correa (ed), *Pharmaceutical Innovation, Incremental Patenting and Compulsory Licensing* (Geneva, South Centre 2013) 73.

[147] Bermudez et al (n 16) 136.

[148] Flynn (n 41) 58; Chavez and Reis, 'Health, Intellectual Property And Innovation' (2011) 74; Bermudez et al (n 16) 136.

[149] Homedes and Ugalde, 'Improving Access To Pharmaceuticals' (2006) 125.

[150] Gabriela Chaves, Marcela Vieira and Renata Reis, 'Access To Medicines And Intellectual Property In Brazil: Reflections And Strategies Of Civil Society' (2008), available at www.scielo.br/pdf/sur/v5n8/en_v5n8a09.pdf (accessed 21 May 2015).

[151] Serra (n 122).

[152] Jillian Clare Cohen and Kristina M Lybecker, 'AIDS Policy And Pharmaceutical Patents: Brazil's Strategy To Safeguard Public Health' (2005) 28 *The World Economy* 220.

[153] Homedes and Ugalde (n 137) 125.

[154] Cohen and Lybecker, 'AIDS Policy And Pharmaceutical Patents' (2005).

currently has the largest pharmaceutical sector and market in Latin America and has one of the top 10 globally. At the time of this research, the sector locally produced 80 per cent of medicine units marketed in the country, totalling 74.6 per cent of market value sales.[155] Of course, foreign firms based in Brazil lobbied heavily against this law, as they feared for loss of market access. The Brazilian transnational pharmaceutical companies association (ABIFERMA) launched campaigns aimed at educating consumers and physicians questioning the quality and safety of generic medicines.[156]

However, in spite of efforts by the Government to mitigate the growing cost of ARV because of the NAP and its constitutional obligations, the federal expenditure on health still remained high. Though the Brazilian state's ability to locally produce majority of its pharmaceutical needs contributed significantly to the improvement of access to highly active antiretroviral therapy (HAART) treatments, it was still not enough to stem the rising costs of new-line HAART treatments that are more efficient but expensive and patent-protected. This inevitably called for expedient political and legal action. In response, the federal government threatened to issue CLs to coax foreign pharmaceutical companies that have patents in Brazil to reduce the cost of ARVs sold. In 2001, the Brazilian Government started price negotiations with foreign companies to reduce the local cost of certain ARVs. In most cases, these negotiations were successful due to the threat of CLs. For instance, according to Cohen and Lybecker, Roche reduced the price of nelfinavir in Brazil by 40 per cent after the Ministry of Health threatened to issue a CL.[157] Merck – another foreign pharmaceutical company – offered a 60 per cent discount on its ARV drug Efavirenz, which was still under patent in Brazil despite being in the public domain due to the pipeline mechanism.[158] Abbott was also able to offer considerable discounts after the Brazilian Government threatened to break its patent.

However, it has been argued that the threat of CLs without their actual use has grown futile. Chaves et al assert that the threat of CLs has become ineffective as the prices agreed in later rounds of negotiations in 2004 and 2005 were unsatisfactory. They posit a need for the Brazilian state to invoke compulsory licensing as it is within its sovereign right and its TRIPS Agreement obligation to do so. For instance, the Government was only able to secure a one per cent cut for the ARV drug lopinavir/ritonavir.[159] The discounts secured for other new-line ARV drugs tenofovir and atazanavir were 5.2 per cent and 7.7 per cent respectively.[160] Yet, even with the reductions, the price of the NAP remained high, threatening its sustainability. In fact, a study by Chaves and Reis showed that the generic versions of the ARV supplied by Indian manufacturers such as Cipla, Ranbaxy and Aurobindo

[155] See Bermudez et al (n 16) 138.
[156] ibid 136.
[157] Cohen and Lybecker (n 152).
[158] Galvão (n 118) 1864; Reis, Terto Jr and Pimenta (n 89) 26.
[159] Chaves, Vieira and Reis, 'Access To Medicines And Intellectual Property' (2008) 170.
[160] ibid.

were much cheaper, with an annual cost of USD 164 per patient compared to Merck's version that costs USD 580 per patient per year.[161] Moreover, even though the Government was able to secure a 60 per cent discount for the price of Merck's *Efavirenz*, Merck was still selling the drugs at cheaper prices in countries at the same development level as Brazil and with still fewer HIV patients.[162]

In May 2007, Brazil granted a CL for Efavirenz, which is patented by Merck under the pipeline mechanism.[163] It is important to note at this point that the Brazilian Government attempted for the second time to negotiate with Merck for its ARV *Efavirenz*. Specifically, Carlos Correa notes that prior to the issuance of the CL, Merck offered USD 1.59 to USD 1.10 per dose, which the Brazilian Government deemed unsatisfactory.[164] Merck, however, did not provide a counter-offer to the Brazilian Government, ignoring the size of the Brazilian market as it was predominantly used by 77,000 patients (or 45 per cent) under the HIV programme as one of the medications for first-line treatment.[165] This explains why the Government issued the CL. In fact, the study by Staffen et al showed that the Government reported a reduction of 72.2 per cent in the cost of supplying this drug.[166] Reis, Terto and Pimenta, on the other hand, found that for 2007 alone, the acquisition of a cheaper version of *Efavirenz* from India saved the Brazilian Government USD 30 million.[167] Nevertheless, one cannot discount the impact of the threat and use of CLs to the sustainability of the government policy of free HIV/AIDS treatment. This is especially so in the context that these drugs are sold at exorbitant prices in other parts of the developing world. Indeed, the Brazilian approach, which consists of local production of majority of its pharmaceutical needs as well as its ability to utilise the flexibilities embedded in its IPLB, increased its bargaining position with foreign multinational pharmaceutical companies. This has contributed significantly in improving domestic access to essential life-saving ARV treatments and has so far ensured that the Government's ARV programme remains sustainable.

V. RESISTANCE FROM BELOW: SOCIAL MOVEMENT AND PATENT LAW

The Brazilian response to the HIV/AIDS epidemic challenges the perception that it is economically impossible to intervene and reverse the tragic HIV trends in

[161] Price estimate is for 2005–06. Reis, Terto Jr and Pimenta (n 89) 27.

[162] Carlos Correa, 'The Use Of Compulsory Licenses In Latin America' in R Hilty and L Kung-Chung (eds), *Compulsory Licensing: Practical Experiences And Ways Forward*, 1st edn (Heidelberg, Springer, 2015) 52.

[163] Chaves, Vieira and Reis (n 150) 170.

[164] Correa, 'The Use of Compulsory Licenses in Latin America' (2015).

[165] ibid; Reis, Terto Jr and Pimenta (n 89).

[166] Rosina, Wang and De Campos (n 59) 191. Based on UNAIDS Programme estimates, 38% of the 200,000 patients benefited from the CL on Efavirenz in 2007. See 'Thematic Segment: HIV And Enabling Legal Environments' (2011), available at www.unaids.org/sites/default/files/en/media/unaids/contentassets/documents/pcb/2011/thematic%20segment_final_correction2Dec.pdf.

[167] Reis, Terto Jr and Pimenta (n 89).

low-income countries.[168] It also attracts attention to the way social movements shape and are shaped by the environment in which institutions and their politics develop.[169] Thus, any analysis of the 'Brazilian Model' should be discussed in light of the roles played by these various actors, particularly the activism of CSOs, and within the context of the 'social mobilisation of Brazilians confronting the military dictatorship and demanding democracy and a return to civilian rule'.[170]

CSOs first rose to prominence in Brazil in the early 1980s – a period characterised by slow transition from 20 years of authoritarian military rule to a gradual return to democratic rule. This transition to democracy spurred the re-emergence of political parties and trade unions as well as the formation of NGOs, which eventually gave rise to strong waves of social activism that changed the course of events in Brazil. These new non-state actors challenged the old military ways such as corruption, cronyism and dilapidated public systems. They called for better infrastructure,[171] a new constitution, election and free congress, among other things.[172] For instance, the Sanitary Reform Movement (*Sanitarista*) formed in the 1980s and comprising healthcare professionals, academics and student groups, was one of the groups that demanded a health system reform, controlled by the public.[173] The group also argued for and defended the right to health as a fundamental human right to be guaranteed by the Constitution.[174] The concomitant effect of this demand was the inclusion of right to health in the Brazilian Constitution and the creation of the SUS, which spurred the development of the Brazilian public health system.[175]

At the local level, the *Sanitarista* led the first response to the initial AIDS cases reported in the city in 1983 partly due to its active involvement at the São Paulo State Health Department.[176] This organisation together with GAPA, the first HIV prevention action group in Sao Paulo, helped develop a strong human rights-oriented perspective in the municipal Government's conception of its health-related responsibilities They also helped develop São Paulo's first AIDS programme that included the free distribution of ART – *Zidovudine* (AZT) – to patients in the state. This jump-started public policy dialogue on the epidemic

[168] João Guilherme Biehl, 'The Activist State: Global Pharmaceuticals, AIDS, And Citizenship In Brazil' (2004) 22 *Social Text* 106.

[169] Balakrishnan Rajagopal, *International Law From Below* (Cambridge, Cambridge University Press 2010) 10.

[170] Berkman et al, 'Brazilian Response To HIV/AIDS' (2005).

[171] Joanildo A Burity, 'Reform of The State And The New Discourse On Social Policy In Brazil' (2006) 33 *Latin American Perspectives* 67.

[172] Berkman et al (n 109) 1166.

[173] ibid 1163; see also Sonia Fleury, 'Brazilian Sanitary Reform: Dilemmas Between The Instituting And The Institutionalized' (2009) 14 *Cien Saude Colet* 744.

[174] Berkman et al (n 109) 1164; Nunn et al (n 133).

[175] Sabine Kleinert and Richard Horton, 'Brazil: Towards Sustainability And Equity In Health' (2011) 377 *The Lancet* 1721.

[176] ibid.

and prompted the federal Government to expand the programme nationally in the form of the NAP. In fact, according to some commentators, the renaissance of the civil society movement in the democratisation process spurred the formation of numerous health-related NGOs throughout the country focusing on the issues of AIDS, access and anti-discrimination on all fronts.[177]

Indeed, this vibrant rebirth of civil society groups – especially in the late 1980s to early 1990s when the reported cases of HIV/AIDS were at an all-time high – saw a rapid growth in the formation of CSOs to include LGBT groups, human rights organisations, policy activists, medical professionals and academics. Encouraged by the prior successful activities of the *Sanitarista*, the newly formed civil society groups made right to health a central demand by co-opting 'galvanized actions aimed at securing civil and human rights mandated by the new progressive constitution of 1988'.[178] They pressured the national Government to create a national AIDS programme and demanded that the Government and fellow citizens respect the rights of people living with HIV/AIDS (PLWHA). Within this context, these civil movements framed the public discourse regarding health services, access to medical care, medicines and medical innovation from a re-democratisation agitation to a legal process backed by the Constitution.

It is important to note that this period was also characterised by protest against the Structural Adjustment Program (SAP) of the IMF and the World Bank, which prioritised currency devaluation and reduced governmental expenditure on social services, such as a reduction in public health financing and privatisation of health services. Thus, though relatively independent of each other, these two issues – the effect of SAP on public services, including health care and the emergence of HIV/AIDS with fatal consequences – came together to produce a new discourse in the field of social policy. This new field of social policy, according to Joanildo Burity, was fleshed out against the backdrop of programmes of state reforms that 'ranged from redefining the State's role in the economy to reconsidering how it should function in relation to society in the field of public policy and advocating the adoption of new management models'.[179] This new social policy, therefore, reconsiders the role and duties of the state from other functions that, though still public in nature, do not explicitly require the direct engagement of the state such as the formulation of social programmes. It was within the formulation of social programmes that the civil society groups established a collective agenda to tackle the problem produced by the AIDS epidemic. To do this, these civil society movements focused on issues of health rights and access to medicine, which blossomed to take on new life within the Brazilian public sphere.

[177] Berkman et al (n 109) 1165.
[178] Biehl, 'The Activist State' (2004) 108.
[179] Burity, 'Reform of The State' (2006) 74.

In recent times, civil society groups have continued to be active in the Brazilian political, legal and social space. To effect the required change and response, these groups adopted several tactics such as policy advocacy, HIV/AIDS de-stigmatisation campaigns and legal suits against government policies that negate the healthcare responsibilities of the Government. Couching their activism on the right to health and right to life as provided for under the Brazilian Constitution, these civil society groups brought class action suits against the state and municipal Governments. In these struggles, the judiciary became an insurgent actor ruling against the state (both federal and municipal) and proved to be a supportive important ally by ruling favourably for citizens and social activists. The courts argued that in most instances, the Brazilian Constitution creates a legal obligation on the part of the Government to take steps to actualise the rights therein. For instance, activist groups filed lawsuits seeking to defend the rights of PLWHA from discrimination in housing, education, the workplace and elsewhere. These lawsuits – in addition to improving the lot of the PLWHA – also helped in strengthening a less discriminatory understanding of the legal person concept[180] and a better definition of collective right. Therefore, these lawsuits aimed at simultaneously improving tangible rights (such as healthcare) and intangible rights (such as social inclusion and representation). Other commentators similarly argue that the lawsuits against all forms of unjustifiable and unconstitutional attitudes against HIV-positive individuals were decisive in fomenting 'the social inclusion of PLWHA, the introduction of the language of human rights in [Brazilian] daily practices, and to stimulate the fight for social efficacy of legal standards for all'.[181] As a result, these lawsuits not only influenced how the AIDS epidemic was understood and addressed but also influenced AIDS-related policies and the broader conceptualisation of public health.

In the same vein, civil society groups played a key role in knowledge and expertise production regarding the adverse effect of patents on medicine access. In this role, the activism of the GTPI/REBRIP was most prominent. Created in 2001, REBRIP is a network of NGOs, patient groups, unions and professional groups engaged in 'the process of regional integration and trade, and committed to the construction of a democratic society grounded in economic, social, cultural, ethical and sustainable development'.[182] GTPI specifically deals with IP-related issues and its repercussions on Brazilian society. Since 2001, GTPI has been involved in various legal cases against the granting of patents.

[180] ibid 236. According to Roger Raupp Rios, the definition of 'legal person' was a previously exclusionary category limited to mean only the heterosexual, middle class, or male person.

[181] Miriam Ventura, 'Strategies To Promote And Guarantee The Rights Of People Living With HIV/AIDS' (2003), available at www.columbia.edu/ itc/hs/pubhealth/p8725/all_week_8_articles.pdf (accessed 21 May 2015).

[182] Reis, Terto Jr and Pimenta (n 89) 31. GTPI also work closely with other international NGOs such as Doctors Without Borders and Oxfam. It actively mobilises other NGOs within and outside Brazil and champions South–South collaborations among HIV organisations in the Global South.

In 2005, the Brazilian Government declared ARV drugs lopinavir and ritonavir (marketed under the brand name Kaletra) as public interest, which would have enabled the Government to issue a CL, allowed for the local manufacture of the drug at a lower price, and enabled the transfer of technology to local firms. Instead, the Government signed a contract with the pharmaceutical company Abbott – the makers of Kaletra. Though the contract lowered the price of the drug, it contained clauses that were in conflict with public interest. Specifically, the Government guaranteed to Abbott that it will not issue a CL for Kaletra, agreed that Abbott will not have any responsibility for technology transfer or FDI to manufacture the drug locally, and accepted a fixed price of USD 1,380 per patient per year until 2011 when the patent expired, regardless of the increase in demand or variations in international prices.[183] In reaction, GTPI filed a public civil action suit against the Brazilian Government and Abbott – the first of its kind – demanding that a CL be issued.[184] The suit received negative preliminary hearing on the grounds that not only would a CL possibly trigger trade retaliation, which would lead to drug stock-outs, but also that Brazilian pharmaceutical companies do not have the technological capacity to locally produce the drug.[185] The GTPI appealed the preliminary decision and the appeal is still pending.

In another notable instance, ABIA[186] and GTPI filed a pre-grant opposition in 2006 in an attempt to stop the Brazilian patent office, INPI, from granting patents for essential medicines. The pre-grant opposition was filed against Gilead's ARV medication Viread (*tenofovir disoproxil fumarate*). ABIA and GTPI presented technical grounds against the grant of the patent by calling into question the 'inventiveness' of the drug and argued that the synthesis of the key substance tenofovir as described in the patent application has been available to the public before the filing date and therefore is not original nor inventive.[187] It is also cited the US Patent and Trademark Office's rejection of Gilead's patent application for the drug. In 2008, the INPI rejected Gilead's application.

In 2015, GTPI also filed several pre-grant oppositions on molecule related to *sofosbuvir* (marketed as Sovaldi by Gilead) used in the treatment of Hepatitis C as well as co-infection of Hepatitis C with HIV/AIDS. Sofosbuvir has high-efficiency cure rates of 97 per cent in Hepatitis C cases. According to GTPI, Gilead's patent for Sofosbuvir does not meet the minimum requirements of patentability for the grant of a patent, notably the novelty requirement under Sections 2 and 3 of Article 11 of Law 9,279 of 1996 and an inventive step

[183] Reis, Terto Jr and Pimenta (n 89) 29.
[184] ibid 34.
[185] ibid.
[186] ABIA was founded in 1987 by Walter Almeida and Hebert De Souza, popularly known as Betinho. Betinho was most active in developing ABIA's strategy of addressing governmental omission or violation of civil and political rights of those living with the virus. For details on the functions of the organisation, visit http://abiaids.org.br (accessed 21 February 2019).
[187] Reis, Terto Jr and Pimenta (n 89) 36.

under Article 13 of said Law.[188] Again in 2017, the organisation filed a pre-grant opposition against the pro-drug PI0809654-6 on the ground that it does not meet patentability requirements as well as on public interest grounds, since the drug in question is a strategic drug for the SUS and thus the grant of the patent is a violation of the human right to health. In 2018, the Brazilian patent office rejected the patent application. At the time of writing, several other patents relating to Sofosbuvir are still pending.

In addition, the GTPI/REBRIP and Médecins Sans Frontières (MSF) conducted an independent study on the feasibility of local Brazilian laboratories to locally manufacture the lopinavir/ritonavir combination. The study found that four Brazilian pharmaceutical firms (two public and two private) could produce anti-retroviral medicines at an even cheaper price offered by Abbott, ie USD 0.41.[189] The report was simultaneously corroborated by another independent report conducted by the Clinton Foundation and the United Nations Development Programme (UNDP) in the same year. Both GTPI and the MSF continue to participate and shape norms even at the international level and have been involved in various high-level meetings at the UN, WIPO and World Health Organization (WHO).

In addition to litigations and patent oppositions, civil society groups are also active in policy advocacy and destigmatisation campaigns. Many HIV/AIDS scholars in Brazil have argued that the mobilisation by civil society groups can singlehandedly be credited in shaping and framing Brazil's HIV/AIDS discourse.[190] This is because the activism of CSOs framed the discourse as a human rights issue rather than a solely medical or social awareness issue. The mobilisation for improved actualisation of health rights, such as access to essential medicines, medical innovation and technology, brought to the fore the issue of IP – specifically patents – on medicine access. This was the case especially after the 1996 International AIDS Conference in Vancouver made public the news that ARV 'when used in combination, could effectively control HIV progression in the human body'.[191] This completely transformed the context of the response to control HIV and changed the notion of AIDS from being a fatal disease to one that could be treatable and considered chronic.[192] In fact, according to Veriano Terto Jr, the Vancouver Conference positively affected HIV and treatment activism in Brazil by 'changing the conception of people living with AIDS from it being a death sentence, it became a person would live and be treated'.[193] This, according to him, helped to finally break that stigma

[188] Paragraph 3 of Grupo De Trabalho Sobre Propriedade Intelectual Opposition (GTPI), 'Opposition, Sofosbuvir (Pi0410846 9 E Divisionais (Pi0419342 3, Pi0419343 1, Pi0419344 0, Pi0419345 8) Wo2005003147)' (Patent Opposition Database 2015) 2 (in Portuguese).
[189] Fieldwork interview with Marcela Viera (Rio de Janeiro, 2014); fieldwork interview with Felipe Carvalho (Rio de Janeiro, 2014).
[190] Fieldwork interview with Viera (ibid).
[191] Reis, Terto Jr and Pimenta (n 89) 27.
[192] Fieldwork interview with Terto Jr (n 126).
[193] ibid.

that linked AIDS to death and gave impetus for the treatment of access to ARVs as a human right.[194]

This watershed moment changed the dynamic of the health right discourse in Brazil, and it was within this new context that the CSOs in Brazil (and elsewhere) adopted a patent-based definition of the HIV crisis. This social construction of patent-based interpretation of the HIV crisis contends that the broad protection provided by the new global IP regime, particularly patent protection on pharmaceutical product and process, has an adverse effect on access to essential HIV/AIDS medicines. It also illuminates patent-based methods of deepened protection (eg evergreening), among others. The AIDS civil society argued that by placing a high price tag on medicine, pharmaceutical companies are making important drugs unavailable to the millions of people desperately in need of the drugs. The effect is that these pharmaceutical companies therefore 'determine [...] those who can benefit from new, improved ARVs and those that will die due to lack of the same medications, most likely the millions of patients from poorer countries'.[195] In response to this, many AIDS advocacy groups forged partnerships among themselves as well as with international organisations such as Oxfam and MSF to publicise the negative impacts of the TRIPS Agreement and bilateral trade treaties on medicine. The aim of these alliances is to lend visibility to the social impact of IP trade agreements, monitor international forums that discuss IP issues and access to medicines, and influence government decisions on patent applications while developing alternatives that can widen access to medicines. The success of these initiatives lies in the fact that the problem of IP was made accessible and understandable to everyone.[196] For instance, Passarelli and Terto note that it was the advocacy operations of AIDS civil groups that brought awareness to 'the need for budget supplement in the Ministry of Health so that drugs and other health materials can be purchased and distributed without interruption'.[197] By raising awareness of the cost of purchasing these drugs thanks to patent monopolies, these activist groups brought to the public, knowledge regarding the influence of IP and patents on drug access. In this way, IP was no longer seen as an arcane subject for the highly educated select few. Further, this awareness enabled ordinary Brazilians to petition their municipal and state – and to a larger extent, national – governments to implement or consider pro-public health policies when processing patent applications and in trade or investment agreements.

Looking back now at the civil society activism through a TWAIL lens, it can be argued that such activism signifies TWAIL in praxis.[198] In other words, by

[194] Passarelli and Terto (n 140) 254.

[195] Reis, Terto Jr and Pimenta (n 89) 30.

[196] 'The Case Of TDF In Brazil' (2012), available at http://patentoppositions.org/case_studies/4f106d0504a7f92f5b000003.

[197] Passarelli and Terto Jr (n 140) 260.

[198] Usha Natarajan, John Reynolds, Amar Bhatia and Sujith Xavier, 'Introduction: TWAIL: On Praxis And The Intellectual (2016) 37 *Third World Quarterly* 1946.

employing the language of right to health in their pursuit for equitable global medicines access, these activists have managed to challenge the strong patent protection regime established in the TRIPS Agreement while articulating counter-hegemonic human rights-focused pharmaceutical patent rules. It is clear that these CSOs are influential in not only shaping policy and generating a common discourse on right to health, medicine access and the HIV epidemic, but have also been successful in establishing lines between seemingly distinct realms of 'science', 'politics' and 'law' by entering in the process policy debates and contesting interpretations that are particularly restrictive of policy space. From a practical standpoint, at the basic level, the activism of these groups underscores key TWAIL themes of resistance and counter-hegemony in the quest to democratise the international patent system and to make it work in a just manner.

VI. ENGAGING WITH THE WORLD: TOWARDS DEVELOPMENT

As stated above, Brazil quickly implemented the full trade agreement package without using the transition period when it joined the WTO. Since the transition into the TRIPS regime, the constitutional obligations of the Government have led to the implementation of innovative regulatory policies, and the consequent export of these policies to international forums such as the WTO and the WIPO, especially given Brazil's growing willingness to challenge WTO-based restrictions. Thus, David Trubek et al observe that as the Brazilian state began to play a more robust role in the promotion of economic growth and social protection, successive administrations protected domestic policy space by challenging restrictive interpretations of global trade rules.[199] In this new environment, trade policy-making became more closely included in the overall development strategy, and Brazil invested in the legal and related skills needed for success in trade disputes.

Brazil was one of the most active countries in the Uruguay Round negotiations, but this did not mean much as it subsequently capitulated to pressures from developed countries.[200] Many scholars have explained the reasons for this, which include but are not limited to the following: (a) the acceptance of the GATT trade package was the *sine qua non* for receiving aid from the US and Europe; (b) several countries in the Global South lacked the technical expertise and

[199] David Trubek, Helena Alviar Garcia, Diogo Coutinho and Alvaro Santos, *Law And The New Developmental State: The Brazilian Experience In Latin American Context* (Cambridge, Cambridge University Press, 2013) 331. David Trubek used the Brazilian experience to describe the emergence of a new developmental state (NDS), its implications for law, new approaches to development, and new legal tools.

[200] To map the weakening of the Brazilian stance at the Uruguay Round, see (a) statement by Ambassador George Marciel, Representative of Brazil, 'General Agreement on Trade and Tariffs: Multilateral Trade Negotiations Group Frameworks' (1977) MTN/FR/W/1; (b) statement by HE Mr Marcos Castrioto de Azambuia, Special Representative of the President of the Republic, General

human resources to fully engage in trade negotiations; and (c) many of the countries in the Global South were either going through economic turmoil in the late 1980s and 1990s or were undergoing the structural adjustment programmes enforced by the IMF and World Bank, which required these countries to sign on the global trade regime.[201] However, as has been shown, Brazil was able to roll back some of the adverse effects of TRIPS Agreement internalisation through concerted effort in law, politics and various administrative frameworks. In doing so, the country has been able to recapture the discourse by balancing public interest and social responsibility with private rights.

At the international level, Brazil faced aggressive responses because of its policies at home. The first was the WTO dispute between Brazil and the US, ie *Brazil–Measures Affecting Patent Protection*.[202] In this case, the US complained that the Brazilian industrial property law (Law Number 9.279/96) and the 'local working' requirement for the grant of patent is discriminatory and therefore violates Articles 27.1 and 28.1 of the TRIPS Agreement. The US also questioned Article 68(4) of the IPLB regarding parallel importation. Analogous to this event was the growing collaboration and sympathetic alliance among countries of the Global South regarding public health flexibilities due to the growing ravages of HIV/AIDS in these countries.[203] The US later withdrew the case before the Dispute Settlement Body panel after Brazil threatened to file a counter-dispute. However, Brazil agreed to inform the US whenever it wished to apply this legal provision against a US company. Nevertheless, the symbolism of this case cannot be ignored. On one hand, the Brazilian condition for CLs creates a legal ambiguity and pushes, in a sense, what is generally understood as the liberal reading of TRIPS Agreement flexibilities. Conversely, the US action appeared to be an attempt to send a signal to developing countries not to adopt

Secretary for Foreign Policy, 'General Agreement on Trade and Tariffs: Multilateral Trade Negotiations Group Frameworks' (1990) MTN.TNC/MIN(90)/ST/38; and (c) statement by HE Mr Celso Amorim, Minister of External Relations, 'General Agreement on Trade and Tariffs: Multilateral Trade Negotiations Group Frameworks' (1995) MTN.TNC/MIN(94)/ST/101.

[201] Brazil was not the only country that played an unsuccessful role at the Uruguay Round. Indeed, one could argue that the Global South in general failed at the Uruguay Rounds negotiations. See Raghavan (n 57), which describes the divide-and-conquer tactics used by the Quad at the negotiations; Peter Drahos, 'Global Intellectual Property Rights In Information: The Story Of TRIPS At The GATT' (1995) 13 *Prometheus* 6, on the use of Section 301 by the US to pressure developing countries into signing the agreements. See also Peter Drahos, 'Trade-Offs and Trade Linkages: TRIPS in a Negotiating Context' (2000), available at www.anu.edu.au/fellows/pdrahos/reports/pdfs/2001tradeoffstradelinkages.pdf (accessed 1 June 2015). For a Twailian view, see BS Chimni, 'Political Economy Of The Uruguay Round Of Negotiations: A Perspective' (1992) 29 *International Studies* 135.

[202] *Brazil–Measures Affecting Patent Protection* (2001) WTO Dispute Settlement Body, WT/DS199.

[203] Two years prior to the *Brazil–Measures Affecting Patent Protection* case, the South African Pharmaceutical Manufacturers Association and 39 mostly multinational pharmaceutical companies took the Government of South Africa to court after the Government approved a legislative proposal which contained the explicit authorisation of parallel imports of patented pharmaceuticals. See Tshimanga Kongolo, 'Public Interest Versus The Pharmaceutical Industry's Monopoly In South Africa' (2001) 4 *The Journal of World Intellectual Property* 609.

measures that are not in line with the US pharmaceutical industry's strategy and interests.[204] Specifically, Shanker observes that the US did not have a strong case against Brazil; rather, its action is part of the American strategy to test the provisions of the TRIPS Agreement through case law and the dispute settlement mechanism.[205]

Outside the WTO, Brazil continues to be to an active advocate of a human rights-based approach to trade, development and IP rules in other forums such as the Mercosur, WHO and WIPO. Together with Argentina, it launched the WIPO Development Agenda (WIPO/DA) in 2004.[206] The proposal argued for the incorporation of the UN Millennium Development Goals to the global IP regime to promote a development-centred approach. Specifically, the WIPO/DA aimed at blocking new advancement in the protection of IPRs while integrating substantive proposals on how to combine public policy interest with the private sector's role in innovation and protection of rights.[207] Indeed, the introduction of this agenda by Brazil and Argentina was a reaction to the growing discourse on certain TRIPS-plus narratives, especially the Substantive Patent Law Treaty (SPLT). The SPLT raises patent protection standards substantially, including initiatives that only consider the rights of patent-holders. Michelle Badin notes that for Brazil, the WIPO/DA was influenced by shifting dynamics at home, especially the interventionist actions of the Brazilian state in fostering national development, particularly in the health sector, as well as institutional changes such as the creation of an IP division within the *Itamaraty*.[208] In the case of the latter, the IP unit benefitted from an uncommon capacity-building to meet the highly technical approach required by WTO issues. This unit is also actively involved in the Inter-Ministerial Group on Intellectual Property (GIPI), which consists of 11 ministries such as the Ministries of Health, Science and Technology, Foreign Affairs, Trade and Development, and others. Additionally, the emergent anxiety among Brazilian policy circles of another Uruguay Round with the growing acceptance of SPLT and its TRIPS-plus clauses, as well as the ever-increasing knowledge gap still separating rich and poor countries, are some of the Brazilian motives behind the WIPO/DA.

The proposal by Brazil and Argentina were supported by other developing countries and at the 2007 General Assembly of WIPO, Member States adopted 45 recommendations that constitute the WIPO Development Agenda. Scholars such as Laurence Helfer champion this regime-shifting strategy as an opportunity for states dissatisfied with several provisions of particular international

[204] Daya Shanker, 'Brazil, The Pharmaceutical Industry And The WTO' (2002) 5 *The Journal of World Intellectual Property* 57.

[205] ibid 99.

[206] Proposal By Argentina And Brazil For The Establishment Of A Development Agenda For WIPO (2004), available at www.wipo.int/edocs/mdocs/govbody/en/wo_ga_31/wo_ga_31_11.pdf.

[207] Sanchez Badin, 'Developmental Responses' (2013) 275.

[208] ibid.

agreements to recalibrate them in a different forum to satisfy their need.[209] Others posit that discussing the same issue in various forums weakens a state's position and could lead to concessions, which may be reflected in future WTO negotiations.[210] Nonetheless, the Brazilian contribution to the operation of new policies and procedures in international circles cannot be ignored or downplayed. In defending its domestic policies while actively engaging at the international level, Brazil has established a norm of constructive engagement with the TRIPS Agreement framework and demonstrated that it is comfortable with 'asserting claims that preserve its discretion over the appropriate balance between access and protection of knowledge assets'.[211]

VII. CONCLUSION

Globally, there is growing recognition of the need for a more balanced IP regime, especially as high prices – an attendant result of market monopoly due to patent protection – affect the availability of life-saving medicines. However, the pharmaceutical industry has been pushing for an ever stronger and more imbalanced IP regime in trying to consolidate its gains.

Analysis of the Brazilian context has shown ways to balance IPRs with socio-economic development goals and the public interest. Though the country quickly implemented the TRIPS Agreement due to external pressures and as part of its trade liberalisation policies without using the transition period, internal circumstances such as the HIV/AIDS crisis, budgetary constraints and the Government's constitutional obligation to provide healthcare for all Brazilians has influenced the evolving role of patent law in Brazilian society.

Furthermore, the confluence of local non-state actors' cultural disposition towards litigation and the technical expertise regarding important patent law issues has helped Brazil substantially adopt innovative regulatory policies. Exploring history as well as local politics shows that the country is not interested in a patent system that does not support health policies. In this sense, health policies underpin and frame Brazil's engagement with patent law.

In fact, at the time of the fieldwork in Brazil, there are bills currently pending at the Brazilian House of Representatives proposing changes to the patent law. If implemented, the bills would include the participation of health professionals in the analysis of pharmaceutical patents,[212] allow third parties to challenge patent application before or after grant,[213] allow the exploitation of

[209] Laurence R Helfer, 'Regime Shifting: The TRIPS Agreement And New Dynamics Of International Intellectual Property Lawmaking' (2004) 9 *Yale Journal of International Law* 54.
[210] Gontijo, 'The Position Of Brazil' (2005) p 20.
[211] Okediji (n 86) 245.
[212] Bill 3.943/2012 and Bill 5.402/2013.
[213] Bill 5.402/2013.

patented products for the purpose of public non-commercial use without the consent of patent-holder,[214] and further increase access to medicines.[215]

By linking its patent regime to the health sector, Brazil has developed a health-oriented patent examination system. Even though opinion remains divided on the ANVISA prior consent system, the fact remains that public health and the right to health perspective considered in patent discourse – an area in which private rights that are contrary to the majority's interest usually prevail. In fact, in recent years, Brazil has adopted the notion of health within the context of national development and industrial policy. Known as the health-industrial complex,[216] the Government has sought to improve access to medicines and advanced medical technology through partnerships with private companies. It is hoped that public-private partnership (PPP) agreements would increase transfer of technology and the production of higher value-added drugs.

[214] Bill 5.402/2013.
[215] Bill 139/1999.
[216] Carlos Augusto Grabois Gadelha, 'Development, Health-Industrial Complex and Industrial Policy' (2006) 40 *Revista de Saúde Pública*, available at http://dx.doi.org/10.1590/S0034-89102006000400003 (accessed 21 February 2019).

5

India: From Little Acorns to Mighty Oaks

I. INTRODUCTION

THIS CHAPTER FOCUSES on India – a country characterised as the 'pharmacy of the developing world'[1] – due to the important role of Indian generic manufacturers in supplying affordable medicines throughout the developing world. Further, due to the shrinking markets of developed countries, many Western pharmaceutical companies are looking to the developing country markets of China, Brazil and India, among others, to compensate for lacklustre drug sales in the US and Europe. As a result, the country continues to be a battleground on contentious patent issues relating to the limits of flexibilities in the TRIPS Agreement, data exclusivity and market competition to mention a few.

By focusing on the Indian pharmaceutical sector, this chapter continues the critical approach to understanding pharmaceutical patent law-making in the Global South. Particularly, it expounds on the understanding of patents by the Indian state based on how the notion of patent is conceptualised in policy and in law highlighting, in the process, the long torturous overlapping interactions of various actors interested in influencing the country's patent policy. Second, this chapter looks into the policy options and priorities embraced by Indian policy-makers in the wake of the Patent (Amendment) Act of 2005 (IPAA), why these policies were embraced, as well as how the current contestations in the post-TRIPS Agreement landscape affect not only the development goals of the country but also access to medicines. This chapter concludes by unpacking the alliances, patterns and schisms among key actors to understand how they challenge and/or influence the state's understanding and application of patents.

Patent laws do not operate in a social, cultural, political and policy vacuum, and the mere implementation of IPRs under the TRIPS Agreement – the history of the Agreement notwithstanding – will not necessarily spur local development. Rather, patent policies twinned with a specific goal within the larger context

[1] Médecins Sans Frontières (MSF), 'Examples Of The Importance Of India As The 'Pharmacy For The Developing World' (MSF 2007), available at www.msfaccess.org/sites/default/files/MSF_assets/Access/Docs/ACCESS_briefing_PharmacyForDevelopingWorld_India_ENG_2007.pdf (accessed 5 March 2015).

of the national economic development plan can be instrumental in balancing the effects of the trade regime to achieve sustainable development. In observing these prosaic mechanics of law, institutional interactions and globalisation, the central argument of this chapter is that patent laws work better in furthering the developmental agenda when implemented to reflect local realities and tied to larger policies, be it industrial, health, or otherwise. As this chapter shows, India leveraged on this to achieve its development and technological goals. Basically, it is this drive for pharmaceutical autonomy and self-sufficiency that underpinned the initial indigenous industrialists' engagement with the patent regime and continues to fuel the roles played by local pharmaceutical industrialists in the patent discourses and law-making.

Nonetheless, that is not to say that civil society actors did not play any role in the development of India's patents. They did and continue to do so. But they only came to the scene due to a series of separate but interconnected actions such as the HIV/AIDS epidemic in sub-Saharan Africa and other parts of the developing world, the challenge of South Africa's Medicines and Related Substances Control Amendment Act of 1997 (which was launched in 1998 by 38 pharmaceutical companies and the corollary publicity campaign launched by transnational civil society), and the aborted US–Brazil WTO dispute. All these came to a head at the Doha Development Round. One of the takeaways from this chapter, therefore, is the significant role of the pharmaceutical sector in patent compliance and governance in India – something that was absent in Brazil (and as we shall see in Nigeria). Importantly, the Brazil and India case studies underscore three key factors that need to be in place in terms of narrative, actors and politics for a successful patent regime to evolve out of the interaction of all those forces – active law, strong private sector engagement, and informed and active civil society movement.

As in the preceding chapter, TWAIL is employed here to delineate the colonial origins of patent law in India and illustrating, in the process, the evolution and globalisation of an inherently hierarchical international patent regime, which entrenched the interest of capital and distribution of wealth and power along European/Non-European axis.[2] As the analysis in this chapter advances, it crystallises the way international law structures our daily existence both in the material and ideological sense.[3] This kind of Twailian-materialist approach, which advocates for a reading of international law scholarship beyond the traditional sites of enactment and performance such as global summits, international interventions, or the latest international criminal tribunal,[4] but instead in the

[2] James Thuo Gathii, 'The Agenda Of Third World Approaches To International Law (TWAIL)' forthcoming in Jeffrey Dunoff and Mark Pollack (eds), *International Legal Theory: Foundations and Frontiers* (Cambridge, Cambridge University Press, 2019) 13.

[3] Luis Eslava, 'The Materiality Of International Law: Violence, History And Joe Sacco's The Great War' (2017) 5 *London Review of International Law* 50.

[4] Luis Eslava, 'Istanbul Vignettes: Observing The Everyday Operation Of International Law' (2014) 2 *London Review of International Law* 2.

daily operation of international law on the mundane or 'material' plane of everyday life,[5] helps us see the counter-hegemonic pharmaceutical patent law-making in India as part of the numerous forms of resistance already at play in the struggle against the (post-)colonial normative order now being institutionalised and administered across the world.

Finally, as this chapter will show, the battle is not over as the dialectical relationship between the state and key actors, and among actors, continues. If anything, the Indian experience could be understood as a local reproduction of the international. That is, a symptomatic reflection of the ongoing battle over 'new' capital knowledge – its access and control – between the developed economies of the North and the new geopolitical constellation called BRICS – Brazil, Russia, India, China and South Africa. The battle is also currently symbolised in many forms, from the proliferation of bilateral and plurilateral agreements, to the creation of the BRICS Development Bank as a possible competitor to the World Bank, and the recent wave of hacks of sensitive information online.

The remainder of the chapter is divided as follows: section II maps the historical development of patent law in India from its colonial, postcolonial and global phases. The objective of this exercise is to provide a broad context for understanding how the development of the Indian generic pharmaceutical sector is tied to the ideas circulating at that time – the exploitative nature of colonial patent law and domestic interests are best served by a certain kind of IP law that could help the development of indigenous pharmaceutical industry. It is these ideas, buttressed by existing socio-economic factors, which shaped the Indian Patent Act of 1970 (IPA).

Section III looks at India's interaction with the TRIPS Agreement at the local level and how it has come to be woven in the fabric of everyday life, materialising in public discourses on patent, national development policies and the activism of non-state actors. From a Twailian perspective, this demonstrates the instructing function that takes place in the interaction between the international order and its materialisation on the ground, especially how ideas circulate, the manner in which particular policy options get constructed, and – as an extension – how others get extinguished. Basically, we see how international law constitutes and reconstitutes spaces, shaping people's everyday life and their local geographies.[6] It also highlights the roles played by industrial alliances created in previous years and by transnational civil society groups which helped in knowledge and expertise production regarding the possible impact of the TRIPS Agreement on India's pharmaceutical sectors and overall development framework. Here, the interactions of nodes (pharmaceutical companies) become apparent in the way

[5] Luis Eslava and Sundhya Pahuja, 'Beyond The (Post)Colonial: TWAIL And The Everyday Life Of International Law' (2012) 45 *Journal of Law and Politics in Africa, Asia and Latin America – Verfassung und Recht in Übersee (VRÜ)* 195.

[6] Eslava, 'Istanbul Vignettes' (2014) 2.

knowledge and expertise are created and mobilised toward the governance of the patent system in India and beyond. In both the contestation of the TRIPS Agreement in local spaces as well as the operationalisation of node in various ways to manage the course of events, one thing becomes clear: a development of counter-hegemonic patent rules that widen the aperture on norms governing global pharmaceutical rules.

Section IV provides an analysis and critique of the IPAA by looking at key aspects of the law, specifically novelty, inventive step, CL and the opposition system. Attendant to this, key jurisprudential cases, decisions and the role of the courts will also be examined to extrapolate an emerging counter-hegemonic Indian patent jurisprudence that recognises the need to balance patent obligations with the constitutional right to life and health (framed in this context as access to medicines). In section V, the focus is on how key actors are coping and adapting since India phased fully into the TRIPS Agreement regime. Specifically, the strategies used by civil society groups to further the specific access to medicines agenda as well as those adopted by the pharmaceutical industry in patent lawmaking are highlighted.

II. HISTORICAL EVOLUTION OF PATENT LAW IN INDIA

A. Colonial Encounters

The first piece of legislation in India relating to patents was Act VI of 1856, which granted 'certain exclusive privileges to inventors of new manufacture for a period of 14 years'.[7] The law was intended to replicate the successes of the British industrial revolution in India by giving impetus to local industries. It remains to be an important improvement on patent law at that time because it 'embodied the most progressive and innovative idea of inventor being given exclusive privilege through the operation of the Act rather than by the Act of the Crown'.[8] That is, instead of an inventor obtaining exclusive privilege or monopoly for his invention from the Crown, he was made entitled to it by operation of law, subject to certain restrictions and upon the fulfilment of certain conditions.

Another interesting aspect of Act VI of 1856 is its definition of the term 'inventor', which included not only the actual and genuine creator of an original product, but also a person who brings or imports an invention into India.[9] The idea behind this, according to legal historian Rajesh Sagar, is to provide an incentive for the importation of inventions by '[encouraging] capitalists of India and abroad to import and commercialise the technologies in India, thereby

[7] P Narayanan, *Patent Law*, 4th edn (Kolkata, Eastern Law House, 2013) 6.

[8] Rajesh Sagar, 'Introduction Of Exclusive Privileges/Patents In Colonial India: Why And For Whose Benefit?' (2007) 2 *Intellectual Property Quarterly* 324.

[9] ibid 6.

increasing India's technological capacity'.[10] The 'inventor' could, under this Act, also authorise others to make, sell or use the invention for a term of 14 years from the time of filing of such specification.[11] This ties into the historical reasoning of granting exclusive privilege to encourage the introduction of knowledge and inventions within the importing country and for increasing diffusion and aggregation of technology.

A major drawback of Act VI of 1856 was the high cost for obtaining exclusive privileges in India, which was set at INR 100. The amount then, according to some commentators, was equivalent to almost '16 months' wages of an average Indian and made the system not conducive to encourage local inventors to take advantage of the system due to a very high cost-prohibitive factor.'[12] This had not only an exclusionary effect, as it means only foreigners with the capacity or extremely wealthy Indians could patent inventions, but also demonstrates how the application of Eurocentric patent rules creates a regime favourable to the interest of imperial powers. However, even though Act VI was later repealed, it was done not because of its hierarchical nature but because it was enacted without the sanction of Her Majesty as the Legislative Council of India consequently did not have the authority to pass Act VI of 1856.[13]

In 1859, Act V replaced Act VI of 1856 and was founded on the provisions of the English Patent Act of 1852. The new Act V retained the original scheme for the grant, refusal and enforcement of exclusive privileges, but significantly departed from the concepts of 'inventor' and 'novelty' of Act VI of 1856. Among the significant aspects of this new Act is its extension of the right of the British patent-holder to 12 months in India instead of the open six months stipulated by Act VI of 1856. In addition, Section XVII of Act V of 1859 also provided that an importer of an invention within India 'shall not be deemed to be an inventor' within the meaning of the Act.[14] This is a significant departure from Act VI of 1856, which included an importer of an invention within the meaning of the term 'inventor'. This provision discouraged the diffusion of technology by making the importation of technology less attractive. This is because under Act V of 1859, an imported invention is not protected, which made the imported product an easy target for free riders. Thus, the only route for an importer of an invention to obtain exclusive privilege is through an application for and the approval of letters of patent in Britain, and subsequently applying for an exclusive privilege in India under Section XX of Act V of 1859 as a British patentee claiming priority rights.

[10] ibid.

[11] Narayanan, *Patent Law* (2013).

[12] Sagar, 'Exclusive Privileges/Patents In Colonial India' (2007) 9.

[13] ibid 7. See also VK Unni, 'Indian Patent Law And TRIPS: Redrawing The Flexibility Framework In The Context of Public Policy and Health' (2011) 324, available at https://scholarlycommons.pacific.edu/cgi/viewcontent.cgi?article=1018&context=globe (accessed 18 December 2018).

[14] Sagar (n 8) 9.

Act V of 1859 also considerably expanded the 'priority rights' of British patentees, much to the detriment of Indian interests, by broadening the 'assessment of novelty of an invention for granting exclusive privilege to include both India and the United Kingdom (UK), which Act of 1856 was limited only to India'.[15] This particular rule was based on a model used at that time by the UK and other countries and was found to be extremely useful in gaining technological advantage, while India, being a colony, was deprived of this benefit.[16] In fact, P Narayanan argues that the purpose of this legislation was 'to enable the English Patent holders to acquire control over Indian markets'.[17] This is not surprising as many Eurocentric patent laws applied to the colonies such as Act VI of 1856, Act V of 1859, and subsequent laws enacted by the British during the colonial period produced a considerable impediment for the direct transfer or importation of technology by creating a time-consuming and costly process to the detriment of India (and other colonies). The economic and political impact, from a TWAIL viewpoint, is the concentration of patents in the hands of foreigners, leading to inadequate levels of economic and technological development in the patent-granting country. Later amendments and refinements of the patent laws in India did not ameliorate the situation. Instead, these laws further burdened the colony and benefited the imperial power.

The Patents and Designs Protection Act, which introduced legislation for the protection of industrial designs, was enacted in 1872, while the Protection of Inventions Act was enacted in 1883. Both laws were consolidated in the Inventions and Designs Act in 1888. In 1911, the British Government enacted the Indian Patent and Designs Act, which created 'a system of patent administration in India under the administration of Controller of Patents'.[18] It allowed for a patent term of 16 years, which can be extended for an additional seven to 10 years if the working of the patent has not been sufficiently remunerative to the patentee.[19]

The Indian Patent and Designs Act of 1911 continued with the imperial legacy of exploitation by establishing a

> form of intra-British Empire priority system such that an applicant for an Indian patent who had within the previous twelve months filed an application for the same invention in the UK was entitled to the benefit of the earlier UK filing date.[20]

[15] ibid.

[16] ibid.

[17] Narayanan (n 7).

[18] Unni, 'Indian Patent Law And TRIPS' (2011) 325; Narayanan (n 7) 6.

[19] Sudip Chaudhuri, citing ss 14 and 15 of the Patent and Designs Act of 1911. See Sudip Chaudhuri, *The WTO And India's Pharmaceuticals Industry: Patent Protection, TRIPS, And Developing Countries* (Oxford, Oxford University Press, 2006) 129.

[20] Janice Mueller, 'The Tiger Awakens: The Tumultuous Transformation Of India's Patent System And The Rise Of Indian Pharmaceutical Innovation' (2007) 68 *University of Pittsburgh Law Review* 507. It is worth mentioning at this point that because of the British colonial expansionism, which meant that British law was applied across Britain's colonies, it can be argued that it was in fact British imperialistic aspirations that first achieved 'harmonisation' and not the TRIPS Agreement.

In addition, it did not categorically state what was patentable, and widely worded claims were permitted. As such, new and old products and processes were described in a patent. This was specifically used by foreign MNCs to prevent indigenous research laboratories and pharmaceutical companies from concentrating on developing the manufacturing process. The MNCs did this by describing all the known, possible and even old processes in patent applications, and because the Indian Patent and Designs Act of 1911 did not categorically state what was patentable, indigenous companies were forbidden by the patent office to use it.[21]

This severely affected indigenous pharmaceutical companies that were already locally manufacturing modern drugs. In fact, several eminent chemists such as Prafulla Chandra Ray, TK Gajjar, and AS Kottibhasker were already producing drugs as early as 1905.[22] Consequently, under the Indian Patent and Designs Act of 1911, indigenous companies were forbidden from processing a patented drug into formulations or from importing it, and MNCs asserted their patent right to proceed legally against firms that tried to manufacture or import the patented drug.[23] For example, an MNC importing a drug for INR 2 would sue an indigenous company importing a similar drug for INR 2.[24] The effect of the colonial patent system was a stunted industrial sector, especially as regards pharmaceuticals, and led to sky-high prices for basic drugs in India. This was confirmed by the Kefauver Committee Report,[25] which found that India was one of the nations with the highest-priced drugs in the world at that time (cited in the Ayyangar Committee Report, discussed in the next section). Critical essential medicines such as penicillin and antibiotics were wholly imported.[26] Estimates suggest that foreign firms controlled 68 to 70 per cent of the Indian market,[27] and essential drugs such as insulin and penicillin were not manufactured locally.[28]

Furthermore, although MNCs were present in the pharmaceutical sector, they mainly engaged in processing imported bulk drugs into formulations, meaning

See Sagar (n 8) for a review of patent law modelled after the British system, which by 1935 was about one-half (63/140) of the world's total number of patent territories that had their patent law either as an extension or a close modification of British patent law.

[21] ibid.

[22] Chaudhuri, *The WTO And India's Pharmaceuticals Industry* (2006) 21–22. According to Chaudhuri, the evolution of the indigenous drug companies can be traced back to a series of public research laboratories set up by provincial governments. These public sector laboratories set up as early as 1899 produced vaccines for local plagues, cholera, typhoid and rabies. By the early 1940s, these laboratories started synthesising new drugs and finding new uses for existing drugs. See Chaudhuri (n 19) 29–36.

[23] Chaudhuri (n 19) 21–22.

[24] ibid 130.

[25] The US Senate Committee headed by Senator Estes Kefauver.

[26] Planning Commission, 'First Pan (1951–1956)' (Government of India, 1951) ch 32.

[27] Amy Kapczynski, 'Harmonization And Its Discontent' (2009) 97 *California Law Review* 1577.

[28] Planning Commission, 'First Pan' (1951).

they did not engage in inventive activity.[29] This is because the patent system provided foreign patent-holders with too little responsibility and too much power such that 'multinational[s] could make onerous technical collaborative deals'.[30] Therefore, importation – as was widely practised by many foreign MNCs – was a way of controlling competition from indigenous drug-makers and preventing the transfer of technological knowledge to India. Essentially, MNCs were more interested in process importing instead of undertaking basic drug manufacturing. As a result, foreign companies did not establish any production units in India, but engaged in assembling bulk drugs into formulation.[31] Colonial laws in force at that time helped these foreign firms calcify their position within the Indian market even though they were not keen on manufacturing. Not only did these laws lack 'a clear policy direction to pave way for industrial development through patents'[32] for the colony, they also prioritised wealth extraction and exploitation of Indian conditions to the benefit of the metropolis.

From a Twailian view, the introduction and transplantation of the alien concept of exclusive privileges, which was hardly of any utility to a larger cross-section of the Indian populace due to systemic bias in the form of high fees and an exclusionary legislative policy, made colonial patent law disadvantageous to colonial India. The colonial patent regime structure, in limiting competition from indigenous manufacturers, also led to the underdevelopment of the pharmaceutical sector. Importantly, this embodies the Twailian insistence of mapping and critically appraising the historical foundations of international law in order to not only reveal international law's relationship to the colonial encounter but also highlight the power imbalance that criss-cross the international legal order. The Indian Government rectified this imbalance by not only changing its patent law, but also by developing public sector laboratories to encourage the improvement of indigenous technological capacity in partnership with private companies.

B. Post-colonial Interventions

When India gained its independence from Great Britain in 1947, the Indian Government wasted no time in crafting an indigenous patent law. Cognisant of its dire socio-economic realities, especially the tragedy of the partition war, and in the spirit of nationalism and economic development circulating among

[29] Rajeev Dhavan, Lindsay Harris and Gopal Jain, 'Whose Interest? Independent India's Patent Law And Policy' (1990) 32 *Journal of the Indian Law Institute* 473.

[30] ibid.

[31] Chaudhuri (n 19) 28.

[32] Srividhya Ragavan, *Patent And Trade Disparities In Developing Countries* (Oxford, Oxford University Press 2012) 31.

the political and capitalist class,[33] the new Government set up committees to look into ways to make the patent system work for the newly independent India: the Patents Enquiry Committee I (1950) under the chairmanship of Dr Bakshi Tek Chand;[34] and the Patent Enquiry Report II (1959) headed by Rajagopala Ayyangar.[35] The Committees were tasked to review the patent law in India with a view to 'ensure that the patent system is more conducive to the national interest and welfare'.[36]

The Tek Chand Report criticised the failure of India's patent system to stimulate invention and encourage exploitation of new inventions for industrial purposes. Consequently, it recommended the use of CLs to prevent abuse of the patent process and curb patent abuse and working of inventions (licences of right).[37] The recommendation of the Tek Chand Report led to the amendment of Sections 22, 23, and 23A to 23G of the Indian Patents and Designs Act of 1911 (*vide* Act 32 of 1950).[38] The Tek Chand Report is primarily viewed as more of a plea for improvement rather than a radical overhaul of the colonial patent system. It was concerned more with the 'management of already existing patent regime rather than a reassessment of the then current law and its impact on the political economy as a whole'.[39] This is not to say that the task of the Tek Chand enquiry was futile, but rather it did no more than emulate, even copy, the provisions pending in the legislation before the UK Parliament at that time. In spite of this cosmopolitan imitation, the Tek Chand Report, if anything, did instigate national discourse on the importance of developing a national patent regime that prioritises national issues and paves the way for national industrialisation.

The Ayyangar Report, on the other hand, suggested a new patent regime for India cognisant of the following: the level of industrial development of the country at that time, with special reference to its economic conditions, and the level of its scientific and technological advancement and its future needs so as to minimise, if not to eliminate, the abuses to which a system of patent monopoly is capable of being subjected to.[40] More aware of economic issues than its predecessor, the Ayyangar Report is noteworthy in many respects. First, it forms the backbone of the current Indian patent regime.[41] Second, the Ayyangar Report

[33] In 1994, a small group of influential business leaders in Bombay drew up and published a plan for the economic development of India. The Bombay Plan will be discussed further in coming sections.

[34] 'Report Of The Patent Enquiry I' (1950) (Tek Chand Report).

[35] Shri Justice N Rajagopala Ayyangar, 'Report On The Revision Of The Patent Laws' (Government of India, 1959), available at http://spicyip.com/wp-content/uploads/2013/10/ayyangar_committee_report.pdf (accessed 10 March 2015).

[36] Narayanan (n 7) 6.

[37] Dhavan, Harris and Jain, 'Whose Interest?' (1990) 511.

[38] ibid 432–42.

[39] ibid 431.

[40] Ayyangar Report (1959), para 44.

[41] Srividhya Ragavan, 'Of The Inequals Of Uruguay Rounds' (2006) 10 *Marquette Intellectual Property Law Review* 301.

is significant in its inquiry into the adaptability of foreign patent laws to meet the needs of the Indian state.[42] Specifically, it examined 'whether and how IP regime can be used effectively to achieve national ambitions, and investigates the history of several foreign patent regimes'.[43] In fact, the Ayyangar Report observed that 90 per cent of patents were owned by MNCs, and that they worked only 10 per cent of these.

Based on the comparative analysis of foreign patent regimes, the Ayyangar Report proposed the amendment of sections of the patent law antithetical to the present needs and development aspirations of India. In order to make patent law work for India, the Ayyangar Report suggested a classification of inventions to which patent protection should be made available. It did this by precisely defining patentable and non-patentable inventions and by removing process patents for food, medicines and chemicals.[44] The Ayyangar Report also suggested the inclusion of a local working requirement so as to establish in India a 'new industry or an improvement of an existing industry, which would profitably employ the labour and capital of the country and thus increase the national wealth'.[45] The Ayyangar Report likewise proposed for the inclusion of a disclosure clause that allows the inventor to make public the invention and the manner of its working so that 'on the expiry of the life of the patent the public are enabled to work the invention themselves and in competition with each other'.[46] Finally, the Ayyangar Report suggested the inclusion of a provision preventing India from joining other international patent regimes such as the Paris Convention.[47]

Opinions vary regarding the legacy of the Ayyangar Report. The debate seems to be divided between those who herald the report as radically changing the patent discourse in India. Narayanan, for example, calls the Ayyangar Report 'the backbone of Indian patent law'[48] while Chaudhuri and Kapczynski laud it as a breakthrough in indigenous postcolonial law-making.[49] However, certain scholars think otherwise. Dhavan et al point out that the Ayyangar Report 'did not seriously consider whether the patent system was actually suited for India'.[50] Consequently, the report curtailed the opportunity for a nationwide discourse on alternatives to the patent system.[51] Not only that, it inadvertently provided unmitigated assurances to foreign patent-holders that India's patent system was not going to be fundamentally changed.[52]

[42] ibid 281. see also Ragavan, *Patent and Trade Disparities* (2012) 34.
[43] Ayyangar Report (n 35), para 2.
[44] ibid, para 45(1).
[45] ibid, para 38.
[46] ibid.
[47] ibid, para 57; see also Unni (n 13) 327.
[48] Narayanan (n 7); see also Unni (n 13) 327 and Ragavan (n 33) 33.
[49] Chaudhuri (n 19); Kapczynski, 'Harmonization' (2009) 1576.
[50] Dhavan, Harris and Jain (n 29) 445–74.
[51] ibid.
[52] Dhavan, Harris and Jain (n 29) 474.

Nevertheless, the suggestions from both the Tek Chand and Ayyangar Committees show the importance of studying the economic situation of a country and tailoring a patent system that works for the newly democratic India, thereby spurring domestic inventions and industries. In deliberately seeking to understand the economic realities of that time while planning for the future, India understood that patents are not just private rights but also tools that – when used appropriately and at the right time – foster development. It highlighted the developmental and nationalistic aspirations and ideas circulating among the domestic capitalist class at that time. It is this understanding that underpins the discourse on the patent regime in India as will be seen 35 years later, and should serve as a lesson for other countries which are similarly placed.

Though the Ayyangar Report was submitted in 1959, it would take a decade before legislative changes were undertaken. This is not surprising, as it is well known that laws are shaped by a multiplicity of influences. In the case of the Ayyangar Report, multinational lobbyists, analyses by Joint Committees set up by the Government, as well as parliamentary debates influenced consequent legislative changes.[53] In the end, the IPA incorporated most of the recommendations of the Ayyangar Report even though some believe that the new law deviated significantly from the ethos of the report.[54]

The IPA[55] introduced salient features to Indian patent jurisprudence. First, it abolished product patents for pharmaceuticals and agrochemicals and only allowed process patents. That is, it allowed an inventor to only claim protection for the best processes known to him/her for the manufacture of pharmaceutical products. Secondly, it reduced the term of drug and food patents from 'at least sixteen years to five years from the date of sealing or seven years from the date of filing complete specifications',[56] whichever is shorter. For other patents, the duration was 14 years. The philosophy behind this change was to encourage the access of Indian society to foreign technologies, especially in pharmaceuticals, that otherwise might be unavailable due to cost and pricing structures under a strong proprietary IP protection system.[57] In addition, Indian policy-makers believed it was a matter of 'national security that India provides medicines and treatment at prices its people could afford for diseases and illnesses that were specific to the Indian subcontinent'.[58] In this regard, the patent law was used as a vehicle to foster pharmaceutical autonomy.

[53] ibid; Mueller, 'The Tiger Awakens' (2007) 512.

[54] Dhavan, Harris and Jain (n 29) 474.

[55] Patent Act (1970) (which came into force in 1972) and subsequent amendments, 'History Of Indian Patent System' (2015), available at http://ipindia.nic.in/ipr/PatentHistory.htm (accessed 2 September 2015).

[56] Chaudhuri (n 19) 37.

[57] Amiya Kumar Bagchi, Parthasarathi Banerjee and Uttam Kumar Bhattacharya, 'Indian Patents Act And Its Relation To Technological Development In India – A Preliminary Investigation' (1984) 19 *Economic and Political Weekly* 294.

[58] Luigi Palombi, 'The Role of Patent Law In Regulating And Restricting Access To Medicines' (2009) 6 *SCRIPTed* 401.

The IPA resuscitated an almost dying Indian pharmaceutical sector, including public and private research laboratories. The prohibition of product patents for pharmaceuticals, it has been argued, led indigenous pharmaceutical firms to focus on generic manufacturing of drugs by copying patented drugs through reverse engineering. It was under the umbrella of the IPA that the Indian pharmaceutical industry grew at the fastest possible rate. Within a decade of its introduction, indigenous pharmaceutical firms were able to domestically reverse-engineer known drugs patented elsewhere. Reverse engineering helped lower the cost of drugs sold to both domestic and international consumers. The sector also exported to many countries that could not afford the original product made in the developed countries.

From a TWAIL perspective, the abolition of product patent protection in pharmaceuticals speaks directly as a response to the colonial ethos of international law to bring about greater material equality. The non-patenting of pharmaceutical processes allowed for technology acquisition, transfer, development, diffusion and incremental innovation in the shortest of time.[59] This is because reverse engineering, subsequent development, and production of patented drugs required only a fraction of time and money compared to the original drug discovery process, thus allowing Indian pharmaceutical firms to produce drugs cheaper and faster than their foreign counterparts.[60] Further, the IPA eliminated the monopoly status enjoyed by many foreign MNCs as it only allowed new process patents.[61] This is a drastic shift from previous colonial laws that allowed the patenting of all known processes, whether new or otherwise, including importation. Under the IPA, only one method or process – the best known to the applicant – could be patented for a particular drug. The effect of this new law was a drop in foreign patent applications in India, as foreign MNCs could no longer engage in frivolous patenting, and consequently increased the share of patents granted to indigenous Indian firms by the US patents office from 0.02 per cent from 1977 to 1987 to 0.06 per cent from 1996 to 2000.[62] That is, the drop in frivolous patenting in India started allowing the development of the Indian pharmaceutical industry, which was then able to increase its own patent filings in the US.

The IPA resulted in making the Indian pharmaceutical sector more diverse and technically competitive. Since the end of the 1980s, India has been exporting more and importing less pharmaceuticals. The sector has grown to be one of the biggest gross domestic product (GDP) generators for the country. For example, while only two indigenous companies were amongst the top 10 firms in terms

[59] Kalpana Chaturvedi, 'Policy And Technology Co-Evolution In The Indian Pharmaceutical Industry' (Open University, 2005), available at www.open.ac.uk/ikd/documents/working-papers/ikd-working-paper-8.pdf (accessed 10 March 2015).

[60] ibid.

[61] Chaudhuri (n 19) 37.

[62] Dwijen Rangnekar, 'No Pills For Poor People: Understanding Disembowelment Of India's Patent Regime' (2006) *Economics and Political Weekly* 411.

of retail sales in 1970, by 1996 this rose to six, and by 2001 it was up to eight.[63] By 1991, domestic firms accounted for 70 per cent of the bulk drugs production while 80 per cent of formulations were produced in the country.[64] Between 1998 to 2008, the export surplus widened from EUR 370 million to EUR 2 billion.[65] Basic manufacturing by MNCs also accelerated after the abolition of product patents because of the removal of the industrial policy restriction on the expansion into formulation unless bulk drugs are produced in specified amounts. Thus, it is also not surprising that the post-independence period saw a shift in drug therapy from treating symptoms to treating the disease itself. Within the next three decades, India emerged as the leading manufacturer and exporter of generic drugs to developing countries in Asia, Latin America and Africa.

In addition to the amendment of its patent law, the Government of India also introduced other policies that worked in tandem with patent laws. Specifically, the Government introduced some form of control on drug prices to ensure access to medicines. The Drugs (Display of Prices) Order of 1962 and the Drugs Control of Prices Order (DPCO) had the effect of freezing the price of drugs. The DPCO set the price of drugs sold within India and put a ceiling on overall prices set by pharmaceutical companies, thus providing affordable medicines for the masses. In essence, the DPCO divided bulk drugs, which are usually basic raw materials or APIs, into essential and 'other' bulk drugs. Prices of essential drugs would be allowed to rise with the prior approval of the Government (or the relevant agency in charge). The prices of 'other' bulk drugs were then frozen 'at the level prevailing immediately before the announcement of the DPCO'.[66] It is important to note at this juncture that the DPCO is strictly an executive decision with no mandate in the statute. Over the years, the DPCO has been reviewed and amended by the Government to reflect the socio-economic needs of the Indian population.

To enhance local production of drugs, the Government introduced investment in local manufacturing firms. The Government also invested in educational institutions to encourage local technological knowledge as well as in chemistry-based reverse engineering, which formed the core of their processes and product development skills, especially in the area of chemistry, pharmaceutical

[63] ibid.

[64] Jean Lanjouw, 'The Introduction Of Pharmaceutical Product Patents In India: "Heartless Exploitation Of The Poor And Suffering"?' (1998) National Bureau of Economic Research, Working Paper No 6366.

[65] Deutsche Bank, 'Indian Pharmaceutical Industry On Course For Globalization' (Deutsche Bank, 2008), available at www.dbresearch.com/PROD/DBR_INTERNET_EN-PROD/PROD000000000022 4095.pdf (accessed 2 April 2015).

[66] The findings from the 1975 Hathi Committee Report on essential drugs played a crucial role in the development of the Indian pharmaceutical industry. The findings from the Committee led the Government to exempt nearly 200 essential drugs from the sway of patenting. See N Lalitha, 'Access To Indian Generic Drugs: Emerging Issues' in K Shadlen, S Guennif, A Guzmán and N Lalitha (eds), *Intellectual Property, Pharmaceuticals And Public Health: Access To Drugs In Developing Countries*, 1st edn (Cheltenham, Edward Elgar Publishing, 2011) 228.

research and biotechnology, and in building sophisticated research institutions.[67] Specifically, the Government created an 'extensive scientific infrastructure and skilled human capital that would be absorbed into the pharmaceutical sector'.[68] This encouraged innovation and meant that Indian firms thrived and invested into several kinds of generic activities. An example of Indian drug innovation was the release in 2001 of the HIV drug Triomune – the world's first fixed-dose anti-retroviral drug. It was produced by Cipla, and sold at USD 600 per year, but reduced to USD 1 per day for MSF. Luigi Palombi asserts that the low price of Triomune encouraged Merck – a US pharmaceutical company – to reduce the price of Crixivan, a highly active ARV therapy to roughly the same price, which in turn caused Bristol Myers Squibb and GlaxoSmithKline to follow suit.[69]

The importance of the IPA became obvious during the HIV/AIDS crisis of the 1990s and early 2000s when Cipla, an Indian generic company, offered to sell the triple therapy ARV drugs of stavudine+lamivudine+nevirapine for USD 350 per year – a stark reduction from the USD 10,000 which the originator company charged.[70] The introduction of cheaper versions of the expensive ARV treatment not only crashed the market price but also helped in scaling up treatment worldwide. Since then, other generic companies from India have entered the ARV market, which further reduced the price.[71] Currently, India is third in global volume terms and fourteenth in global value terms. It also meets 70 per cent of in-country needs for bulk drugs, formulations, dry intermediaries and others.[72] India is the top drug exporter into the US.[73] In fact, some estimates suggest that India's pharmaceutical industry supplies 40 per cent of over-the-counter and generic prescription drugs consumed in the US.[74] However, even though the drug industry is one of the country's most important economic engines, exporting USD 10 to 15 billion in products annually,[75] the sector is hugely dependent on imports of APIs from China, with cumulative imports going up from USD 2.5 billion in 1996 to USD 15 billion in 2010.[76]

[67] Gehl Sampath Padmashree, 'Economic Aspects Of Access To Medicine After 2005: Product Patent Protection And Emerging Firm Strategies In The Indian Pharmaceutical Industry' (Commission on Intellectual Property Rights, Innovation and Public Health (CIPIH), 2005).

[68] ibid 13; see also Palombi, 'The Role of Patent Law' (2009) 402 and Chaturvedi, 'Policy And Technology Co-Evolution' (2005) 15–17.

[69] Palombi (n 58) 402.

[70] Chaudhuri (n 19) 8. See also Deutsche Bank, 'Indian Pharmaceutical Industry' (2008) 3.

[71] ibid.

[72] Sakthivel Selvaraj, Dinesh Abrol and K Gopakumar, *Access to Medicines in India* (Haryana, Academic Foundation, 2014) 22.

[73] Heather Timmons, 'India Expands Role as Drug Producer' *New York Times* (2010), available at www.nytimes.com/2010/07/07/business/global/07indiadrug.html?_r=0 (accessed 14 March 2015).

[74] Gardiner Harris, 'Medicines Made In India Set Off Safety Worries' *New York Times* (2014), available at www.nytimes.com/2014/02/15/world/asia/medicines-made-in-india-set-off-safety-worries.html (accessed 15 March 2015).

[75] ibid. See also Gardiner Harris and Katie Thomas, 'Low-Cost Drugs In Poor Nations Get A Lift In Indian Court' *New York Times* (2013), available at www.nytimes.com/2013/04/02/business/global/top-court-in-india-rejects-novartis-drug-patent.html (accessed 15 February 2015).

[76] Fieldwork interview with Dinesh Abrol (Delhi, August 2014) (transcript on file with author).

C. Global Struggle

Prior to phasing fully into the TRIPS Agreement regime in 2005, India used the TRIPS Agreement's transitional provisions under Article 65, which gave developing countries a 10-year window from 1995 to 2005 to make necessary changes to their IP regimes. It shows how a large developing country has played the TRIPS Agreement implementation game and underscores the importance for less developed countries to utilise the flexibilities available in the TRIPS Agreement.[77] According to Peter Yu, by experimenting with different policy options and delaying the introduction of TRIPS Agreement standards, India successfully maintained an IP system that was tailored to its local needs, interests, conditions and priorities.[78] Although Article 65 of the TRIPS Agreement allowed for a transition period, only 13 countries used this provision. Of these 13, only six used up the complete period.[79]

Despite using the transition clause, the period leading up to the 2005 deadline was not easy or smooth. This is not surprising as even though India accepted the TRIPS Agreement as part of the single undertaking, it was one of the countries from the Global South (along with Argentina, Brazil, Nigeria and Thailand) that opposed the inclusion of IP rules in the wider body of global trade rules. India has always taken the position that substantive matters relating to IP are outside the purview of global trade rules. It viewed the inclusion of an IP regime in the international trade framework as a tool by which wealthy nations could impose strong IPRs as the cost of much-needed access to Western markets.[80] Specifically, the inclusion of both process and product patents in all areas of technology, including pharmaceuticals, was heavily criticised as it meant the country must now provide for patent protection in areas where it previously did not do so.[81] Thus for India, any IP regime should strike a balance between the rights of patentees and the public interest, and between the promotion of industrialisation and securing the transfer of technology. It is this understanding of IP (and patents in particular) that formed the lynchpin of amendment-related politics and discourse during the transition period, and the subsequent revisions to India's patent law.

The contentious politics of India's compliance with its obligations under the TRIPS Agreement led to three implementation stages. The *first amendment* added Chapter IVA, titled 'exclusive marketing rights', to the IPA and

[77] ibid.

[78] Peter K Yu, 'Are Developing Countries Playing A Better TRIPS Game?' (Social Science Research Network, 2013), available at http://ssrn.com/abstract=1915117 (accessed 2 March 2015).

[79] Swaraj Paul Barooah, 'India's Pharmaceutical Innovation Policy: Developing Strategies For Developing Country Needs' (2013) 5 *Trade, Law and Development* 150.

[80] Mueller (n 20) 517.

[81] Fieldwork interview with Amit Sengupta (Delhi, August 2014) (transcript on file with author). See also the report by Economic and Political Weekly, 'Intellectual Property Rights: The Geneva Surrender' (Economic and Political Weekly, 1989) 1201–04, on the Indian stance and specific objections throughout the Uruguay Round negotiations.

provided for mechanisms for receiving pharmaceutical product patent applications – the so-called 'mailbox' filing – as stipulated by Articles 70(8) and 70(9) of the TRIPS Agreement, which required countries to have adequate infrastructure for receiving and filing patent applications from the date of enforcement of the TRIPS Agreement. The *second amendment*, the Patent Amendment Bill of 1999, introduced over 70 changes such as CLs, working requirements and non-patentable inventions. This second amendment was in accordance with Article 65(2) of the TRIPS Agreement, which entitles a developing country member 'to delay for a further period of four years the date of application, as defined in paragraph 1, of the provisions of this Agreement other than Articles 3, 4 and 5'.[82] The *third amendment* included new criteria for patentability. The intricacies of this amendment will be discussed in the ensuing sections.

III. DEVELOPMENT AND COMPETING INTERESTS

Analysing the interaction of international law – in this case, the TRIPS Agreement – at the local spaces in India (ie the politics of the implementation of the TRIPS Agreement and how the TRIPS Agreement interfaced with local institutions, non-state actors and laws) requires a historical and economic backstory on how India conceptualised the idea of development, and laws that could affect development such as patent laws, post-independence. This back story performs two functions: first, it illuminates how the multiplicity of actors influence and circulate ideas, and the manner in which particular policy options get constructed – and, as an extension, how others get extinguished – with regards to IP, development and access to medications in India. The multiplicity of these influences provides a lens through which to understand India's engagement at the Uruguay Round negotiations, the politics in the lead up to the 2005 patent law amendment, as well as the ongoing national engagement on patent jurisprudence within India today. Second, it illustrates how international norms shape people's everyday lives and their local geographies. Seen this way, local events, disputes, contestations and discourses are not only imbued with meaning of global importance, but *as part of* the global.

A. Planned Economy and the Bombay Plan

The newly independent Indian state inherited an impoverished economy from the British Government. Life expectancy and literacy levels were low, poverty levels were high, communicable diseases were rife, and the country was capital-deficient due to its proxy involvement in the Second World War. Except for

[82] TRIPS Agreement, Art 65(2).

a few pockets of items within the manufacturing sector, the sector itself was underperforming. Based on these conditions, the Indian Government set out to promote a rapid rise in the standard of living of the people and to improve the country's overall economic performance. One of the targeted sectors was health and drug technology due to the magnitude and significance of health issues, which included non-existent to limited access to and availability of medicines as local prices of drugs were one of the highest in the world.[83]

This price anomaly could be attributed to numerous factors, but the most glaring was the patent laws, which led to availability to be significantly controlled by foreign companies operating a 'small number of plants that formulated a limited range of medicines while importing the balance'.[84] This caused, in addition to high prices, market manipulation of drugs by MNCs. Citing the case of Parke Davis' promotion of choloramphenicol – an antibiotic usually prescribed for typhoid but marketed as a common cure for infections such as cough and common cold, thus leading to the build-up of resistance and which proved to be fatal during the typhoid outbreak – Rangnekar contends that it was this scenario that augmented the need for reform of the patent law, the local drug system, and the development of local technological and research capacity to enable India to become self-sufficient.[85] In fact, this need for self-sufficiency underscored the Ayyangar Report, which sought to make patents work for the Indian nation, thereby reversing the negative impact of colonial law.

The planned economic development in India in the form of the Five-Year Plans (FYPs) and the review of relevant laws to complement the development process had already begun prior to independence. The Bombay Plan, for example, provided for a 15-year economic plan for India in January 1944.[86] It was authored by leading Indian industrialists and technocrats at that time, including JRD Tata (son of a cousin of Jamsedji Tata, one of India's pioneer industrialists), GD Birla (founder of the Birla group of industries), Sir Ardeshir Dalal (administrator and technocrat), Lala Shriram (industrialist, Delhi Cloth Mills), Kasturbhai Lalbhai (textile and shipping magnate), D Shroff and Purushottamdas Thakurdas (businessmen). It specified clear objectives to be kept in mind in the economic planning of India as well as the general lines on which development should proceed.

Significantly, the Bombay Plan foreshadowed the first FYP launched in 1951, just three years after independence. One of the purposes of the Bombay

[83] The Kefauver Committee mentioned this in its report. See Michael Kidron, *Foreign Investments In India* (Oxford, Oxford University Press, 1965) 251.

[84] Rangnekar, 'No Pills for Poor People' (2006) 410.

[85] ibid.

[86] The official title is 'A Brief Memorandum Outlining a Plan of Economic Development for India' and was named after the city where the authors convened. See PS Lokanathan, 'The Bombay Plan' (1945), available at www.foreignaffairs.com/articles/70448/p-s-lokaathan/the-bombay-plan; see also Amal Sanyal, 'The Curious Case Of The Bombay Plan' (2010) 6 *Contemporary Issues and Ideas in Social Sciences* 1.

Plan was to initiate some form of planned domestic industrialisation after independence and attain in 15 years' time 'a general standard of living which would leave a reasonable margin over the minimum requirements of human life'.[87] Other commentators such as PS Lokanathan consider the Bombay Plan to be a concrete statement of 'the objectives to be kept in mind in economic planning in India, the general lines on which development should proceed and the demands which planning is likely to make on the country's resources'.[88] The Bombay Plan was therefore, in a sense, a compass in the way development and economic growth should proceed.

The Bombay Plan emphasised the importance of developing basic industries for the exploitation of India's large industrial potentials. It is no wonder that key sectors such as power, mining and metallurgy, engineering, agriculture, chemicals, armaments, transport and cement were among the industries listed to be developed within the 15-year period of the Bombay Plan.[89] What is interesting about the Bombay Plan, apart from its admirable objectives, was the group of gentlemen who authored it. It highlights the role of industrialists in pushing forward a particular agenda for the development of an indigenous technology sector with a strong research development base. This agenda was not only adopted by the newly independent India but was also one of the cornerstones in policy decisions for many decades to come. As a result, the Bombay Plan came to be very much seen as a nationalistic aspiration of the domestic capitalist class.[90]

Although the Bombay Plan was not officially adopted, it has been considered a reflection of the interests and ideas circulating among the capitalist class and, by extension, the policy-makers of the time as some of the initial authors of the Bombay Plan went on to become practitioners in government. For example, Purushottamdas Thakurdas and GD Birla were involved in building business associations such as the India Chamber of Commerce and the Federation of Indian Chamber of Commerce and Industry. D Shroff became the founder-director of the Investment Corporation of India as well as chairman of the Bank of India.

The Bombay Plan was also important in shaping many government policies afterwards, especially the FYPs.[91] In his analysis of the history of Indian

[87] Sanyal (ibid) 6–10.

[88] Lokanathan, 'Bombay Plan' (1945), s II.

[89] ibid.

[90] Vivek Chibber, *Locked In Place: State-Building And Late Industrialization In India* (Princeton, Princeton University Press, 2003) 88.

[91] In a 2004 speech, the then prime minister of India, Dr Manmohan Singh, extolled the significance of the Bombay Plan in the making of modern India. He remarked that the Plan laid great emphasis on public investment in the social and economic infrastructure, in both rural and urban areas. Above all, it defined the framework for India's transition from agrarian feudalism to industrial capitalism, but capitalism that is humane, that invests in the welfare and skills of the working people. In many ways, it encapsulated what all subsequent Plans have tried to achieve. See Paranjoy Guha Thakurta, 'Bombay Plan And Mixed-Up Economy' *The Hindu Businessline* (2004), available at www.thehindubusinessline.com/2004/09/07/stories/2004090700010800.htm (accessed 16 April 2015).

businesses, Dwijendra Tripathi noted that the Bombay Plan helped shift government attention that previously exclusively focused on commercial trade to manufacturing.[92] According to him, the authors of the Plan 'recognised the need for planned development, state ownership and control of key industries, and the idea of a centrally directed authority to ensure successful implementation of the economic plans'.[93] Of course, opinions differ regarding the reasons for state failure in spite of the development efforts of the business class in India. On one hand, it has been argued that such failure is due to the inability of the state to take advantage of the enthusiasm of the business class. Instead, the state instituted a system that stifled business initiative, overextended administrative capacity, and lost coherence in a dense web of bureaucratic tape.[94] On the other hand, the argument is that the Indian capitalist class did not support the developmental state in any relevant sense and opposed disciplinary planning that would allow the Government to regulate the flow of investment and punish non-compliance.[95]

Irrespective of this, the striking similarities between the Bombay Plan and the Government's FYPs cannot be denied. Noting the resemblance between the Bombay Plan and the first three FYPs, M Naidu argues that it is an example of the muddled relationship between law-makers and the Indian bourgeoisie and how easy it is for one to influence the other and vice versa.[96] Others observe that the similarity between the Bombay Plan and the FYPs is an example of the impact of capitalist preferences on state-building.[97] If anything, the resemblance between both documents shows how ideas circulate, the manner in which particular policy options get constructed, and, as an extension, how others get extinguished vis-à-vis the capitalist and political class.

India has come a long way since the time of the Bombay Plan, but the ethos of the Plan – the need for planned development and economic independence, building indigenous technological and scientific competency, and improving standard of living – still echoes in government policy and public discourse. These same sentiments permeated the contours of India's involvement in the negotiations leading up to the creation of the WTO, as well as in local discussion regarding joining a new world organisation. At the Uruguay Round negotiations, the country maintained a position based on the principle that any IP matter was outside the purview of the GATT. Focusing on patents, the Indian representative

[92] Dwijendra Tripathi and Jyoti Jumani, *The Concise Oxford History Of Indian Business* (New Delhi, Oxford University Press, 2007) 333.

[93] ibid.

[94] Sanyal, 'Curious Case' (2010) 13.

[95] Chibber, *Locked In Place* (2003) 30.

[96] M Naidu, 'The Bombay Plan' (Workers' International News, 1944), available at www.marxists.org/history/etol/newspape/win/vol05a/no07a/naidu.htm (accessed 16 June 2015).

[97] Chibber (n 90) 85.

at the Uruguay Round specifically stated that 'India is not in favour of raising the levels of patent protection unduly, particularly in the area of pharmaceuticals, because of its adverse implications for the growth of indigenous industry as well as research and development efforts'.[98] This is not surprising because India has made it increasingly clear through its IPA that it will pursue laws that will work for the nation. It believed that 'IPRs are not trade-related and instead, the WIPO is the appropriate forum to deal with IP issues'.[99]

For India, bringing IP issues to the WTO through the TRIPS Agreement was a mistake, as the WIPO exists to deal with global IP-related mandates. According to India's chief negotiators at the Uruguay Round, AV Ganesan, the country was firmly opposed to the inclusion of substantive norms and standards for the protection of IPRs within the negotiating mandate.[100] This is because it believed that the inclusion of IP rules in GATT is inimical to its national interest as it 'intrudes into domestic policy space and would constrain their freedom to pursue economic and social policies best suited to their individual needs'.[101] These attitudes framed not only the perception of the legitimacy of, but also interaction with and consequent resistance to, the TRIPS Agreement in the local spaces in India.

About the time when the Uruguay Round negotiation activities began, there was an ongoing paradigm shift among the developing countries at the international level in the form of the NIEO. This shift in thinking, based on the belief of a just and equitable international economic order, influenced India's stance at the Ministerial negotiations and diffused into the debates at the home front. The NIEO thinking adopted a 'reformist approach' in transnational governance and international law-making. Promulgated by the UN Declaration in 1974, it sought to restructure and reform the asymmetry in international economic relations and systems, and transfer economic benefits from developed to developing states.[102]

The NIEO, it has been argued, was the 'most important international law initiative taken by the developing world in attempting to remedy colonial

[98] 'Statement by Dr Subramanian Swamy, Union Minister of Commerce, Law and Justice', Multilateral Trade Negotiation: Uruguay Round (MTN/TNC/MIN(90)/ST/46) (1990). See also Economic and Political Weekly, 'The Geneva Surrender' (1989) 1201.

[99] Peter Drahos, 'Global Intellectual Property Rights In Information: The Story Of TRIPS At The GATT' (1995) 13 *Prometheus* 6; see also TN Srinivasan and Suresh D Tendulkar, *Reintegrating India With The World Economy* (Washington DC, Peterson Institute for International Economics, 2003).

[100] AV Ganesan, 'Negotiating For India' in J Watal and A Taubman (eds), *The Making Of The TRIPS Agreement: Personal Insights From The Uruguay Round Negotiations* (Geneva, World Trade Organization, 2015) 3.

[101] ibid.

[102] United Nations General Assembly, 'Declaration On The Establishment Of A New International Economic Order (3201 (S-VI)' (United Nations, 1974), available at www.un-documents.net/s6r3201.htm (accessed 19 April 2015). See also Nils Gilman, 'The New International Economic Order: A Reintroduction' (2015) 6 *Humanity* 1.

inequities'.[103] It was not a single entity but rather a political brand holding together a set of loosely compatible agendas with interrelated agendas.[104] In particular, the NIEO sought for control of the extraction and marketing of domestic natural resources by Third World states,[105] the regulation of transnational corporations,[106] a no-strings-attached transfer of technology from the rich to the poor countries of the Global South,[107] the cancellation of debts,[108] and the right of every country to adopt the economic and social system that it deems most appropriate for its own development and not to be subjected to discrimination of any kind as a result.[109] If anything, the NIEO discourse represents an attempt by many formerly colonised nations to enter global debate – once the purview of an old boys' European network – as equal members, if not partners. It also sought to challenge trading and investment rules that are unfair to Third World countries,

Although the NIEO failed[110] to achieve many of its stated objectives, it underscored India's participation at the Uruguay Round as well as that of many post-colonial countries, including Brazil. Viewed from this conjuncture, the NIEO explains the political and economic thought in India – international co-operation based on improving the economic position of the Global South in relation to the Global North. For the country, any international agreement that did not further this agenda did not warrant signing up to.

The various events mentioned above – from crafting a development plan by the newly independent India capitalist class to resistance against the inclusion of IP into the global trade framework to the NIEO philosophy growing among developing countries – might seem unrelated but in actuality are. The single thread binding these events was the need to better the allotment of India both at home and abroad. This is borne out of the realisation that as the international economic order is unjust towards fulfilling the needs of developing countries, deliberate intentional intervention from the state was needed 'to address the

[103] Antony Anghie, *Imperialism, Sovereignty And The Making Of International Law* (Cambridge, Cambridge University Press, 2005) 313.

[104] Gilman, 'Reintroduction' (2015) 3.

[105] NIEO Declaration (1974), para 4(e).

[106] ibid, para 4(g).

[107] ibid, para 4(p).

[108] ibid, para 4(o).

[109] ibid, para 4(d).

[110] See D Otto, 'Subalternity And International Law: The Problems Of Global Community And The Incommensurability of Difference' (1996) 5 *Social and Legal Studies* 337, on why the NIEO failed. According to her, the NIEO failed due to many reasons, which included but are not limited to: the consensus adoption of a new blueprint for global economic co-operation by the General Assembly in 1990 which made no reference to the NIEO; the seeming futility of reshaping the international economic environment and transferring economic benefits from developed to developing states; and the fact that two central disputes of the Charter of Economic Rights and Duties of States (CERDS) were never resolved: first, the issue of expropriation or nationalisation of property owned by foreigners in decolonised states and the associated questions of compensation; and, second, the justification of commodity cartels. Gilman also notes that the various factors that contributed to the failure of NIEO, which includes the unravelling of political solidarity of the Third World states,

blind spot and level the playing field for third world countries within the free market economy model of international economic governance'.[111] If anything, these actions and events predicate the TWAIL philosophy to revise rules, norms and systems unjust to the interest and development of Third World countries.

B. Interest Groups and Patent Reform

On the home front, India pursued statist economic policies, which saw excessive government control over the economy and the 'Licence Permit Raj' – a vast system of national and state-level quotas and licences[112] – were in force. This led to a balance of payment crisis. Although liberalisation had already begun, there existed among policy-makers and the general public a protectionist stance, which saw the opening up of the economy to FDI as well as to international trade as either unnecessary or anti-self-reliance.

These left-leaning policies and philosophies created considerable opposition to globalisation and India's integration into the global economy. Significantly, this anti-globalisation stance allowed for the fusion of expertise and allegiance between indigenous pharmaceutical companies and civil society groups. At home, various civil society groups spearheaded the campaign against the TRIPS Agreement and played an important role in knowledge formation and expertise production on the TRIPS Agreement's possible impact on the country's robust generic sector because these civil society groups understood the likely negative effects on health rights, knowledge access and food security.[113]

The Indian Drug Manufacturers' Association (IDMA), the largest and best-known association that represents the domestic Indian pharmaceutical industry, was one of the most outspoken industry bodies on this issue. Working towards this end, the IDMA heavily lobbied the Government and prepared draft letters to various members of the Parliament, urging them to protect the health rights of citizens and the pharmaceutical sector. Together with CSOs, professional bodies and student groups, the IDMA pushed for public resistance thereby generating a negative image of the TRIPS Agreement, the Dunkel Draft and the GATT in public media.

Among the CSOs, the National Working Group on Patent Laws (NWGPL), which was headed by BK Keayla, specifically played an active role in providing studies for informed debate in the Parliament and in the public regarding the

fragmentation and forum shopping that weakened the attempt to use international law to rein in the sovereign prerogatives of powerful countries, as well as the economic might of the developed countries of the North. See Gilman (n 102) 9.

[111] James Thuo Gathii, 'Third World Approaches to International Economic Governance' in R Falk, B Rajagopal and J Stevens (eds), *International Law And The Third World, Reshaping Justice* (London, Routledge-Cavendish, 2008) 258.

[112] Mueller (n 20) 516.

[113] Fieldwork interview with BS Chimni (Delhi, 2014) (transcript on file with author).

Uruguay Round agenda and the effect of the new international body on the availability and affordability of medicines. A former bureaucrat in the Finance Ministry, Keayla joined Ranbaxy around 1990, and he was influential in the counter-hegemonic resistance by organising national and international seminars or conferences and facilitating research on the constitutional issue of the implementation of the TRIPS Agreement. Keayla's dual role as head of NWGPL and executive at Ranbaxy underscores the ability of big corporations to mobilise leading sources of expertise to elaborate, interpret and defend their agendas and influence standard-setting. Ranbaxy also financed the work of NWGPL to develop research and build public opinion, and even provided office space in a prime location for the NWGPL.[114]

Ranbaxy was not the only Indian generic company working in collaboration with civil society groups. Other companies such as Cipla and Dr Reddy's funded research activities on the potential impact of the proposed IP regime on the country's pharmaceutical sector and public health.[115] Since the amendments were bringing in monopoly protection for pharmaceutical inventions for the very first time, they were obviously a concern for the IDMA. The association was most interested in ensuring the protection of the interests of its members and was the most vocal in opposing the TRIPS Agreement at home and abroad.

The pharmaceutical sector continued to play a vocal role in the lead-up to the 2005 amendments to the IPA. The IDMA was also active during the Doha Round as some of its members were present during the negotiations. In the lead-up to the 2005 IPA amendments, it was the IDMA which provided the language of the important Section 3(d). According to Amit Sengupta, the Left parties had asked for a more stringent definition of patentability, and the IDMA provided the text, which limited patents for pharmaceutical substances to 'new chemical entities' or to 'new medical entities involving one or more inventive steps'.[116] This particular clause protects not only public health interests by ensuring that only genuine patent applications are approved, but also protects the generic sector by preventing patent 'evergreening'. 'Evergreening' refers to the patenting strategy of seeking and securing multiple patents around a single invention and is not exclusive to pharmaceuticals. Commentators such as Biswajit Dhar remarked that Section 3(d) was 'included for innovation purposes as [India] cannot allow minor innovations to be treated at par with something, which we

[114] Fieldwork interview with N Raghuram (Delhi, September 2014) (transcript on file with author).
[115] ibid.
[116] Fieldwork interview with Sengupta (n 81). It is worth mentioning that besides IDMA, the other major player was the farmer's movement. During the Uruguay Round Negotiations, nearly 200,000 farmers were mobilised by Karnataka Rajya Raitha Sangha – a farmer's movement in Bangalore – to protest against the Dunkel Draft. This protest was picked up by other farmers in different parts of India. See Shefali Bhimal and Saritha Rai, 'Attack On Cargill By Karnataka Rajya Raitha Sangha Brings Dunkel Draft Issue in Focus' (1993) *India Today*, available at http://indiatoday.intoday.in/story/attack-on-cargill-by-karnataka-rajya-raitha-sangha-brings-dunkel-draft-issue-in-focus/1/302677.html (accessed 10 October 2015).

consider a breakthrough'.[117] Thus, by successfully including the limiting and clearer language of only new chemical entities (NCEs) in patent application, the IDMA was able to achieve a more tempered patent regime for India, thereby reducing the space for frivolous patenting.

In opposition to the IDMA is the Organisation of Pharmaceutical Producers in India (OPPI), which is primarily an association of foreign pharmaceutical MNCs operating in India. The OPPI pushed a pro-Dunkel Draft agenda in a very quiet manner at the top government level[118] and lobbied for the adoption of the TRIPS Agreement, which it argued 'would encourage genuine scientific and technological research, reverse years of brain drain in the science and technology sector and spur foreign direct investment'.[119] The OPPI also opposed the pre-grant patent opposition clause in the IPA, believing that it unduly prolonged the patent application process. In so doing, the OPPI opposed several of the policy provisions pushed for by both the NWGPL and the IDMA by hedging its argument on the potential economic and innovation benefit to India by joining the global economy.

If anything, the dichotomy between the IDMA and the OPPI shows how fragmented the Indian pharmaceutical sector is. The interaction between the IDMA and the OPPI indicates how a reform preferred by one sectorial player might be seen as damaging by another as well as the predictable bipolarity among actors with divergent interests. In fact, the formation of a third group, the Indian Pharmaceutical Alliance,[120] heightens this fragmentation. Founded in 1999, the Indian Pharmaceutical Alliance consists of the biggest generic companies, namely Cipla, Dr Reddy's, Ranbaxy, Lupin Laboratories, Alembic Limited, Primal India, Sun Pharmaceutical and Wockhardt Limited. Together, these companies account for 50 per cent of domestic production and 80 per cent of domestic export.[121] In the lead-up to the 2005 IPA amendments, the Indian Pharmaceutical Alliance lobbied for the inclusion of a specific limitation on patentability preventing the patenting of new uses of known substances, as well as the patenting of many new forms of known substances.[122]

Paradoxically, the OPPI found support from the Indian Pharmaceutical Alliance in the lead-up to the 2005 IPA amendments in areas including but not limited to licences of rights and CLs. This is not surprising as most members of the Indian Pharmaceutical Alliance engage in significant independent R&D, a move away from reverse engineering of branded drugs which is still employed

[117] Fieldwork interview with Biswajit Dhar (Delhi, 2014) (transcript on file with author).

[118] Fieldwork interview with Raghuram (n 114).

[119] Homi R Khusrokhan, 'Letter To The Ministry Of Science And Technology From The Organization Of Pharmaceutical Producers In India (OPPI), dated 28 April 1999' (Spicy IP, 1999) (document on file with the author).

[120] See Rangnekar (n 62) 414.

[121] 'Indian Pharmaceutical Alliance' (2019), available at www.ipa-india.org/about-ipa/profile.aspx (accessed 17 March 2019).

[122] Fieldwork interview with Sengupta (n 81).

by a majority of the members of the IDMA.[123] In a 2002 letter from the Indian Pharmaceutical Alliance to the Minister of Commerce and Industry, Shri Murasali Maran, notes that the Indian Pharmaceutical Alliance supports patent protection for pharmaceutical products, provided such protection is balanced by public health requirements.[124] Working towards this end, the Indian Pharmaceutical Alliance made a strong pitch for strengthening CLs, licences of rights and the Bolar provisions[125] – the latter being a form of legal exemption from the right conferred by patent for the purposes of obtaining regulatory approval or other commercial purposes.

The fragmentation within domestic manufacturers provides significant complexity when explaining the multiplicity of factors in the way the TRIPS Agreement regime interacts in local spaces. The sector's diversity, according to Janice Mueller, also illustrates the fallacy of viewing the patent debate in India as a purely two-sided argument between foreign and domestic drug companies.[126] As will be seen below, the lack of homogeneity is significantly changing the landscape many years post-TRIPS Agreement.

Indian civil society groups played an integral role in the Uruguay Round negotiations by keeping up the public discourse on GATT in mass media. This is vastly different from the Brazilian example as discussed in the previous chapter. In India, these actors that included academics and patient groups, as well as professional groups such as journalists and health workers, played crucial roles in knowledge, expertise production and framing policy discourse on IP-related issues vis-à-vis India's economic needs and development aspirations. They successfully influenced the agenda of government by ensuring that adequate flexibilities and public interest protections were included in the TRIPS Agreement. Indeed, India is credited for the inclusion of the TRIPS Agreement flexibilities.[127]

The interregnum period from 1995 to 2005, especially the lead-up to the final amendment to the IPA in 2005, saw active local civil society demonstrations. Significantly, the second wave of activism saw increased participation of and partnership between, transnational civil society groups and local NGOs. The MSF, the South African Treatment Action Congress, and the ABIA organised protests in their home countries in solidarity with their counterparts in India.

Locally, NGOs and health groups such as the Delhi Network of Positive People (DNP+), the People's Health Movement, the Lawyers Collective and the Human Rights Network, among others, organised protests against the

[123] Mueller (n 20) 537.

[124] Letter From DG Shah (Secretary General Of The Indian Pharmaceutical Alliance) To Shri Murasali Muran (Honourable Minister Of Commerce And Industry) Dated 23 March 2000 (document on file with the author).

[125] ibid.

[126] ibid.

[127] Kapczynski (n 27) 1573.

implementation of a sweeping interpretation of the TRIPS Agreement into local law that does not consider the nuances of Indian realities and without including the broadest flexibilities in place.[128] In 2001, for example, the Lawyers Collective HIV/AIDS Unit launched the Affordable Medicines and Treatment Campaign (AMTC) – a coalition of networks of PLWHA, NGOs and individuals – to campaign for the inclusion of public health safeguards in the IPAA and the exclusion of TRIPS-plus provisions.[129] The objective of the AMTC was to demand and create an environment that will ensure sustained accessibility and affordability of all medicines and treatment for every individual in India, including access to affordable medicines for PLWHA.[130] The Lawyers Collective, together with national and international civil society actors, engaged in extensive advocacy in the form of dialogues, seminars and white papers. According to Julia George, the advocacy campaigns of CSOs in India successfully led to the retention and inclusion of key public health safeguards in the IPA when Parliament finally amended the law in 2005. These safeguards include the retention of the pre-grant opposition provided in the IPA, the inclusion of post-grant opposition proceedings, and the amendment of provisions relating to compulsory licensing.[131] The latter, according to Gopakumar and Tahir Amin, underscores India's role as a generic drug supplier to developing countries.[132]

Civil society groups have continued their activism post-TRIPS Agreement implementation through the submission of *amicus curiae* briefs in legal cases and through civil protests. The Lawyers Collective, NWGPL, Drug Action Forum and MSF all provided submissions to the Technical Expert Group on Patent Law Issues (Mashelkar Committee Report).[133] The Mashelkar Committee was set up following the introduction in Parliament of the Patents (Amendment) Bill of 2005. It was specifically tasked to examine two important questions, ie whether it would be TRIPS-compatible to limit the grant of patents for pharmaceutical substances to NCEs or to new medical entities (NMEs) involving one or

[128] Fieldwork interview with Vikas Sharma (Delhi, August 2014) (transcript on file with author); see also Ethan B Kapstein and Joshua W Busby, *AIDS Drugs For All: Social Movement And Market Transformations* (Cambridge, Cambridge University Press, 2013) 117–18.

[129] Julia George, 'India, Intellectual Property And Access To Medicines: Developments And Civil Society Initiatives In India' in R Reis, V Terto Jr and M Pimenta (eds), *Intellectual Property Rights And Access To ARV Medicines* (São Paulo, ABIA, 2009) 130.

[130] 'Affordable Medicines And Treatment Campaign' (2001), available at www.lawyerscollective.org/access-to-medicine/atm-background.html (accessed 6 May 2015).

[131] George, 'India, Intellectual Property And Access To Medicines' (2009) 130.

[132] See also KM Gopakumar and Tahir Amin, 'Patents (Amendment) Bill 2005: A Critique' (2005) 40 *Economic and Political Weekly* 1.

[133] According to the popular Indian IP website, Spicy IP, the Patents (Amendment) Act of 2005 that introduced pharmaceutical product patents in India suffered fairly long innings prior to coming into force. It first began as the Patents (Amendment) Bill of 2003 under the BJP Government but soon lapsed due to a change in government and the consequent dissolution of the Lok Sabha. The new Congress-led coalition Government endorsed the Patents (Amendment) Bill of 2003, but since they were unsure of whether it would go through Parliament well in time to meet the TRIPS Agreement

more inventive steps,[134] and whether it would be TRIPS-compatible to exclude microorganisms from patenting.[135]

In this respect, the mandate of the Mashelkar Committee was restricted to TRIPS Agreement analysis and not the broader policy consideration of how best to balance public health goals with pharmaceutical innovation goals. In its submission, the NWGPL argued that patents should be made available

> for basic novel inventions including pharmaceutical substances as defined in Section 2 and 3 whether products or processes in all fields of technologies excluding invention of the Indian Patent Act provided they are new, involve an inventive step and are capable of industrial application.[136]

The Lawyers Collective, for its part, argued that it would be TRIPS-compatible to limit the grant of patent to NCEs.[137] The Mashelkar Committee Report concluded that it would not be TRIPS-compliant to limit the granting of patents for pharmaceutical substances to NCEs only and to exclude microorganisms from patents.[138] However, it reiterated the importance of providing drugs to the people of India at affordable prices. It also reaffirmed the importance of preventing the grant of frivolous patents. In doing so, the Mashelkar Committee Report reaffirmed the Government's understanding that patent rights should be balanced and calibrated with public health, national security and public interest concerns.

Nevertheless, these acts of counter-hegemonic resistance, especially among local actors within India, are important in spearheading instances of dialogue, scrutiny and education. Civil society groups, through their activism, have been able to shape the contours of national dialogue and international law norms and exemplify the Twailian tenet of resistance. If anything, their persistent opposition to the TRIPS Agreement shows that they never ceded to its domination.

deadline of 1 January 2005, they had it passed as a Presidential Ordinance. Due to pressure from the Left parties, changes were immediately made to the Ordinance and cleared by the Parliament in the third week of March as the Patents (Amendment) Bill of 2005. This is not to say that the Left was completely satisfied. Some issues remained outstanding and rather than risk any further delays, the Government strategically did what it does best when caught in a spot – it appointed a committee. If anything, the Mashelkar Committee was nothing more than a deft move by the Government to prevent any further stalling of the passage by the Left parties of the IPA by raising the issue of the TRIPS Agreement, particularly after being summoned twice earlier to the WTO over allegations of violating it. See Shamnad Basheer, 'The Mashelkar Committee Report On Patents: Placing It In Context OR Reading The Lines And Not "Between" Them' (2019), available at http://spicyip.com/2007/01/mashelkar-committee-report-on-patents_28.html (accessed 17 October 2015).

[134] RA Mashelkar, Goverdhan Mehta, Asis Datta, NR Madhava Menon and Moolchand Sharma, 'Report Of The Technical Expert Group On Patent Law Issues' (Department of Industrial Policy and Promotion, Government of India, 2006) 6, available at http://ipindia.nic.in/ipr/patent/mashelkar_committee_report.doc (accessed 27 August 2014).

[135] ibid, p 8.

[136] Mashelkar Report (n 134) 27.

[137] ibid 30.

[138] Mashelkar Report (n 134) 8–12.

IV. INDIAN PATENTS (AMENDMENT) ACT OF 2005: UNPACKING KEY ISSUES

As mentioned above, in order to come into full compliance with its obligations under the TRIPS Agreement, India amended the IPA three times, with the third and final amendment coming into force on 4 April 2005.[139] This section examines and critiques the IPAA, focusing on significant provisions that touch on public health and innovation – the latter being imperative for continued development of the pharmaceutical sector. This chapter specifically focuses on the following areas – patentable subject matters (ie what can and cannot be patented), criterion for patentability, CL provisions, opposition systems and the limitation on exclusive right, along with analyses of their interpretation by judicial authorities. The analysis in this section shows that while India was able to exploit the residual flexibility and legal ambiguity in the TRIPS Agreement, it did not go far enough to deepen the space for law-making and regulatory diversity. That is, while it determined what works best from a national policy perspective and included certain clauses to that effect, it did not tighten up the patent provisions, as will be seen. Yet, it provides a learning tool for Nigeria and many other developing countries. The section concludes by arguing that the mantle falls on the courts to close the legal loopholes that still exist in the IPAA through progressive judgments.

A. Patentable Subject Matters

Section 2 defines key terms used throughout the IPAA. Importantly, it explains the definition of terms such as invention, inventive step, new inventions[140] and pharmaceutical substance. Specifically, Section 2(j) defines an invention to mean '*a new product or process involving an inventive step*'[141] while an inventive step is explained to mean 'a feature of an invention that involves *technical advance as compared to the existing knowledge* or *having economic significance* or *both that makes the invention not obvious to the person skilled in the art*'.[142] It broadens the definition of pharmaceutical substance to mean '*any new entity involving one or more inventive steps*'.[143] Thus a patent is granted only to a new product or process involving an inventive step and capable of industrial application. The inclusion of the patentability of pharmaceutical products and processes is the cornerstone of bringing Indian patent law into full compliance

[139] There was an executive ordinance before this, which was passed in order to have it ready for the 1 January deadline, but the bill was passed only in April 2005.

[140] New invention is explained to mean 'any invention or technology, which has not been anticipated by publication in any document or used in the country or elsewhere in the world before the filing of patent application with complete specification': IPAA, s 2(l).

[141] IPAA, s 2(j).

[142] IPAA, s 2(ja) (emphasis added).

[143] IPAA, s 2(ta).

with the TRIPS Agreement and the major point of advocacy of the generic industry and civil society.

In their review of the IPAA, Gopakumar and Amin point out that the provision is too broad and allows for the patenting of all types of pharmaceutical substances.[144] To rectify this lacuna, they suggest the addition of the term 'chemical', ie new *chemical* entity, to limit pharmaceutical patents to just chemical entities and not any pharmaceutical entity. Gopakumar and Amin also believe that economic significance should not be the sole criterion for evaluating the inventive step of an invention. In their estimation, 'it is not the purpose of patents to recognise economic significance of an invention as economic significance of an invention depends on many other factors'.[145]

B. Exceptions to Patentability

Like the Brazilian Patent Act, the IPAA includes an extensive list of exclusions from patentability. Found in Sections 3 and 4, some of these include frivolous inventions, traditional knowledge, methods of agriculture or horticulture, inventions against public order or morality, and others. However, the most significant exclusion from patentability is the derivatives of known substances enshrined in Section 3(d), which reads:

> The mere discovery of a new form of a known substance which does not result in the enhancement of the known efficacy of that substance or the mere discovery of any new property or new use for a known substance or of the mere use of a known process, machine or apparatus unless such known process results in a new product or employs at least a new reactant.[146]

What is significant about Section 3(d) is the scope and extensive list of non-patentable items, with the aim of preventing evergreening,[147] thereby limiting the negative impact of such frivolous patenting on medicine access. It is well known that obtaining patents on new uses of known substances as well as the use of a compound in a particular way is a regular practice in the US and is employed by pharmaceutical companies to extend the life of their patent rights. According to the National Institute for Health Care Management, of the 1,035 new drug

[144] Gopakumar and Amin, 'A Critique' (2005) 2.

[145] KM Gopakumar, 'Product Patents And Access To Medicines In India: A Critical Review Of The Implementation Of TRIPS Patent Regime' (2010) 3 *The Law and Development Review* 333.

[146] IPAA, s 3(d). An explanation was appended to the clause, which notes that salts, esters, ethers, polymorphs, metabolites, pure form, particle size, isomers, mixtures of isomers, complexes, combination and other derivatives of a known substance will be considered to be the same substance, unless they differ significantly in properties with regard to efficacy.

[147] Evergreening is defined as pursuing patent thickets by seeking and securing multiple patents around a single invention. See Dwijen Rangnekar, 'Context And Ambiguity In The Making Of Law: A Comment On Amending India's Patent Act' (2007) 10 *The Journal of World Intellectual Property* 31; see also Amy Kapczynski, 'Engineered In India – Patent Law 2.0' (2013) 369 *New England Journal of Medicine* 2.

applications approved by the US Food and Drug Administration from 1989 to 2000, majority (65 per cent) were for incrementally modified drugs.[148] Also, a study by Kapczynski et al on secondary patents in the pharmaceutical industry found that secondary claims are common, thereby technically providing substantial additional patent life.[149] This negates the time limit of patent terms as new patents continue to keep the subject matter under protection.[150] Thus, when placed within the wider context of national IP laws and pharmaceutical patent practice, the importance of Section 3(d) becomes significant.

By stipulating that only new and more efficacious forms are patentable, Section 3(d) – in contrast to the rhetoric often peddled by the US – encourages innovation, thereby creating substantial scope for competition in the pharmaceutical sector. Section 3(d) was recently tested in the Novartis case.[151] Basel-headquartered Novartis contested the rejection of its patent application for anti-cancer drug Glivec by the Indian Patent Office and subsequently by the Intellectual Property Appellate Board (IPAB) and had challenged the IPAB's interpretation of Section 3(d). Novartis argued that its betacrystal form of imatinib mesylate is more 'efficacious' than the base compound imatinib (which was discovered prior to 1995 and is therefore not patentable) as it is easier to store and process, and is also 30 per cent more bioavailable than imatinib.[152]

The Indian Supreme Court ruled that the

> new form of a drug must demonstrate an improvement in its therapeutic effect or curative property as compared to the old form to secure a patent and the beta crystalline form of *Imatinib Mesylate*, fails the test of section 3(d).[153]

The Supreme Court also discussed at length the meaning of therapeutic efficacy with respect to pharmaceutical products, and observed that there are different possible meanings. The definition may be limited only to action resulting in a curative effect, or it might be more broadly extended to cover improved safety or reduced toxicity. In the end, the Supreme Court decided to leave open what is the appropriate definition of enhanced (therapeutic) efficacy – the narrower or broader interpretation – because it did not need to reach that conclusion in this particular case.[154] Furthermore, noting the claim made by Novartis regarding increased 'bioavailability', the Supreme Court observed that 'bioavailability' measures the level at which the drug is made available in the human body and may or may not have an influence on the therapeutic or curative effect of

[148] The National Institute for Health Care Management Research and Educational Foundation, 'Changing Patterns Of Pharmaceutical Innovation' (NIHCM Foundation, 2002), available at www.nihcm.org/pdf/innovations.pdf (accessed 5 March 2015).

[149] See Amy Kapczynski, Chan Park and Bhaven Sampat, 'Polymorphs And Prodrugs And Salts (Oh My!): An Empirical Analysis Of "Secondary" Pharmaceutical Patents' (2012) 7 *PLoS ONE* 1.

[150] Rangnekar, 'Context and Ambiguity in the Making of Law' (2007) 376.

[151] *Novartis AG v Union of India* (2013) Supreme Court of India, Civil Appeal Nos 2706-2716 Of 2013 (Supreme Court of India).

[152] ibid, paras 14 and 23.

[153] ibid, para 190.

[154] ibid, para 192.

the drug.[155] As a result, the Supreme Court held that such effect was not demonstrated.

While the Novartis judgment is seen as a vindication of not just India's legislative process but also a triumph of human rights over profit,[156] it has led to various interpretative tussles. Some scholars, for instance, assert that the ruling was not far-reaching enough, as it did not explain the meaning of 'therapeutic efficacy'. Dinesh Abrol, Convener of the NWGPL, for instance contends that 'the Court could have even strengthened the therapeutic efficacy concept by clarifying and defining in concrete terms and could have directed the state on patent guideline by creating jurisprudence on it'.[157] This view is supported by KM Gopakumar of the Third World Network (TWN), who agrees that because the court did not clarify the meaning of 'therapeutic efficacy', ie whether it meant 'technological efficacy' or 'economic efficacy', India opened itself up to future contestation.[158] According to him, the courts opened the door for the patenting of known substances by insisting on therapeutic efficacy and as a result, missed a very useful opportunity to stop the patenting of known substances and do away with this discretionary element.[159] From his perspective, this leaves the country and millions of people that depend on generic drugs vulnerable, as there is a threat of diluting policy concerns regarding the patenting of known substances through subsequent judicial interpretation or the practices of patent offices.[160]

In contrast, Justice Prabha Sridevan, the judge who ruled on the Novartis case at the Chennai High Court, believes that the fact that the court left out the definition of 'therapeutic efficacy' is a good thing. Addressing the reasoning behind the non-definition of 'therapeutic efficacy', Sridevan notes

> it would be foolhardy for [the court] to limit it today because it does not know what could happen tomorrow. Therefore, it is better to leave it to the wisdom of a future court to decide whether what we said was therapeutic efficacy would include this new quality that is now being argued.[161]

It can be argued therefore that by leaving open the definition, the court is protecting the interest of not only the public but of the manufacturers as well. In not capping what is termed 'therapeutic efficacy', the court leaves the room open for future innovations and circumstances. If anything, the Novartis case has shown the importance of Section 3(d) in limiting practices that might result in the grant of patents for insubstantial technological contributions. It also provides

[155] ibid, para 184.

[156] Leena Menghaney, 'Drop The Case' (2013) 48 *Economic and Political Weekly* 56; Amit Sengupta, 'Two Decades Of Struggle' (2013) 48 *Economic and Political Weekly* 43.

[157] Fieldwork interview with Abrol (n 76).

[158] Fieldwork interview with KM Gopakumar (Delhi, September 2014) (transcript on file with author).

[159] ibid.

[160] KM Gopakumar, 'The Need To Curb Patents On Known Substances' (2013) 48 *Economic and Political Weekly* 55.

[161] Fieldwork interview with Prabha Sridevan (Chennai, September 2014) (transcript on file with author).

an intelligent balance for India's obligations under the international treaty and its commitment to protect and promote public health considerations, not only of its own people but also in many other parts of the world.[162]

In spite of considerable focus on the jurisdictional decision on 'therapeutic efficacy', other scholars have pointed out that the discourse on Section 3(d) needs to focus on the interpretation by patent offices. Sakhtivel Selvaraj points out that the issue should be on the number of patent officers with skills and expertise to examine patents using the 3(d) provision.[163] Patent officers are the first point of contact on any patent issue and therefore should be thoroughly informed about what this provision means and how to interpret it, what is and is not a frivolous patent, and what is a real objective blockbuster drug.[164] It is well known that the Indian Patent Office suffers from a chronic shortage of adequately trained and specialised personnel. As a result, they lack access to leading prior art databases to undertake a thorough and comprehensive examination of complex patent applications.

Section 3(d) is currently seen as an example of a judicial innovation tool[165] – a form of counter-hegemonic resistance from a developing country in recalibrating a seemingly inequitable global IP rule.[166] But none of these matters if the first point of call of a patent application is not well-trained in the technical and complex text of patent examinations. Thus, having a well-trained patent officer is tantamount to strengthened and effective patent jurisprudence. It is therefore not surprising that many patent examiners are now being sponsored by foreign pharmaceutical associations to train in the US. While this training has the potential of improving the technical skills of India's patent examiners, it would also likely compromise the policy under Section 3(d) as the examiners imbibe standards of evaluation not relevant to India. In so doing, orienting them to the narrative of (foreign) pharmaceutical companies appears to be detrimental to the public interest.

C. Opposition Systems

Another important aspect of the IPAA is the inclusion of pre-grant and post-grant patent opposition. Section 25 on pre-grant opposition allows any person to file an opposition at any time before the grant of a patent on certain specified grounds.[167] The section delineates 11 specified grounds in which interested parties can oppose a patent application. These include 'prior publication

[162] Novartis case (n 151), para 66.

[163] Fieldwork interview with Sakhtivel Selvaraj (Delhi, September 2014) (transcript on file with author).

[164] ibid.

[165] Ruth L Okediji, 'Legal Innovation In International Intellectual Property Relations: Revisiting Twenty-One Years Of The TRIPS Agreement' (2014) 36 *University of Pennsylvania Journal of International Law* 233.

[166] Dwijen Rangnekar, 'Drugs In 3(d) And What Matters In The Novartis Case at Supreme Court' (2012), available at http://kafila.org/2012/08/21/drugs-in-3d-and-what-matters-in-the-novartis-case-at-supreme-court-dwijen-rangnekar (accessed 6 April 2012).

[167] IPAA, s 25.

of a patent application but a patent has not been granted',[168] 'lack of inventive step, non-invention under Section 3 of the Patents Act',[169] insufficient or unclear description of the invention in the specification,[170] and failure to disclose the source of biological material used for the invention.[171] The pre-grant opposition is noteworthy as it signifies the first instance when a challenge can be made before the grant of a patent. In addition, it conserves administrative time otherwise spent on examining a patent application that could later be invalidated.[172] It is important to note that pre-grant opposition is not a new inclusion via the IPA amendment. It was carried from the Patent Act of 1911 and was retained in the IPA and its subsequent amendments.

The IPAA also requires the Patent Office to grant the person a hearing.[173] Ragavan points out that the pre-grant opposition provision was retained because it was felt that the approximately 6,000 applications pending in the mailbox protection system would escape scrutiny. Retaining the pre-grant opposition was intended to weed out frivolous patent applications.[174] In this instance, the pre-grant opposition works as a mechanism to check the genuineness of the patent application and allows any third party to contest the application before it is granted.[175]

Furthermore, the IPAA added a post-grant opposition system to the patent law. Post-grant opposition allows an interested person to oppose a patent within one year after the application has been granted.[176] Many Indian generic pharmaceutical companies, CSOs, as well as patient groups keenly knowledgeable of the esoteric IPAA have often invoked this law. Indeed, both the pre- and post-grant opposition clauses are seen by many as a key victory for health activists and civil society groups alike, and these groups have often invoked these provisions in recent times. It shows how non-state actors actively participating in the judicial setting are shaping emerging patent jurisprudence in India. Importantly, it represents a mechanism uniquely used to get around one of India's debilitating constraints, particularly backlog, and reduces the time taken to resolve disputes in India.[177] Key cases are discussed in the subsequent section.

D. Compulsory Licence

The IPAA provides for four grounds for the issuance of a CL, which many contend is 'the broadest and most comprehensive of all the world's

[168] IPAA, s 25(b).
[169] IPAA, s 25(e).
[170] IPAA, s 25(g).
[171] IPAA, s 25(j).
[172] Ragavan (n 32) 8.
[173] IPAA, s 25(1).
[174] Ragavan (n 32) 48.
[175] ibid.
[176] IPAA, s 25(2).
[177] Fieldwork interview with Sridevan (n 161).

patent systems'.[178] These grounds are broadly divided into: (a) abuse of patent; (b) government use for public interest; (c) national health emergency; and (d) dealing with the licensing of related patents. These will be elaborated on below. Chapter XVI of the IPAA, comprising of Sections 82 to 94 and titled 'Working of Patents, Compulsory Licences and Revocation', deals with the broad principles and context for the issuance of CLs.

(a) Abuse of Patent

Section 84 specifically refers to abuse of patent as a basis for the granting of a CL. In this instance, the patentee is culpable for the issuance of a CL on the ground that reasonable requirements of the public with respect to the patented invention have not been satisfied[179] because of the non-availability of the patented invention to the public at a reasonable affordable price,[180] and due to the non-working of the patented invention within India.[181] Section 84(7)(a)–(e) provides the definition for 'reasonable requirement of the public', which includes the following: refusal of the patentee to grant licence on reasonable terms;[182] prejudiced conditions imposed by the patentee for the grant of licence;[183] the patent is not worked in India on a commercial scale to an adequate extent or not worked to the fullest extent that is reasonably practicable;[184] and the working of the patented invention in India on a commercial scale is being prevented or hindered by the importation from abroad of the patented article.[185] It thus appears that Section 84(7) seeks to cover possible impediments such as anti-competitive practices.

On reasonable price, the IPAA did not define or explain what it deems to be such, but commentators including Basheer and Kochupillai suggest that the context for reasonable price of a patented article will depend upon the circumstances of each case.[186] Using a case of HIV medicines, they contend that if the price being charged in the US and the European Union (EU) is the same as that charged in India, this could raise a prima facie case.[187]

It is important to note at this junction that Section 84 allows for a lapse of three years from the date of grant of a patent and allows any person, despite being

[178] Mueller (n 20), p 580.
[179] IPAA, ss 84(1)(a) and (7)(a)–(e).
[180] ibid, s 84(1)(b).
[181] ibid; as mentioned above, non-working is also a ground for issuing a compulsory licence in Brazil.
[182] IPAA, s 84(7)(a).
[183] IPAA, s 84(7)(b).
[184] IPAA, s 84 (7)(c).
[185] IPAA, s 84 (7)(d).
[186] Shamnad Basheer and Mrinalini Kochupillai, 'The "Compulsory Licence" Regime In India: Past, Present And Future' (Social Science Research Network, 2005) 9, available at http://ssrn.com/abstract=1685129 (accessed 21 March 2015).
[187] ibid.

already a holder of a licence under the patent,[188] to apply for a CL. However, the applicant should make out a prima facie case in order to be granted a CL. This means that the onus to prove the conditions for the grant of a CL is on the applicant and not on the patent holder.

Under Section 84, the Controller – with a view to securing certain purposes – should review a CL application by making sure that the patented invention is worked on a 'commercial scale within India without undue delay and to the fullest extent that is reasonably practicable'[189] and to safeguard that the 'interests of any person working or developing an invention in India under the protection of patent are not prejudiced'.[190]

The licensee also has the right to enforce the patent against infringers if the patentee refuses or neglects to do so within two months after being called upon. In such instances, the licensee 'may institute proceedings for the infringement in his own name as though he were the patentee, making the patentee a defendant'.[191]

So far, there has been only one successful case of CL application in India. In 2011, Natco, an indigenous generic pharmaceutical company, applied for a CL under Section 84(1) to manufacture and sell a generic version of Nexavar (the generic name is *sorafenib tosylate*) used in the treatment of primary kidney cancer and advanced primary liver cancer. Bayer Pharmaceutical Corporation (Bayer) currently holds the patent for Nexavar.[192] Couching its application on the 'reasonable price' requirement, Natco argued that Nexavar has a limited availability in India, as it is only available in pharmacies attached to large hospitals in select cities of Delhi, Mumbai, Kolkata and Chennai.[193] The company pointed out that the price of Nexavar (sold at INR 280,428 per month or INR 33,65,136 per year) makes the drug out of reach for over a million Indians diagnosed with the disease.[194] Specifically, when Bayer sells the product, it reaches less than one per cent of patients while almost 99 per cent of patients who are unable to afford the drug are left to die every year.[195]

Furthermore, Natco underscored the 'non-working' requirement provision, stating that the patentee Bayer imports and sells the drug *sorafenib* instead of locally manufacturing in India.[196] The applicant also mentioned the inherent difficulty in obtaining a licence to manufacture and sell the product *sorafenib* in India and the subsequent refusal of the patentee to grant a licence

[188] IPAA, s 84(2).
[189] IPAA, s 89(a).
[190] IPAA, s 89(b).
[191] IPAA, s 110 titled 'Right of the Licensee under Section 84 to Take Proceedings against Infringement'. In the event that the patentee is called as a defendant, he is not liable for any cost unless he enters an appearance and takes part in the proceedings.
[192] PH Kurian, 'The Compulsory License Application From M/S Natco Pharma Ltd' (2011).
[193] ibid, paras 2 and 7(b).
[194] ibid, para 7(a).
[195] ibid, para 7(c).
[196] ibid, para 7(a).

(refusal to grant licence on reasonable term clause). Finally, Natco argued that it will not only manufacture the drug in India but that it will be sold at a fraction of the current price at INR 8,880 per month.[197] It will also donate the tablets to patients who cannot afford even the proposed price. Noting the aforementioned points, the Controller found that Natco met all the requirements for a CL application and thus granted the applicant the licence to produce Nexavar in India. However, he ruled that Natco should pay Bayer six per cent royalty.

One area in the *Natco v Bayer* case which has garnered the attention of experts is the 'non-working' requirement. The requirement of 'non-working', usually used as a tool for domestic economic enhancement, raises an important question of compatibility with the TRIPS Agreement. While Section 83(b) of the IPA explicitly states that importation does not mean 'work' (it reads patents are not 'granted merely to enable patentees to enjoy monopolies for the importation of the patented article'),[198] the TRIPS Agreement, on the other hand, mandates the grant and enjoyment of patent rights regardless if the products are manufactured locally or imported.[199] Taken at face value, provisions of 'non-working' which are also present in the Indian patent law is not compatible with the TRIPS Agreement. Janice Mueller, in her extensive analysis of Indian patent law, believes that India and many other developing countries with the 'non-working' requirement will undoubtedly be challenged by MNCs that 'strongly prefer to consolidate production facilities in order to achieve economies of scale and related efficiencies'.[200] Rangnekar, on the other hand, argues that in maintaining the non-working requirement, India demonstrates its intent to explore space left open by legal ambiguity.[201] In a similar vein, Basheer and Kochupillai firmly believe that 'non-working' does not contravene the TRIPS Agreement. Specifically, they note:

> The Paris Convention clearly stated that 'importation' would not amount to working of a patent, and that if a patent wasn't worked, this could be treated as an 'abuse'. Secondly, TRIPS is premised on the promise of technology transfer to developing countries. And a local working provision is geared towards encouraging such technology transfer. By forcing patentees to 'work' their patents in India, the regime encourages local use/transfer of the said technology.[202]

In the *Natco v Bayer* case, the Controller found that the mere importation of Bayer's drug into India did not amount to 'working' and is convinced that 'worked

[197] ibid, para 9(e).
[198] IPAA, s 83(b).
[199] Article 27(1) reads 'Subject to the provisions of paragraphs 2 and 3, patents shall be available for any inventions, whether products or processes, in all fields of technology, provided that they are new, involve an inventive step and are capable of industrial application.5 Subject to paragraph 4 of Article 65, paragraph 8 of Article 70 and paragraph 3 of this Article, patents shall be available and patent rights *enjoyable without discrimination as to the place of invention, the field of technology and whether products are imported or locally produced*' (emphasis added).
[200] Mueller (n 20) 596.
[201] Rangnekar (n 147) 375.
[202] Basheer and Kochupillai, 'The "Compulsory Licence" Regime In India' (2005) 9–11.

in the territory of India' means manufactured to a reasonable extent in India.[203] It held that Bayer could not give reasons as to why working (ie manufacture) of the patented drug was not possible in India. This decision therefore makes it distinctly clear that 'working' as used in the IPA cannot include 'importation'. Bayer challenged the decision at both the IPAB and the Bombay High Court. Both petitions were dismissed.

Apart from the Natco case, there have only been two other instances of CL application in India. BDR Pharmaceutical filed a CL application for an anti-cancer drug *Dasatinib*, which is sold under the trade name Sprycel and patented by Bristol-Myers Squibb. The application was rejected.[204] Lee Pharmaceutical Company also filed a CL application for AstraZeneca's diabetes management drug *Saxagliptin*. The decision was rejected in January 2016.[205] Opinions vary on why there has been a low number of CL applications in India. Gopakumar Nair, former president of IDMA, attributes the lack of data to support CL applications as one of the reasons.[206] India, according to him, suffers from a dearth of accurate or even up-to-date data on diseases, patient usage, production of generics, or drug consumption. In instances where data is available, their authenticity is questioned.[207] This hampers CL application and is the reason for the high incidence of prima facie rejection. However, DG Shah, the secretary general of the Indian Pharmaceutical Alliance, posits that the pressure exerted by the USTR and the US International Trade Commission on the Government of India is the reason why the Government is reluctant to grant another CL.[208] In fact, at a recent conference, DG Shah stated that the industry does not see CLs as a viable business model, as there are bigger profits to be made outside India.[209]

(b) Government Use for Public Interest

Section 92(1) deals with the instances for which a CL may be issued for public interest purposes by notification in the Patent Office journal, regardless of the

[203] Kurian, 'M/S Natco Pharma Ltd' (2011), para 9(e).

[204] See Dilasha Seth and Soma Das, 'DIPP Defers Decision On Issuance Of Compulsory Licence For Cancer Drug Dasatinib' (2014), available at http://articles.economictimes.indiatimes.com/2014-10-16/news/55106950_1_cancer-drug-dasatinib-health-ministry-compulsory-licence (accessed 5 November 2015).

[205] See Balaji Subramanian, 'Compulsory Licence Application Filed Over Astrazeneca's Saxagliptin' (2015), available at http://spicyip.com/2015/07/compulsory-licence-application-filed-over-astrazenecas-saxagliptin.html (accessed 5 September 2015).

[206] Fieldwork interview with Gopakumar Nair (Mumbai, September 2014) (transcript on file with author).

[207] ibid.

[208] Fieldwork interview with DG Shah (Mumbai, September 2014) (transcript on file with author).

[209] See http://spicyip.com/wp-content/uploads/2016/08/Consilience-2016-Report.pdf (accessed 12 August 2016).

time that has elapsed since the grant of the patent. These instances include national emergency, extreme urgency, or public non-commercial use. It further mandates the Controller to grant a licence to 'any private entity' that applies on such terms and conditions he thinks fit[210] while ensuring that the articles manufactured under the patent will be available to the public at the lowest prices consistent with the patentees deriving a reasonable advantage from their patent rights.[211]

The difference between Sections 84 and 92 is that the patent-holder is culpable for the grant of a CL in the former while the CL is granted irrespective of the patent holder in the latter. Further, Section 84 allows for a time lapse of three years while the applicant need not wait for such period to apply for a CL under Section 92. Also, the Controller has discretionary powers regarding the terms and procedure of a CL application within the context of Section 92, which many believe makes the procedure long and cumbersome, as 'both the Act and Rules do not prescribe any time limit for the conclusion of the proceeding'.[212] The possible effect is an indefinite delay on the grant of a CL. Further, according to IP and health economist Shaktivel Selvaraj, Section 92 allows the Government to make medicines available for public health facilities.[213] However, due to political pressure from foreign pharmaceutical companies, the Indian Government is yet to avail itself of this provision despite the constant stock-out of drugs in public health facilities.

(c) National Health Emergency

Added in the IPAA, Section 92(A) allows for the grant of a CL for the export of patented pharmaceutical products in certain exceptional circumstances, such as to countries with insufficient or no manufacturing capacity for the concerned product to address public health, and provided that a CL has been granted by such a country.[214] These exceptional circumstances include situations relating to HIV/AIDS, tuberculosis, malaria or other epidemics.[215] Section 92(A) fits into the Doha Declaration, which emphasised that flexibilities were available in the TRIPS Agreement to address public health needs.[216] Many commentators

[210] IPAA, s 92(1)(i).
[211] IPAA, s 92(1)(ii).
[212] Fieldwork interview with Nair (n 206).
[213] Interview with Selvaraj (n 163).
[214] IPAA, s 92A(1). The explanation for pharmaceutical products reads: 'For the purposes of this section, "pharmaceutical products" means any patented product, or product manufactured through a patented process, of the pharmaceutical sector needed to address public health problems and shall be inclusive of ingredients necessary for their manufacture and diagnostic kits required for their use.'
[215] IPAA, s 92A(3).
[216] 'Implementation-Related Issues And Concerns' (2001), available at www.wto.org/english/thewto_e/minist_e/min01_e/mindecl_implementation_e.htm (accessed 27 April 2015).

contend that it was the position of India and other developing countries at the beginning of the negotiations that the Doha Declaration should cover their current and future health needs, which led to the inclusion of pharmaceutical manufacturing capability in the Doha Declaration and in the subsequent August 2003 Decision on the Implementation of Paragraph 6 of the Doha Declaration.[217] Where a CL is applied for export, the Controller 'shall grant a compulsory licence solely for manufacture and export of the concerned pharmaceutical product to such country under such terms and conditions as may be specified and published by him'.[218] This will be without prejudice to the extent to which pharmaceutical products are produced under CLs.

(d) Licensing of Related Patents

Section 91 deals with the licensing of related rights. In this instance, a CL is granted to alleviate the situation where a patentee or licensee is hindered or prevented from his right to work any other patented invention without infringing on another's pre-existing 'basic' or 'dominant' patent.[219] The provision also specifies two conditions for the grant of a Section 91 CL: first, the CL applicant should show that it is in a position to grant to the first patentee a cross-licence under the second patent on 'reasonable terms';[220] and second, that the other invention has 'made substantial contribution to the establishment and development of commercial or industrial activities in India'.[221]

Part of the reason that a patent regime has flourished in India is because it has been able to carve out a regime that reflects its socio-economic realities and development needs. In fact, in 2018, the country released a policy Report outlining its stance on it IPR.[222] Specifically, the Report takes a strong stance against TRIPS-plus measures for data exclusivity and patent linkages, noting that these would have a negative effect on public health in India.[223] Importantly, by redeploying TRIPS Agreement laws in a progressive way, as the analysis of Section 3(d) has shown, the IPA embodies TWAIL praxis towards the reform and revision of hegemonic global IP laws.

[217] ibid. See also Duncan Matthews, 'From The August 30, 2003 WTO Decision To The December 6, 2005 Agreement On An Amendment To TRIPS: Improving Access To Medicines In Developing Countries?' (2006) 2 *Intellectual Property Quarterly* 91, which discusses the 2005 amendment to Art 31 of the TRIPS Agreement, which intended to improve access to medicines in developing countries by waiving pharmaceutical licensing requirements.

[218] IPAA, s 92A(2).

[219] IPAA, s 91; Mueller (n 20) 605.

[220] IPAA, s 91(2)(i); Mueller (n 20) 605.

[221] IPAA, s 91(2)(ii).

[222] Centre for IPR Promotion and Management (CIPAM), 'Intellectual Property Rights Regime In India – An Overview' (The Centre for IPR Promotion and Management (CIPAM) at the Department of Industrial Policy and Promotion, 2018), available at https://spicyip.com/wp-content/uploads/2018/01/IPR-Regime-in-India-An-Overview.pdf (accessed 20 September 2018).

[223] ibid, 8–9.

V. MEDICINE ACCESS AND THE NATION-STATE AS SITE OF GLOBAL STRUGGLES

How are key stakeholders adjusting to post-TRIPS Agreement India? How are policies, jurisprudence, norms and counter-norms relating to patent rights and access to medicines shaped (and continues to be shaped) post-TRIPS Agreement? This section focuses on these issues by looking into the performative strategies adopted by key actors in the dense configurations and reconfigurations of patent jurisprudence, justice and medicine access discourse in post-TRIPS Agreement India. While India has fully phased into the TRIPS Agreement, it is demonstrated herein that the battle is by no means over as various actors have developed strategies to expand their autonomy within the Indian legal space. Focusing on the use of pre-emptive injunctions by foreign pharmaceutical companies, pre- and post-patent opposition by CSOs and indigenous pharmaceutical firms alike, as well as legal tie-ups via voluntary licences (VLs), this chapter demonstrates emerging alliances, patterns and schisms among key actors to highlight how they challenge and/or influence the state's understanding and application of patents.

A. Pre-emptive Injunctions

According to the Oxford Law Dictionary, an injunction is a court order by 'which an individual is required to perform, or is restrained from performing, a particular act'.[224] There are two types of injunction. A temporary injunction is a temporary stay pending a trial and is 'predicated on the assumption that if the patentee were to ultimately win at trial, the non-grant of a temporary injunction would detrimentally impact the patentee and her rights in the interim'.[225] A permanent injunction, on the other hand, is awarded only after the conclusion of a trial and the patent is found to be valid and infringed.

In India, the law governing the grant of injunctions is set down in the Civil Procedure Code, and is conditioned upon the following pre-requisites: (a) there is a prima facie case in favour of the plaintiff; (b) irreparable injury would be suffered by the plaintiff if the injunction is not granted; (c) the balance of convenience is in favour of the plaintiff; and (d) the public would not be harmed by the grant of injunction. The reason for these conditions, according to Basheer, is the protection of an IP owner against the 'vicissitudes of a long trial, where the alleged infringer could flood the market with competing products and destroy the value of a time-sensitive IP rights'.[226] Thus, the court should

[224] Jonathan Law and EA Martin, *A Dictionary Of Law* (Oxford, Oxford University Press, 2009).

[225] Shamnad Basheer, Jay Sanklecha and Prakruthi Gowda, 'Pharmaceutical Patent Enforcement', *Patent Law in Global Perspective* (Oxford, Oxford University Press, 2014) 607.

[226] Shamnad Basheer, 'Jugaad Justice?' (2015), available at www.livemint.com/Opinion/HUvXJ9hMCRnNpPg9GDMmZJ/Jugaad-justice.html (accessed 7 June 2015).

scrutinise the plaintiff's application to ensure that the pre-requisites are present before an injunction is granted.

There is growing evidence to show that foreign MNCs are pre-emptively using injunctions against local generic players to protect the market of patented drugs and delay the entry of low-cost generic medicines.[227] Courts are also granting these ex parte injunctions prima facie. That is, the courts are granting restraining orders without hearing from the defendants (usually generic firms) or making sure that the pre-requisites apply. The *Economic Times*, for example, reported that the number of ex parte injunctions has grown from six in 2012, to 10 in 2013 and over 15 in 2014.[228] Table 5.1 below provides a snapshot of recent cases:

Table 5.1 Snapshot of pharmaceutical patent injunctions

Date	Appellant	Defendant(s)	Patented compound	Decision
2009	Bristol-Myers Squibb (BMS)	Dr BPS Reddy, HeteroDrugs, BDR Pharmaceuticals, Shilpa Medicare and Natco	Dasatinib	Interim injunctions against all of them except Shilpa Medicare
2011	Vifor (International) AG	Symed Laboratories	Indian patent number 221536[229]	Ex parte interim injunction
2012	Pfizer and Sugen Pharmaceuticals	Cipla, Natco	Sunitinib	Ex parte interim injunction
2014	Novartis	Ranbaxy Laboratories, Wockhardt Ltd, Biocon, Alembic Pharmaceuticals, Glenmark Generics, Cadila Healthcare and Bajaj Healthcare	Vildagliptin	Permanent injunction against Bajaj Healthcare and interim injunction to the rest
2015	Novartis	Cipla	Indacaterol	Permanent injunction against Cipla
2015	Merck	Glenmark	Sitagliptin	Permanent injunction

[227] Aparajita Lath, 'Analysing The Pitfalls Of Indian Patent Injunctions Based On Fear Of Infringement' (2014) 19 *Journal of Intellectual Property Rights* 255. See also Times of India-Economic Times, 'Pharma MNCs Use RTI Law To Protect Market For Patented Drugs & Delay Entry Of Generics' (2013), available at http://articles.economictimes.indiatimes.com/2013-01-24/news/36526946_1_generic-firms-generic-version-bayer-spokesperson (accessed 7 March 2015).
[228] ibid.
[229] Process for preparation of water-soluble iron carbohydrate complex of a particular weight.

Several scholars and health activists have expressed concerns regarding the negative impact of such interim restraining orders to the public and patent law in India. In their extensive analysis of ex parte injunctions in Indian courts, Basheer et al note that these injunctions have a 'draconian' effect on competitors, who are forced to desist from manufacturing and selling the allegedly infringing good, as well as on consumers, who are denied access to cheaper goods.[230] Leena Meenghaney describes these injunctions as 'tactics employed by foreign MNCs in post-TRIPS India to not only limit market access of competitor but also to control the access of cheaper generic versions'.[231] This, according to her, impacts everyday lives of people as generic firms are forced to withdraw these products from the market while the fears of financial damage discourages investment of new product development and launch.[232] Similarly, Justice Sridevan Prabha points out that granting ex parte injunctions causes irreparable hardship to the public who are denied access to important medicines. As damage to health cannot be compensated, the court therefore should not only think of the two adversaries before it but also the effect on the public.[233]

The rise of injunctions points to a deeper and potentially more troubling trend among pharmaceutical MNCs and a departure from their earlier strategy of launching patent infringement suits only after a generic firm has rolled out a competing drug in the market. The use of ex parte injunctions not only has an adverse impact on access to medicines, as it affects the rights of patients to access cheaper generic versions of drugs, but also helps foreign pharmaceuticals maximise their monopoly and increase their profits.

B. Pre- or Post-patent Opposition

As mentioned above, Section 25 of IPA allows for both pre- and post-grant oppositions. Patent opposition allows interested parties to file an opposition at any time before or after grant of a patent. Indian civil society groups have always been cognisant of the dangers posed by IP to access to medicines. As a result, these groups have been able to employ opposition clauses against what they see as frivolous patent applications or applications deemed injurious to public health.

Recent years have seen a spike in patent opposition. For example, in 2013, Natco and a group of civil society and patient groups comprising of I-MAK, Sankalp Rehabilitation Trust and DNP+ successfully filed a pre-grant patent

[230] Basheer, Sanklecha and Gowda, 'Patent Enforcement' (2014) 605.

[231] Fieldwork interview with Leena Menghaney (Delhi, August 2014) (transcript on file with author).

[232] ibid.

[233] Fieldwork interview with Sridevan (n 161).

opposition against Gilead's Sovaldi (generic name *sofosbuvir*).[234] The application sought to prevent Gilead or Pharmasset from gaining a patent in India on sofosbuvir – a drug for Hepatitis C. In the opposition filings, I-MAK argued that the technologies comprising these patent applications are known (old science), while the patent document describing the invention is not sufficient, and therefore does not fully comply with patent law requirements.[235] Natco's opposition was also based on the grounds that the patent for *sofosbuvir* is not inventive, and thus does not meet the standards for patent protection in India. Sankalp Rehabilitation Trust and DNP+ presented their argument on grounds of access, citing the high cost of the drug, which retails at USD 80,000 (or USD 1,000 per pill).[236] This, they argued, makes the drug out of reach for the estimated 12 million Indians who are chronically infected with Hepatitis C.[237] In 2015, the patent was rejected, which Gilead appealed. In 2016, the Deputy Controller handed down a clear victory to Gilead, dismissing the contentions raised in the various oppositions that had been filed against the patent application.

In the same vein, the Indian Network of Positive People and the Positive Women Network successfully filed a pre-grant patent opposition in 2008 against Boehringer Ingelheim's patent application for *nevirapine* (a pediatric ARV). Indeed, the practice of patent opposition has seen civil society groups and generic pharmaceutical companies being on the same side against foreign pharmaceuticals.

According to DG Shah, there is an increase in the number of patent oppositions filed by Indian generic companies, and the Indian Pharmaceutical Alliance files 20 to 25 patent oppositions per month.[238] For instance, in 2012, Cipla successfully filed a post-grant opposition against Pfizer/Sugen's patent on the drug Sutent (generic name *sunitinib malate*), a liver and kidney cancer drug.[239] Pfizer and Sugen were granted the patent for the cancer drug in 2007. The following year, Cipla opposed the patent grant on the following grounds: (a) the claimed invention was publicly used in India before the priority date of claim;[240] (b) the invention as claimed is obvious and did not include an inventive step;[241]

[234] 'I-MAK And DNP+ Pre-Grant Opposition to Opposition to Sofosbuvir (India)' (2014), available at www.i-mak.org/sofosbuvir (accessed 15 January 2019).

[235] ibid.

[236] Sankalp Rehabilitation Trust Petition (documents on file with author).

[237] ibid.

[238] Fieldwork interview with Shah (n 208).

[239] CH Unnikrishnan, 'India Revokes Patent For Pfizer's Sutent' (2012), available at www.livemint.com/Companies/nAHUvoEXEzEXXiC66jG6ZI/India-revokes-patent-for-Pfizers-Sutent.html (accessed 12 March 2015). Natco has previously filed a CL application on public health grounds to supply Sutent to neighbouring Nepal. The application was rejected. See Shamnad Basheer, 'Natco's Doha CL Application: Patent Office Rules In Favour of Pfizer' (2008), available at http://spicyip.com/2008/07/natcos-doha-cl-application-patent.html (accessed 29 November 2018).

[240] Rajiv Choudhry, 'Cipla Succeeds In Revoking Pfizer / Sugen's Patent on Sunitinib' (2012), available at http://spicyip.com/2012/10/breaking-news-cipla-succeeds-in.html (accessed 12 April 2019).

[241] ibid.

and (c) the patentee failed to disclose information as required under Section 8 of the IPA.[242]

In analysing the Pfizer/Sugen patent case, Rajiv Choudhry notes that the lack of inventiveness was the main thrust of the opposition as the claimed compound is prima facie obvious, which is based on the concept of 'structural obviousness'.[243] Thus, in a case of prima facie obviousness, the patentee should demonstrate that 'there are actual differences between the claimed compound and the prior art such that the invention as a whole is non-obvious'.[244] Though Pfizer/Sugen sought to distinguish the claims from the cited prior art document, they could not prove actual difference between the claimed compound and the cited prior art document. As a result, the Controller annulled the patent. In deciding the case, the Controller held that 'the invention that is claimed in the patent does not involve any inventive step … and hence not patentable under section 2 (1) j of the Indian Patents Act'.[245]

The opposition system provides a unique opportunity for Indian civil society groups to build their capacity on matters relating to patents. It also brought networks of patient groups together with other CSOs and generic drug manufacturers to rally for the cause of access to medicines. Of course, the partnership of CSOs and generic pharmaceutical companies does not mean that both groups are always in agreement. It shows how networks can successfully promote the idea that patents equate to denial of access to people desperately in need. It is a good example of Peter Drahos's general point on how socially mediated acts of nodal interpretation and mobilisation have influenced collective action in the IP regime.

It is important to mention at this point that in these patent opposition cases, civil society groups often invoke the human right-to-life argument. This is unlike in Brazil where treatment activism is based on the human right to health. This is because the Indian Constitution does not formally recognise the right to health as a fundamental right. As a result, in most pharmaceutical patent opposition cases, CSOs invoke the right to life, which is recognised by the Indian Constitution.

In mooring the treatment access activism on the right to life, CSOs in India have been able to reinterpret and even strike down IP laws that impede access to medications. In fact, in the *F Hoffmann-LA Roche AG v Cipla Ltd* case,[246] the court based its decision on the right to life, which it interpreted as the right to health. In this case, the plaintiff Roche sought an interim injunction to restrain Cipla from manufacturing and selling the generic version of the cancer drug *Erlotinib* (sold under the brand name Tarceva), for which the plaintiff holds a patent. In his decision, the judge ruled that the right to life will be denied if the

242 ibid.
243 ibid.
244 ibid.
245 ibid.
246 *F Hoffmann-LA Roche AG v Cipla Ltd* (2008) IA 642/2008 IN CS (OS) 89/2008, IA 642/2008 IN CS (OS) 89 (IA 642/2008 IN CS (OS) 89/2008).

general public is denied access to life-saving drugs and the effect of such denial is uncompensable. In this regard, in granting the injunction, the 'Court would in effect be stifling Article 21 [which protects the right to life] so far as those [who] would have or could have access to Erloticip are concerned'.[247] Based on this, the court dismissed the injunction.

C. Voluntary Licence

A VL is where an 'innovator pharmaceutical company of a patented product offers, on his own accord, a licence to a third party (usually a generic producer) to produce, vend and distribute the patented product'.[248] In exchange, the generic producer(s) 'pays royalty to the innovator company on the net sales made by the licensee'.[249]

Since India harmonised its law with TRIPS Agreement standards, there has been a gradual increase in the number of VLs between Indian generic companies and foreign MNCs. Indian companies such as Dr Reddy's, Aurobindo, Cadila Healthcare and Torrent have entered into supply agreements with MNCs such as GSK, AstraZeneca and Abbott. For example, when Gilead's patent for the HIV drug Viread was rejected in 2006, it signed voluntary non-exclusive licences with 11 Indian generic companies for the manufacturing and sale of the drug while awaiting the decision on its appeal.[250] It also signed further licences that included patents on the product *Emtricitabine* (*FTC*), sold under the trade name Emtriva, and combinations of *Tenofivir disoproxil fumarate* (*TDF*) and FTC, sold under the trade name Truvada, or the once-a-day triple combination product *TDF+FTC+Efavirenz* (*EFV*), sold under the trade name Atripla.[251] The licensees in India include Emcure Pharmaceuticals, Hetero Drugs, Strides Arcolab, Alkem Laboratories, Aurobindo Pharma, FDC Ltd, JB Chemicals & Pharmaceuticals, Matrix Laboratories, Medchem International, Ranbaxy Laboratories and Shasun Chemicals & Drugs, and the licence covers 99 countries. In addition, Gilead reportedly required companies seeking VLs to withdraw patent oppositions.[252]

[247] ibid, para 85.

[248] Tahir Amin, 'Voluntary Licensing Practices In The Pharmaceutical Sector: An Acceptable Solution To Improving Access To Affordable Medicines?' (Oxfam, 2007), available at www.i-mak.org/storage/Oxfam%20-%20Voluntary%20Licensing%20Research%20IMAK%20Website.pdf (accessed 12 January 2019).

[249] ibid.

[250] See 'KEI Request For Investigation Into Anticompetitive Aspects Of Gilead Voluntary Licenses For Patents On Tenofivir And Emtricitabine' (Knowledge Ecology International, 2007), available at www.keionline.org/misc-docs/ftcgilead12feb07.pdf (accessed 9 March 2015). According to KEI.org, Gilead's licence further prohibits the supply of APIs to firms and markets not approved by Gilead. Licensed sellers are also required to purchase APIs from Gilead affiliated and licensed suppliers.

[251] ibid.

[252] ibid.

Many scholars and health activists view the latest wave of VLs as unconscionable and objectionable. As Gilead does not have patents for two of the FTC or combinations involving FTC in India while the patent decision for TDF is still pending, Gilead is able to control the Indian competition by signing an agreement with potential competitors whilst undermining India's progressive patent laws. According to MSF, this leads to 'restricted competition'.[253] The significance of the agreement is that it neutralises competition from generic companies, which would have otherwise filed patent oppositions and/or CLs to manufacture the drugs.

In 2014, Gilead also issued another set of VLs to 11 Indian companies to manufacture and sell Sovaldi, a patented Hepatitis C drug in several low- and middle-income countries.[254] The deals entitle the licensees to full technology transfer of the Gilead manufacturing process to enable them to boost production, and the licensees are free to fix their own prices for their versions against a seven per cent royalty payment on low generic sales to Gilead.[255] In addition, the geographical scope of the agreements excludes certain middle-income countries with high rates of Hepatitis C, such as Brazil and Ukraine. The deals have generated a lot of division among health activists within and outside India as many see it as a move by Gilead to tightly control competition. This type of tie-ups, activists assert, will mean fewer patent challenges.[256] Tahir Amir contends that 'Gilead's action is a strategic move to leverage its relevant drugs' potential and save its patent protection'.[257] According to James Love, the highly restrictive licensing 'falls short of ensuring widespread affordable access to these new drugs in middle-income countries, where over 70 [per cent] of people with hepatitis C live today'.[258] However, other actors do not see this as an issue. DG Shah believes that this will promote competition and further drive down prices.[259]

Regardless, it is clear that a VL, in the manner being pursued by Gilead and others, limits the option of full use of flexibilities such as CLs and patent oppositions. This is not surprising as big Indian generics, in collaboration with

[253] 'MSF Review Of The July 2011 Gilead Licences To The Medicines Patent Pool' (MSF, 2011), available at www.msfaccess.org/sites/default/files/MSF_assets/HIV_AIDS/Docs/AIDS_Briefing_GileadLicenceReview_ENG_2011.pdf (accessed 9 January 2019).

[254] 'Gilead Announces Generic Licensing Agreements To Increase Access To Hepatitis C Treatments In Developing Countries' (Gilead.com, 2014), available at www.gilead.com/news/press-releases/2014/9/gilead-announces-generic-licensing-agreements-to-increase-access-to-hepatitis-c-treatments-in-developing-countries (accessed 20 January 2019).

[255] ibid.

[256] Fieldwork interview with Gopakumar (n 158).

[257] Tahir Amin, 'OPINION: The Dirty Motivation Behind Gilead's Hepatitis C Agreement' (2014), available at http://america.aljazeera.com/opinions/2014/11/pharmaceuticals-gileadhepc.html (accessed 12 March 2015).

[258] James Love, 'The Gilead HCV License: Glass Half Empty, Or Half Full?' (2014), available at http://keionline.org/node/2083 (accessed 9 January 2019).

[259] Fieldwork interview with Shah (n 208).

foreign MNCs, will be reluctant to file CL applications because it would be seen as a direct affront to the MNCs. Besides, collaboration with foreign MNCs via VL tie-ups means that the Indian counterparts have better chances of tapping those markets. Further, the growing number of VLs between foreign MNCs and foreign generic companies has led to schism between parts of the generic industry and parts of civil society. This is because the collaboration between foreign MNCs and local generic companies diminishes the propensity of local generics to team up with civil society groups on patent challenges.

D. Mergers and Acquisitions

Mergers and acquisitions (M&As) within the Indian pharmaceutical industry is not a new phenomenon. What is new in the post-TRIPS Agreement situation is the drive with which MNCs are trying to expand not only in the patented markets, but also in the generic markets.[260] In recent years, the share of MNCs in the domestic formulations market has dramatically increased from less than 20 per cent in March 2008 to 28 per cent in December 2010.[261] Notable takeovers include the takeover of Ranbaxy by Daiichi Sankyo in June 2008, Orchid by Hospira USA, Piramal by Abbott (US), Shantha by Sanofi Aventis, Matrix by Mylan (US) and Para by Reckitt Benkiser, to mention a few.

Also, most of these acquisitions are brown field in nature, which is when a company purchases or leases existing production facilities to launch a new production activity. While various factors point to the reason for these M&As, what should be worrying is the position and independence of indigenous firms to push forward counter-hegemonic norms on patent law. It also raises the question of India's self-sufficiency and health security as key indigenous firms are now in foreign hands. It also affects manufacturing as most of the foreign firms are interested in importation instead of local manufacturing. According to Gopakumar of the TWN, M&As are akin to India 'giving away its prime companies, and raises question on of Indian ability to independently use the flexibilities in [its] patent law'.[262] Public health activist Leena Menghaney further adds: 'Today Indian [pharma] industries no longer an Indian industry. What we have are big pharma's little mini-GSKs. It would be stupid to say that [we] have Indian generic industry, which is independent, and takes on challenges'.[263] Other key actors do not see this as a problem. According to Gopakumar Nair, president

[260] Sudip Chaudhuri, 'The Pharmaceutical Industry In India After TRIPS' in H Löfgren and O Williams (eds), *The New Political Economy of Pharmaceuticals: Production, Innovation and TRIPS in the Global South* (Hampshire, Palgrave Macmillan, 2013) 113.

[261] ibid 115.

[262] Fieldwork interview with Gopakumar (n 158).

[263] Fieldwork interview with Menghaney (n 231).

of IDMA, M&As are a good opportunity for medium-sized Indian companies to take over the mantle of leadership and fill the vacuum left by big generics.[264]

The insight from the above analysis of the local space in India as a site of global struggles grasps what Eslava has called termed 'autochthonous internationalization' – a process where international aims and obligations are routinised within nation states, facilitating a subsequent process of internationalisation from within.[265] This internationalisation, according to him, occurs through states' electoral and legislative happenings, in the manoeuvrings of their administrative and judicial bureaucracies, and the often violent proceedings unleashed by their anxiety to develop and compete in the global marketplace.[266] In the case of India, the seemingly benign activities of tie-ups via voluntary licensing, injunctions and M&As embody the multifarious operation of the international normative order through national, and increasingly through local, jurisdictions. Even though these legal manoeuvrings operate within the domestic legal framework, it is and always will be linked to issues of global economic, political and cultural powers manifesting both within and beyond the national jurisdiction.

VI. CONCLUSION

This chapter has shown the sophisticated space in which law, in this case patent law, interacts with actors in the local spaces. It has also been shown that there is a hegemonic order and counter-hegemonic contestation co-existing in the Indian IP sphere.

Adopting a Twailian lens in the form of a historiographical mapping of the patent regime in India provides complementary insights into the specific 'rationalities' setting the parameters of colonial patent law. Specifically, it revealed how MNCs exercised their patent rights and prevented Indian companies from undertaking basic drug manufacturing. This not only stunted the growth of the sector but made essential medicines in India one of the most expensive at that time. By introducing the IPA, which abolished product patent protection in pharmaceuticals, the post-colonial Indian state developed a regime to suit its own distinctive set of concerns. This led to the growth of a globally competitive domestic industry. This signifies, from a Twailian lens, a pertinent example of a dynamic subaltern resistance and reform – a capacity to revolt effectively against misappropriations of the formal norms and institutions of international law.[267] Adoption of Section 3(d) marked a turning point for health and development policy in India. Instituting a stricter standard of non-obviousness and novelty

[264] Fieldwork interview with Nair (n 206).

[265] Eslava (n 4) 9.

[266] ibid.

[267] Luis Eslava and Sundhya Pahuja, 'Between Resistance And Reform: TWAIL And The Universality Of International Law' (2011) 3 *Trade, Law and Development* 128.

for obtaining a patent reaffirmed India's primary commitment to protecting its citizens' lives and health.

Using nodal governance theory, it can be seen how the expansion of IP law among non-state actors responded not just to material interests, but also to acts of framing that allowed these actors to interpret their interests, build alliances and persuade the court and the state to support their cause. The IPAA and subsequent use of flexibility clauses enshrined within the law exemplifies how civil society groups and generic manufacturers have both used the language of the human right to life and the need for pharmaceutical autonomy in political action to promote public policy change. In fact, the activism of CSOs in invoking the opposition clauses provides a rich account of the new politics of IP and the way nodal mobilisation has co-evolved in the shadow of law.

Thus far, Indian scholars, health activists and pharmaceutical companies (both foreign and generic) continue to disagree on the overall best patent policy fit for India. Some argue in favour of higher and tighter thresholds to prevent evergreening and ensure access. Others are against this, suggesting that patents would limit the innovation and R&D required for developing new drugs. Admittedly, India's patent law contains provisions targeting industry development and enabling transfer of technology by ensuring local manufacturing and preventing frivolous patents that could jeopardise access. This contestation has also spilled out into other areas; key actors are working within both the legal and market spaces to carve out counter-norms, thereby increasing the aperture on discourse on medicine access and patent law. This will undoubtedly shape how Indian patent law will be construed in the future. Nonetheless, the prosaic events happening within India has shown the move to local jurisdictions as the foci of legal development.

Lastly, the Indian Government's position with IP policy in recent years has been a confusing one, with the Government seemingly trying to placate the US, while also trying to placate civil society, thus having contrary positions. With respect to the latter, the Government recently set up an IP think tank to develop a national IPR policy that will lay the future roadmap for IP in India. Recommendations from the think tank include the setting up of a National Institute of Excellence on IPRs to enhance awareness of IPRs among all stakeholders, expedited patent examination, an IP exchange, and the encouragement of Corporate Social Responsibility funds into open innovation. It remains to be seen if these will be implemented by the Government.

6

Nigeria: Disconnects, Discontinuities and the Spectacle of Reform

I. INTRODUCTION

IN THIS CHAPTER, the focus is on Nigeria. It continues the thematic thread that runs through previous chapters in employing TWAIL to provide a broad historical lens of the origins of patent law in Nigeria. Secondly, TWAIL is used to illustrate the exploitative relationship between foreign pharmaceutical companies and the host state, Nigeria, and the myriad ways in which power is exercised by the dominant groups (Western corporations) to the detriment of the disempowered (Nigeria). These practices, as shall be seen, reproduce the colonial way of knowing and being by impeding technological transfers and access, thereby further perpetuating the continued exploitation of Third World people. Furthermore, the significance of the presence (or the absence) of nodal networks in influencing and shaping the rule-making process becomes apparent as the analysis in this chapter will show. The absence of these actors in governance processes means there is a deficit in the awareness and conceptualisation of and engagement with the patent regime by both the state and non-state actors. Consequently, patent is not seen as a useful tool in development policy nor as a problem to be solved. The result, then, is that the patent regime has never been significant in the Nigerian context, with little or no socio-economic and developmental impact in law and policy the way it does in Brazil and India.

The rest of the chapter is divided as follows: section II provides a detailed evolution of patent law in Nigeria in order to contextualise and unpack the Nigerian encounter with patent law. While this exercise shows a legal and historical disconnect caused by the absence of interaction between foreign patent law and local actors or institutions, resulting in little direct benefit to the country, the hasty implementation of a post-colonial patent law by the military government also laid a shaky ground for rewriting patent law that is reflective of the country's socio-economic reality and of benefit to the Nigerian people. With focus on key aspects of the law, section III situates the current Nigerian Patent Act vis-à-vis the TRIPS Agreement to show how the latter interacts with laws, institutions and actors at the domestic level. In this section, the role of courts in deciding the substantive issue of patent law is also discussed. Section IV captures the attitude of the Nigerian state towards patents by reflecting on the 'official' use of patents provided in the Patents and Designs Act of 1990 (PDA) as an effective mechanism for achieving the cardinal goals of public healthcare and economic development. In essence, this chapter looks at how the language of patent is employed and deployed by the National Office for Technology Acquisition and Promotion (NOTAP) and among policy-makers. In so doing, it maps how ideas circulate – the particular way in which policy options are selected and others rejected. Section V examines the dynamics of patent discourse by probing into how the private sector and civil society groups engage, if at all, with patent discourse. To do this, this section examines the impact of events such as years of military government and of certain government policies such as the Nigerian Enterprises Promotion Decree, the ISI policy and the way the IMF/World Bank SAP eviscerated the pharmaceutical manufacturing sector, greatly impacting the way the sector pursues and engages in the project of patent knowledge production and lawmaking. Section VI concludes this chapter.

The crux of the argument in the chapter is this: the ongoing legal innovations and contestations found in local spaces in Brazil and India is absent in Nigeria because the patent regime – as a legal phenomenon, a constructed knowledge and a policy tool – is largely seen as irrelevant and not applicable. The cause of this thinking – of patent as irrelevant and not applicable – is a result of the potent mixture of policy disconnect and discontinuities stemming from various dynamics, which include legal indeterminacies, market logics and failure, poor governance, influential donor presence, fractured regulatory system and absence of competing interests, such as strong pharmaceutical manufacturing industry and vocal civil society groups – the last two of which are particularly important and required in the cognitive shaping and knowledge production of the patent discourses. Therefore, any future discourse, legal reform and policy recommendation on patent law in Nigeria should be cognisant of not only the country's past failures and its unique environment, but also the structural and governance gaps that have hindered the development of a progressive patent regime in Nigeria.

II. HISTORICAL EVOLUTION OF THE PATENT REGIME IN NIGERIA

A. Colonial Encounters

As a former British colony, patent law was first introduced to the Lagos colony and the Southern Protectorate[1] in 1900 through the Patent Ordinance[2] and

[1] The Southern Protectorate consisted mainly of Lagos and the Southwest region of Nigeria. The British annexed Lagos in 1861.

[2] Patent Ordinance No 27 (1900). See Bankole AA Sodipo, 'Piracy And Counterfeiting: The Freedom To Copy Vs Intellectual Property Rights', PhD thesis (Queen Mary, University of London, 1995) 41.

the Patent Proclamation.[3] Two years later, the Patent Proclamation of 1902 introduced patent law and protection to the Northern Protectorate.[4] Each of these enactments contained full-scale provisions for the recognition, grant and control of patents in Nigeria and were comparable to the English law on the subject at that time. Applications for patents were made to the patent office, appeals from the decisions of the Registrar were brought before the Attorney-General, who had the power to consider such appeals, and patents were granted to a successful applicant by the High Commissioner in the name of the Crown.[5]

In 1914, the Southern and Northern protectorates were amalgamated to create modern-day Nigeria. In 1916, a new patent law – the Patent Ordinance of 1916 – repealed previous patent ordinances and made the new ordinance applicable throughout the newly formed country. The UK Patent Ordinance of 1925 was subsequently introduced in Nigeria, replacing the Patent Ordinance of 1916. Titled the Registration of UK Patent Ordinance,[6] it disallowed patent application in Nigeria and instead provided for the registration in Nigeria of patents already granted in the UK as long as the application for registration was made within three years from the date of issue of the patent.[7] This law established a dependent patent regime[8] in which patent application could no longer be made in Nigeria while only patents granted in the UK can be registered in Nigeria. It also conferred rights and privileges in Nigeria to the extent that these were granted by the UK law. In other words, the Patent Ordinance of 1925 only allowed for and recognised British patents.

Furthermore, the Patent Ordinance of 1925 also excluded patents granted in other countries from registration in Nigeria – a ploy employed to maintain a British monopoly of the Nigerian market.[9] For example, a seminal study by Owen Adekibi on the Nigerian patent system between 1949 to 1970 found that out of the 2,250 patents registered between 1949 to 1970, about 64 per cent were owned by UK citizens or enterprises and the rest by citizens of other countries.[10] This shows bias for patents based in the UK. Furthermore, about 90 per cent of this figure was registered during the decade following Nigeria's independence from Britain in 1960. This scramble for patent protection, according to Adekibi, suggests the 'apprehension of foreigners, mainly British, about the change in government and the possibility of increased competition in the industrial

[3] Patent Ordinance No 17 (1900).

[4] The Northern Protectorate consisted of the North Central, Northeast and Northwest of modern Nigeria.

[5] Gaius Ezejiofor, 'The Law Of Patents In Nigeria: A Review' (1973) 39 *African Legal Studies* 40.

[6] Patent Ordinance No 6 (1925).

[7] Ezejiofor, 'The Law Of Patents In Nigeria' (1973).

[8] Edith Penrose, 'International Patenting And The Less-Developed Countries' (1973) 83 *The Economic Journal* 770.

[9] Owen T Adikibi, 'The Multinational Corporation And Monopoly Of Patents In Nigeria' (1988) 16 *World Development* 512.

[10] ibid 512.

capabilities in the Nigerian market'.[11] Importantly, it shows that the colonial patent regime, which lasted over five decades, was not only created from the perspective and for the benefit of colonial authorities but also for the protection of colonial territorial rights and privileges acquired under a patent granted in the metropolitan country.[12]

An analysis of the Patent Ordinance of 1925 in Nigeria and Act VI of 1856, Act V of 1859, and subsequent laws enacted by the British during the colonial rule in India – which were discussed in the previous chapter – shows their marked similarity. These laws were introduced by Britain and instituted dependent patent regimes in the respective colonies. This is not surprising; neither is it a strictly British endeavour. Colonial metropoles such as France, Belgium and Portugal often applied legal rule from the centre to the colonies. Indeed, the Paris Convention allowed patent laws of the colonial metropolis to regulate issues of patent in the various colonies.[13] The consequence of this is Nigeria's adoption of both the strength and weakness of the English system without regard for prevailing local circumstances such as economic and infrastructural underdevelopment, high poverty and illiteracy rates, and other compelling factors affecting security and otherwise.

The institutionalisation of English patent laws in Nigeria have been critiqued as unnecessary and irrelevant to the local population by many scholars because it did not consider already existing indigenous laws and customs for recognising and rewarding creative inventions. From a TWAIL point of view, it typifies the exploitative nature of colonial patent laws introduced when industrialisation was still at a nascent stage in Nigeria for the exploitation of local resources and market instead of the encouragement of local innovation.[14] This is because patents registered in foreign countries are not taken for the interests of the economy granting the patents or with a view to manufacture there, but with the main objective of protecting an export market from rival manufacturers, particularly those in other parts of the world.

The patent regime in existence at that time, according to commentators, was not based on one of the justifications for patents, which is to reward the inventor for his/her invention, thereby encouraging creativity. Rather, it was put in place for the interest of the imperial powers.[15] Echoing the same sentiment, George Sipa-Adjah Yankey agrees that colonial patent laws were never

[11] ibid 517.

[12] Ezejiofor (n 5).

[13] See GHC Bodenhausen, 'Guide To The Application Of The Paris Convention For The Protection Of Industrial Property, As Revised At Stockholm In 1967' (United International Bureaux for the Protection of Intellectual Property, 1968) 18.

[14] See Okechukwu Timothy Umahi, 'Access To Medicines: The Colonial Impacts On Patent Law Of Nigeria', available at http://papers.ssrn.com/sol3/papers.cfm?abstract_id=1975928 (accessed 15 March 2015).

[15] Adebambo Adewopo, 'Public Health, Access To Medicines And Role Of Patent System In Nigeria' (2011) 1 *NIALS Journal of Intellectual Property Law* 169.

meant to encourage either indigenous innovation, research and development, or effective transfer of technology, but geared instead towards the exploitation and exportation of resources in the colonies.[16] This illustrates the research by Adekibi who found that of the 2,250 patents granted in Nigeria between 1949 to 1970, 67 per cent of patented processes were standardised and widely available, 22 per cent were obsolete, while only 11 per cent were considered worthy for the grant of a patent.[17] In this vein, the system was calculated to benefit British patent owners and exploit the local population. Much of the funds accumulated went into reserve in Britain to serve the metropole's post-war needs.[18]

Further, most of the patents granted were not locally worked or utilised in Nigeria. That is, the patented items were not produced in the patent-granting developing country but were imported. This distorted market forces and enabled foreign patent-holders to charge prices higher than they could expect under more competitive conditions in the absence of patents. This underscored the points put forward by Vaitsos and Penrose that the introduction of a patent regime in a least developed country – which Nigeria was at that time – negates the industrialisation objectives of those countries because the system encourages foreign monopolies.[19] These patents, Penrose specifically notes, did not assist in industrialisation, benefit local industry, encourage foreign investment, nor stimulate local manufacturing by local businessmen. This is because these patents were sought primarily to enhance the monopoly position of the foreign patentees in the local market.[20] As a result, the patent system stifled the growth of indigenous technological capacities and innovation which could have developed through imitation and adaptation.

Looking back, patent law was imposed on Nigeria when the country was at a nascent industrialisation stage. Similar to the Brazilian and Indian experiences, none of the patents granted were exploited by patent-owners or even licensed to local producers. Since it had very few inventions worth patenting in developed countries, the country did not receive the 'expected reciprocal advantages from granting patents to foreigners on inventions worked in those countries'.[21] Consequently, instead of achieving its stated objectives such as contributing to research, development and transfer for technology, the colonial patent regime achieved the contrary. The system instead allowed patent-owners – mostly

[16] George Sipa-Adjah Yankey, 'The Role of International Patent System in the Transfer of Technology to West Africa: Case Studies of Ghana and Nigeria', PhD thesis (University of Warwick, 1987) 106.

[17] Adikibi, 'Monopoly Of Patents In Nigeria' (1988) 517.

[18] Bill Freund, 'Oil Boom And Crisis In Contemporary Nigeria' (1978) 5 *Review of African Political Economy* 91, 92.

[19] See Constantine Vaitsos, 'Patents Revisited: Their Function In Developing Countries' (1972) 9 *The Journal of Development Studies* 71; Penrose, 'International Patenting' (1973) 785.

[20] Penrose (n 8) 785.

[21] ibid.

foreigners – monopoly control of the local market, stifling local development and restricting the transfer of technology as a result.

B. Post-colonial Spectacle

On 1 October 1960, Nigeria obtained its independence from Great Britain. However, it was not until *Rhone-SA Poulenc and May & Baker v Lodeka Pharmacy*[22] – which tested the applicability of colonial patent laws – that the first patent case was heard. In the *Rhone-Poulenc* case, the parties were importers of chemical products and other pharmaceutical preparations. The claimants, Rhone-SA Poulenc and May & Baker, took out a UK patent for *chlorpromazine* in 1951, which they subsequently registered in Nigeria in 1957 under the Patent Ordinance of 1925 as Patent Number 367. In 1964, the Federal Ministry of Health placed a supply order for the patented product *chlorpromazine* under the market name Largactil. The defendant, an indigenous pharmaceutical company called Lodeka Pharmacy, supplied large quantities of the patented product to the Federal Ministry of Health. Additionally, the defendant displayed the drug at a National Trade Fair that same year.

The claimants sued Lodeka Pharmacy, alleging that the latter infringed on their patent by selling, storing and offering for sale the patented product. During trial, the defendant acknowledged the patent right of the claimants, but argued that the importation of the patented product was no infringement as the product was imported under the request of the Federal Ministry of Health on behalf of the Nigerian Government for public use. The defendant relied on Section 46(1) of the UK Patents Act of 1949, which stated that

> notwithstanding anything in this Act, any Government department, and any person authorized in writing by a Government department, may make, use and exercise any patented invention for the service of the Crown in accordance with the provisions of this section.[23]

The judge issued an interim injunction against Lodeka Pharmacy to prevent further infringement pending the determination of the case. In deciding the case, the judge ruled that the patent law did not apply to the Nigerian Government in its totality as the Patent Ordinance of 1925 as well as Section 46 of the UK Patents Act of 1949 do not permit the Nigerian Government to exercise the prerogative of the British Crown.[24] In his ruling, Justice Ikepeazu specifically held that the re-registration law does not permit the Nigerian Government to exercise the Crown prerogative under the Act to supply a patented drug, as the only significant effect the 1949 Act had in Nigeria was in respect of the

[22] (1965) LLR 9.
[23] Umahi, 'Access To Medicines' (n 14) 10–11.
[24] Ezejiofor (n 5).

rights and privileges that ensued from the issuance of a certificate after the registration of a UK patent in Nigeria.[25] Consequently, His Lordship gave judgment in favour of the applicant and issued a permanent injunction against the defendant.

The negative ruling of the *Rhone-Poulenc* case prompted the then federal military Government to repeal the Patent Act of 1925 in 1968 and introduce the Patents (Limitation) Decree of 1968.[26] This new decree allowed the Government to purchase patented pharmaceutical products (under the Government Use clause). Specifically, Section 15 of the Patents (Limitation) Decree empowered the Health Commissioner to authorise any person, including government departments, to purchase, make, use and vend any patented articles for the services of a government agency in the Federation if he was satisfied it is in the public interest to do so.[27] The Decree also exempted the Government from infringement of a patent granted with respect to the articles concerned or the liability to pay royalties or compensation to the patentee.[28] Further, the Decree authorised the Permanent Secretary of the concerned Ministry to give the patentee such information as he pleased concerning the extent of use.[29] Finally, special provision was made for the use of these powers in times of national emergency such as war, for the service of the war and the maintenance of the economy. According to Yankey, the Decree was modelled after the BIRPI[30] Model Law for developing countries[31] because of Nigeria's active participation as the Acting Registrar of Patents in the various proceedings that eventually resulted in the birth of the BIRPI Model Law.[32] The BIRPI Model has often been criticised as unreflective of the specificities of different socio-economic realities and aspirations of developing countries.[33] Thus, it is not surprising that the essence of the policy behind the patent system still remains elusive in the face of a public health and development crisis in Nigeria.[34]

The Patents (Limitation) Decree was a reaction to the *Rhone-Poulenc* case, and was created to essentially limit the powers of the patentee and protect the Government from infringement. It was introduced at a time when Nigeria had no robust national technological or industrial base. In this respect, the law was not enacted to positively encourage domestic inventiveness, support the

[25] Ezejiofor (n 5). See also Umahi (n 14) 10–11; Sodipo, 'Piracy And Counterfeiting' (1995) 46–47.
[26] Patents (Limitation) Decree No 8 (1968).
[27] Patents Limitation Decree, s 15.
[28] Patents Limitation Decree, s 1(3).
[29] Patents Limitation Decree, s 1.
[30] BIRPI stands for *Bureaux Internationaux Reunis pour la Protection de la Propiete Intellectuelle* (United International Bureaux for the Protection of Intellectual Property). It was the predecessor of the WIPO, the global governing body for IP-related issues.
[31] Yankey, 'Case Studies of Ghana and Nigeria' (1987) 213.
[32] ibid.
[33] Ulf Anderfelt, *International Patent-Legislation And Developing Countries* (The Hague, Martinus Nijhoff, 1971) 210.
[34] Umahi (n 14) 6.

local industrial base to harness economic development objectives, or address a particular policy need. This was unlike the situation in Brazil and India where extensive studies were carried out to understand the utility of a patent regime for development. Those studies found that patents not only encouraged monopoly practices but also stunted technological development. It was based on the findings on the impact of patents that the Indian Patent Act of 1972 and Brazil's Law Number 5.772/71 of 1971 – which respectively prohibited the patentability of processes for food, chemical and medicines – were enacted. In both countries, the new patent laws were developed to ensure that patents were more conducive to and worked for national development interests.

This was not the case in Nigeria as the post-independent patent law was a knee-jerk reaction to the decision of the *Rhone-Poulenc* case. It was a serious counter-movement against the strengthening and modernisation of the patent regime to make it favourable to economic development. If anything, it shows an acute lack of understanding of the linkages between law and development and at worst, makes a spectacle of the whole legislative process. This law was not crafted to encourage indigenous inventive activity and continues to be a handicap to various sectors and national development. It is important to note that this was during the first military junta following the 1966 counter-coup that overthrew a civilian government. The military era is known by arbitrary decrees and the flagrant disregard of established legal rules and system. Historical studies of Nigeria's military regime have observed that several socio-economic, political and legal policies implemented during that period had little or no positive impact on the socio-economic development of the country.[35] As will be seen, the lack of evidence-based patent lawmaking (and development policy in general) was insidiously felt a couple of years later when Nigeria could not effectively marshal the windfall of high oil prices to develop an indigenous manufacturing base.

C. Global Struggle

Nigeria was among the Group of Ten countries,[36] led by Brazil and India, that initially opposed the inclusion of IP rules within the global trade framework. The Nigerian delegate at the Brussels Ministerial Meeting, for example, argued

[35] Ajibola A Abdulrahman, 'The Impact Of Military Rule On Nigeria's Nation Building, 1966–1979' (2014) 15 Historical Research Letter; Patrick Oluseun Bamgboye, 'The Military And Socio-Economic Development In Nigeria (1983–1999) A Critical Appraisal' (2014) 5 *Mediterranean Journal of Social Sciences* 2340; Max Siollun, *Nigeria's Military Coup Culture: From Major Nzeogwu To LT-Colonel Dimka (1966–1976)* (New York, Algora Publishing, 2009).

[36] Known as the Group of Ten, these countries were Argentina, Brazil, Cuba, Egypt, India, Nicaragua, Nigeria, Peru, Tanzania and Yugoslavia.

that GATT should confine itself to only trade-related issues and not the regime of protection and enforcement of IPRs as the latter would impose an unbearable burden on the country, stifling its aspirations towards access to technology.[37] Thus, from the beginning, Nigeria saw the whole process of the TRIPS Agreement as an imposition by the developed countries.

As part of the Single Undertaking package, Nigeria signed up to and accepted the TRIPS Agreement when it acceded to the WTO. Being a developing country, Nigeria was given a 10-year transition period to phase into the TRIPS Agreement. However, even though the country was supposed to change its IP laws to be TRIPS-compliant in 2005, it has yet to fully do so. In fact, efforts by several foreign organisations such as the WIPO and the WHO to help the country bring its patent law into compliance with the TRIPS Agreement by 2005 were futile. A WHO official who worked closely on the issue shared that after

> extensive seminars and sensitization classes with both law makers and civil society groups to prepare policymaker for 2005 transition nothing happened as lawmakers were not interested and the civil society groups were simply interested in basic service delivery and access to donor funds.[38]

Currently, there is a Patent and Design (Amendment) Bill on the floor of the Senate at the National Assembly, Nigeria's legislative arm. The Amendment Bill underwent a second reading in March 2018 and, at the time of writing, has been referred to the Committee on Trade and Investment. The (Amendment) Bill, according to a government official who is aware of its content, will be progressive because the West African Health Organization (WAHO)[39] provided the guideline for the drafting of the Bill.[40] The guidelines provide for a harmonised TRIPS Agreement implementation across the Economic Community of West African States (ECOWAS) Member States and strengthen the maximum utilisation of the TRIPS Agreement flexibilities and safeguards. In January 2017, Nigeria notified the WTO of its acceptance of the Protocol Amending the TRIPS Agreement.

Despite not amending its patent law fully in light of its TRIPS Agreement commitments, Nigeria has not yet been subject to full WTO dispute settlement procedures (DSP) or US Section 301 sanctions. The last WTO Trade Policy Review of Nigeria published in 2017 notes not only that the national law on IP remains unchanged, but also that the country has a weak enforcement and

[37] Senas J Ukpanah, 'Statement At The Ministerial Level Meeting In Brussels (MTN.TNC/MIN (90)/ST/34, Multilateral Trade Negotiations, Uruguay Rounds)' (1990).

[38] Fieldwork interview with WHO official (Abuja, October 2014) (transcript on file with author).

[39] The WAHO is the regional Agency of the Economic Community of West African States (ECOWAS) and is charged with the responsibility of safeguarding the health of the peoples in the sub-region. ECOWAS members include Benin, Burkina Faso, Cape Verde, Côte d'Ivoire, The Gambia, Ghana, Guinea, Guinea Bissau, Liberia, Liberia, Mali, Niger, Nigeria, Senegal, Sierra Leone and Togo.

[40] Fieldwork interview, Abuja, November 2014 (transcript on file with author).

management system.[41] Similarly, the 2018 USTR Special 301 Report found the country to have ineffective or inadequate IPR protection systems and is an 'entry point […] into Africa for counterfeit and pirated goods – often threatening health and safety'.[42] This raises the important question of why the country has not undergone DSP. As will be seen, the answer lies in the absence of countervailing forces in the form of a strong pharmaceutical sector to move the country towards compliance. At the time of writing, Nigeria has not yet updated its laws to comply with the TRIPS Agreement even though aspects of its legal regime conform to relevant provisions of the TRIPS Agreement.[43]

III. UNPACKING THE PATENTS AND DESIGNS ACT OF 1990

The patent regime currently in force in Nigeria stems from the Patent Ordinance Decree promulgated by the military after the decision in the *Rhone-Poulenc* case. In 1970, the Patent Ordinance Decree was changed into the Patent Design Act (PDA) of 1970.[44] The PDA was updated in 1990 and is still in force to date.

This section specifically focuses on five areas – patentable subject matters (ie what can and cannot be patented as well as the criterion for patentability), rights granted by the PDA, and flexibilities within the PDA (such as compulsory licence provisions and government use). Focusing on these sections allows for a critique and analysis of the PDA to show how it interacts with laws, institutions and actors in Nigeria. The analysis from this section shows that although flexibilities and safeguards exist in Nigerian patent law, such law can still be exploited for health purposes. The section concludes by arguing that the mantle falls not only on the courts but also on the legislative arm of the Government (House of Assembly) to marshal and approve progressive patent legislation, the civil society to educate the legislators on existing progressive alternatives elsewhere, and the regulatory agencies to enforce the modus operandi of IPRs. At this juncture, it is important to note there exists a new yet-to-be-approved IP Bill[45] pending before the Nigerian House of Assembly, however, the analysis in this section will focus on the current PDA.

[41] World Trade Organization, 'Trade Policy Review: Nigeria' (WTO, 2011) 57–58.

[42] Office of the US Trade Representative, 'The 2018 Special 301 Report' (USTR, 2018) 21, available at www.ustr.gov/sites/default/files/files/Press/Reports/2018%20Special%20301.pdf.

[43] Nigeria has been a member of the Paris Convention since 1963, a member of the WTO since 1995, and a member of the Patent Cooperation Treaty (PCT) since 2005.

[44] 'Patents and Designs Act' (1990), available at www.nigeria-law.org/Patents%20and%20Designs%20Act.htm (PDA).

[45] This Bill – known as *An Act to Provide for the Protection and Administration of Intellectual Property Rights and for Other Related Matters* – provides for the establishment of an Intellectual Property Commission of Nigeria responsible for all matters relating to IPR administration and enforcement, as well as the creation of the Intellectual Property Appeal Board responsible for hearing and determining all IP matters. The Bill also codifies existing diverse legislation regarding the different categories of IP in Nigeria (such as the Copyright Act (2011), Trademarks Act (1990), and

A. Patentable Subject Matters

According to the PDA, an invention is patentable if it falls under two categories: (a) if it is new, results from inventive activity, and is capable of industrial application;[46] and (b) if it constitutes an improvement upon a patented invention.[47] The PDA defines a 'new' invention to be that which does not form part of the state of the art,[48] while an invention is deemed to result from 'inventive activity' when it does not obviously follow from the state of the art, either as to the method, application, combination of methods or product which it concerns, or as to the industrial result it produces.[49] Finally, an invention is capable of industrial application if it 'can be manufactured or used in any kind of industry, including agriculture'.[50] The PDA defines 'state of the art' as everything concerning that art or field of knowledge which has been made available to the public anywhere and at any time through any means (ie a written or oral description, by use, or in any other way).[51]

A close reading of Section 1(1)(b) reveals one of the many lacunae present in the PDA. Section 1(1)(b) could be deemed to refer to utility models or petty patents although there is no specific reference to such in the PDA. According to the WIPO, a petty patent or utility innovation is an 'exclusive right granted for an invention, which allows the right holder to prevent others from commercially using the protected invention, without his authorization, for a limited period of time'.[52] Unlike patents, utility models are much cheaper to obtain, with less stringent requirements and for a shorter term – usually between seven to 10 years. Further, protection for utility models is often sought for innovations of a rather incremental character which may not meet the patentability criteria.[53] In fact, while the requirement of 'novelty' should be met for utility models, the requirement for 'inventive step' or 'non-obviousness' may be much lower or altogether absent. This may lead to evergreening or patent thickets – the latter described as a dense network of overlapping patents that slows down the commercialisation of new inventions.

For an emerging economy like Nigeria with excruciating health burdens, patent application (and IP registration of any kind) should require a stringent examination procedure to prevent abuse of the system and protect public interest. When juxtaposed against the larger goal of harnessing the IP regime for

the PDA into a single document and provides for new legislation regarding utility models, layout designs, and the protection of traditional knowledge and expressions of folklore.

[46] PDA, s 1(1)(a).

[47] PDA, s 1(1)(b).

[48] PDA, s 2(a).

[49] PDA, s 2(b).

[50] PDA, s 2(c).

[51] PDA, s 3.

[52] World Intellectual Property Organization, 'Protecting Innovations by Utility Models', available at www.wipo.int/sme/en/ip_business/utility_models/utility_models.htm.

[53] ibid.

innovation and economic development and considering the fact that there is no examination of either novelty or inventive activity, the PDA creates a loophole that could be exploited at the expense of the country and public interest. As such, any specific or vague reference to utility models in the PDA needs to be excluded.

B. Exceptions to Patentability

Under the PDA, non-patentable inventions include those that contravene public order or morality, plant or animal varieties or biological processes for the production of plants or animals,[54] as well as principles and discoveries of a scientific nature. Unlike the Brazilian[55] and Indian Patent Acts, which include a broad list of non-patentable subject matters, the limited list in the PDA leaves the option open to all sorts of inventions and indeed, interpretations.

Moreover, the inclusion of 'principles and discoveries of scientific nature' raises the pertinent question of whether pharmaceutical products and processes are patentable as there is no guideline on what can be classified as discoveries of scientific nature. This lacuna creates a particular conundrum as pharmaceuticals and petrochemicals are the most patented inventions in Nigeria.[56] According to the Patent Registrar, seven out of 10 patent applications received by the Patent Office are for pharmaceutical products and are mostly filed by foreign applicants.

In fact, this issue of non-patentability of principles and discoveries of nature was raised in the case of *Beijing Cotec New Technology Corp & Churchbell Pharmaceutical v Greenlife Pharmaceuticals Co Ltd & Ors*.[57] Here, the plaintiffs Beijing Cotec New Technology Corp (a foreign company) and Churchbell Pharmaceuticals (its Nigerian affiliate) filed an ex parte injunction and Anton Piller order against the defendant Nigerian company Greenlife Pharmaceuticals. According to the plaintiffs, their patent for *dihydroartemisinin* – an antimalarial drug registered in Nigeria as Patent Number 13566 and sold under the brand name Cotecxin – was infringed upon when Greenlife Pharmaceuticals imported and marketed the patented article without their permission.[58] In this light, the plaintiffs contended that they had the sole right to import, sell and market anti-malaria drugs containing dihydroartemisinin in Nigeria. Subsequent to the

[54] PDA, ss 1(4)(a), 1(4)(b), and 1(5).

[55] While the list of non-patentable matters is not explicitly codified in the Brazilian Patent Act, the Brazilian INPI Guidelines for the Examination of Patent Filings in the areas of Biotechnology and Pharmaceuticals as well as the ANVISA subject matter guideline on what is held patentable in Brazil provide the parameter for patentable objects.

[56] Interview with Patent Official, Commercial Law Department, Ministry of Trade, Commerce and Investment, Abuja, (February 2015) (transcript on file with author).

[57] (2003) FHC/L/CS/718/03 (Federal High Court Lagos Division).

[58] ibid 499.

suit, an action was also brought against the national drug regulatory body, the National Agency for Food and Drug Administration and Control (NAFDAC), whose role is akin to the US Food and Drug Administration for approving the sale of Alaxin, the generic version marketed by Greenlife Pharmaceuticals.

Based on prima facie evidence and the fact that the defendant did not file a counter-affidavit, Justice CPN Senlong ruled that the plaintiffs/applicants were indeed the owners of registered Patent Number 13566 and issued an ex parte order restraining Greenlife Pharmaceuticals and its agents from making, importing or selling Alaxin pending the determination of the Motion of Notice for Interlocutory Injunction.[59]

However, in a later countersuit, Greenlife Pharmaceuticals and its agents applied for a motion to discharge the ex parte order on the ground that Beijing Cotec New Technology Corp and Churchbell Pharmaceuticals concealed, suppressed and misrepresented facts when they applied for the ex parte injunction. They further averred that the alleged patent is not patentable as '*Artemesinin* is a generic compound from which *Dihydroartemsinin* was derived and that even though *Dihydroartemsinin* constitutes an improvement, *Artemisinin* itself is not an invention or a patented invention but *mere principles and discoveries of scientific nature*'.[60]

Furthermore, Greenlife Pharmaceuticals also argued that because *Dihydroartemsinin* is a derivative of *Artemisinin*, it follows that it cannot be patented as the latter forms part of state of the art, having been known and used in China for over 2,000 years.[61] Greenlife Pharmaceuticals also claimed that the specification for *Dihydroartemsinin* did not 'give the description of relevant invention with any appropriate plans and drawings but simply a process of producing a drug called Cotecxin, which according to section 9(1)(b) is not registrable'.[62] As such, the invention did not comply with the appropriate registration procedure under the PDA and therefore should not be granted patent protection.

In deciding the countersuit, Justice Mohammed Shuaibu ruled that even though the patent right does not confer to the plaintiff absolute right, it does confer to the plaintiff some recognisable right that should be protected by the court. However, based on the evidence before the court, which included (a) NAFDAC's prior letter to the plaintiff requesting for letter of patent; (b) an 18-month delay by the plaintiffs in providing the said letter, which shifted the

[59] ibid.
[60] ibid, paras 7(a)–(o) (emphasis added).
[61] ibid.
[62] *Beijing v Greenlife* (n 57) para 37; Section 9(1)(b) stipulates that 'Subject to this section, on the application of any person (including a public officer acting in the exercise of his functions) the court shall declare a patent null and void – (b) if the description of the invention or the claim does not conform with section 3(2) of this Act and section 3(2) states every patent application shall disclose the relevant invention in a manner sufficiently clear and complete for the invention to be put into effect by a person skilled in the art or field of knowledge to which the invention relates; and the claim or claims referred to in subsection (1)(a)(iii) of this section shall define the protection sought and shall not go beyond the limits of the said description.'

balance of convenience to the defendants; and (c) the inability of the plaintiffs to prove that they will suffer irreparable damage, with an order of injunction being the only adequate remedy, Justice Shuaibu vacated the ex parte injunction against Greenlife Pharmaceuticals. The issue of patentability of 'principles and discoveries of scientific nature' was left undecided. In failing to tackle this, the court missed an opportunity to not only clarify the law but also to advance patent jurisprudence in Nigeria.

C. Rights Conferred

The PDA does not allow for substantive examination of a patent application. Unlike in Brazil where ANVISA thoroughly examines a pharmaceutical patent application,[63] and in India where Section 3(d) of the IPA provides the lens through which patents are examined,[64] the PDA allows only for a simple formal examination of applications, ie checking whether required documents are in order.

Specifically, Section 4(1) of the PDA requires the Registrar to examine every patent application as to its conformity with Sections 3(1), (3), and (4), which deal with written declarations showing the name of the application, its specifications and its claims. If the Registrar is satisfied, the patent is then granted 'without further examination'.[65] In fact, Section 4(2) explicitly forbids asking the following questions: (1) 'whether the subject of the application is patentable under section 1',[66] ie if it is new, results from inventive activity and is capable of industrial application; and (2) whether the 'description and claims satisfy the requirements of section 3(2) on claims', ie if the relevant invention is disclosed in a clear and complete way for the invention to be put into effect by a person skilled in the art or field of knowledge[67] and on prior application.[68] Thus, while the PDA stipulates that only new inventions that result from an inventive step and are capable of industrial application, or are improvements from an earlier patented invention, are to be granted patent rights, it does not scrutinise such patent applications to see if they conform to the stated criteria. According to one of the officials at the Patent Office in Abuja, patent registrars do not substantially examine patents as the law does not allow it. The official is 'only mandated to conduct regulatory checks – if the application is in order, if the application form is properly filled out, all the attachments such as the specification claims and PCT documents are clearly and legibly written out'.[69] Once all the required documents are in place, the Registry usually issues patent certificates. According

[63] See ch 4 on Brazil.
[64] See ch 5 on India.
[65] PDA, s 4(2).
[66] PDA, s 4(2)(a).
[67] PDA, s 4(2)(b).
[68] PDA, s 4(2)(c).
[69] Interview with Patent Official (n 56).

to this official, the Patent Office hardly ever rejects an application, and in cases where an application is incomplete, it is kept in view pending the applicant's delivery of the complete document.[70] When probed further on the capacity of the Patent Office to examine patents, the official explained that 'the manpower for patent examination is not something that has been considered yet since Nigerian patent laws do not provide for the substantive examination'.[71]

Of course, there are many problems, especially from a public interest perspective, that could arise due to the lack of substantive examination, such as granting patents to unqualified inventions, ie inventions that are not new, do not result from inventive activity, and are incapable of industrial application. This is especially pertinent considering the various health crises in the country such as malaria, HIV/AIDS and tuberculosis, to mention a few. However, some legal practitioners contend that the registration system for patents is suitable for Nigeria where there is a dearth of expert patent examiners and limited resources for the due diligence required in conducting substantive examinations.[72] Therefore, the registration system not only saves government funds but also reduces long delays usually prevalent in jurisdictions that allow for substantive examination. While it may be argued in some cases that substantive examination leads to delays, Nigeria does not have a high volume of patent applications compared to those in other emerging economies like Brazil, China or India. In fact, data collected from the Nigerian Patent Registry shows that the country receives less than 1,000 patent applications in a year (see Tables 6.1 and 6.2). The total pendency time for the grant of patents in Nigeria is two to three months, according to the Nigerian Patent Official interviewed.[73] This voids the argument regarding undue delays and volumes in relation to Nigeria.

Table 6.1 Patent applications in Nigeria, 2000–2018 (including pharmaceuticals, chemicals, petrochemicals, utility models, etc)

Year	Indigenous applicants	Foreign applicants	Total
2000	40	403	443
2001	31	472	503
2002	35	461	496
2003	60	454	514
2004	74	448	522
2005	81	297	378
2006	98	248	346

(continued)

[70] ibid.

[71] ibid.

[72] Allen and Ogunkeye cited in Onyeka Uche Ofili, *Intellectual Property Rights Protection And Economic Development: The Case Of Nigeria*, 1st edn (Archamps, European Scientific Institute, 2014), available at www.eujournal.org/files/journals/1/books/OnyekaUcheOfili.pdf.

[73] Interview with Patent Official (n 56).

Table 6.1 *(Continued)*

Year	Indigenous applicants	Foreign applicants	Total
2007	93	562	655
2008	92	711	803
2009	83	631	714
2010	75	855	930
2011	64	747	811
2012	42	676	718
2013	50	869	919
2014	150	810	960
2015	410	930	1340
2016	200	686	886
2017	200	552	752
2018	300	459	759

Table 6.2 Data on pharmaceutical patents granted, 2000–2018

Year	Indigenous applicants	Foreign applicants	Total
2000	0	2	2
2001	0	9	9
2002	0	12	12
2003	2	12	14
2004	3	5	8
2005	5	9	14
2006	3	9	12
2007	1	8	9
2008	0	17	17
2009	2	21	23
2010	0	22	22
2011	1	18	19
2012	1	15	16
2013	0	12	12
2014	3	10	13
2015	4	9	13
2016	3	13	15
2017	5	14	19
2018	4	11	15

Where a patent is granted, the PDA accords patent rights solely to a statutory inventor,[74] defined as 'the person who, whether or not he is the true inventor, is the first to file, or validly to claim a foreign priority for, a patent application in respect of the invention'.[75] However, in situations where the statutory inventor is not the true inventor, ie when the primary inventor licences the right to a third party for furtherance of research, Section 2(2) allows for the primary inventor to be named in the application.

The PDA allows for protection for 20 years from date of filing, provided that annual fees are duly paid,[76] although a six-month grace period is given in situations of late payment. Once a patent is granted, Section 6 of the PDA accords the patentee the right to preclude any other person from making, importing, selling or using the product, or stocking it for the purpose of sale or use.[77] The same applies where the patent has been granted in respect of a process.[78]

The High Court exercises jurisdiction to the exclusion of any other court on matters of infringement.[79] While there is no explicit clause allowing for post-grant opposition, patent rights can still be challenged once granted. Section 4(4) of the PDA specifically stipulates that 'patents are granted at the risk of the patentee and without guarantee of their validity'.[80] In this view, the courts do not recognise a presumption of validity for issued patents. This means that an ownership of a patent in Nigeria does not mean that the patent is valid, and when the validity of the patent is challenged, the onus is on the patentee to prove such validity.

While a patent application can be filed only for one invention, it may include, in connection with that invention, claims 'for any number of products or for any number of manufacturing processes for those products, and for any number of applications of those products'.[81] In addition, an application may include claims for 'any number of processes, and for the means of working those processes, for the resulting product or products and for the application of those products'.[82] While claims infringement lawsuits (or even patent cases, for that matter) are neither prominent nor popular in Nigeria, two cases in recent past are worth

[74] PDA, s 2(1).
[75] PDA, s 2(1).
[76] PDA, ss 7(1) and (2).
[77] PDA, s 6(1)(a).
[78] PDA, s 6(1)(b).
[79] PDA, s 26(1); also according to s 251(1)(f) of the 1999 Constitution of the Federal Republic of Nigeria, the High Court has and exercises jurisdiction to the exclusion of any other courts in civil causes and matters, which include any federal enactment relating to copyrights, patents, designs, trademarks and passing-off, industrial designs and merchandise marks, business names, commercial and industrial monopolies, combines and trusts, standards of goods and commodities, and industrial standards.
[80] PDA, s 4(4).
[81] PDA, s 3(a).
[82] PDA, s 3(b).

noting. The first case, *Pfizer Incorporated v Polyking Pharmaceutical Limited and Anor*,[83] highlights the question of claims where the defendants question the validity of a plaintiff's patent right since it registered for patent on the product and not the process. In this case, plaintiff/applicant Pfizer sued the defendants for infringing on its Patent Number RP 9708, which covers the chemical compound with the generic name *Piroxicam*. *Piroxicam* is used in treating fever, pain and inflammation in the body. According to Pfizer, the defendants were importing, selling and stocking for sale the patented article under the generic name Rossiden without its permission. Consequently, Pfizer sought for an ex parte injunction and Anton Piller order against the class sued[84] until the court further orders.

In its defence, Polyking Pharmaceuticals asserted that the patent in question is null and void as the specification claim used by Pfizer in its Nigerian patent application is derived from its UK patent application, and thus does not represent specification claim under Nigerian law. Further, the defendant averred that Patent Number RP 9708 held by Pfizer has not been infringed upon because, according to Nigerian law, one can either claim for a *product* patent or a *process* patent. Explicating on this, the defendant argued that the process used in the manufacturing of *Piroxicam* is not the same as the process used in manufacturing the Rossiden capsules. Therefore, since Pfizer registered a claim for the product Patent Number RP 9708 and not the process patent, its patent has not been infringed upon in the importation and sale of the Rossiden capsules as the manufacture of the latter, even though it contains the said patented article, was arrived at using a different process.

Pfizer countered that the assertion that one can only claim for either a *product* patent or a *process* patent but not for both is erroneous. The PDA allows for an application to be made for only one invention, thus a patentee can – in connection with that invention – include claims for any number of products or manufacturing processes for those products, and for any number of applications of those products.[85] Moreover, with the onus of proving the validity of the patent, the plaintiff called an expert witness who disagreed with the view of the defendant and averred that 'regardless of the possibility of producing any chemical product by different processes, so long as the products of different processes were the same compound, they cannot differ in potency'.[86]

Finding for the plaintiff, the judge ruled that the Rossiden capsules stocked and sold by the defendants is the same organic compound contained in the plaintiff's patent and as such, the defendants have infringed the plaintiff's Patent Number RP 9708.

[83] (1992) FHC/L/CS/178/1992 (Federal High Court, Lagos Division).
[84] ibid, paras 6–12.
[85] PDA, s 3(a).
[86] (1992) FHC/L/CS/178/1992 (Federal High Court, Lagos Division).

Another case of patent infringement in which the court found the patent to be valid and infringed upon is that of *Pfizer Limited v Tyonex Nigeria Limited and Ebamic Pharmacy Limited*.[87] In this case, Pfizer filed an injunction against two pharmaceutical companies, Tyonex Nigeria Limited and Ebamic Pharmacy Limited, for importing, stocking and selling in Nigeria a generic version of Norvasc (the generic name is *Amlovas*), which contained the patented article amlodipine besylate and was used in treating hypertension. According to Pfizer, the active ingredient contained in Amlovas was amlodipine besylate, which was invented by Pfizer and patented in Nigeria under Patent Number RP 9970. In deciding the case, the judge ruled that the defendants infringed on Pfizer's patent by importing, stocking and selling an item containing a patented product without the permission of the right-holder. The court subsequently granted an injunction and awarded damages in favour of Pfizer.

D. Compulsory Licence

Section I of the First Schedule to the PDA allows for the grant of a CL and defines the conditions for its use in Nigeria. The PDA allows for the grant of two classes of CLs: (a) court-sanctioned CL (ie a judicial order); and (b) minister-sanctioned CL.

i. Court-sanctioned Order

A court can issue an order for CL at any time after the expiration of a period of four years after the filing of a patent application or three years after the grant of a patent. An application for a CL through the courts is allowed in four instances: (a) when 'the patented invention, being capable of being worked in Nigeria, has not been so worked';[88] (b) when the working of the patented invention does not reasonably meet the demand for the product;[89] (c) the refusal of the patentee to grant licences on reasonable terms or the grant of a licence that unfairly and substantially prejudices the establishment or development of industrial or commercial activities in Nigeria;[90] and (d) if an invention protected by a patent in Nigeria cannot be worked without infringing rights derived from a patent granted on an earlier application or benefiting from an earlier foreign priority. In the case of the latter, a CL may be granted to the patentee of the later patent to the extent necessary for the working of his invention.[91]

[87] (2010) CA/L/25/08 (Court of Appeal (Lagos Division)).
[88] PDA, First Schedule, s 1(a).
[89] PDA, s 1(b).
[90] PDA, s 1(c).
[91] PDA, s 2.

In applying for a CL, the applicant should prove to the court that he has attempted to obtain a contractual licence from the patentee within a reasonable time and under reasonable terms but has been unable to do so.[92] In addition, he should guarantee to the court to work the relevant invention sufficiently to remedy the deficiencies that gave rise to his application.[93] However, a CL will not be granted if the patentee satisfies the court that his actions in relation to the patented invention are justifiable in the circumstances and not merely shows that the patented article is freely available for importation.[94] A CL is transferable with the consent of the court[95] and the court can cancel a CL if the licensee fails to comply with the terms or conditions of the licence.[96] The court may also vary the terms of the CL if new facts justify such variation or if the patentee has granted contractual licences on more favourable terms.[97]

The court-sanctioned CL raises various points of possible contention. First, the local working requirement of the PDA highlights germane questions of compatibility with the TRIPS Agreement. Section 14 of the First Schedule of the PDA explains 'working of patented invention' to mean either 'the manufacture of a patented article',[98] 'the application of a patented process',[99] or 'the use in manufacture of a patented machine by an effective and serious establishment existing in Nigeria on a scale which is adequate and reasonable in the circumstances'.[100] Importantly, Section 6 explicitly forbids the importation of a patented article in the utilisation of a CL.

On the other hand, Article 27(1) of the TRIPS Agreement requires patents to be 'available and patent rights enjoyable without discrimination as to the place of invention, the field of technology and whether products are imported or locally produced'.[101] Of course, it could be argued that local working that requires manufacturing in the locality of the patent protection fulfils the ethos of Article 7, which requires IP protection to contribute to the promotion of technological innovation, transfer, and dissemination of technology, to the mutual advantage of producers and users of technological knowledge and in a manner conducive to social and economic welfare, and to a balance of rights and obligations.[102] In this vein, all three requirements of Article 7 – technological innovation, transfer and dissemination of technology and use of technological knowledge – fit into the justification of local working. Nevertheless, the position

[92] PDA, s 5.
[93] PDA.
[94] PDA, First Schedule, s 4.
[95] PDA, s 7.
[96] PDA, s 9.
[97] PDA, s 10.
[98] PDA, s 14(a).
[99] PDA, s 14(b).
[100] PDA, s 14(c).
[101] TRIPS Agreement, Art 27.
[102] TRIPS Agreement, Art 7.

of the WTO Dispute Settlement Body on the issue of local working remains unclear, as it is yet to interpret this important provision which will be significant for future strategies of national governments and pharmaceutical companies.

Another possible point of contention is the fact the PDA does not define what would amount to 'reasonable terms' or 'reasonable time' in the context of which a CL should be granted by the patentee to a third party. However, it has been argued that the incidence of reasonability in all cases would have to be determined by the courts in all circumstances, and each case has to be determined on its own merits.[103] Nevertheless, the fact that the courts need to approve CL applications can itself be confusing, time-consuming and prone to undue delays. With Nigerian courts known to be slow and bureaucratic, this judicial provision clearly favours transnational corporations who are majority patent-holders over local producers or the public interest. Moreover, the prerogative of the patentee to approach the court to establish his actions in relation to the patent are justifiable could give rise to the withholding of a CL if the patent holder presents legitimate reasons.

ii. Minister-sanctioned Order

Section 13 of the First Schedule allows a minister, by order in the *Federal Gazette*, to approve a CL for certain patented products and processes declared by the order to be of vital importance for defence, economic or public health purposes.[104] Within this context, a CL can be sanctioned before the expiration of the period mentioned in Section 1 of the First Schedule, ie before the expiration of the four-year period after the filing of a patent application or the three-year period after the grant of a patent while importation is also permitted. A CL under this instance falls within the ambit of public health purposes of the Doha Declaration. According to Adewopo, a Minister-sanctioned CL is a practical justification for the supply of drugs by way of production, importation, or necessary measures to procure supplies of drugs and other treatment during dire times without weakening or undermining the patents on those medicines.[105] The Government of Nigeria, through the minister, is yet to issue a CL for health purposes despite the various health epidemics experienced in Nigeria in recent times, such as the polio and meningitis outbreaks and the current HIV/AIDS crisis. As will be discussed below, factors such as the absence of a patent regime framework, and the strong influence of donor presence in the delivery of medicines explains why this this clause has not been invoked by the state.

[103] Templars Law Firm, 'Patentability Under The Nigerian Patents And Designs Act (PDA): An Introductory Analysis' (2012), available at www.templars-law.com/wp-content/uploads/2015/05/Patentability-Under-the-Nigerian-Patent-Act.pdf (accessed 4 March 2015).

[104] PDA, First Schedule, s 13.

[105] Adewopo, 'Public Health' (2011) 177.

E. Government Use

Section 20 of the PDA allows a minister, who is satisfied that it is in the public interest to do so, to authorise any person to purchase, make, exercise or vend any patented article or invention for the service of a government agency in the Federal Republic.[106] This ministerial authorisation may be exercised before or after the relevant patent has been granted and to any person, whether or not he is authorised directly or indirectly by the patentee to make, use, exercise or vend the relevant article or invention.[107] The PDA defines a 'minister' to mean a Minister of the Federation, including a State Commissioner, and exempts him as well as any person authorised by the Government from liability for the infringement of any patent relating to the relevant article or invention, and from liability to make any payment to the patentee by way of royalty or otherwise.[108] Although the TRIPS Agreement does not specifically refer to government use of patents, it recognises such use in its references to the concept of public non-commercial use and of patents 'used by or for the government'.[109] The 'government use' clause has only been invoked once, when the Federal Ministry of Health placed a supply order for the patented product chlorpromazine in 1964. This led to the first patent case in Nigeria – the *Rhone-Poulenc* case.

Government use as specified in the PDA is prone to misuse in many ways. It does not, for instance, define nor provide a guideline on what would amount to an exercise 'in the public interest'. Moreover, the definition for 'minister' is too broad and poses a problem of consistency. Although the PDA technically allows a State Commissioner to invoke government use of patented article, in reality, a State Commissioner does not have the power to do so as patents and designs are under the Exclusive Legislative List. The Exclusive Legislative List deals with specific items which only the National Assembly has the sole prerogative to legislate on, to the exclusion of the state and local governments. Thus, it is only the Minister of Health, with explicit approval from the National Assembly, who can invoke the government use clause. Also, the PDA gives the minister the choice of whether or not to inform the patent-holder of the government use of the patented object 'if it is clear to the Minister such information is not contrary to the public interest to do so'.[110] This is in fact incompatible with the TRIPS Agreement, which mandates the Government or contractor to inform the right-holder.[111]

Finally, even if the PDA allows for the grant of a CL in Nigeria, it may not work because the country currently does not have the manufacturing capability to engage in such, as will be discussed below. Nevertheless, it should be included under safeguards for future use.

[106] PDA, First Schedule, s 16.
[107] PDA, First Schedule, s 16.
[108] PDA, First Schedule, s 17.
[109] TRIPS Agreement, Art 31(b).
[110] PDA, First Schedule, s 18.
[111] TRIPS Agreement, Art 31(b).

In sum, although the PDA incorporates certain aspects of the TRIPS Agreement, it is still lacking in key respects, particularly on patentable subject matters as well as relevant TRIPS Agreement flexibilities to ensure maximum health safeguards. For example, both the Bolar exceptions and parallel importing are not included in the PDA. Bolar exceptions allow a company (usually generic) to conduct research on a patented drug in order to have it ready for the market as soon as the patented drug version goes off patent. Due to the long-term nature of pharmaceutical research, Bolar exceptions ensure that the generic drug is available immediately after the expiration of patent.

Parallel importing, on the other hand, allows a country to 'shop around' for the lowest price of the same product wherever it may be distributed. This is based on the principle that one's patent right is exhausted once the patented invention is released into the market. The TRIPS Agreement allows for national, regional and global parallel importation. Inclusion of these flexibilities is also in line with the Doha Declaration, which recognises the gravity of the public health problems afflicting many developing and least developed countries and therefore recommends the implementation of the TRIPS Agreement in a 'manner supportive of WTO members' right to protect public health and, in particular, to promote access to medicines for all'.[112] However, the high incidence of counterfeit drugs in Nigeria could prevent the use of this clause. According to the NAFDAC, 48 per cent of drugs available in Nigeria are fake or below standard.[113] Therefore, in the case of Nigeria, parallel importation may not be advisable for the sake of public safety, as the country does not have a good record of careful supervision and storage by government authorities.

Nevertheless, it could be argued that the language of the PDA shows that the Nigerian state understands and is aware of the patent regime. However, as the next section shows, there is a disconnect in the extent to which this awareness is employed in policy framework and for what purpose.

IV. STATE REGULATORY AGENCIES AND PATENT REGIME

This section attempts to capture the attitude of the Nigerian state towards patents by reflecting on the 'official' use of patents provided in the PDA as an effective mechanism for achieving the cardinal goals of public health care and economic development. By 'official', the research refers to state actors created to deal with patents or those whose oversight duties interfaces with the patent regime. The focus here is how the language of patent is employed and deployed

[112] 'Implementation Of Paragraph 6 Of The Doha Declaration On The TRIPS Agreement And Public Health' (2001), para 4, available at www.wto.org/english/tratop_e/trips_e/implem_para6_e.htm (Doha Declaration).

[113] Dora Akunyili, 'Counterfeit And Substandard Drugs, Nigeria's Experience: Implications, Challenges, Actions And Recommendations' (Washington DC, World Bank, 2005).

by governmental bodies in the monitoring, approval and audit of pharmaceutical-related and industrial development in Nigeria. Thus, the notion of how ideas circulate among these actors and the manner in which particular policy options are crafted – and, as an extension, how others are extinguished – is explored.

Over the years, Nigerian policy-makers at the federal and state levels have created various regulatory and monitoring agencies concerning all activities in relation to manufacturing and technology transfer. The agencies whose work intersect on the issue of patents for development purposes are NOTAP and NAFDAC. These agencies ensure the establishment of co-ordination mechanisms among various agencies to improve detection, investigation and prosecution of cases of counterfeit medical products and the commercialisation of technology transfer, respectively. In looking into the circulation of ideas, the book has found that there is little understanding of the patent regime within these agencies in terms of its relationship to their mandate. Thus, despite the content of the PDA, patents are of limited impact in development frameworks.

NOTAP was initially created as the National Office of Industrial Promotion by Decree 70 of 1979. Its current acronym was introduced in 1992 by virtue of Decree 82 of 1992.[114] NOTAP is tasked with the acquisition, promotion and development of technology, as well as the commercialisation of foreign technology brought into the country.[115] Within this remit, NOTAP assists in the patenting of all inventions and innovations carried out by government-funded research institutes and others in the private sector. The agency is tasked with commercialising all R&D results and inventions brought into the country by liaising with local research institutes for the adaptation of such imported technology, promoting locally generated technologies in the process.[116] Furthermore, NOTAP helps inventors by linking them with patent offices worldwide and by assisting the inventor in drafting patent applications. However, in reality, the commercialisation of such processes is non-existent. As stated by a NOTAP official,

> the Agency is not notified of most of the technology that come into this country because most government ministries work in silos and are disorganised. The effect is that the Agency is unaware of the inflow of technology into the country, and therefore, cannot facilitate technology registration and commercialisation in the country.[117]

This suggests that although NOTAP is aware of its regulatory role and has the capacity to fulfil its functions, institutional bottlenecks prevent it from doing so. In many occasions, foreigners seeking to commercialise their technology in Nigeria are put off by the contract terms, which require the sharing of technological information with NOTAP.[118] In other instances, contractual agreements

[114] Kristin Peterson and Olatubosun Obileye, 'Access To Drugs For HIV/AIDS And Related Opportunistic Infections In Nigeria' (US Agency for International Development, 2002) 45.

[115] Fieldwork interview with NOTAP Official (Abuja, 2015) (transcript on file with author).

[116] ibid.

[117] ibid.

[118] ibid

between the Nigerian Government and foreign entities are usually unfavourable to the country, which further hinders the transfer of technology.

Besides the issue of non-notification of foreign technology, the communication between government ministries responsible for patent issuance is generally almost non-existent. For example, the patent registry is located in the Ministry of Trade and Investment, which deals with foreign trade, investment and all other commercial activities. On the other hand, NOTAP, which deals with patent registration and technology transfer, is located in the Ministry of Science and Technology. Also, the WTO Department is under the Trade Department at the Ministry of Trade and Investment while the patent registry is under the Commercial Law Department, which is under the Legal Department. This has created mission confusion and creep, leading to a tug of power between the various departments, where each feels threatened by the other and any interaction is seen as an intrusion into the other's turf.[119] This sentiment is echoed by other interviewees at the Ministry of Trade.[120] This has led to the lack of synergy and fragmentation of IPR administration under different agencies, departments and ministries, which has not worked effectively for the development of IP.[121]

Another important player to take into consideration is NAFDAC, which was created to tackle the issue of fake and pirated drugs. Pirated products began to emerge in the Nigerian market in the early 1980s due to the oil bust, affecting government expenditure and causing the scarcity of essential goods. In response, the Government decided to award import licences, although these licences were awarded on the basis of political patronage. Many people who were unqualified to import drugs started importing drugs and flooding the market with substandard and counterfeit drugs.

The situation was further exacerbated by the implementation of the SAPs (discussed below), which mandated an end to government-subsidised health programmes. Because the state was massively downsized, regulatory bodies were incapacitated to do the work of the law.[122] Thus, Nigeria had become a dumping ground for fake and counterfeit medicines by the early 1990s. For instance, 109 children died in 1990 after ingesting paracetamol syrup that contained toxic diethylene glycol solvent instead of propylene glycol.[123] In 1995, Nigeria donated

[119] Fieldwork interview with Official 1 at the WTO Department, Ministry of Trade and Investment (Abuja, 2014) (transcript on file with author).

[120] Fieldwork interview with official at the Commercial Law Department (Abuja, 2014) (transcript on file with author); Fieldwork interview with Official 2 at the WTO Department, Ministry of Trade and Investment (Abuja, 2014) (transcript on file with author).

[121] Adebambo Adewopo, 'According To Intellectual Property: A Pro-Development Vision Of The Law And The Nigerian Intellectual Property Law And Policy Reform In The Knowledge Era' (Nigerian Institute of Advanced Legal Studies (Lagos) 5th Inaugural Lecture, 2012) 66.

[122] Kristin Peterson, 'Intellectual Property Designs: Drugs, Governance, And Nigerian (Non-) Compliance With The World Trade Organization' in P Geissler, R Rottenburg and J Zenker (eds), *Rethinking Biomedicine and Governance in Africa: Contributions from Anthropology*, 1st edn (Bielefeld, Transcript Verlag, 2012) 143.

[123] Akunyili, 'Counterfeit And Substandard Drugs' (2005).

88,000 doses of meningitis vaccine to its neighbour Niger, but before the authorities realised that these vaccines were fake, about 60,000 people had already been 'inoculated'.[124] These incidents prompted the Government to create a regulatory agency tasked with ensuring the safety of food and drugs in Nigeria.

Created in 1993, NAFDAC is responsible for the regulation and control of the importation, exportation, manufacture, advertisement, distribution, sale, and use of food and drugs.[125] In addition to this, the agency also conducts appropriate tests to ensure that the quality of these items is up to the standard specified and approved by the Governing Council. It also investigates production premises, investigates imported drugs and compiles standard specification guidelines for the production, importation, exportation, sale and distribution of drugs.

The duties of NAFDAC place it in the role of ensuring effective and efficacious medicines in Nigeria. Specifically, the fact that it should also approve the importation and distribution of medicines means that it engages with patents one way or the other. In fact, the *Beijing Cotec New Technology Corp & Churchbell Pharmaceutical v Greenlife Pharmaceuticals* case discussed above is a pertinent example of how this was applied. However, there is no mention of patents in the NAFDAC Act. An interview with a NAFDAC official is even more revealing. According to him, while

> NAFDAC understands patent as something required to protect an intellectual work, however, it is not considered in the Agency's line of work. Rather, [the Agency's] focus is on counterfeit and fake drugs, not patents and to protect Nigerians from fake, substandard and counterfeit drugs.[126]

This legal indeterminacy creates a system where contradiction and incoherence thrive. Instead of a single cohesive strategy and an effective enforcement mechanism, an arbitrary system is created where even authoritative regulatory agencies permit conflicting outcomes with devastating consequences.

V. PATENT LAW-MAKING AND NIGERIAN PHARMACEUTICAL MANUFACTURING SECTOR

Despite the size of the sector, currently estimated at USD 1.28[127] billion and anticipated to more than double to USD 1.3 trillion by 2020,[128] there appears to

[124] Abiodun Raufu, 'Nigeria Leads Fight Against "Killer" Counterfeit Drugs' (2006), available at www.who.int/bulletin/volumes/84/9/06-020906/en (accessed 7 February 2016).

[125] 'National Agency for Food and Drug Administration and Control Act' (Federal Government of Nigeria, 1993), available at www.nafdac.gov.ng/wp-content/uploads/Publications/Laws/NAFDAC-Act.pdf.

[126] Fieldwork interview with NAFDAC Official (Abuja, 2015) (transcript on file with author).

[127] Frank Gumel, 'Investment Opportunities In The Pharmaceutical Sector – Nigeria/Pakistan' (PwC, 2014) 16.

[128] Pharmaceutical Manufacturers Group of Manufacturers Association of Nigeria (PMG-MAN) Nigeria Pharma Expo 2015, 'West Africa Pharma Market Biggest Show Nigeria Pharma

be an ongoing deficiency in the pharmaceutical manufacturing sector's engagement with patent law as it plays a different role in Nigeria than it does in either Brazil or India. This is because there are very few original researches being carried out by companies in Nigeria to warrant monopoly protection provided by patents. Of the five pharmaceutical company executives interviewed for this book (coming from three local firms and two foreign affiliates), none of their companies conduct original pharmaceutical research and development of drugs. The industry, according to these executives, does not need patents to operate because monopoly and market protection guaranteed by patent is not important in what they do. For instance, according to Ms Y Ali, who works for a foreign affiliated company, [the company] in Nigeria 'has not produced any new chemical entity that requires the company to apply for patent because it does not engage in original research and development of new drugs'.[129] Even though the parent company abroad has registered a patent in Nigeria, the patented molecule was discovered and produced outside Nigeria even though [the company] had to undertake clinical trials when the chemical entity was introduced to the Nigerian market.[130] The interviewee further added that in spite of the patent registration, the products still get copied within two to three years. Patent are not respected here.[131]

Commenting on this, Mr A Okeke explained the situation:

> [The company] does not engage in any original research and development of drugs here in Nigeria. These countries you mentioned [India and Brazil] have the structural facilities like electricity, the infrastructure and even educated population that can undertake such intensive research. We don't have such in Nigeria. We only do basic packaging and formulation of elementary items like vitamins, analgesics and paracetamol. Just basic items, nothing innovative. Nothing is manufactured locally here. That is why patent is not our focus. We have nothing to protect, really.[132]

Similarly, another pharmaceutical company executive commented further:

> The situation is different in Nigeria in that every single pharmaceutical company currently operating in the country, both foreign and local, are not doing any substantive research. We are not developing new drugs; we are not even in the process of developing new drugs. It is very expensive to engage in such here. The pharmaceutical companies here are involved in tertiary manufacturing – the manufacturing of

Manufacturers Expo 2015 Is Set To Display Above 200 Exhibitors From 11 Countries & More Than 4,000 Products / Services On Pharma Manufacturing Technologies For Central & West African Pharma Markets', available at www.nigeriapharmaexpo.com/press_release.html.

[129] Fieldwork interview with Y Ali, Pharmaceutical Company A, (Lagos, July 2016) (transcript on file with author).

[130] ibid.

[131] ibid.

[132] Fieldwork interview with A Okeke, Pharmaceutical Company B (Lagos, July 2016) (transcript on file with author).

> finished goods without any research input. We make basic items that do not require patents. We are not into original research and development yet.[133]

Similarly, an interviewee from the PMG-MAN, an umbrella organisation for manufacturers of pharmaceuticals and allied products in Nigeria, concurred. According to him, the organisation does not engage with Nigerian policy-makers on patent issues as the group is more concerned with ensuring government assistance. He clarified:

> Patents are not our focus right now. Maybe they will be in the future but not currently. We are instead engaging with the government on other issues. We are engaging the Executive who gives out the contract for drug procurement. We are also engaging with the Legislature who will put it in the law that [drug] companies need to be encouraged if they are making efforts to produce locally and the quality is top notch. So, we are pushing hard in both directions and we asking both the Executive and the Legislature to patronise local drug manufacturers. So, we are working hard to make sure jobs stay in Nigeria; we are also working hard to make sure that Nigerian medicines are of the highest international quality. This is why we are not focusing on patents.[134]

In this context, the sector does not need to engage with in the patent discourse either to theorise its interests, build alliances or mobilise government support. Consequently, the ongoing legal innovations and contestations found in local spaces in Brazil and India are non-existent in Nigeria because the patent regime – as a legal phenomenon, a constructed knowledge and a policy tool – is largely seen as irrelevant and inapplicable.

The Nigerian situation echoes the principles of nodal governance, which emphasises the role of nodes in governance especially in the way nodal networks link up to create concentrations of power for purposes of exercising governance. For nodes to be able to influence governance, they should have three essential characteristics:

(1) A node should have a way of thinking (mentalities) that cognitively shapes how individuals and organisations see the world and act accordingly, technologies for applying and exercising influence over the course of events at issue, resources to support and mobilise the operation of the node and fuel its influence, and the existence of institutions that enable the directed mobilisation of resources, mentalities and technologies over time.[135] How then does the nodal governance theory apply to Nigerian pharmaceutical actors?

[133] Fieldwork interview with M A Pharmaceutical Company C (Ogun State, July 2016) (transcript on file with author).

[134] Fieldwork interview with interviewee from PMG-MAN (Lagos, July 2016) (transcript on file with author).

[135] Jennifer Wood and Clifford D Shearing, *Imagining Security* (Cullompton, Willan, 2007) 26; Scott Burris, Peter Drahos and Clifford Shearing, 'Nodal Governance' (2005) 30 *Australian Journal of Legal Philosophy* 12.

Going by the interview excerpts, the pharmaceutical actors in Nigeria do not have the mentality, ie the attitude towards and engagement with patent law. They do not see patents as valuable because they are not engaging in original research that deserves monopoly protection. Due to this lack of engagement, there is no need to seek state compliance on patent issues. While they do have technologies for applying and exercising influence as well as resources to fuel mobilisation because of the size of the sector, the institution (effective patent regime) does not exist. This ties back to the law in place as well as the ability of state institutions to enforce protection, ie prevent copying. Since the patent regime is predicated on the development of innovative products, it means that the patent regime will also be absent in contexts where development of innovative drugs is absent. Conversely, since the country lacks widespread patent infrastructure, industry actors cannot challenge and/or influence the conceptualisation of patent into law and policy.

This is in stark contrast to Brazil and India which have large generic manufacturing sectors with the technological capabilities to not only reproduce patented drugs, but to also undertake original research and development of new drugs. In those jurisdictions, both the brand name and generic companies have a vested interest in an effective and enforceable patent regime. In other words, because the drug companies in those countries have the ability to undertake the development of new pharmaceutical entities, they are able to activate their nodal networks to mobilise government compliance on patent regimes because the existence and enforcement of such a regime ensures market-segmented monopoly that allows them to recoup the financial expenses associated with pharmaceutical research. It also explains why foreign MNCs adopt various tactics to restrict competition from Indian generics either through legal tie-ins of VLs or outright purchase of generic competitors. This is because for brand name companies, indigenous drug manufactures pose a considerable threat due to their capacity to formulate and manufacture more advanced patented drugs, thereby reducing their market profit. It is the existence of a fair market structure in Brazil and India in the form of a strong generic industry as well as the ability of patent law to affect monopoly and market access which explain the strong use of patent language in policy and legal decisions and in public debates.

Investigating the extent of the engagement of Nigerian drug manufacturers with patent law raises the question of why there is no original research being undertaken in the sector. What are the issues that prevent the sector from developing the technical and technological capacity required for pharmaceuticals, and consequently improve sectoral participation in patent discourse? Key events and policies such as the Indigenisation Decree, ISI policy and the SAPs can be pinpointed as the factors that eviscerated the pharmaceutical manufacturing companies by weakening critical infrastructure, creating an unhealthy environment both for business development as well as for the brain power required by the sector to undertake important research. In turn, these factors weakened the pharmaceutical manufacturing sector from growing, developing necessary research and development infrastructure to engage in domestic inventiveness and, to a larger extent, patent law-making.

Since Nigeria became independent in 1960, achieving economic development through rapid industrialisation has remained a major challenge. Nigeria started exporting oil in 1957, however, it was the oil boom of the 1970s due to the two price hikes orchestrated by the Organization of Petroleum Exporting Countries in 1973–74 and 1979–80 that triggered a substantial windfall for the country and resulted in a large transfer of wealth to the state's coffers.[136] In the wake of the oil boom, the country suddenly became wealthy, completely restructuring the economy from agrarian-based to oil-exporting. This sudden large increase in income subsequently led to a general decline of national production in other sectors – or what is known as Dutch Disease – which had serious repercussions on important segments of the country's economy. For example, the oil sector accounted for less than three per cent of GDP and a modest USD 370 million in exports in 1969, but by 1980, the oil sector had come to account for nearly 30 per cent of GDP and oil exports totalled USD 25 billion.[137] It also accounted for 90 per cent of foreign exchange earnings and 70 per cent of budgetary revenues.[138] The country also saw a decline in agricultural exports (cash crops such as groundnut, cotton and palm oil), which formed the main non-oil tradable sector and source of GDP prior to the export of oil. Moreover, the oil boom also led a significant shift in emphasis from planning for industry to primary product export and possibly deindustrialisation. According to Bill Freund, the oil boom increased the importation of luxury consumer goods which poured into the country on an unprecedented scale to the detriment of Nigerian exports. In 1974, Nigerian imports were worth NGN 1.737 million; by 1976, they reached NGN 5.140 million and in 1977, NGN 7.297 million. By mid-1978, they were running at an annual rate of NGN 8.76 million.[139] Importation of items such as cars, electronics and other finished goods increased exponentially. According to Mr. Freund, car importation surpassed

[136] Ngozi Okonjo-Iweala, 'Point Of View: Nigeria's Shot At Redemption' (International Monetary Fund, 2008), available at www.imf.org/external/Pubs/FT/fandd/2008/12/okonjo.htm (accessed 3 July 2015).

[137] National Centre for Economic Management and Administration (NCEMA), 'Understanding Structural Adjustment Programme In Nigeria' (Global Development Network (GDN), 2004) 11, available at www.gdn.int/html/GDN_funded_papers.php?mode=download&file=Nigeria-first-draft_176.pdf (accessed 9 March 2015).

[138] Benno J Ndulu, Stephen A O'Connell, Robert H Bates, Paul Collier, Chukwuma C Soludo and others, *The Political Economy Of Economic Growth In Africa, 1960–2000* (Cambridge, Cambridge University Press, 2007) 148–49.

[139] Freund, 'Oil Boom' (1978) 94.

the 10,000 mark such that Nigerian roads were increasingly clogged by fleets of motorised two-wheeled vehicles.[140]

In the drugs sector, the attendant increase in oil export earnings led to three structural changes. First, it led to an increase in the number of brand name pharmaceutical companies setting up manufacturing plants in Nigeria, which expanded pharmaceutical manufacturing in the country.[141] Previously, companies such as Beecham, May and Baker, Pfizer and Glaxo had distribution and trading outlets in the 1940s and 1950s while others such as Bayer, Wellcome, Roche, Hoerst and Boots arrived later in the 1960s. In fact, although the first production plant was registered in Nigeria in 1942, actual production activities did not start until the late 1960s.[142] By 1970, these companies had already scaled up their presence by building manufacturing plants or expanding distribution plants to be able to distribute to other parts of West Africa. In so doing, these companies took advantage of the lucrative oil market and the emergent middle class. With the success of these pharmaceutical companies, Nigeria metamorphosed into a regional hub for the export of pharmaceuticals into other parts of West Africa.[143]

(2) As a corollary, the oil boom increased the presence and relative wealth of the Nigerian middle class. This resulted in an expanded income, thereby resulting in new waves of consumerism and creating a growing demand for finished and imported goods. According to Kristin Peterson, the members of the emergent middle class were able to 'afford luxury goods and with sensibilities oriented toward the high symbolic value associated with brand name drugs'.[144] This emergent middle class, flush with new wealth, became not only the marketing focus of these companies but also spent heavily in purchases. In addition, increased rent from oil export led to the introduction of subsidised health programmes such as free drugs in government hospitals, which also added to the sales output for pharmaceutical companies. In fact, data from industry earnings were estimated at around USD 48 million in 1973, and by 1980 earnings increased to about USD 200 million and the employment of nearly 10,000 Nigerians.[145] Between 1977 and 1981, the pharmaceutical subsector grew by 110 per cent.[146]

(3) The expansion of pharmaceutical manufacturers led to the increase and professionalisation of pharmacists. The increased presence of

[140] ibid.

[141] Kristin Peterson, *Speculative Markets: Drug Circuits And Derivative Life In Nigeria* (Durham, Duke University, 2014) 41.

[142] SI Ebohon, 'Nigerian Policy Towards Foreign Companies: Case Study Of The Multinational Pharmaceutical Formulation Plants, 1972–1983', PhD thesis (University of Manchester, 1985) 146.

[143] Peterson, *Speculative Markets* (2014) 41.

[144] ibid, 42.

[145] ibid.

[146] Ebohon, 'Nigerian Policy Towards Foreign Companies' (1985) 147.

> pharmaceutical manufacturers triggered by the profitable oil boom led to an increase in the number of pharmacists, especially those who worked as marketers for brand name pharmaceutical companies.[147] The new crop of pharmacists did not only receive marketing training by attending conferences and seminars abroad – all sponsored by pharmaceutical companies – but were also given credit lines and bulk discounts on drug purchases. These pharmacists, not traders, dominated the drug supply and marketing chain. At the same time, new pharmacy schools at major universities were opening up to meet demands for local pharmacists, which at the time of independence were only three.

With the above in mind, certain questions arise – did the substantial presence of foreign drug producers result in increased participation of the sector in patent law and jurisprudence? Was any local value added in terms of organising and reshaping the politics of patent law and governance in Nigeria, either through transfer of technology to local producers or pushing forward reformist patent law? The answers lie in the structure and organisational frame of the foreign pharmaceutical companies in Nigeria as well as the policy instruments introduced to reconfigure the economy following the oil crisis of the 1980s.

In the period leading up to the 1970s, indigenous pharmaceutical manufacturing companies were almost non-existent while foreign drug companies were not engaged in original R&D. It has been argued that the research intensity of the global pharmaceutical industry was not replicated in Nigerian pharmaceutical affiliates due to the high cost of maintaining facilities and the slim chance of major discoveries due to lack of local facilities and technical know-how.[148] Most of the raw materials and heavy-duty machines required to produce the drugs were imported. Simple items such as spare parts for machines were also imported; in the event of breakdown, machines were shipped outside the country for repair. This made the cost of local manufacturing exorbitant. In addition to this, the country also lacked the skilled labour force able to engage in intensive pharmaceutical research. Therefore, even though these companies opened manufacturing plants, they all engaged in basic formulation of drugs. Even the Nigerians working in these plants were not placed in managerial and research positions due to the lack of professional and technical experience in pharmaceutical and allied research. The few Nigerians engaged in the production value chain were mostly limited to quality control positions. However, Terisa Turner contends that the lack of local expertise were excuses given by foreign companies to retain control and dominance of their companies.[149]

[147] Peterson (n 141) 42.

[148] SI Ebohon, 'Globalization, Technology Transfer And The Knowledge Gap: Case Study Of The Global Pharmaceutical Industry in Nigeria' (2012) 11 *Global Journal Of Social Sciences* 27.

[149] Terisa Turner, 'Multinational Corporations And The Instability Of The Nigerian State' (1976) 3 *Review of African Political Economy* 63, 65.

Nonetheless, the boomerang effect of this was the failure to locally capture know-how and know-why of pharmaceutical manufacture. That is, imported technology was not adapted to the local situation and therefore did not lead to any significant transfer of technology, which would have led to local industrialisation. Thus, because the subsector lacked any meaningful integration and linkage with the Nigerian economy, it created a knowledge gap that made technological transfer impossible, perpetuating a regime of technological dependency as a result. Unfortunately, evidence from the fieldwork in Nigeria shows this knowledge gap still plagues the subsector till this day. The implication of this structure of production is that the country is perennially trapped in knowledge dependence mode and restricted innovation growth. If no new research is being undertaken, then there is no need to apply for patents to protect newly developed pharmaceutical entities as patent monopoly acts as a mechanism for generating high earnings needed to cope with the extreme financial endeavour of pharmaceutical research. In fact, looking at this from a TWAIL perspective, the reluctance to adapt technology to local context so as to encourage domestic inventiveness can be seen as a vestige of colonial exchanges. That is, it perpetuates a structure wherein the Global North continues to be the privileged centre of knowledge and technological advancement to the exclusion and detriment of the subaltern. This continues the ownership and concentration of technology in the Global North, forestalling the development of and continuing the technology dependency of developing countries. However, responsibility also lies with the Nigerian Government that did not take deliberate steps to ensure the development of local technological knowledge. This is unlike in India where the Government, in addition to changing its patent law, also invested in education especially in the areas of chemistry, pharmaceutical research and biotechnology, and built sophisticated research institutions. In a similar vein, the Brazilian Government also created the Central Medicines Agency (CEME) in order to develop the country's pharmaceutical technology base.

Furthermore, even though foreign drug companies were engaged in pharmaceutical manufacturing, they were not financially equipped nor ideologically engaged to participate in cognitive shaping and expertise production in relation to patent governance. That is, many of the local affiliates of foreign companies were concerned with repatriating profits to the parent company, usually located in Europe or North America.[150] For example, 50 per cent of Nigeria's foreign exchange outlay on imported drugs at that time, Ebohon states, went to Britain where most of the companies producing drugs in Nigeria have their headquarters.[151] This is still being practised by the subsector. Commenting on this, Mr A Okeke notes that 'once his company achieves its

[150] Raymond Baker, 'Plundering A Continent' (2012), available at www.gfintegrity.org/press-release/plundering-a-continent (accessed 29 March 2016); Peterson (n 141) 42.
[151] Ebohon (n 142) 154.

financial target, the money is immediately wired abroad'.[152] It can be suggested, therefore, that foreign subsidiaries were not focused on active participation in any form of contestation of the domestic patent regime introduced five years prior. Unlike in India, which had its home-grown drug industry that proved to be highly competitive because of the Patent Act, Nigerian subsidiaries were not set up to compete with multinationals but to work with them.

Thus, even though the Nigerian economy was growing thanks to the oil boom, this growth was largely ephemeral, ie characterised largely by foreign-owned and foreign-managed industries, often dependent on imported raw materials and engaged in aggressive transfer pricing and money laundering schemes where profits are shifted from the country where they are in business into locations where they are often not in business. This structural contradiction in the pharmaceutical industry became obvious when the oil boom began to decline. To reconfigure the dominance of foreigners in the economy, which was also apparent in other sectors, the Government introduced the Nigerian Enterprises Promotion Decree of 1972 – often referred to as the Indigenisation Decree.[153]

The Indigenisation Decree was a series of private-sector-focused policy instruments introduced by the federal military Government to prevent continued foreign monopoly of the vital productive sectors of the country's economy.[154] Through this Decree, the Government sought to reserve certain categories of industrial activity for Nigerian citizens by compelling foreign businesses in a large number of specified activities to transfer their ownership wholly or partly to private Nigerian investors and businessmen.

The aim of the policy was three-pronged. First, to encourage more involvement of Nigerian citizens in the ownership, management, and control of productive enterprises in the country.[155] Second, to reduce profit repatriations and ensure greater retention of profits accruing from the economic sector.[156] Third, to enhance industrial development by substantially encouraging transfer of technology from foreign investment in intermediate and capital goods production.[157]

[152] Fieldwork interview with Okeke (n 132).

[153] Prior to the Nigerian Enterprises Promotion Decree of 1972, the Nigerian Government implemented various laws to increase the participation of Nigerians in the economy. These included the Immigration Law of 1962, which sought to control the entry of foreign business into Nigeria; the Companies Decree of 1968, which aimed to bring under the control of the Nigerian Government 'local' subsidiaries of foreign firms, and later to secure the participation of Nigerians in such businesses; and the Industrial Training Fund Decree of 1971, which sought to encourage the acquisition of relevant industry skills in order to create a ready source of indigenous manpower capable of playing a more meaningful role in the fast-growing Nigerian economy.

[154] Chibuzo SA Ogbuagu, 'The Nigerian Indigenization Policy: Nationalism Or Pragmatism' (1983) 82 *African Affairs* 241.

[155] ibid.

[156] ibid, 251.

[157] Andrew H Apter, *The Pan-African Nation: Oil And The Spectacle Of Culture In Nigeria* (Chicago, University of Chicago Press, 2005) 38.

The Decree was introduced in two phases. The first phase of the Decree in 1972 promulgated that Nigerians had to hold at least 40 per cent equity shares in certain industries, while the second phase in 1977 mandated that 60 per cent of transnational corporate assets be sold to Nigerian indigenes.[158] It was the 1977 Decree which targeted industries with local manufacturing and production presence that affected the pharmaceutical subsector.

The Indigenisation Decree was predicated on a strong feeling of political and economic nationalism and not based on the actual existing capability or readiness of Nigerian indigenes to perform higher functions in the productive sector of the economy. Of course, this new nationalistic thinking did not happen in a vacuum. It grew out of two factors. First, the experience of the Nigerian civil war, which changed the country's attitude towards foreign capital. According to Ebohon, the refusal of Britain and America – Nigeria's traditional allies – to come to the aid of the federal Government in nipping the secessionist agenda reversed the country's official thinking against the open-door policy towards Western capital.[159] Second, the emergence of ideas regarding the development of a New Economic Order further propelled the enactment of the Decree. Like Brazil and India, there was growing discontent – circulation of ideas of some sort – within the Nigerian Government regarding the unequal exchange and exploitation between developed and developing nations. For Nigeria, this deepening shift and perspective on global economic systems manifested in its readiness to canvass for a new international economic system where developing countries would attain economic parity. Thus, it is not surprising that the emerging intellectual discourse and politics reflected – at the time – the suspicion of Nigerian policy-makers of private foreign investors and the emergent concern against colonial and neo-colonial structures anywhere in Africa. By promulgating the Indigenisation Decree, the Government hoped to achieve an exclusion or complete elimination of foreign personnel from commercial and industrial activities.

The Indigenisation Decree succeeded in transferring a significant percentage of transnational assets into local hands. For example, in the pharmaceutical sector and prior to the Indigenisation Decree, foreign pharmaceutical companies were private with 100 per cent foreign equity capital.[160] By 1974, two years after the implementation of the first phase, the stake of indigenous stakeholders in the subsector increased. According to Ebohon, by this period, seven of the 13 foreign plants operating in the country divested at least 40 per cent of their equity holdings for purchase by Nigerian investors, while the remaining 60 per cent were still retained by the parent companies.[161] By 1979, two years after the

[158] ibid.

[159] SI Ebohon, 'Conflict And Accommodation In A Post-Imperial Order: Reflections On Nigerian Policy Towards Foreign Capital, 1972–2010' (2012) 1 *International Journal of Developing Societies* 62.

[160] Ebohon (n 142) 189.

[161] ibid, 190.

second phase was enacted, 12 out of the 13 foreign drug plants were completely indigenised.[162] This, in turn, led to an unprecedented growth of local entrepreneurs and succeeded in including Nigerians in this key sector.

However, some commentators take the view that the Decree also fostered the growth of a comprador class – members of a national business class of senior corporate managers who derive their position and status from their connection to foreign corporations of developed nations.[163] In his analysis of the Indigenisation Decree, Ogbuagu argues that the comprador class lacked the 'capital, skilled managerial and technical knowledge in manufacturing to effectively and meaningfully replace the foreigners in the industries reserved for them by law'.[164] In fact, Ebohon mentions that most of the new equity-holders in the pharmaceutical companies were retired army officers, traditional rulers and local businessmen who had little or no knowledge on how to run technology- and research-intensive pharmaceutical companies. Not only that, most of these indigenous investors were able to buy their pharmaceutical equity due to their connection to the Government or foreign executives.[165] This view is supported by Andrew Apter, who notes that the equity shares from the indigenisation policy

> were privately distributed to connected partners who would tow management line with their dividends and as a result, led to less active involvement of Nigerians in the management and more the rise of a newly connected elite who formed a tight circle of comprador cronies around foreign capital.[166]

Other scholars such as Iwuagwu further reports that the Decree hardly changed company control or relationships with parent companies, but instead changed the leadership (eg chairman of the Board).[167] As a result, the Nigerians were mostly figureheads without any serious executive or administrative responsibilities bequeathed to them, while foreign owners continued to occupy almost all strategic positions. This often led to cases of indigenous managers colluding with foreign companies.[168] The negative effect of this cronyism, Thomas Biersteker goes on to report, was that dividends of shares were not productively invested back into the business but favoured patterns of conspicuous consumption.[169] Subsequently, the indigenous managerial class which the

[162] ibid.

[163] Kenneth Roberts, *Key Concepts In Sociology* (China, Palgrave Macmillan, 2008) 41.

[164] Ogbuagu 'The Nigerian Indigenization Policy' (1983) 264.

[165] Ebohon (n 142) 199.

[166] Apter, 'The Pan-African Nation' (2005) 37.

[167] Obi Iwuagwu, 'Nigeria And The Challenge Of Industrial Development' (2009) 37 *African Economic History* 161.

[168] Ebohon (n 142) 124.

[169] Thomas Biersteker, 'Indigenization And The Nigerian Bourgeoisie: Dependent Development In An African Context' in P Lubeck (ed), *The African Bourgeoisie: The Development of Capitalism in Nigeria, Kenya and the Ivory Coast* (Boulder, Lynne Rienner Publishers 1987) 148.

Decree sought to construct became effectively 'denationalized since it acted as a peripheral managerial class to foster the growth of global accumulation'.[170]

In essence, although the Indigenisation Decree reduced the presence of foreign participation, it did not really lead to positive structural change in the subsector. The fact that foreign pharmaceutical companies were engaged in elementary formulation and packaging activities in the first place meant that new Nigerian managers were not privy to advanced technological information that could have been adapted locally. In fact, Ebohon states that despite the rudimentary production activities in these plants, expatriates still controlled their daily management.[171] These expatriates were in collaboration with their headquarters abroad which made critical corporate decisions while Nigerian managers only rubber-stamped decisions already taken outside the country. Thus, though the Decree indigenised equity, it did not indigenise technology nor facilitate technology acquisition that would have enabled original drug production.

The Indigenisation Decree was not the only policy implemented by the Nigerian Government in its attempt to facilitate technology transfer and subsequently attain industrialisation. Like most other post-colonial states at that time, Nigeria also introduced and implemented the ISI policy.[172] As previously discussed (see chapter four on Brazil), the ISI strategy sought to mobilise national economic resources in order to establish domestic production facilities for manufacturing goods which were formerly imported. The same ethos underpinned the ISI policy instruments introduced in Nigeria. Precisely, the Government hoped that in eliminating importation, it would kick-start domestic production and initiate local industrialisation. Industrialisation would subsequently produce much needed dynamic change in the economic structure of the country, with attendant substantial benefits trickling down to the people.

It has been argued that economic performance in the decades after the implementation of the ISI strategy was unimpressive. Instead of reducing the country's over-dependence on imported goods, it intensified Nigeria's external dependence since the country relied on imported raw materials, foreign technology and

[170] Ebohon (n 142) 125.

[171] ibid, 221.

[172] For an assessment of the ISI implementation in Nigeria, see Tom Forrest, *The Advance Of African Capital: The Growth Of Nigerian Private Enterprise* (Charlottesville, University Press of Virginia, 1994); Charles Chukwuma Soludo, Michael Osita Ogbu and Ha-Joon Chang, *The Politics Of Trade And Industrial Policy In Africa* (Trenton, Africa World Press, 2004); Adebayo Olukoshi, *The Politics Of Structural Adjustment In Nigeria* (Suffolk, James Currey, 1993); Festus O Egwaikhide, 'Import Substitution Industrialisation In Nigeria: A Selective Review' (1997) 39 *The Nigerian Journal of Economic and Social Studies* 183; Ana Paula F Mendes, Mário A Bertella and Rudolph FAP Teixeira, 'Industrialization In Sub-Saharan Africa And Import Substitution Policy' (2014) 34 *Brazilian Journal of Political Economy* 120; LN Chete, JO Adeoti, FM Adeyinka and O Ogundele, 'Industrial Development And Growth In Nigeria: Lessons And Challenges' (2012), available at www.brookings.edu/~/media/Research/Files/Papers/2014/11/learning-to-compete/L2C_WP8_Chete-et-al.pdf?la=en.

even skilled manpower.[173] In the pharmaceutical sector, the ISI policy proved to be antithetical to growth and was a highly ineffective strategy for development. This is due to the sector's heavy reliance on imported raw materials, foreign technology and skilled manpower. For example, estimates show that 80 to 90 per cent of raw materials required by foreign companies with manufacturing bases in Nigeria in the 1970s and early 1980s were imported.[174] The situation has not changed to any great extent in recent decades, with a 2011 report by the UN Industrial Development Organization stating that Nigerian drug manufacturers still imported all their active pharmaceutical ingredients and virtually all their inactive pharmaceutical ingredients such as adhesives, syrups, etc.[175] Evidence from the fieldwork interviews for this book further corroborates this. All pharmaceutical executives that were interviewed mentioned that they wholly import the items used in their factories.[176] One executive explained the situation:

> We import all our products even packaging. Everything is imported in this country including our packing such as cartons and outer packing including paper. The only thing we do not import is water, however, the ingredient we use in purifying the water are all imported. No pharmaceutical raw material is manufactured in Nigeria. None.[177]

Like the Indigenisation Decree, the Government ignored many of the factors needed for overseeing the emergent industrial sector such as the management of technologies transferred or acquired. Chete et al, in their analysis of the ISI programmes, note that it was the need to rectify the shallow nature of Nigeria's technological capacity, among other factors, which fuelled the implementation of the Indigenisation Decree.[178] However, as the analysis above has shown, the unsuccessful indigenisation of human capital such as techno-managerial capabilities and skills required for initiating, implementing and managing pharmaceutical projects subsequently limited implementation. Consequently, there is a near complete absence of indigenous R&D in Nigeria's drug sector. Balance of payments problems also affected imports and other resources required for industrial production, thereby imposing additional obstacles to industrial development.[179] The end of the oil boom in the 1980s and the SAP further exacerbated the obstacles.

[173] Mendes, Bertella and Teixeira 'Industrialization in Sub-Saharan Africa' (2014) 121; Chete, Adeoti, Adeyinka and Ogundele, 'Industrial Development and Growth in Nigeria' (2012) 2.
[174] Ebohon, 'Conflict and Accommodation in a Post-Imperial Order' (2012) 27.
[175] Charles Wambebe and Nelson Ochekpe, 'Pharmaceutical Sector Profile: Nigeria' (United Nations Industrial Development Organization (UNIDO), 2011) 35, available at www.unido.org/fileadmin/user_media/Services/PSD/BEP/Nigeria_Pharma%20Sector%20Profile_032011_Ebook.pdf.
[176] Fieldwork interview with senior executive, Pharmaceutical Company D (Lagos, July 2016) (transcript on file with author).
[177] Fieldwork interview with M A Pharmaceutical Company C (n 133).
[178] Chete, Adeoti, Adeyinka and Ogundele (n 172) 2.
[179] ibid.

The oil bust of the early 1980s left the country fiscally and structurally exposed. This led to a deterioration of public finances, a balance of payments crisis, foreign exchange shortage and a debt crisis. To rectify this, the World Bank and IMF recommended a series of fiscal and economic policy reforms which the Nigerian Government accepted and implemented in 1986. These included the devaluation of the Nigerian naira, removal of subsidies and grants on food, agricultural and petroleum products, the curtailment of loans to state government, and the privatisation of public enterprises.[180] The SAP policies aimed at realigning domestic expenditure and production patterns so as to reduce dependence on imports, enhance the non-oil export base and put the economy on the path of steady and balanced growth.[181]

The effects of the SAP policies have been diverse in Nigeria. While the microeconomic reforms have yielded little result, the negative social ramifications were immense. The devaluation of the currency led to price inflation and massive job loss, plummeting many into below the poverty line. The privatisation of healthcare also led to the introduction of user fees and increased domestic expenses, while the removal of the subsidy on fuel and agricultural goods increased hardship and household poverty incidence, especially for Nigeria's middle class and poor, who depend on government-subsidised programmes.

Of all the policies introduced, the devaluation of the Nigerian currency had the most negative impact on the pharmaceutical sector. Devaluation decreased earnings and increased the prices of food and other basic necessities, which in turn caused a sharp deterioration in the living standards of the majority of the people. Per capita income declined from USD 949.4 in 1985 to USD 280.7 in 1987 and fluctuated between USD 240 and USD 361 between 1988 and 2000.[182] Consequently, the proportion of the population living below the poverty line rose from 34.7 per cent (75.0 million) in 1985 to 67.1 per cent (102.3 million) in 1996.[183] A general decline in per capita income meant that the previously relatively affluent middle class could no longer indulge in luxury goods and expensive brand-name drugs, which affected the sales output and turnover of drug companies. Peterson asserts that drug companies which had previously occupied a major chunk of the Nigerian market could no longer operate in the country because the naira was rapidly losing value, leading to a general decline in sales.[184] As a result, 'the brand-name companies in operation at that time

[180] Yusuf Bagura, 'IMF and World Bank Conditionality And Nigeria's Structural Adjustment Programme' in K Havnevik (ed), *The IMF And The World Bank In Africa: Conditionality, Impact And Alternatives* (Uppsala, Scandinavian Institute of African Studies, 1987) 100.

[181] NCEMA, 'Understanding Structural Adjustment Programme In Nigeria' (2004).

[182] ibid, 35.

[183] ibid.

[184] Peterson (n 141) 55.

either completely ended their product lines and manufacturing or attempted to move their activities to other existing markets'.[185]

Furthermore, devaluation also increased the cost of imports as these companies mostly imported the APIs needed in drug manufacturing. The market effect was increased price of drug manufacturing but poor sales, as consumers could no longer afford the now-expensive products. The situation further worsened as the Government scaled back on financing and providing essential health services. Consequently, the brand name parent companies ended credit extensions to local distributors and when the pharmacists could not pay off their debts, their businesses folded. With high financial and market loss, the brand name companies divested from their Nigerian businesses – or what Peterson termed 'market abandonment'[186] – which generated a massive shortage of drugs. Within 10 years of the implementation of the SAP, the domestic production of pharmaceuticals ceased.[187]

The above analysis of select Nigerian industrial policies shows how these policies incapacitated the ability of the pharmaceutical sector from developing. Also, in not engaging in adaptive research on patented drugs, foreign drug companies blocked the transfer of technology to the host country, Nigeria. Since the research intensity of the foreign pharmaceutical industry was not replicated in the Nigerian affiliates beyond basic formulation and minor quality control activities, this severely limited the prospect for local technological development. Consequently, due to the absence of indigenous R&D in the subsector, the attendant regime of patents necessary to protect and reward the development of innovative products will be lacking. In this scenario, there will be no need for local pharmaceutical companies to engage and mobilise the Government on patent issues. This explains the absence of the pharmaceutical private sector in the patent regime and discourse in Nigeria.

A. Civil Society Organisations

Nigeria's CSOs are complex and have a highly varied socio-economic history and taxonomy. Their activism is marked by their proliferation and fragmentation, which has subsequently impacted the ideation of civil society participation. While some commentators contend that up until the early 1980s, civil society activism was neither popular nor mainstream in Nigeria,[188] others disagree.

[185] Kristin Peterson, 'On The Monopoly: Speculation, Pharmaceutical Markets, And Intellectual Property Law In Nigeria' (2014) 41 *American Ethnologist* 131.

[186] ibid (emphasis added).

[187] Peterson (n 141) 54.

[188] Abdul Raufu Mustafa, 'Civil Rights And Pro-Democracy Groups In And Outside Nigeria' in D Bach, Y Lebeau and K Amuwo (eds), *Nigeria During The Abacha Years (1993–1998): The Domestic And International Politics Of Democratization* (Ibadan, Institut Français de

According to Kew and Kwaja, Nigeria has always had active civil society advocacy even from the precolonial times. Civil society activism in pre-colonial times were religious, ethnic and traditional institutions and were not created for the purpose of influencing the state.[189] It was from 1914 to 1980 when the current form of civil society with a purpose of influencing the state emerged. To achieve this purpose, this second-generation civil society groups, which ranged from trade and student unions to professional associations and others engaged in various forms of civil disobedience such as trade union strikes, picketing and protests in reference to issues of marginalisation or to demand of the government provision of welfare services such as education, health, jobs, better wages, etc. Fuelled by the oil boom of the 1960s and 1970s, these groups were deeply concerned with democratising the Nigerian state with the belief that democracy is the ideal form of governance and system in which their interests were likely to be best served over time.[190] They also immersed in 'exalting and defending the distinctive interests of their members, especially in the area of private practice in various professional occupations or along ethnic/tribal lines'.[191]

The 1980s and 1990s saw the emergence of third-generation civil society groups. Growing authoritarianism as a result of military government as well as the attendant rise in educational standards meant that the language of human rights gained currency in Nigeria and was co-opted by these groups in the framing and contestation of advocacy issues. Since then, groups such as pro-democracy groups, professionals, labour unions and the organised private sector Academic Staff Union of Universities (ASUU), National Association of Nigerian Students (NANS), Nigerian Bar Association, and Nigeria Labour Congress dominate the civic engagement space and agitate against repression by the military, deterioration of the Nigerian economy and growing corruption.

Using the language of human rights, these groups campaigned for specific economic and social demands such as improved conditions for the masses, environmental rights and resistance against state corruption. For example, when the SAP was implemented, student-led riots and trade union strikes, which ground the country to a halt, were framed on social and economic rights to education, health and social safety nets which the programme destroyed. Likewise, when

Recherche en Afrique, 2001) 145. See also Chidi A Odinkalu, 'The Management Of Transition To Civil Rule By The Military In Nigeria (1966–1996)' in D Bach, Y Lebeau and K Amuwo (eds), *Nigeria During The Abacha Years (1993-1998): The Domestic And International Politics Of Democratization* (Ibadan, Institut Français de Recherche en Afrique, 2001).

[189] Darren Kew and Chris M A Kwaja, 'Civil Society In Nigeria' in AC Levan and P Ukata (eds), *The Oxford Handbook of Nigerian Politics* (Oxford, Oxford University Press, 2018). Darren Kew in *Civil Society, Conflict Resolution, And Democracy In Nigeria* (Syracuse, Syracuse University Press, 2016) identifies three generation of civil society in Nigeria ranging from first generation during the precolonial times, second generation *c* 1914–1980; third generation from 1980 to present.

[190] Kew and Kwaja, 'Civil Society In Nigeria' (2018).

[191] Matthew Todd Bradley, 'Civil Society And Democratic Progression In Postcolonial Nigeria: The Role Of Non-Governmental Organizations' (2005) 1 *Journal of Civil Society* 61, 66.

the military regime annulled the 1993 election that was widely seen by many as free and fair, civil society activity was further galvanised to assume a pointed organisational focus on the civil and political right to vote. These groups were able to organise massive protests that pushed General Babangida – the then military dictator – from office in 1993 when his long transition programme finally proved fraudulent. In fact, according to Kew and Oshikoya, CSO activism 'spearheaded by human rights organizations, joined forces with trade unions, the Bar, student unions, and most importantly, the leading political opposition party to force Babangida to hand power to a transitional government offering to hold new elections'.[192]

The return to democratic rule in 1999 increased the number and variety of civil society activism in the public space to include patient groups, foreign donor-funded organisations and even foreign NGOs working on various issues such as election monitoring, lesbian and gay issues, religious rights and public health implementation programmes. In a study conducted by Ogbogu and Idogho, it was shown that CSOs comprising of community development associations, support groups for PLWHA and other health groups played important roles in the earlier phase of Nigeria's response to the HIV/AIDS epidemic.[193] Today, these CSOs are significant actors in the implementation of the public health programme on malaria, HIV/AIDS, tuberculosis and infant or maternal care, to mention a few, with these programmes ranging from prevention to care and support. This new generation of public health CSOs is more cosmopolitan and has ties with international organisations such as the UN, the WHO and the GFATM. They attend international conferences, receive funds from foreign governments and donor organisations, and are party to a global discourse on public health management, especially regarding diseases that plague Nigeria.

In spite of this, there is paucity of Nigerian CSO engagement and activism around IP-related issues and their impact on public health. This raises the question of why these organisations have not gone beyond basic implementation programmes and service delivery roles to a substantial role bordering on the problematising of institutional frameworks that create barriers to access and treatment. That is, why is civil society activism in Nigeria not targeting structural issues such as fixing patent laws in Nigeria to ensure medicine access and sustainable public health management? The answers to this question are three-pronged.

First, the psychological effect of military dictatorship adversely affected civil society psyche and blunted the once dynamic civil society activism. Since

[192] Darren Kew and Modupe Oshikoya, 'Escape From Tyranny: Civil Society And Democratic Struggles In Africa' in E Obadare (ed), *The Handbook Of Civil Society In Africa* (New York, Springer, 2013) 15.

[193] Irene Ogbogu and Omokhudu Idogho, 'The Role Of Civil Society Organizations In HIV/AIDS Control' in O Adeyi (ed), *AIDS In Nigeria: A Nation On The Threshold* (Cambridge, Harvard University Press, 2006) 297.

independence from Britain in 1960, Nigeria has experienced civilian rule (1960–66, 1979–83 and 1999 onwards) and military rule (1966–79 and 1983–99). The period of military regime stands out clearly as the architect of collective disenchantment in civil society engagement.

Due to the austerity measures introduced by the military Government at the onset of the oil bust, many civil society groups participated in acts of civil disobedience such as public demonstrations and strikes as a way to voice their displeasure with the austerity measures. In response, the military Government proscribed several CSOs, mostly labour unions and professional associations, that dared to criticise its policies or which embarked on public demonstrations and strikes. Key figures were arrested, detained and sometimes tortured without recourse to legal processes. As Remi Aiyede has pointed out, the military regime introduced decrees that not only allowed for persons to be detained for a period of three months without trial for any act prejudicial to state security, but also placed the Government above the law by protecting the military Government against court proceedings by public sector workers.[194]

In addition to overt repression, which created an extremely oppressive climate, the military Government bought out political and civil actors through bribery and material inducement, thereby co-opting the civil society movement and corrupting its moral foundations. Kew and Oshikoya, for example, observed the devastating effect of the SAP, which gutted public infrastructure and social safety nets and increased government largesse, proving increasingly irresistible to political leaders and some civil society actors.[195] This worsened economic situation made it easy for some activists to be easily influenced. Likewise, Peter Lewis states that the Government 'diversified its strategies of control to include political manipulation, populist side-payments, elite dispensations, expansion of the parallel economy and political patronage'.[196] The regime bankrolled several groups to openly canvass for the prolonging of military rule and countering of democratisation pressures, subsuming the rest under various government ministries, undermining their effectiveness and affecting their focus.[197] By co-opting CSO activism, the Government was able to quell their influence.

Even the coming of General Sani Abacha in 1993, who continued the military dictatorship in Nigeria, did not abate the repression of civilian and democratic activism. If anything, the Abacha regime intensified the climate of fear and authoritarian control. Particularly, the hanging of the environmental rights activist Ken Saro-Wiwa along with eight others in 1995 created a collective feeling of despair, despondency and powerlessness among key activist groups. Even though the return to civilian rule in 1999 added a new lease on life to

[194] E Remi Aiyede, 'The Dynamics Of Civil Society And The Democratization Process in Nigeria' (2003) 37 *Canadian Journal of African Studies/Revue Canadienne des Études Africaines* 1, 8–9.

[195] Kew and Oshikoya, 'Escape From Tyranny' (2013) 15. See also Kew and Kwaja, (n 189).

[196] Peter Lewis, 'From Prebendalism To Predation: The Political Economy Of Decline In Nigeria' (1996) 34 *The Journal of Modern African Studies* 79, 88.

[197] Aiyede, 'The Dynamics Of Civil Society' (2003) 10.

CSO advocacy in Nigeria as the various groups recovered their strength and bargained major reforms with the democratic Government, the state continues to use, on certain occasions, intimidation techniques. The overall impact of this on the national psyche is the pacification of even the most ardent of groups, sapping civil society influence. Therefore, it is not surprising that CSOs working on public health continue to demonstrate this weakened position, especially with their inability to foment policy-deepening coalitions.

Second, the overwhelming presence of donor funding in the provision of health services also explains why Nigerian public health-focused CSOs have not directed their gaze towards patents. This is largely due to the fact that most of the essential medicines for diseases such as HIV/AIDS, malaria and tuberculosis dispensed in hospitals are provided by donor organisations. In an interview, an official at the National Agency for the Control of AIDS (NACA) mentioned that majority of drugs used in the treatment of HIV/AIDS, malaria and tuberculosis are donated to the Nigerian Government. She explains further:

> Majority of the drugs we dispense are given to us by international organizations such as Global Funds, the US President's Emergency Plan for AIDS Relief (PEPFAR), United Nations AIDS Program (UNAIDS). Domestic HIV funding has been very low and unstable, and that is why we largely depend on international funding sources.[198]

Similarly, the Director of foreign sponsored non-government organisations states:

> Majority of the NGOs here receive donor funding which they use to procure the drugs. In this environment, there will be no need to look at patent issue as patent is not seen a problem or hindrance to medicines access.[199]

In fact, the President's Comprehensive Response Plan for HIV/AIDS in Nigeria states that 74.65 per cent of the HIV/AIDS fund is donor-sourced while the remaining 25 per cent is from the Nigerian Government.[200] In contrast, 100 per cent of Brazil's HIV/AIDS programmes is funded by the Brazilian state (federal, state and municipal governments) while the Indian Government provides 90 per cent of the funds for its AIDS programmes.[201] In another report, the 2014 National HIV/AIDS Epidemiological and Impact Analysis, which provides scientific insight into the nature of Nigeria's HIV/AIDS epidemic and the impact of government efforts, state that international funding steadily increased to USD 445.2 million in 2012 from USD 317.2 million in 2009

[198] Fieldwork interview with Official A, NACA (Abuja, February 2015) (transcript on file with author).

[199] Fieldwork interview with KO (Abuja, January 2015) (transcript on file with author).

[200] Federal Ministry of Health, 'President's Comprehensive Response Plan For HIV/AIDS In Nigeria' (Federal Ministry of Health, 2013) 19.

[201] 'HIV And AIDS In India' (2015), available at www.avert.org/professionals/hiv-around-world/asia-pacific/india.

(35 per cent of this was spent on treatment and care).[202] It follows, therefore, that the overwhelming presence of donor funds has a noticeably disempowering effect on CSO engagement on patent issues in Nigeria. Since majority of funds for medicine purchase are internationally sourced, then patents – which are problematised in Brazil and India as the reason for high drug prices and encumbrance to medicine access – are eliminated. In other words, patents are not seen as a problem. This means that there is less tendency for CSO groups to engage the state on patent law reform or to insist on the use of TRIPS Agreement flexibilities to ensure availability of and access to medicines.

Third, there is a general lack of patent knowledge or awareness on patent issues. While Nigeria is active at the international level, often championing the cause of the African Group,[203] local awareness of the IP regime is deficient. For example, a health activist who was interviewed stated:

> I don't know intellectual property because it is not an issue for us in Nigeria. Our problem is corruption and the mismanagement of donor funds. Patent is not the issue here, corruption is. There is the GAVI problem that is heating up the Ministry of Health right now. It is issues like these that we focus on. There is also the bureaucracy problem that causes drugs stock-outs. We have instances where ARVs worth thousands of dollars have been destroyed because they were unused and some even expired, yet if you go to Garki [Government hospital] they tell you they don't have drugs. But the money is there, the drug is there so what happened to them?[204]

Correspondingly, an interviewee elucidates:

> Patent is a non-issue here and there are many reasons for that. There is no strong policy space to trigger the kind of discussions and activisms you have in Brazil and India. Donors provide the funds for procurement and for many of these CSOs, procurement is opportunity for graft. Also, donor organisations are not really interested in setting up frameworks on IP and access related issues mainly because result and monitoring is ambiguous. Add to the fact that these organisations are looking for value for their money.[205]

[202] National Agency for the Control of AIDS (NACA), 'National HIV/AIDS Epidemiology And Impact Analysis (NHEIA) Report' (NACA, 2014) 47. Nigeria has the second highest HIV burden in Africa after South Africa, with 3.4 million people living with HIV and only 491,021 receiving ARV drugs. The country's tuberculosis burden is equally high at 100,401. For assessment of HIV/AIDS burden in Nigeria, see National AIDS/STI Control Programme, 'Integrated National Guidelines for HIV Prevention, Treatment and Care' (Federal Ministry of Health, 2014).

[203] Ukpanah, 'Statement' (1990).

[204] Fieldwork interview with a health activist (Abuja, January 2015) (transcript on file with author). The GAVI issue the interviewee referred to was the cash programme audit report on funds disbursed to Nigeria to support immunisation activities from 2011 to 2013. The audit was undertaken by GAVI's Programme Fiduciary Oversight team. The report describes systemic weaknesses regarding the operation of controls and procedures in national systems used to manage GAVI cash-based support. As a result of specific findings, the Government of Nigeria has agreed to repay funds deemed to have been misused, which are quantified as USD 2.2 million (copy of report on file with author).

[205] Fieldwork interview with KO (n 199).

In fact, a report by a local newspaper showed how significant government and donor funding in the HIV/AIDS campaign failed to translate to good numbers due to corruption. According to the report, Nigeria spent more than USD 4.4 billion between 2008 and 2012 on HIV/AIDS treatment, yet the number of people living with HIV/AIDS in Nigeria rose from 2.98 million to 3.5 million; AIDS-linked deaths climbed from 192,000 to 217,000; and new infections increased from 336,000 to 388,000 during that same period.[206] These statistics provide glaring evidence to support the argument that huge amounts of money donated to fight HIV/AIDS are being siphoned away. Therefore, when faced with issues of corruption, it is perhaps unsurprising that the legal consciousness about the possibilities of patents is absent among CSO circles in Nigeria. For these actors, treatment activism is about ensuring availability of drugs and vaccines donated by foreign organisations as well as ensuring that there are effective systems to deliver these to all who need them. In this context, priority is given to the development of stronger, sustainable and efficient health systems and not on the reform of patent law as the latter is not seen as problematic.

Furthermore, in Nigeria, patent law is not part of life. That is, it is not living law. It also does not help that that law as it stands is old. As discussed in the previous section, the current patent law was passed 45 years ago in 1970 and though it was modified in 1990, the modifications are minor and not up to date. This, coupled with the problem of insufficient legal knowledge on patent issues, explains why many CSOs do not engage with it. As a result, there is also little or no understanding in NGO circles of how international regimes such as the TRIPS Agreement affect access to drugs. This points to the need for the law to adapt to changing social needs. In the analyses of the Brazil and Indian patent regimes, the 'living law' of patents was observed. In those jurisdictions, law in action was evident – in policy tools, in commerce, and engaged with by many associations, not only by those that the law has recognised (inventors) but also by those that it has overlooked or passed by (patient groups, the sick, and health activists). In these jurisdictions, patent law is seen as an instrument which could be used to solve social problems, ie to protect and incentivise invention, while also used to resolve social issues, eg access to medicines. In engaging in claims and counter-claims put forward and bargained over by these competing groups, patent norms are expanded and amplified.

If anything, the analysis in this section has underscored an omission prevalent in the literature on access to medicines, ie the patent regime as one of the impediments to access. Particularly, it advances existing knowledge on how the use of legal and regulatory tools of patents is linked to the practices of different actors, such as inventors (in this case, brand name or generic pharmaceutical manufacturers) and civil society groups, that underpin the regime.

[206] Bunno Esdiake, 'Nigeria's HIV/AIDS Fight Gulps Billions of Dollars, Yields Little' *Telegraph* (2013), available at http://telegraphng.com/2013/10/nigerias-hivaids-fight-gulps-billions-dollars-yields-little.

VI. CONCLUSION

This chapter has critically discussed the patent regime in Nigeria. Specifically, its origins, the main sections governing patent rights and how it interacts with the TRIPS Agreement. It also highlighted the ways in which regulatory agencies and non-state actors engage with patent law.

As mentioned in previous chapters, pharmaceutical patents operate under the notion that an inventor should disclose the invention to facilitate development and for public consumption of the patented invention. In turn, the inventor is given the exclusive right to price and sell the invention for a limited time in a competition-free environment in order to recoup the investment for developing said invention. Thus, the patent system is a social institution created to facilitate this exchange.

Underlying this notion of exchange between inventors versus the state or consumer is the assumption of fair market; that is, an equitable just structure that allows buyers (in this case, the state or consumers) and sellers (in this case, inventors) to exchange any type of good (patented invention). However, how the market should work to facilitate this fair exchange is not defined in patent law even though actions such as CLs exist as corrective measures against market failures. This structure of patents raises the crucial question of what happens when the market *does not exist*, as was the case in Nigeria when brand name companies pulled out of the country and indigenous manufacturers were unable to fill the vacuum.

Importantly, this structure also raises the question of what is the actual purpose of patent law when key actors (inventors or in this case, pharmaceutical companies) that underpin the fair exchange are absent? In the case of Nigeria where widespread pharmaceutical manufacturing infrastructure is absent, patent regime is inconsequential. The concomitant effect is that actors (pharmaceutical industry stakeholders) that normally push for a robust patent regime in policy-making circles and in influencing government decisions cannot do so. This is unlike in India where the patent regime was hugely influenced by the existence of a strong pharmaceutical sector. It would not be unreasonable to presume that the level of interest in the various epochs of Indian patent regime development – from the 1970s when the country changed its colonial law to the 2000s when it transitioned into the TRIPS Agreement regime – is proportionate to the size of the Indian market and of the entities interested in accessing it. Further, the existence of a fair market structure in India in the form of a strong generic industry as well as the ability of patent law to affect monopoly and market access explain the strong patent language in policy and legal decisions and in public debates. The Nigerian pharmaceutical market discontinuity and ensuing lacuna in the patent regime evokes the question of the impact of patent policy and regime on prospects of development.

Moreover, the inability of local civil society actors to engage with patent law also explains the absence of an organised pressure group, determined to make the Government reformulate a richer patent policy in such a way that it can enhance the indigenous pharmaceutical sector while simultaneously protecting public interest. This relates back to the concerted effort of civil society activism in Brazil and India, especially the active role which civil society played in reshaping these countries' laws. The civil society groups in these countries were able to instigate, promote and legitimise ideas regarding patent law and its effect on sectoral development and health. It is their engagement with law that changed the national architecture, discourse and strategies on patent law. This underscores the nodal governance literature which emphasises that strong nodes have strong purposes, can formulate demands, and can create concentrations of power for purposes of influencing governance.[207] Conversely, weak nodes are unable to formulate these demands or work together, thus are incapable of influencing governance. Nigeria, having a weak pharmaceutical sector and CSO without the capacity to mobilise the Government, has proven this.

The lesson from this chapter is that laws and policies alone are not enough in the multi-scalar and longitudinal understanding of the issues arising from patent governance as regards socio-economic development. Rather, the strong presence of relevant interest groups is also required to not only elevate discourse but also to produce expertise and govern knowledge in related issue areas. It is hoped that analyses from this chapter contribute to the understanding of the importance of local actors and strong institutions in the creation of national patent law and its relationship with economic development and the protection of public interests.

[207] Peter Drahos, 'Intellectual Property and Pharmaceutical Markets: A Nodal Governance Approach' (2004) 77 *Temple Law Review* 404.

7

General Conclusions

I. APPRAISING THE DISCUSSION

ANALYSES IN THIS book explored pharmaceutical patent law-making in Brazil, India and Nigeria. To do this, it looked at the history and origin of patent law in each country, the conceptualisation of patent law, and how this understanding framed (and continues to frame) the politics, interpretation and patent law-making to achieve national goals. In general terms, this study has found that various key factors that unfolded over time influenced the circulation of ideas regarding patents, thereby leading to the emergence of narratives and counter-narratives on patent regime discourse. These factors include colonial experience, development aspirations, the confluence of local politics (which could be either political or socio-economic in nature) and international political processes that unfolded over time.

Colonialism was one of the factors that influenced ideas on patents in the countries studied. Brazil, though one of the original members of the Paris Convention, was dissatisfied with the Paris Convention due to the rampant abuses of patent monopolies by foreign pharmaceutical companies. As a result, the country demanded for a patent system both at home and at the UN that is favourable to its economic development, including proper controls against abuse, thereby putting 'development' issues and 'public interest concerns' on the international IP agenda. Whilst the country was not successful in pushing forward this counter-hegemonic stance at the UN, it succeeded at home in revising the Brazilian patent law in 1971 and removed patent protection for both pharmaceutical products and processes to allow and encourage the transfer of technology. In making this reform, the country understood and conceptualised patent as a deliberate industrial policy to encourage transfer of technology and industrial development. With these goals in mind, Brazil implemented a patent regime in 1971 that did not grant protection to pharmaceutical products and processes to allow for transfer of technology.

However, due to external pressure from the US and panels at the WTO, the country quickly implemented the TRIPS Agreement. This led to the Brazilian Congress's introduction and approval of Industrial Property Law 9.279/96 in 1996 – much earlier than the WTO deadline of 2005 for middle income countries.[1] However, as analyses in chapter four have shown, Brazil passed Law 9313 (also known as the Sarney Law) to provide free access to ARVs due to internal circumstances such as the HIV/AIDS crisis and widespread social mobilisation and activism waged by health CSOs. Because Brazil had already phased into the TRIPS Agreement, thereby making it difficult to locally produce ARV drugs patented elsewhere, the cost of free ARV drugs ballooned, threatening the AIDS programme. The combination of budgetary constraints, ballooning health costs, and the Government's constitutional obligation to provide healthcare for all Brazilians spurred the Government to introduce Law 9787/99, known as the Law of Generic Medicines, in 1999. The law required all purchasing contracts under the government system to be generic, while all prescriptions are to be written using the generic name, essentially introducing generics into the Brazilian market.[2] The Law of Generic Medicines also made the use of CLs more flexible and simpler, while regulatory reforms were introduced to accelerate the market entry of generics after the expiration of their on-patent versions. Brazil also amended its patent policy to adopt a human rights approach wherein a patent application is examined vis-à-vis its impact on public health. Thus, Law 10196/2001 was added as Article 299c to Brazil's IP legislation, which instituted the 'prior consent' (*Anuência Prévia*) mechanism.[3] This empowered ANVISA to grant patents for pharmaceutical products and processes on public health grounds. In other words, ANVISA examines pharmaceutical patent applications to make sure the grant of patents will not negatively affect public health. However, this power and role have recently been curtailed to limit ANVISA's decision to mere recommendation and not as an essential requirement for patent approval.

As it stands, there is incoherence on the country's understanding and approach towards patents. This incoherence can be seen in the tension within the local administrative spaces, eg between INPI (which seems to align with private sector interests) and ANVISA, between the state and civil society groups. The early transition into the TRIPS Agreement significantly affected the human rights and public health safeguards instituted by the Brazilian Constitution. Growing health needs, coupled with the threat to the country's policy of universal access to AIDS medicines due to the high cost of patented medicines and the social mobilisation of health activism, as well as the need to attract FDI in the

[1] Amy Nunn, *The Politics And History Of AIDS Treatment In Brazil* (New York, Springer, 2008) 3.

[2] Matthew Brian Flynn, 'Pharmaceutical Governance In Brazil: Globalization, Institutions And AIDS', PhD thesis (University of Texas at Austin, 2010) 58; Gabriela Chavez and Renata Reis, 'Health, Intellectual Property And Innovation: A Case Study Of Brazil' (2011) *South Centre* 74; Jorge A Bermudez, Ruth Epsztejn, Maria Auxiliadora Oliveira and Lia Hasenclever, *The WTO TRIPS Agreement And Patent Protection In Brazil: Recent Changes And Implications For Local Production And Access to Medicines* (Rio de Janeiro, Oswaldo Cruz Foundation, 2002) 136.

[3] Monica Steffen Guise Rosina, Daniel Wang and Thana Cristina De Campos, 'Access to Medicines: Pharmaceutical Patents And The Right To Health' in L Shaver (ed), *Access To Knowledge In Brazil: New Research On Intellectual Property, Innovation And Development* (Connecticut, Yale Law School, 2008) 191.

form of technological transfers and pharmaceutical innovation, have continued to act as pulls regarding the country's understanding and conceptualisation of patents.

India, from the onset, conceptualised and implemented patent law based on its socio-economic realities and development goals of pharmaceutical autonomy or self-sufficiency. As such, patents are seen as an instrument of industrial policy and patent laws were implemented in ways to preserve and enhance the competitiveness of the local pharmaceutical industry.[4] Similar to Brazil, the colonial patent regime in India, for instance, encouraged the abuse of patent monopoly which led to high drug prices, non-working patented articles that stifled transfer of technology, and often delayed the introduction and production of essential drugs and stifled industrial development.[5] This led to the emergence of a general movement towards reforming the colonial patent regime seen by many, especially indigenous drug manufacturers, as an encumbrance to the development of a robust pharmaceutical sector and achievement of pharmaceutical autonomy. In response, India amended its patent law in 1970 and removed product patents on medicines and agro-chemicals. It also limited the protection term for processes to seven years. The Indian patent reform, it has been argued, was an icon of the thinking that prevailed in terms of patent reform.[6]

The quest for pharmaceutical autonomy continued in the post-TRIPS Agreement era as the Government availed itself of the transitional period and interpreted the TRIPS Agreement in ways that ensured the use of flexibilities. Specifically, Section 3(d) considers derivative forms of known substances, ie salts, esters, ethers and polymorphs, to be the same substance, unless it is shown that the new derivative improved efficacy of the known substance. Thus, as chapter five argued, the Indian Patent Act appears to be a successful attempt at striking a balance between protecting IPRs and promoting local innovation. The Brazilian and Indian examples provide attempts by Third World countries to make modern technology more freely accessible for commercial development within their respective countries. Abolishing patent protection in the case of Brazil and severely limiting the patent framework in the case of India represent a radical departure from the traditional concept that patent ownership rights should be afforded the highest degree of protection.[7]

Furthermore, analyses herein have shown how counter-hegemonic campaigns and activism by non-state actors, referred to in this book to mean the private sector and civil society groups, achieved a reform of patent laws in Brazil and

[4] Amy Kapczynski, 'Harmonization And Its Discontents' (2009) 97 *California Law Review* 1571.

[5] Sudip Chaudhuri, *The WTO And India's Pharmaceuticals Industry: Patent Protection, TRIPS, And Developing Countries* (Oxford, Oxford University Press, 2006) 54.

[6] Pedro Roffe and Gina Vea, 'The WIPO Development Agenda In An Historical And Political Context' in N Netanel (ed), *The Development Agenda: Global Intellectual Property And Developing Countries*, 1st edn (Oxford, Oxford University Press, 2008) 92.

[7] Frederick M Abbott, 'Intellectual Property, International Protection' (2009) Florida State University – College of Law Public Law Research Paper No 601, 2.

India. As mentioned earlier, Brazil phased into the TRIPS Agreement early without using the transition period accorded to developing countries. It also implemented standards which many believed to be higher than what is required by the TRIPS Agreement. However, the HIV/AIDS epidemic amplified the engagement of civil society groups that couched their activism on the terms of the constitutional right to health.[8] These groups played a key role in producing knowledge, expertise and awareness regarding the impact of patents on access to ARV drugs. To effect the required change and response, these groups adopted several tactics such as policy advocacy, HIV/AIDS destigmatisation campaigns, and legal suits against government policies that negated the Government's healthcare responsibilities. This led to the introduction of Law 9313/96 (Sarney Law), which guarantees free access to ARVs for AIDS treatment for all people in Brazil living with HIV/AIDS.[9]

It can be argued that the legal battle waged by civil society groups, especially in relation to the right to health as codified in the Brazilian Constitution, was decisive behind the change in Brazil's patent law. If anything, it led to a more structured and organised response by the Government. In fact, the policy of universal ARV access was initially undermined by the early implementation of the TRIPS Agreement as it meant the country cannot copy drugs patented elsewhere and should therefore purchase the required ARV drugs at full price. By expressing the threat to the AIDS programme during campaigns and protests as a patent issue due to the price of expansive patented drugs, civil society movements forced the Government to break patents and issue a CL for the ARV medicine Efavirenz.[10]

In India, the primacy of local industry vis-à-vis the patent law has seen indigenous drug manufacturers play an active role in the initial post-colonial patent amendment as well as in the post-TRIPS Agreement era. The country's unique position as a supplier of generic drugs to the world was achieved as a result of the changes to its patent law in 1970. The post-TRIPS Agreement era deepened popular activism of Indian civil society groups, which became dominant prior to the final amendment of India's patent law in 2005 to comply with its TRIPS Agreement obligation. Since the final amendment of the IPA in 2005, new social movements, radical legal decisions and business partnerships have led to the development of novel conceptions of patents advanced by the different actors. For example, CSO groups are actively pushing forward a rights-based patent regime that enables the provision of drugs at affordable prices to the people

[8] Renata Reis, Veriano Terto Jr and Maria Cristina Pimenta, *Intellectual Property Rights And Access To ARV Medicines* (São Paulo, ABIA, 2009); Gabriela Chaves, Marcela Vieira and Renata Reis, *Access To Medicines And Intellectual Property In Brazil: Reflections And Strategies Of Civil Society* (2008), available at www.scielo.br/pdf/sur/v5n8/en_v5n8a09.pdf.

[9] A Nunn, F Da Fonseca and S Gruskin, 'Changing Global Essential Medicines Norms To Improve Access To AIDS Treatment: Lessons from Brazil' (2009) 4 *Global Public Health* 134.

[10] Chaves, Vieira and Reis, *Access To Medicines* (2008).

of India.[11] They have adopted patent opposition strategies against what they see as frivolous patent applications or applications deemed injurious to public health. The courts have also become the battleground in the development and expansion of patent law and policies. The private sector is also employing various tactics to increase its space within post-TRIPS Agreement India. In seeking out favourable rules via pre-emptive injunctions and legal tie-ups through VLs and outright purchase of competitor firms, MNCs are gaining control of generic markets and are pursuing capitalist goals that are contrary to CSO and, sometimes, state objectives.

Nigeria, however, continues to move in the opposite direction. Like Brazil and India, the country was vocal and active in opposing the inclusion of IP to global trade rule. Yet, its policies at home do not display the sophisticated understanding it seems to display at the international level. For starters, the country does not have a concise conceptualisation or understanding of patent law or how it relates to social development aspirations. Unlike Brazil and India where the post-colonial patent regime was a deliberate act of the Government, bearing in mind the needs and realities of the country, the reverse was the case in Nigeria. In Nigeria, post-colonial patent law – the Patent Rights Limitation Decree (1968) – was implemented as a response to the court ruling of the first patent case in Nigeria, which the military Government found offensive to its powers to issue orders in pursuance of the Government use clause under the patent law. This showed that patents were not conceptualised in the first place by the Nigerian state either as a matter of deliberate industrial policy or as part of its development pursuits. As Nigeria has not fully phased into the TRIPS Agreement, the 1968 patent law – though renamed and slightly updated in 1990 – has continued to this day. This shows, if anything, a lack of deliberate patent conceptualisation in law and policy, which has underscored the Government's general movement towards a patent regime even in the post TRIPS Agreement era.

Whilst Nigeria also experienced high incidents of monopoly abuse,[12] the first post-colonial patent law was a response to the *Rhone-SA Poulenc and May & Baker v Lodeka Pharmacy* case.[13] The then military Government implemented the first post-colonial patent law to allow the Nigerian Government to purchase patented pharmaceutical products and to also exempt the Government from infringement of a patent granted with respect to the articles concerned or the liability to pay royalties or compensation to the patentee.[14] In this regard, the PDA did not take into account the country's development level at the time,

[11] Julia George, 'India, Intellectual Property And Access To Medicines: Developments And Civil Society Initiatives In India' in R Reis, V Terto Jr and M Pimenta (eds), Intellectual Property Rights And Access To ARV Medicines, 1st edn (São Paulo, ABIA, 2009).

[12] Owen T Adikibi, 'The Multinational Corporation And Monopoly Of Patents In Nigeria' (1988) 16 *World Development* 512.

[13] (1965) LLR 9.

[14] Patents (Limitation) Decree No 8 (1968), s 1(3).

leading to an absence of relevant underlying policy for using the patent regime to attain certain social development purposes.

Meanwhile, the discovery of oil in commercial quantities, especially the oil boom of the 1970s, drastically changed the structure of the economy.[15] Specifically, it increased the importation of finished goods, which severely weakened the industrial sector. Thus, while Brazil and India had to look inwards to develop policies that would encourage technology transfer and industrial development, Nigeria relied on the windfall from oil to grow its economy and did not implement a strategic and deliberate development policy towards ensuring the transfer and development of technological capacities.

Moreover, the influx of foreign drug companies to Nigeria[16] – a by-product of the oil boom – created an illusion of industrial growth and expansion. Analyses in chapter six showed that the growth was largely ephemeral as it was mainly characterised by foreign-owned and foreign-managed industries, often dependent on imported raw materials and engaged in aggressive transfer pricing and money laundering schemes.[17] This became obvious when the oil boom ended and the introduction of austerity measures, which negatively affected the purchasing power of Nigerians, forced foreign pharmaceutical companies to divest from the country.

Specifically, this study showed that pharmaceutical technology imported by foreign drug-makers operating in Nigeria in the early 1960s and 1970s was not adapted to the local situation and therefore did not lead to any significant transfer of technology, which would have led to local industrialisation. Government policies such as the Indigenisation Decree – instituted to reconfigure the dominance of the foreign nationals in the Nigerian economy – also failed to increase technology transfer. This is because the Indigenisation Decree was improperly implemented and instead encouraged the transfer of company ownership to individuals connected to the ruling class but who had no prior experience in running a drug manufacturing plant. Furthermore, the ISI policy enforced at the time made the importation of raw materials expensive and made local production unsustainable. This forced drug manufacturers to resort to importing finished goods instead of engaging in local manufacturing. On the other hand, the SAP – introduced to curtail fiscal mismanagement triggered by the oil boom and bust of the 1970s and the 1980s – eviscerated the pharmaceutical manufacturing companies, in turn weakening the ability of the pharmaceutical manufacturing sector to engage in domestic inventiveness. Thus, while the

[15] Bill Freund, 'Oil Boom And Crisis In Contemporary Nigeria' (1978) 5 *Review of African Political Economy* 91, 92.

[16] Kristin Peterson, *Speculative Markets: Drug Circuits And Derivative Life In Nigeria* (Durham, Duke University, 2014) 41.

[17] SI Ebohon, 'Globalization, Technology Transfer And The Knowledge Gap: Case Study Of The Global Pharmaceutical Industry In Nigeria' (2012) 11 *Global Journal of Social Sciences* 27; Raymond Baker, 'Plundering A Continent' (2012), available at www.gfintegrity.org/press-release/plundering-a-continent.

1970s witnessed a wave of legal reforms in Brazil and India that created a counter-narrative on patents that translated into important changes in IP-related legislation, the counter-hegemonic movement was absent in Nigeria because the windfall from oil prevented the state from seriously engaging in patent reform or using patents to effect development.

Furthermore, the non-state actors' contestation and engagement in Brazil and India are absent in Nigeria. Years under a military regime blunted CSO activism, while the presence of donor organisations further weakened the ability of CSOs to participate in patent law-making. As a result, these actors that normatively would have played an important role in the cognitive shaping of and knowledge production on patent law are not doing so. The inability of local civil society actors to engage with patent law also explains the absence of an organised pressure group, determined to make the Government reformulate patent policy in such a way that it can enhance the indigenous pharmaceutical sector while simultaneously protecting public interest. This relates back to the concerted effort of civil society activism in Brazil and India, especially the active role which civil society played in reshaping these countries' IP laws.

II. WHAT IS THE WAY FORWARD FOR NIGERIA?

As this book has shown, both Brazil and India provide a comprehensive legal framework for IPR protection. These countries implemented the TRIPS Agreement in a different manner and time. Each country had a different set of challenges, and a different strategy or model of protection. Both Brazil and India have opened their markets to foreign investments and competition, aiming to become part of the globalised prosperity envisaged with the creation of the WTO. In this regard, Nigeria has something to learn from these countries.

First, the lesson from the Brazilian and Indian IP law regime has shown that patent law and policy cannot be implemented in a vacuum and is dependent on the cultural, political and economic lives of the country. It has many other components going far beyond the IPR regime. Brazil framed and marketed its patent regime as part of its health policy, whereas India mainly promoted its patent regime as an industrial tool and social development policy. Nigeria should adopt a patent law bearing in mind its economic and social circumstances and aspirations, technological capabilities and industry profile. This research therefore recommends developing a patent regime framed as a health policy tool due to the various health challenges faced by Nigeria, especially with HIV/AIDS, malaria and tuberculosis. Adopting a right to health framework, as Brazil did, will not only allow the country to invest in healthcare but to also collaborate with foreign MNCs through PPP agreements to locally develop and manufacture drugs in the country. Doing so would encourage technology transfer whilst developing the manufacturing sector.

Second, in terms of patents and access to medicines, Brazil and India have shown the way that policy-makers have tailored the implementation of TRIPS Agreement obligations to fit their particular circumstances. This was absent in the first post-colonial patent law in Nigeria. As Nigeria is yet to fully implement the TRIPS Agreement, the analyses here suggest framing a patent regime cognisant of Nigeria's health challenges and needs as well as its development aspirations. Specifically, this study recommends that patent protection for pharmaceutical products and processes be explicitly included in the list of patentable inventions in Section 1(4) of the PDA, and such right be enjoyable without discrimination as stipulated by Article 27(1) of the TRIPS Agreement. In addition, the new policy should not be too restrictive to hinder innovation nor too wide to engender abuse. If anything, the TRIPS Agreement still allows some degree of flexibility for countries to determine how the criteria for patentability should be applied.[18] In this regard, Nigeria could borrow from India to exclude new uses of known products or processes in order to promote access to medicines and to ensure that only inventions which are new, involving an inventive step, and are capable of industrial application can be patented. This would also prevent evergreening.

Third, the current patent law in Nigeria does not allow for substantive examination of patents. This research suggests an amendment of the patent law to include a substantial examination clause. This is to ensure that only inventions that meet patentability standards are approved. In addition, Nigeria should also borrow from Brazil and allow the participation of the health sector in the examination and analysis of pharmaceutical patents. This would ensure that a patent application is examined in light of its impact on public health. This is also in line with Article 8 of the TRIPS Agreement, which permits members to adopt measures necessary to protect public health when formulating domestic laws.

Fourth, the book reveals the gap in communication among government regulatory agencies, which has created a system where contradiction and incoherence thrive. This study therefore recommends the institution of a committee similar to the Brazilian GIPI. This committee should consist of agencies and government departments whose oversight duties interface with the patent regime and should be required to meet on a monthly basis to ensure that each department or agency is well-informed of the workings and activities of the other. This will not only reduce fragmentation and policy contradiction, but would also encourage the development of a cohesive patent regulatory strategy and effective enforcement mechanisms.

Sixth, as analyses in Brazil and India show, strong advocacy remains at the heart of achieving progress on access issues. Civil society in Nigeria needs a reorientation and further education on IP. In this regard, IP and trade law courses should be made available in order to build IP capacity especially for

[18] TRIPS Agreement, Art 27.

those who do not have a legal background. This is important as these actors will act as bulwark against the implementation of TRIPS-plus provisions when Nigeria amends and updates its patent laws.

Finally, more efforts should be devoted by the Nigerian Government in terms of creating public research institutions to develop the technical and scientific capabilities and workforce that will engage in research and development of pharmaceutical and health technologies. Investment in these publicly funded institutions will help in developing essential medicines and health technologies to research and treat diseases that affect millions of Nigerians.

Bibliography

ARCHIVE MATERIAL

Kurian, P, The Compulsory License Application From M/S Natco Pharma Ltd (2011).

Letter From DG Shah (Secretary General Of The Indian Pharmaceutical Alliance) To Shri Murasali Muran (Honourable Minister Of Commerce And Industry) Dated 23 March 2000, Letter.

Sankalp Rehabilitation Trust Petition.

BOOKS

Adusei, P, *Patenting Of Pharmaceuticals And Development In Sub-Saharan Africa* (Heidelberg, Springer, 2013).

Aginam, O, Rupiya, M and U Press, *HIV/AIDS And The Security Sector In Africa* (Tokyo, United Nations University Press, 2012).

Anderfelt, U, *International Patent-Legislation And Developing Countries* (The Hague, Martinus Nijhoff, 1971).

Anghie, A, *Imperialism, Sovereignty And The Making Of International Law* (Cambridge, Cambridge University Press, 2005).

Anghie, A, Chimni, B, Okafor, O and Mickelson, K, *The Third World And International Order: Law, Politics, And Globalization* (Alphen aan den Rijn, Kluwer Law International, 2003).

Apter, A, *The Pan-African Nation: Oil And The Spectacle Of Culture In Nigeria* (Chicago, University of Chicago Press, 2005).

Arup, CW Caenegem, *Intellectual Property Policy Reform* (Cheltenham, Edward Elgar Publishing, 2009).

Banakar, RM Travers, *Theory And Method In Socio-Legal Research* (Oxford, Hart Publishing, 2005).

Basso, ME Rodrigues Jr, *Intellectual Property Law In Brazil* (Alphen aan den Rijn, Kluwer Law International, 2010).

Bedjaoui, M, *International Law* (Dordrecht, Martinus Nijhoff, 1992).

Bermudez, J, Epsztejn, R, Oliveira, M and Hasenclever, L, *The WTO TRIPS Agreement And Patent Protection In Brazil: Recent Changes And Implications For Local Production And Access To Medicines* (Rio de Janeiro, Oswaldo Cruz Foundation, 2002).

Boateng, B, *The Copyright Thing Doesn't Work Here* (Minneapolis, University of Minnesota Press, 2011).

Bodenhausen, G, *Guide To The Application Of The Paris Convention For The Protection Of Industrial Property, As Revised At Stockholm In 1967* (Geneva, United International Bureaux for the Protection of Intellectual Property, 1968).

Bottomore, T, L Harris, V Kiernan and R Miliband, *A Dictionary Of Marxist Thought*, 2nd edn (Oxford, Blackwell, 1985).

Braithwaite, J and Drahos, P, *Global Business Regulation* (Cambridge, Cambridge University Press, 2000).

Cardoso, F and Winter, B, *The Accidental President Of Brazil* (New York, PublicAffairs, 2006).

Cassese, A, *International Law In A Divided World* (Oxford, Clarendon Press, 1986).

Chatterjee, P, *The Politics Of The Governed* (New York, Columbia University Press, 2006).

Chaudhuri, S, *The WTO And India's Pharmaceuticals Industry: Patent Protection, TRIPS, And Developing Countries* (Oxford, Oxford University Press, 2006).
Chibber, V, *Locked In Place: State-Building And Late Industrialization In India* (Princeton, Princeton University Press, 2003).
Chimni, B, *International Law And World Order* (New Delhi, Sage Publications, 1993).
Cimoli, M, Dosi, G, Maskus, K, Okediji, R, Reichman, J and Stiglitz, J, *Intellectual Property Rights* (Oxford, Oxford University Press, 2014).
Comaroff, J and Comaroff, JL, *Law And Disorder In The Postcolony* (Chicago, University of Chicago Press, 2006).
De Beer, J, *Innovation Et Intellectual Property* (Cape Town, UCT Press, 2014).
Deere, C, *The Implementation Game: The TRIPS Agreement And The Global Politics Of Intellectual Property Reform In Developing Countries* (Oxford, Oxford University Press, 2008).
Denscombe, M, *The Good Research Guide*, 3rd edn (London, Open University Press, 2007).
Doyle, M, *Ways Of War And Peace* (New York, Norton, 1998).
Drahos, P, *The Global Governance Of Knowledge: Patent Offices And Their Clients* (Cambridge, Cambridge University Press, 2010).
—— *A Philosophy Of Intellectual Property* (New Hampshire, Dartmouth University Press, 1996).
Drahos, P and Braithwaite, J, *Information Feudalism* (Oxford, Oxford University Press, 2003).
Drahos, P and Mayne, R, *Global Intellectual Property Rights: Knowledge, Access And Development* (Hampshire, Palgrave Macmillan, 2002).
Dreyfuss, R and Rodriguez-Garavito, C, *Balancing Wealth And Health: The Battle Over Intellectual Property And Access To Medicines In Latin America* (Oxford, Oxford University Press, 2014).
Dutfield, G and Suthersanen, U, *Global Intellectual Property Law* (Cheltenham, Edward Elgar Publishing, 2008).
Elahi, S, de Beer, J, Kawooya, D and Rizk, N, *Knowledge & Innovation In Africa* (Cape Town, Open AIR, 2013).
Epelle, S, *Nigeria Speaks / Alhaji Sir Abubakar Tafawa Balewa; Speeches Made Between 1957 And 1964* (Ikeja, Longmans of Nigeria, 1964).
Epstein, S, *Impure Science: AIDS, Activism, And The Politics Of Knowledge* (Oakland, University of California Press, 1996).
Escobar, A, *Encountering Development: The Making And Unmaking Of The Third World* (Princeton, Princeton University Press, 2004).
Eslava, L, *Local Space, Global Life* (Cambridge, Cambridge University Press, 2015).
Falk, R, Stevens, J and Rajagopal, B, *International Law And The Third World: Reshaping Justice* (London, Routledge-Cavendish, 2008).
Falzon, M, *Multi-Sited Ethnography* (Farnham, Ashgate Publishing, 2009).
Fanon, F, *Black Skin, White Masks* (New York, Grove Press, 2008).
Faúndez, J, *Law And Development* (Abingdon, Routledge, 2012).
Flynn, M, *Pharmaceutical Autonomy And Public Health In Latin America: State, Society And Industry In Brazil's AIDS Program* (Abingdon, Routledge, 2014).
Forrest, T, *The Advance Of African Capital: The Growth Of Nigerian Private Enterprise* (Charlottesville, University Press of Virginia, 1994).
Gereffi, G, *The Pharmaceutical Industry And Dependency In The Third World* (Princeton, Princeton University Press, 1983).
Goldsmith, J and Posner, E, *The Limits Of International Law* (Oxford, Oxford University Press, 2007).
Hoen, E, *The Global Politics Of Pharmaceutical Monopoly Power: Drugs, Access, Innovation And The Application Of The WTO Doha Declaration On TRIPS And Public Health* (Diemen, AMB Publishers, 2009).
Kapczynski, A and Krikorian, G, *Access To Knowledge In The Age Of Intellectual Property* (New York, Zone Books, 2010).

Kapstein, EJ Busby, *AIDS Drugs For All: Social Movement And Market Transformations* (Cambridge, Cambridge University Press, 2013).

Kew, D, *Civil Society, Conflict Resolution, And Democracy In Nigeria* (Syracuse, Syracuse University Press, 2016).

Kidron, M, *Foreign Investments In India* (Oxford, Oxford University Press, 1965).

Koskenniemi, M, *From Apology To Utopia: The Structure Of International Legal Argument*, 2nd edn (Cambridge, Cambridge University Press, 2005).

Kothari, A and Shrivastava, A, *Churning The Earth: The Making Of Global India* (New Delhi, Penguin Books, 2014).

Kuanpoth, J, *Patent Rights In Pharmaceuticals In Developing Countries* (Cheltenham, Edward Elgar Publishing, 2010).

Law J and Martin, E, *A Dictionary Of Law* (Oxford, Oxford University Press, 2009).

Lewis-Beck, M, Bryman, A and Liao, T, *The SAGE Encyclopedia Of Social Science Research Methods Volume 1* (Thousand Oaks, Sage Publications, 2004).

MacQueen, H and Waelde, C, *Intellectual Property: The Many Faces Of The Public Domain* (Cheltenham, Edward Elgar Publishing, 2007).

May C and Sell, S, *Intellectual Property Rights* (Boulder, Lynne Rienner Publishers, 2006).

Mbembe, A, *On The Postcolony* (Oakland, University of California Press, 2001).

McGoey, L, *No Such Thing As A Free Gift* (New York, Verso, 2016).

Mgbeoji, I, *Global Biopiracy: Patents, Plants And Indigenous Knowledge* (Vancouver, UBC Press, 2014).

Moyo, D, *Dead Aid* (New York, Farrar, Straus and Giroux, 2009).

Narayanan, P, *Patent Law*, 4th edn (Kolkata, Eastern Law House, 2013).

Ndulu, B, O'Connell, S, Bates, R, Collier, P and Soludo, C, *The Political Economy Of Economic Growth In Africa, 1960–2000* (Cambridge, Cambridge University Press, 2007).

Nunn, A, *The Politics And History Of AIDS Treatment In Brazil* (New York, Springer, 2008).

Oguamanam, C, *International Law And Indigenous Knowledge* (Toronto, University of Toronto Press, 2008).

Olukoshi, A, *The Politics Of Structural Adjustment In Nigeria* (Suffolk, James Currey, 1993).

Pahuja, S, *Decolonising International Law: Development, Economic Growth, And The Politics Of Universality* (Cambridge, Cambridge University Press, 2011).

Patton, M, *Qualitative Research And Evaluation Methods* (Thousand Oaks, Sage Publications, 2002).

Peterson, K, *Speculative Markets: Drug Circuits And Derivative Life In Nigeria* (Durham, Duke University Press, 2014).

Pieterse, J, *Development Theory: Deconstructions/Reconstructions* (London, Sage Publications, 2009).

Pogge T, Rimmer, M and Rubenstein, K, *Incentives For Global Public Health* (Cambridge, Cambridge University Press, 2010).

Ragavan, S, *Patent And Trade Disparities In Developing Countries* (Oxford, Oxford University Press, 2012).

Raghavan, C, *Recolonization: General Agreement On Tariffs And Trade, The Uruguay Round And The Third World* (Penang, Third World Network, 1990).

Rajagopal B, *International Law From Below: Development, Social Movements and Third World Resistance* (Cambridge, Cambridge University Press, 2003).

Reis, R, Terto Júnior, V and Pimenta, M, *Intellectual Property Rights And Access To ARV Medicines* (São Paulo, ABIA, 2009).

Richards, D, *Intellectual Property Rights And Global Capitalism: The Political Economy Of The TRIPS Agreement* (New York, ME Sharpe Inc, 2004).

Ricoeur, P, *Oneself As Another* (Chicago, University of Chicago Press, 1992).

Robert, Y, *Postcolonialism: An Historical Introduction* (Massachusetts, Blackwell Publishing Ltd, 2001).

Roberts, K, *Key Concepts In Sociology* (China, Palgrave Macmillan, 2008).
Robin, A, 'Transfer Of Technology Agreement And The Access To HIV/AIDS Drugs: The Brazilian Case' (2008) (Cheltenham, Edward Elgar Publishing).
Roett, R, *The New Brazil: From Backwater To BRIC* (Washington DC, Brookings Institution Press, 2010).
Roffe P, Tansey, G and Vivas-Eugui, D, *Negotiating Health: Intellectual Property And Access To Medicines* (London, Earthscan, 2006).
Roth, B, *Governmental Illegitimacy In International Law* (Oxford, Oxford University Press, 1996).
Said, E, *Orientalism: Western Conceptions Of The Orient* (London, Penguin Books Ltd, 2003).
Santos, B and Rodríguez-Garavito, C, *Law And Globalization From Below Towards A Cosmopolitan Legality* (Cambridge, Cambridge University Press, 2005).
Santos, B, *Epistemologies Of The South: Justice Against Epistemicide* (Boulder, Paradigm Publishers, 2014).
Scott, D, *Conscripts Of Modernity* (Durham, Duke University Press, 2004).
—— *Refashioning Futures: Criticism After Postcoloniality* (Princeton, Princeton University Press, 1999).
Sell, S, *Private Power, Public Law: The Globalization Of Intellectual Property Rights* (Cambridge, Cambridge University Press, 2003).
Selvaraj, S, Abrol, D and Gopakumar, K, *Access To Medicines In India* (Haryana, Academic Foundation, 2014).
Sen, A, *Development As Freedom* (Oxford, Oxford University Press, 2001).
Shaver L, Subramanian, R and Shaver, L, *Access To Knowledge In India* (London, Bloomsbury Publishing, 2011).
Shaw, M, *International Law*, 5th edn (Cambridge, Cambridge University Press, 2003).
Simpson, G, *Great Powers And Outlaw States: Unequal Sovereigns In The International Legal Order* (Cambridge, Cambridge University Press, 2004).
Siollun, M, *Nigeria's Military Coup Culture: From Major Nzeogwu To LT-Colonel Dimka (1966–1976)* (New York, Algora Publishing, 2009).
Soludo, C, Ogbu, M and Chang, H, *The Politics Of Trade And Industrial Policy In Africa* (Trenton, Africa World Press, 2004).
Soludo C and Mkandawire, P, *African Voices On Structural Adjustment: A Companion To Our Continent, Our Future* (Ottawa, International Development Research Centre, 2003).
Srinivasan, T and Tendulkar, S, *Reintegrating India With The World Economy* (Washington DC, Peterson Institute for International Economics, 2003).
Stack, A, *International Patent Law* (Cheltenham, Edward Elgar Publishing, 2011).
Stiglitz, J, *The Price Of Inequality* (New York, WW Norton and Co Inc, 2013).
Stone M, Rua Wall, I and Douzinas, C, *New Critical Legal Thinking* (New York, Birkbeck Law Press–Routledge, 2011).
Tripathi, D and Jumani, J, *The Concise Oxford History Of Indian Business* (New Delhi, Oxford University Press, 2007).
Trubek D, Alviar Garcia, H, Coutinho, D and Santos, A, *Law And The New Developmental State: The Brazilian Experience In Latin American Context* (Cambridge, Cambridge University Press, 2013).
UNCTAD-ICTSD, *Resource Book On TRIPS And Development* (Cambridge, Cambridge University Press, 2005).
Verzijl J, Heere, W and Offerhaus, J, *International Law In Historical Perspective* (Leyden, AW Sijthoff, 1968).
Verzijl, J, *International Law In Historical Perspective* (Leyden, AW Sijthoff, 1970).
Vojacek, J, *A Survey Of The Principal National Patent Systems* (New York, Prentice-Hall Inc, 1936).
Wade, R, *Governing The Market* (Princeton, Princeton University Press, 1990).
Werbner, R and Ranger, T, *Postcolonial Identities In Africa* (London, Zed Books, 1996).
Weyland, K, *Democracy Without Equity* (Pittsburgh, University of Pittsburgh Press, 1996).

World Intellectual Property Organization, *WIPO Intellectual Property Handbook*, 2nd edn (Geneva, WIPO, 2004).

Wood J and Shearing, C, *Imagining Security* (Cullompton, Willan, 2007).

Yamane H, *Interpreting TRIPS: Globalisation Of Intellectual Property Rights And Access To Medicines* (Bloomsbury, Bloomsbury Publishing, 2010).

CHAPTERS OF AN EDITED BOOK

Abbott, F, Correa, C and Drahos, P, 'Emerging Markets And The World Patent Order – The Forces Of Change' in F Abbott, C Correa and P Drahos (eds), *Emerging Markets and the World Patent Order* (Cheltenham, Edward Elgar Publishing, 2013).

Aggarwal, V and Mukherji, R, 'India's Shifting Trade Policy: South Asia And Beyond' in V Aggarwal and M Koo (eds), *Asia's New Institutional Architecture: Evolving Structures for Managing Trade, Financial, and Security Relation* (New York, Springer, 2008).

Badin, M, 'Developmental Responses To The International Trade Legal Game: Cases Of Intellectual Property And Export Credit Law Reforms In Brazil' in D Trubek, H Alviar Garcia, D Coutinho and A Santos (eds), *Law and the New Developmental State: The Brazilian Experience in Latin American Context* (Cambridge, Cambridge University Press, 2013).

Bagura, Y, 'IMF And World Bank Conditionality And Nigeria's Structural Adjustment Programme' in K Havnevik (ed), *The IMF and the World Bank in Africa: Conditionality, Impact and Alternatives* (Uppsala, Scandinavian Institute of African Studies, 1987).

Banerji, S, 'The Indian Intellectual Property Regime And The Trips Agreement' in C Long (ed), *Intellectual Property Rights in Emerging Markets* (Washington DC, American Enterprise Institute (AEI) Press, 2000).

Barbosa, D, 'Patent And The Emerging Markets In Latin America – Brazil' in F Abbott, C Correa and P Drahos (eds), *Emerging Markets and the World Patent Order* (Cheltenham, Edward Elgar Publishing, 2013).

Basheer, S, Sanklecha, J and Gowda, P, 'Pharmaceutical Patent Enforcement' in R Okediji and M Bagley (eds), *Patent Law in Global Perspective* (Oxford, Oxford University Press, 2014).

Baxi, U, 'Geographies Of Injustice: Human Rights At The Altar Of Convenience' in C Scott (ed), *Torture as Tort: Comparative Perspectives on the Development of Transnational Human Rights Litigation* (Oxford, Hart Publishing, 2001).

Bermudez, J, Oliveira, M and Andrade de Oliveira, E, 'Expanding Access To Essential Medicines In Brazil: Recent Regulation And Public Policies' in J Bermudez and M Oliveira (eds), *Intellectual Property in the Context of the WTO TRIPS Agreement: Challenges for Public Health*, 2nd edn (Rio de Janeiro, Oswaldo Cruz Foundation, 2004).

Bhandari, S, 'From The Era Of Colonialism To Globalization: Making Rules In The GATT/WTO' in JH Paik, SW Lee and KYL Tan (eds), *Asian Approaches to International Law and the Legacy of Colonialism: The Law of the Sea, Territorial Disputes and International Dispute Settlement* (London, Routledge, 2013).

Biersteker, T, 'Indigenization And The Nigerian Bourgeoisie: Dependent Development In An African Context' in P Lubeck (ed), *The African Bourgeoisie: The Development of Capitalism in Nigeria, Kenya and the Ivory Coast* (Boulder, Lynne Rienner Publishers, 1987).

Calboli, I, 'The Role Of Comparative Legal Analysis In Intellectual Property Law: From Good To Great?' in G Dinwoodie (ed), *Methods and Perspectives in Intellectual Property* (Cheltenham, Edward Elgar Publishing, 2013).

Cassier, M and Correa, M, 'Patents, Innovation And Public Health: Brazilian Public-Sector Laboratories' Experience In Copying AIDS Drugs' in JP Moatti (ed), *Economics of AIDS and Access to HIV/AIDS Care in Developing Countries; Issues and Challenges* (Paris, ANRS, 2003).

Chavez, G and Reis, R, 'Health, Intellectual Property And Innovation: A Case Study Of Brazil' in C Correa (ed), *Pharmaceutical Innovation, Incremental Patenting and Compulsory Licensing* (Geneva, South Centre, 2013).

Chaudhuri, S, 'The Pharmaceutical Industry In India After TRIPS' in H Löfgren and O Williams (eds), *The New Political Economy of Pharmaceuticals: Production, Innovation and TRIPS in the Global South* (Hampshire, Palgrave Macmillan, 2013).

Chimni, B, 'Critical Theory And International Economic Law: A Third World Approach To International Law (TWAIL) Perspective' in J Linarelli (ed), *Research Handbook on Global Justice and International Economic Law* (Cheltenham, Edward Elgar Publishing, 2013).

Chon M, 'PPPs In Global IP (Public–Private Partnerships In Global Intellectual Property)' in G Dinwoodie (ed), *Methods and Perspectives in Intellectual Property* (Cheltenham, Edward Elgar Publishing, 2013).

Correa, C, 'The Use Of Compulsory Licenses In Latin America' in R Hilty and L Kung-Chung (eds), *Compulsory Licensing: Practical Experiences and Ways Forward* (Heidelberg, Springer, 2015).

dos Santos Tarragô, P, 'Negotiating For Brazil' in J Watal and A Taubman (eds), *The Making of the TRIPS Agreement: Personal Insights from the Uruguay Round Negotiations* (Geneva, World Trade Organization, 2015).

Dosi, G and Stiglitz, J, 'The Role Of Intellectual Property In The Development Process, With Some Lessons From Developed Countries: An Introduction' in M Cimoli, G Dosi, K Maskus, R Okediji, J Reichman and J Stiglitz (eds), *Intellectual Property Rights: Legal and Economic Challenges for Development* (Oxford, Oxford University Press, 2014).

Drahos, P, 'The Jewel In The Crown: India's Patent Office And Patent-Based Innovation' in C Arup and W van Caenegem (eds), *Intellectual Property Policy Reform: Fostering Innovation and Development* (Cheltenham, Edward Elgar Publishing, 2009).

—— '"IP World" – Made By TNC Inc.' in G Krikorian and A Kapczynski (eds), *Access to Knowledge in the Age of Intellectual Property* (New York, Zone Books, 2010).

Dreyfuss, R, 'Intellectual Property Lawmaking, Global Governance, And Emerging Economies' in R Okediji and M Bagley (eds), *Patent Law in Global Perspective* (Oxford, Oxford University Press, 2014).

Flynn, M, 'Corporate Power And State Resistance: Brazil's Use Of TRIPS Flexibilities For Its National AIDS Program' in K Shadlen, S Guennif, A Guzmán and N Lalitha (eds), *Intellectual Property, Pharmaceuticals and Public Health* (Cheltenham, Edward Elgar Publishing, 2011).

Ganesan, A, 'Negotiating For India' in J Watal and A Taubman (eds), *The Making of the TRIPS Agreement: Personal insights from the Uruguay Round Negotiations* (Geneva, World Trade Organization, 2015).

Gathii, J, 'Third World Approaches To International Economic Governance' in R Falk, B Rajagopal and J Stevens (eds), *International Law and the Third World, Reshaping Justice* (London, Routledge-Cavendish, 2008).

—— 'Approaches To Accessing Essential Medicines And The TRIPS Agreement' in P K Yu (ed), *Intellectual Property and Information Wealth* (Santa Barbara, Greenwood Publishing Group, 2006).

—— 'The Agenda Of Third World Approaches To International Law (TWAIL)' in J Dunoff and M Pollack (eds), *International Legal Theory: Foundations and Frontiers* (Cambridge, Cambridge University Press, 2019).

George, J, 'India, Intellectual Property And Access To Medicines: Developments And Civil Society Initiatives In India' in R Reis, V Terto Jr and M Pimenta (eds), *Intellectual Property Rights And Access To ARV Medicines* (São Paulo, ABIA, 2009).

Gopalakrishnan, N and Anand, M, 'Compulsory License Under Indian Patent Law' in R Hilty and L Kung-Chung (eds), *Compulsory Licensing: Practical Experiences and Ways Forward* (Heidelberg, Springer, 2015).

Ho, C, 'Current Controversies Concerning Patent Rights And Public Health In A World Of International Norms' in *Patent Law and Theory: A Handbook of Contemporary Research* (Cheltenham, Edward Elgar Publishing, 2008).

Hudson, R, 'Import-Substitution Industrialization, 1945–64' in R Hudson (ed), *Brazil: A Country Study* (Washington DC, Library of Congress Federal Research Division, 1998).

Kew, D and Kwaja, C, 'Civil Society In Nigeria' in A Levan and P Ukata (eds), *The Oxford Handbook of Nigerian Politics* (Oxford, Oxford University Press, 2018).

Kew, D and Oshikoya, M, 'Escape From Tyranny: Civil Society And Democratic Struggles In Africa' in E Obadare (ed), *The Handbook of Civil Society in Africa* (New York, Springer, 2013).

Lalitha, N, 'Access To Indian Generic Drugs: Emerging Issues' in K Shadlen, S Guennif, A Guzmán and N Lalitha (eds) *Intellectual Property, Pharmaceuticals and Public Health: Access to Drugs in Developing Countries* (Cheltenham, Edward Elgar Publishing, 2011).

Le Loup, G, Pereira de Assis, A, Costa-Couto, M, Fleury, S, de Camargo, K and Thoenig, J, 'The Brazilian Experience Of "Scaling Up": A Public Policy Approach' in B Coriat (ed), *The Political Economy of HIV/AIDS in Developing Countries: TRIPS, Public Health Systems, and Free Access* (London, Edward Elgar Publishing, 2008).

Love, J, 'Access To Medicine And Compliance With The WTO TRIPS Accord' in P Drahos and R Mayne (eds), *Global Intellectual Property Rights* (Hampshire, Palgrave Macmillan, 2002).

Loxely, J, 'The IMF, The World Bank, And Sub-Saharan Africa: Policies And Politics' in K Havnevik (ed), *The IMF and the World Bank in Africa: Conditionality, Impact and Alternatives* (Uppsala, Scandinavian Institute of African Studies, 1987).

Mamattah, T, 'Building Civil Society In West Africa: Notes From The Field' in E Obadare (ed), *The Handbook of Civil Society in Africa* (New York, Springer, 2013).

Mgbeoji, I, 'A False Dawn? TRIPS And TRIPS-Plus Impacts In Africa' in D Gervais (ed), *Intellectual Property, Trade and Development* (Oxford, Oxford University Press, 2014).

Mustafa, A, 'Civil Rights And Pro-Democracy Groups In And Outside Nigeria' in D Bach, Y Lebeau and K Amuwo (eds), *Nigeria during the Abacha Years (1993–1998): The Domestic and International Politics of Democratization* (Ibadan, Institut Français de Recherche en Afrique, 2001).

Natarajan, U, 'Third World Approaches To International Law (TWAIL) And The Environment' in A Philippopoulos-Mihalopoulos and V Brooks (eds), *Research Methods in Environmental Law* (Cheltenham, Edward Elgar Publishing, 2017).

Nayar, J, 'Between Hope And Despair: The Iraq War And International Law Futures?' in P Shiner and A Williams (eds), *The Iraq War and International Law* (Oxford, Hart Publishing, 2008).

Obasanjo, I and Oduwole, M, 'Influencing HIV/AIDS Policies And Programs Through A Participatory Process' in O Adeyi (ed), *AIDS in Nigeria: A Nation on the Threshold* (Cambridge, Harvard University Press, 2006).

Odinkalu, C, 'The Impact Of Economic And Social Rights In Nigeria: An Assessment Of The Legal Framework For Implementing Education And Health As Human Right' in V Gauri and D Brinks (eds), *Courting Social Justice: Judicial Enforcement of Social and Economic Right in the Developing World* (Cambridge, Cambridge University Press, 2008).

—— 'The Management Of Transition To Civil Rule By The Military In Nigeria (1966–1996)' in D Bach, Y Lebeau and K Amuwo (eds), *Nigeria during the Abacha Years (1993–1998): The Domestic and International Politics of Democratization* (Ibadan, Institut Français de Recherche en Afrique, 2001).

Ogbogu, I and Idogho, O, 'The Role Of Civil Society Organizations In HIV/AIDS Control' in O Adeyi (ed), *AIDS in Nigeria: A Nation on the Threshold* (Cambridge, Harvard University Press, 2006).

Okediji, R, 'Public Welfare And The International Patent System' in R Okediji and M Bagley (eds), *Patent Law in Global Perspective* (Oxford, Oxford University Press, 2014).

—— 'History Lessons For The WIPO Development Agenda' in N Netanel (ed), *The Development Agenda: Global Intellectual Property and Developing Countries* (Oxford, Oxford University Press, 2008).

Oliveira, M, Chaves, G and Epsztejn, R, 'Brazilian Intellectual Property Legislation' in J Bermudez and M Oliveira (eds), *Intellectual Property in the Context of the WTO TRIPS Agreement: Challenges for Public Health*, 2nd edn (Rio de Janeiro, Oswaldo Cruz Foundation, 2004).

Orsi, F, Hasenclever, L, Fialho, B, Tigre, P and Coriat, B, 'Intellectual Property Rights, Anti-AIDS Policy And Generic Drugs. Lessons From The Brazilian Public Health Program' in JP Moatti, T Barnett, B Coriat, Y Souteyrand, J Dumoulin and YA Flori (eds), *Economics of AIDS and Access to HIV/AIDS Care in Developing Countries* (Paris, Agence Nationale de Recherches sur le Sida, 2003).

Park, C and Jayadev, A, 'Access To Medicines In India: A Review Of Recent Concerns' in R Subramanian and L Shaver (eds), *Access to Knowledge in India: New Research on Intellectual Property, Innovation & Development* (London, Bloomsbury Academic, 2011).

Parthasarathy, S and Walker, A, 'Observing The Patent System In Social And Political Perspective: A Case Study Of Europe' in R Okediji and M Bagley (eds), *Patent Law in Global Perspective* (Oxford, Oxford University Press, 2014).

Peterson, K, 'Intellectual Property Designs: Drugs, Governance, And Nigerian (Non-) Compliance With The World Trade Organization' in P Geissler, R Rottenburg and J Zenker (eds), *Rethinking Biomedicine and Governance in Africa: Contributions from Anthropology* (Bielefeld, Transcript Verlag, 2012).

Pogge, T, 'The Health Impact Fund: Better Pharmaceutical Innovations At Much Lower Prices' in T Pogge, M Rimmer and K Rubenstein (eds), *Incentives for Global Public Health: Patent Law and Access to Essential Medicines* (Cambridge, Cambridge University Press, 2010).

Rajagopal, B, 'International Law And Third World Resistance: A Theoretical Inquiry' in *The Third World & International Order: Law, Politics and Globalization* (Alphen aan den Rijn, Kluwer Law International, 2003).

Roffe, P and Vea, G, 'The WIPO Development Agenda In An Historical And Political Context' in NW Netanel (ed), *The Development Agenda: Global Intellectual Property and Developing Countries* (Oxford, Oxford University Press, 2008).

Roffe, P, Spennemann, C and von Braun, J, 'From Paris To Doha: The WTO Doha Declaration On The TRIPS Agreement And Public Health' in P Roffe, G Tansey and D Vivas-Egui (eds), *Negotiating Health: Intellectual Property and Access to Medicines* (London, Earthscan Publications, 2006).

Rosina M, Wang, D and De Campos, T, 'Access To Medicines: Pharmaceutical Patents And The Right To Health' in L Shaver (ed), *Access To Knowledge In Brazil: New Research On Intellectual Property, Innovation And Development* (Connecticut, Yale Law School, 2008).

Shaffer, G and Sell, S, 'Transnational Legal Ordering And Access To Medicines' in R Okediji and M Bagley (eds), *Patent Law in Global Perspective* (Oxford, Oxford University Press, 2014).

Sweet, C, 'The Political Economy Of Pharmaceutical Production In Brazil' in H Löfgren and O Williams (eds), *The New Political Economy of Pharmaceuticals: Production, Innovation and TRIPS in the Global South* (Hampshire, Palgrave Macmillan, 2013).

Teixeira P, Vitória, M and Barcarolo, J, 'Brazilian Experience In Providing Universal Access To Antiretroviral Therapy' in JP Moatti (ed), *Economics of Aids and Access to HIV/AIDS Care in Developing Countries; Issues and Challenges* (Paris, ANRS, 2003).

Teubner, G, 'Global Bukowina: Legal Pluralism In The World Society' in G Teubner (ed), *Global Law Without a State* (Brookfield, Aldershot, 1997).

—— 'Legal Irritants: How Unifying Law Ends Up In New Divergences' in P Hall and D Soskice (eds), *Varieties of Capitalism: The Institutional Foundations of Comparative Advantage* (Oxford, Oxford University Press, 2001).

Trubek, D, Coutinho, D and Schapiro, M, 'New State Activism In Brazil And The Challenge For Law' in D Trubek, H Alviar Garcia, D Coutinho and A Santos (eds), *The Brazilian Experience in Latin American Context* (Cambridge, Cambridge University Press, 2013).

Walker, RBJ, 'Space/Time/Sovereignty' in M Denham and MO Lombardi (eds), *Perspectives on Third World Sovereignty: The Postmodern Paradox* (New York, St Martin's Press, 1996).

Watal, J, 'Developing Countries And The Protection Of Intellectual Property Rights: Current Issues In The WTO' in G Bermann and P Mavroidis (eds), *WTO Law and Developing Countries* (Cambridge, Cambridge University Press, 2007).

CONFERENCE PROCEEDINGS

Blackhurst R, Lyakurwa, B and Oyejide, A, 'Improving African Participation In The WTO', *World Bank for a Conference at the WTO* (World Bank, 1999).

Mutua M and Anghie, A, 'What Is TWAIL' (2000) 94 *Proceedings of the Annual Meeting* (American Society of International Law).

Odinkalu, C, 'Do Our People Matter To Our Courts?: The Case Of Justiciable Socio-Economic Rights In Nigeria', *1st Annual Human Rights Conference of the Nigerian Bar Association* (Unpublished (hard copy with author), 2009).

Schulz, C and Wu, M, 'The TRIPS Agreement And Intellectual Property Protection In Brazil' (2004) 98 *Proceedings of the Annual Meeting* (American Society of International Law).

Serra J, 'The Political Economy Of The Brazilian Struggle Against AIDS' (2004).

'Statement By Dr Subramanian Swamy, Union Minister Of Commerce, Law And Justice', *Multilateral Trade Negotiation: Uruguay Round (MTN/TNC/MIN(90)/ST/46)* (1990).

DISSERTATIONS

Adebola, T, 'The Regime Complex For Plant Variety Protection: Revisiting TRIPS Implementation In Nigeria', Ph D (University of Warwick, 2017).

Ebohon, S, 'Nigerian Policy Towards Foreign Companies: Case Study Of The Multinational Pharmaceutical Formulation Plants, 1972–1983', PhD (University of Manchester, 1985).

Eslava, L, 'Local Space, Global Life: The Everyday Operations Of International Law And Development', PhD (Melbourne Law School, University of Melbourne, 2012).

Flynn, M, 'Pharmaceutical Governance In Brazil: Globalization, Institutions And AIDS', PhD (University of Texas at Austin, 2010).

Kılıç, B, 'Boosting Pharmaceutical Innovation In The Post-Trips Era; The Real Life Lessons For The Developing World', PhD (Queen Mary, University of London, 2011).

Mahajan, M, 'The Politics Of Public Health Emergencies: AIDS Epidemics In India And South Africa', PhD (Cornell University, 2008).

Massard da Fonseca, E, 'Reforming Pharmaceutical Regulation: A Case Study Of Generic Drugs In Brazil', PhD (University of Edinburgh, 2011).

Mohammed, I, 'The Nigerian Enterprises Promotion Decrees (1972 And 1977) And Indigenisation In Nigeria', PhD (University of Warwick, 1985).

Owen, T, 'Patents, Pills, The Press And The Poor: Discourse And Hegemony In News Coverage Of The Global 'Access To Medicines' Dispute, 1997–2003', PhD (Massey University, 2012).

Sodipo, B, 'Piracy And Counterfeiting: The Freedom To Copy Vs Intellectual Property Rights', PhD (Queen Mary, University of London, 1995).

Yankey, G, 'The Role Of International Patent System In The Transfer Of Technology To West Africa: Cases Studies Of Ghana And Nigeria', PhD (University of Warwick, 1987).

ENCYCLOPEDIA ARTICLES

Abbott, F, 'Intellectual Property, International Protection' (2009) *Florida State University College of Law Public Law Research Paper No 601*.

Beckett, J, 'Critical International Legal Theory' in *Oxford Bibliographies Online Datasets* (2012).

Mutua M, 'What Is TWAIL?' in *The American Society of International Law Proceedings* (2000).
National AIDS/STI Control Programme, 'Integrated National Guidelines for HIV Prevention, Treatment And Care' (Federal Ministry of Health, 2014).

GOVERNMENT PUBLICATIONS

Federal Ministry of Health, 'President's Comprehensive Response Plan For HIV/AIDS In Nigeria' (Federal Ministry of Health, 2013).
Federal Ministry of Health, 'National Guidelines For HIV Prevention, Treatment And Care' (Federal Ministry of Health, 2013).
Laws of the Federation of Nigeria, 'Patents And Designs Act' (1990).
Planning Commission, 'First Plan (1951–1956)' (Government of India, 1951).
World Intellectual Property Organization, 'Paris Convention For The Protection Of Industrial Property' (1883).
United Nations Conference on Trade and Development, 'Report On The TRIPS Agreement And Developing Countries' (United Nations, 1996).

JOURNAL ARTICLES

Abbott, F, 'The Trips Agreement, Access To Medicines, And The WTO Doha Ministerial Conference' (2005) 5 *The Journal of World Intellectual Property* 15.
Abdulrahman, A, 'The Impact Of Military Rule On Nigeria's Nation Building, 1966–1979' (2014) 15 *Historical Research Letter* 18.
Abrol, D, Prajapati, P and Singh, N, 'Globalization Of The Indian Pharmaceutical Industry: Implications For Innovation' (2011) 3 *International Journal of Institutions and Economics* 327.
Aderibigbe, M, 'The Nigerian Patent System And The New Industrial Policy' (1990) 12 *World Patent Information* 95.
Adewopo, A, 'Public Health, Access To Medicines And Role Of Patent System In Nigeria' (2011) 1 *NIALS Journal of Intellectual Property Law* 164.
Adikibi, O, 'The Multinational Corporation And Monopoly Of Patents In Nigeria' (1988) 16 *World Development* 511.
Aiyede, E, 'The Dynamics Of Civil Society And The Democratization Process In Nigeria' (2003) 37 *Canadian Journal of African Studies / Revue Canadienne des Études Africaines* 1.
Al Attar, M and Miller, R, 'Towards An Emancipatory International Law: The Bolivarian Reconstruction' (2010) 31 *Third World Quarterly* 347.
Alexander, R, 'The Import-Substitution Strategy Of Economic Development' (1967) 1 *Journal of Economic Issues* 297.
Anghie, A, 'The Evolution Of International Law: Colonial And Postcolonial Realities' (2006) 27 *Third World Quarterly* 739.
—— 'Time Present And Time Past: Globalization, International Financial Institutions, And The Third World' (2000) 32 *New York University Journal International Law & Politics* 243.
—— 'LATCRIT And TWAIL' (2011) 42 *California Western International Law Journal* 311.
Anghie, A and Chimni, B, 'Third World Approaches To International Law And Individual Responsibility In Internal Conflicts' (2003) 2 *Chinese Journal of International Law* 77.
Appiagyei-Atua, K, 'Ethical Dimensions Of Third-World Approaches To International Law (TWAIL): A Critical Review' (2015) 8 *African Journal of Legal Studies* 209.
Attaran, A and Champ, P, 'Patent Rights And Local Working Under The WTO TRIPS Agreement: An Analysis Of The U.S.-Brazil Patent Dispute' (2002) 27 *Yale Journal of International Law* 365.

Baer, W, 'Import Substitution And Industrialization In Latin America: Experiences And Interpretations' (1972) 7 *Latin American Research Review* 95.

Bagchi, A, Banerjee, P, and Bhattacharya, U, 'Indian Patents Act And Its Relation To Technological Development In India-A Preliminary Investigation' (1984) 19 *Economic and Political Weekly* 287.

Bamgboye, P, 'The Military And Socio-Economic Development In Nigeria (1983 – 1999). A Critical Appraisal' (2014) 5 *Mediterranean Journal of Social Sciences* 2340.

Bandeira Galindo, G, 'Force Field: On History And Theory Of International Law' (2012) 20 *Rechtsgeschichte – Legal History* 86.

Barooah, S, 'India's Pharmaceutical Innovation Policy: Developing Strategies For Developing Country Needs' (2013) 5 *Trade, Law and Development* 150.

Basheer, S, 'Turning Trips On Its Head: An "IP Cross Retaliation" Model For Developing Countries' (2010) 3 *The Law and Development Review* 141.

Bass, N, 'Implications Of The Trips Agreement For Developing Countries: Pharmaceutical Patent Laws In Brazil And South Africa In The 21St Century' (2002) 34 *George Washington International Law Review* 191.

Baxi, U, 'New Approaches To The History Of International Law' (2006) 19 *Leiden Journal of International Law* 555.

—— 'What May The 'Third World' Expect From International Law?' (2006) 27 *Third World Quarterly* 713.

Bazzle T, 'Pharmacy Of The Developing World: Reconciling Intellectual Property Rights In India With The Right To Health' (2010) 42 *Georgetown Journal of International Law* 785.

Bennett, W, 'Indian Pharmaceutical Patent Law And The Effects Of Novartis Ag V. Union Of India' (2014) 13 *Washington University Global Studies Law Review* 535.

Berkman, A, Garcia, J, Munoz-Laboy, M, Paiva, V and Parker, R, 'A Critical Analysis Of The Brazilian Response To HIV/AIDS: Lessons Learned For Controlling And Mitigating The Epidemic In Developing Countries' (2005) 95 *American Journal of Public Health* 1162.

Biehl, J, Socal, M, Gauri, V, Diniz, D, Medeiros, M, Rondon, G and Amon, J, 'Judicialization 2.0: Understanding Right-To-Health Litigation In Real Time' (2018) 14 *Global Public Health* 190.

—— 'Patient-Citizen-Consumers: Judicialization Of Health And Metamorphosis Of Biopolitics' (2016) 98 *Lua Nova: Revista de Cultura e Política* 77.

—— 'The Activist State: Global Pharmaceuticals, AIDS, And Citizenship In Brazil' (2004) 22 *Social Text* 105.

Bird, R, 'The Emerging BRICS Economies: Lessons From Intellectual Property Negotiation And Enforcement.' (2007) 5 *Northwestern Journal of Technology and Intellectual Property* 400.

Boltwood, R, 'Basic Patent Law In Brazil, And Recent Developments' (2008) 1 *International In-house Counsel Journal* 1.

Bradley, M, 'Civil Society And Democratic Progression In Postcolonial Nigeria: The Role Of Non-Governmental Organizations' (2005) 1 *Journal of Civil Society* 61.

Braga, C, 'The Economics Of Intellectual Property And The GATT: A View From The South' (1989) 22 *Vanderbilt Journal of Transnational Law* 243.

Bravo, G, 'From Paris Convention To Trips: A Brief History' (2000) 12 *Journal Contemporary Legal Issues* 445.

Buchanan, R, 'Writing Resistance Into International Law' (2008) 10 *International Community Law Review* 445.

Burity, J, 'Reform Of The State And The New Discourse On Social Policy In Brazil' (2006) 33 *Latin American Perspectives* 67.

Burris, S, Drahos, P and Shearing, C, 'Nodal Governance' (2005) 30 *Australian Journal of Legal Philosophy* 3.

Carty, A, 'Critical International Law: Recent Trends In The Theory Of International Law' (1991) 2 *European Journal of International Law* 66.

Cassier, M and Correa, M, 'Intellectual Property And Public Health: Copying Of HIV/Aids Drugs By Brazilian Public And Private Pharmaceutical Laboratories' (2007) 1 *RECIIS* 83.

Chang, H, 'Intellectual Property Rights And Economic Development: Historical Lessons And Emerging Issues' (2001) 2 *Journal of Human Development* 287.

Chimni, B, 'A Just World Under Law: A View From The South' (2007) 22 *American University International Law Review* 199.

—— 'Political Economy Of The Uruguay Round Of Negotiations: A Perspective' (1992) 29 *International Studies* 135.

—— 'The Past, Present And Future Of International Law: A Critical Third World Approach' (2007) 8 *Melbourne Journal of International Law* 499.

—— 'The World Of TWAIL' (2011) 3 *Trade, Law and Development* [x].

—— 'Third World Approaches To International Law: A Manifesto' (2006) 8 *International Community Law Review* 3.

Chon, M, Barbosa, D and Hase, A, 'Slouching Towards Development In International Intellectual Property' (2008) 1 *Michigan State Law Review* 71.

Cohen, J and Lybecker, K, 'AIDS Policy And Pharmaceutical Patents: Brazil's Strategy To Safeguard Public Health' (2005) 28 *The World Economy* 211.

Comaroff, J and Comaroff, J, 'Theory From The South: Or, How Euro-America Is Evolving Toward Africa' (2012) 22 *Anthropological Forum* 113.

Correa, C, 'Is Section 3(D) Consistent With TRIPS?' (2013) 48 *Economic and Political Weekly* 49.

Dhavan, R, Harris, L and Jain, G, 'Whose Interest? Independent India's Patent Law And Policy' (1990) 32 *Journal of the Indian Law Institute* 429.

—— 'Conquest By Patent: The Paris Convention Revisited' (1990) 32 *Journal of Indian Law Institute* 131.

—— 'Power Without Responsibility: On Aspect Of Indian Patent Legislation' (1991) 33 *Journal of the Indian Law Institute* 1.

Drahos, P, 'Developing Countries And International Intellectual Property Standard-Setting' (2005) 5 *The Journal of World Intellectual Property* 765.

—— 'Global Intellectual Property Rights In Information: The Story Of TRIPS At The GATT' (1995) 13 *Prometheus* 6.

—— 'Intellectual Property And Pharmaceutical Markets: A Nodal Governance Approach' (2004) 77 *Temple Law Review* 401.

Drahos, P and Braithwaite, J, 'Intellectual Property, Corporate Strategy, Globalisation: TRIPS In Context' (2002) 20 *Wisconsin International Law Journal* 451.

Ebohon S, 'Conflict And Accommodation In A Post-Imperial Order: Reflections On Nigerian Policy Towards Foreign Capital, 1972–2010' (2012) 1 *International Journal of Developing Societies* 61.

—— 'Globalization, Technology Transfer And The Knowledge Gap: Case Study Of The Global Pharmaceutical Industry In Nigeria' (2012) 11 *Global Journal Of Social Sciences* 21.

—— 'Nigeria: State, Oil And Malignant Underdevelopment' (2012) 36 *The Western Journal of Black Studies* 201.

Edson Beas Jr, R and Murphy, B, 'Brazil's Prior Consent Law: A Dialogue Between Brazil And The United States Over Where The TRIPS Agreement Currently Sets The Balance Between The Protection Of Pharmaceutical Patents And Access To Medicines' (2006) 16 *Albany Law Journal of Science and Technology* 423.

Egwaikhide, F, 'Import Substitution Industrialisation In Nigeria: A Selective Review' (1997) 39 *The Nigerian Journal of Economic and Social Studies* 183.

El-Said, H and El-Said, M, 'TRIPS, Bilateralism, Multilateralism & Implications For Developing Countries: Jordan'S Drug Sector' (2005) 2 *Manchester Journal of International Economic Law* 59.

El-Said M, 'The Road From TRIPS-Minus, To TRIPS, To TRIPS-Plus' (2005) 8 *The Journal of World Intellectual Property* 53.

Eslava L, 'Istanbul Vignettes: Observing The Everyday Operation Of International Law' (2014) 2 *London Review of International Law* 3.

—— 'The Materiality Of International Law: Violence, History And Joe Sacco's The Great War' (2017) 5 *London Review of International Law* 49.
—— 'TWAIL Coordinates' (forthcoming) *Groningen Journal of International Law*.
Eslava, L and Pahuja, S, 'Between Resistance And Reform: TWAIL And The Universality Of International Law' (2011) 3 *Trade, Law and Development* 104.
—— 'Beyond The (Post)Colonial: TWAIL And The Everyday Life Of International Law' (2012) 45 *Journal of Law and Politics in Africa, Asia and Latin America – Verfassung und Recht in Übersee (VRÜ)* 195.
Ezejiofor. G, 'The Law Of Patents In Nigeria: A Review' (1973) 9 *African Legal Studies* 39.
Fagbongbe. M, 'The Future Of Women's Rights From A TWAIL Perspective' (2008) 10 *International Community Law Review* 401.
Fakhri, M, 'Third World Sovereignty, Indigenous Sovereignty, And Food Sovereignty: Living With Sovereignty Despite The Map' (2019) *Transnational Legal Theory* 218.
Fasan, O, 'Commitment And Compliance In International Law: A Study Of The Implementation Of The WTO TRIPS Agreement In Nigeria And South Africa' (2012) 20 *African Journal of International and Comparative Law* 191.
Ferraz O, 'The Right To Health In The Courts Of Brazil: Worsening Health Inequities?' (2009) 11 *Health and Human Rights Journal* 33.
—— 'Human Rights And Healthcare' (2008) 5 *SCRIPT-ed* 611.
Fidler, D, 'Revolt Against Or From Within The West? TWAIL, The Developing World, And The Future Direction Of International Law' (2003) 2 *Chinese Journal of International Law* 29.
Fleury, S, 'Brazilian Sanitary Reform: Dilemmas Between The Instituing And The Institutionalized' (2009) 14 *Cien Saude Colet* 743.
Flynn, M, 'Public Production Of Anti-Retroviral Medicines In Brazil, 1990–2007' (2008) 39 *Development and Change* 513.
Foster, G, 'Opposing Forces In A Revolution In International Patent Protection: The U.S. And India In The Uruguay Round And Its Aftermath: Comment' (1998) 3 *UCLA Journal of International Law & Foreign Affairs* 283.
Freund, B, 'Oil Boom And Crisis In Contemporary Nigeria' (1978) 5 *Review of African Political Economy* 91.
Gadelha, C, 'Development, Health-Industrial Complex And Industrial Policy' (2006) 40 *Revista de Saúde Pública* 11.
Galvão, J, 'Access To Antiretroviral Drugs In Brazil' (2002) 360 *The Lancet* 1862.
—— 'Brazil And Access To HIV/AIDS Drugs: A Question Of Human Rights And Public Health' (2005) 95 *American Journal of Public Health* 1110.
Gathii, J, Richardson, H and Knop, K, 'Introduction To Symposium On Theorizing TWAIL Activism' (2016) 110 *AJIL Unbound* 18.
Gathii, J and Roth, B, 'Neoliberalism, Colonialism And International Governance: Decentering The International Law Of Governmental Legitimacy' (2000) 98 *Michigan Law Review* 1996.
Gathii, J, 'International Law And Eurocentricity' (1998) 9 *European Journal of International Law* 184.
—— 'Rejoinder: Twailing International Law' (2000) 98 *Michigan Law Review* 2066.
—— 'TWAIL: A Brief History Of Its Origins, Its Decentralized Network, And A Tentative Bibliography' (2011) 26 *Trade, Law and Development* 26.
Gilman, N, 'The New International Economic Order: A Reintroduction' (2015) 6 *Humanity* 1.
Gontijo, C, 'Changing The Patent System From The Paris Convention To The TRIPS Agreement: The Position Of Brazil' (2005) 26 *Global Issues Paper* 1.
Gopakumar, K, 'Product Patents And Access To Medicines In India: A Critical Review Of The Implementation Of TRIPS Patent Regime' (2010) 3 *The Law and Development Review* 326.
—— 'The Need To Curb Patents On Known Substances' (2013) 48 *Economic and Political Weekly* 55.

Gopakumar, K and T Amin, 'Patents (Amendment) Bill 2005: A Critique' (2005) 40 *Economic and Political Weekly* 1503.
Grangeiro, A, Teixeira, L, Bastos, F and Teixeira, P, 'Sustainability Of Brazilian Policy For Access To Antiretroviral Drugs' (2006) 40 *Revisita de Saude Publica* 60.
Greco, D and Simao, M, 'Brazilian Policy Of Universal Access To AIDS Treatment: Sustainability Challenges And Perspectives' (2007) 21 *AIDS* 37.
Grover, A, 'Analysing The Supreme Court Judgment' (2013) 48 *Economic and Political Weekly* [x].
Halewood, M, 'Regulating Patent Holders: Local Working Requirements And Compulsory Licences At International Law' (1997) 35 *Osgoode Hall Law Journal* 243.
Helfer, L, 'Regime Shifting: The TRIPS Agreement And New Dynamics Of International Intellectual Property Lawmaking' (2004) 9 *Yale Journal of International Law* 1.
Hettinger, E, 'Justifying Intellectual Property' (1989) 18 *Philosophy & Public Affairs* 31.
Hippolyte, A, 'Correcting TWAIL'S Blind Spots' (2016) 18 *International Community Law Review* 34.
Homedes, N and Ugalde, A, 'Improving Access To Pharmaceuticals In Brazil And Argentina' (2006) 21 *Health Policy and Planning* 123.
Hunt, A, 'The Theory of Critical Legal Studies' (1986) 6 *Oxford Journal of Legal Studies* 1.
Iwuagwu, O, 'Nigeria And The Challenge Of Industrial Development' (2009) 37 *African Economic History* 151.
Jones, P, 'When 'Development' Devastates: Donor Discourses, Access To HIV/AIDS Treatment In Africa And Rethinking The Landscape Of Development' (2004) 25 *Third World Quarterly* 385.
Jouannet, E, 'Universalism And Imperialism: The True-False Paradox Of International Law?' (2007) 18 *European Journal of International Law* 379.
Kangave, J, 'Taxing' TWAIL: A Preliminary Inquiry Into TWAIL's Application To The Taxation Of Foreign Direct Investment' (2008) 10 *International Community Law Review* 389.
Kapczynski, A, Park, C and Sampat, B, 'Polymorphs And Prodrugs And Salts (Oh My!): An Empirical Analysis Of "Secondary" Pharmaceutical Patents' (2012) 7 *PLoS ONE* 1.
—— 'Engineered In India – Patent Law 2.0' (2013) 369 *New England Journal of Medicine* 497.
—— 'Harmonization And Its Discontents' (2009) 97 *California Law Review* 1571.
Khosla, M, 'The TWAIL Discourse: The Emergence Of A New Phase' (2007) 9 *International Community Law Review* 291.
Kiyani, A, 'Third World Approaches To International Criminal Law' (2016) 109 *AJIL Unbound* 255.
Kleinert, S and Horton, R, 'Brazil: Towards Sustainability And Equity In Health' (2011) 377 *The Lancet* 1721.
Kongolo, T, 'Public Interest Versus The Pharmaceutical Industry's Monopoly In South Africa' (2005) 4 *The Journal of World Intellectual Property* 609.
Koskenniemi, M, 'The Fate Of Public International Law: Between Technique And Politics' (2007) 70 *Modern Law Review* 1.
Koskenniemi, M and Leino, P, 'Fragmentation Of International Law? Postmodern Anxieties' (1999) 15 *Leiden Journal of International Law* 553.
Lanjouw, J, 'Intellectual Property And The Availability Of Pharmaceuticals In Poor Countries' (2002) Center for Global Development Working Paper No 5.
—— 'The Introduction Of Pharmaceutical Product Patents In India: "Heartless Exploitation Of The Poor And Suffering"?' (1998) National Bureau of Economic Research, Working Paper No 6366.
Lath, A, 'Analysing The Pitfalls Of Indian Patent Injunctions Based On Fear Of Infringement' (2014) 19 *Journal of Intellectual Property Rights* 253.
Levi, G and Vitória, M, 'Fighting Against AIDS: The Brazilian Experience' (2002) 16 *AIDS* 2373.
Levy, M and Rizansky Nir, A, 'The Pricing Of Breakthrough Drugs: Theory And Policy Implications' (2014) 9 *PLoS ONE* [x].
Lewis, P, 'From Prebendalism To Predation: The Political Economy Of Decline In Nigeria' (1996) 34 *The Journal of Modern African Studies* 79.

Lokanathan P, 'The Bombay Plan' (1945) *Foreign Affairs* 23.

Loup, G, de Assis, A, Costa-Couto, MH, Fleury, S, de Camargo Jr, K and Thoenig, JC, 'The Brazilian Experience Of 'Scaling Up': A Public Policy Approach' in B Coriat (ed), *The Political Economy Of HIV/AIDS In Developing Countries: TRIPS, Public Health Systems, and Free Access* (London, Elgar Edward Publishing, 2008).

Low, P, 'WTO Decision-Making For The Future' (2011) World Trade Organization, Working Paper Series.

Mahajan, M, 'Designing Epidemics: Models, Policy-Making, And Global Foreknowledge In India's AIDS Epidemic' (2008) 35 *Science and Public Policy* 585.

Marcus, G, 'Ethnography In/Of The World System: The Emergence Of Multi-Sited Ethnography' (1995) 24 *Annual Review of Anthropology* 95.

Maskus, K, 'Intellectual Property Challenges For Developing Countries: An Economic Perspective' (2001) 457 *University of Illinois Law Review* 457.

Matthews, D, 'From The August 30, 2003 WTO Decision To The December 6, 2005 Agreement On An Amendment To TRIPS Improving Access To Medicines In Developing Countries' [2006] 2 *Intellectual Property Quarterly* 91.

Mayer, C, 'The Brazilian Pharmaceutical Industry Goes Walking From Ipanema To Prosperity: Will The New Intellectual Property Law Spur Domestic Investment?' (1998) 12 *Temple International and Comparative Law Journal* 377.

Mbao, M and Osinibi, O, 'Confronting The Problems Of Colonialism, Ethnicity And The Nigerian Legal System: The Need For A Paradigm Shift' (2014) *Mediterranean Journal of Social Sciences* 168.

Mendes, A, Bertella, M and Teixeira, R, 'Industrialization In Sub-Saharan Africa And Import Substitution Policy' (2014) 34 *Brazilian Journal of Political Economy* 120.

Menescal, A, 'Changing WIPO's Ways? The 2004 Development Agenda In Historical Perspective' (2005) 8 *Journal of World Intellectual Property* 761.

Menghaney, L, 'Drop The Case' (2013) 48 *Economic and Political Weekly* 52.

Menon, P, 'Self-Referring To The International Criminal Court: A Continuation Of War By Other Means' (2016) 109 *AJIL Unbound* 260.

Mgbeoji, I, 'The Civilised Self And The Barbaric Other: Imperial Delusions Of Order And The Challenges Of Human Security' (2006) 27 *Third World Quarterly* 855.

Mickelson, K, 'Rhetoric And Rage: Third World Voices In International Legal Discourse' (1998) 16 *Wisconsin International Law Journal* 353.

—— 'Taking Stock Of TWAIL Histories' (2008) 10 *International Community Law Review* 355.

Monateri, P, 'Black Gaius: A Quest For The Multicultural Origins Of The 'Western Legal Tradition' (2000) 51 *Hastings Law Journal* 479.

Moser, P, 'Patents And Innovation: Evidence From Economic History' (2013) 27 *Journal of Economic Perspectives* 23.

Mueller, J, 'The Tiger Awakens: The Tumultuous Transformation Of India's Patent System And The Rise Of Indian Pharmaceutical Innovation' (2007) 68 *University of Pittsburgh Law Review* 491.

Mutua, M, 'Savages, Victims, And Saviors: The Metaphor Of Human Rights' (2001) 42 *Harvard International Law Journal* 201.

—— 'Why Redraw The Map Of Africa: A Moral And Legal Inquiry' (1995) 16 *Michigan Journal of International Law* 1113.

Muzaka, V, 'Developing Countries And The Struggle On The Access To Medicines Front: Victories Won And Lost' (2009) 30 *Third World Quarterly* 1343.

—— 'The State As Facilitator And Legitimator Of 'New' Capital Accumulation: The Case Of Patent Reform In India' (2015) 20 *Journal of International Relations and Development* 434.

Natarajan, U, Reynolds, J, Bhatia, A and Xavier, S, 'Introduction: TWAIL – On Praxis And The Intellectual' (2016) 37 *Third World Quarterly* 1946.

Nesiah, V, 'The Ground Beneath Her Feet: Third World Feminisms' (2003) 4 *Journal of International Women's Studies* 30.

Ngugi, J, 'Making New Wine For Old Wineskins: Can The Reform Of International Law Emancipate The Third World In The Age Of Globalization' (2002) 8 *UC Davis Journal of International Law and Policy* 73.

—— 'The World Bank And The Ideology Of Reform And Development In International Economic Development Discourse' (2006) 14 *Cardozo Journal of International and Comparative Law* 313.

Nunn, A, Dickman, S, Nattrass, N and Cornwall, A, 'The Impacts Of AIDS Movements On The Policy Responses To HIV/AIDS In Brazil And South Africa: A Comparative Analysis' (2012) 7 *Global Public Health* 89.

Nunn, A, Fonseca, E and Gruskin, S, 'Changing Global Essential Medicines Norms To Improve Access To AIDS Treatment: Lessons From Brazil' (2009) 4 *Global Public Health* 131.

O'Brien, P, 'Developing Countries And The Patent System: An Economic Appraisal' (1974) 2 *World Development* 27.

Oddi, A, 'The International Patent System And Third World Development: Reality Or Myth?' (1987) 1987 *Duke Law Journal* 831.

Odumosu, I, 'Challenges For The (Present/) Future Of Third World Approaches To International Law' (2008) 10 *International Community Law Review* 467.

Ogaji, J, Alawode, A and Iranloye, T, 'Pharmaceutical Industry Capacity Utilization In Nigeria' (2014) 8 *African Journal of Pharmacy and Pharmacology* 579.

Ogbuagu, C, 'The Nigerian Indigenization Policy: Nationalism Or Pragmatism' (1983) 82 *African Affairs* 241.

Oguamanam, C, 'IP In Global Governance: A Venture In Critical Reflection' (2011) 2 *World Intellectual Property Organization Journal* 196.

—— 'Patents And Pharmaceutical R&D: Consolidating Private-Public Partnership Approach To Global Public Health Crises' (2010) 13 *The Journal of World Intellectual Property* 556.

—— 'Patents And Traditional Medicine: Digital Capture, Creative Legal Interventions, And The Dialectics Of Knowledge Transformation' (2008) 15 *Indiana Journal of Global Legal Studies* 489.

Okafor, O, 'Enacting Twailian Praxis In Nonacademic Habitats: Toward A Conceptual Framework' (2016) 110 *AJIL Unbound* 20.

—— 'Newness, Imperialism And International Legal Reform In Our Time: A TWAIL Perspective' (2005) 43 *Osgoode Hall Law Journal* 171.

Okediji R, 'Back To Bilateralism? Pendulum Swings In International Intellectual Property Protection' (2004) 1 *University of Ottawa Law and Technology Journal* 125.

—— 'Legal Innovation In International Intellectual Property Relations: Revisiting Twenty-One Years Of The TRIPS Agreement' (2014) 36 *University of Pennsylvania Journal of International Law* 191.

—— 'The International Relations Of Intellectual Property: Narratives Of Developing Country Participation In The Global Intellectual Property System' (2003) 7 *Singapore Journal of International and Comparative Law* 225.

Oliveira, M, 'Has The Implementation Of The TRIPS Agreement In Latin America And The Caribbean Produced Intellectual Property Legislation That Favours Public Health?' (2004) 82 *Bulletin of World Health Organization* 815.

Osuji, O and O Umahi, 'Pharmaceutical Companies And Access To Medicines – Social Integration And Ethical CSR Resolution Of A Global Public Choice Problem' (2012) 8 *Journal of Global Ethics* 139.

Otto, D, 'Postcolonialism And Law?' (2000) 15 *Third World Legal Studies* 337.

—— 'Subalternity And International Law: The Problems Of Global Community And The Incommensurability Of Difference' (1996) 5 *Social and Legal Studies* 337.

Oyedepo, O, 'The Impact Of TRIPS Agreement On Patent Law In Nigeria' (2010) 2 *Confluence Journal of Private and Property Law* [x].

Oyewunmi, A, 'Health Access To Medicines And Intellectual Property Options For African Countries In Light Of The WTO TRIPS Agreement' (2013) 1 *Journal of International Law and Diplomacy* [x].

Palombi, L, 'The Role Of Patent Law In Regulating And Restricting Access To Medicines' (2009) 6 *SCRIPTed* 394.

Parker, R, 'Civil Society, Political Mobilization, And The Impact Of HIV Scale-Up On Health Systems In Brazil' (2009) 52 *Journal of Acquired Immune Deficiency Syndromes* 49.

Parmar, P, 'TWAIL: An Epistemological Inquiry' (2008) 10 *International Community Law Review* 363.

Patel, S, 'Intellectual Property Rights In The Uruguay Round: A Disaster For The South?' (1989) 24 *Economic and Political Weekly* 978.

Penrose, E, 'International Patenting And The Less-Developed Countries' (1973) 83 *The Economic Journal* 768.

Peterson, K, 'Benefit Sharing For All?: Bioprospecting Ngos, Intellectual Property Rights, New Governmentalities.' (2001) 24 *Political and Legal Anthropology Review* 78.

—— 'On The Monopoly: Speculation, Pharmaceutical Markets, And Intellectual Property Law In Nigeria' (2014) 41 *American Ethnologist* 128.

Pogge, T, 'Human Rights And Global Health: A Research Program' (2005) 36 *Metaphilosophy* 182.

Poulsen, L, 'Bounded Rationality And The Diffusion Of Modern Investment Treaties' (2013) 58 *International Studies Quarterly* 1.

Purvis, N, 'Critical Legal Studies In Public International Law' (1991) 32 *Harvard International Law Journal* 81.

Ragavan, S, 'A "Patent" Restriction On Research & Development: Infringers Or Innovators?' (2004) 1 *Journal of Law, Technology & Policy* 73.

—— 'Can't We All Get Along – The Case For A Workable Patent Model' (2003) 35 *Arizona State Law Journal* 117.

—— 'Of The Inequals Of Uruguay Rounds' (2006) 10 *Marquette Intellectual Property Law Review* 273.

Rahmatian, A, 'Neo-Colonial Aspects Of Global Intellectual Property Protection' (2009) 12 *The Journal of World Intellectual Property* 40.

Rajagopal, B, 'Counter-Hegemonic International Law: Rethinking Human Rights And Development As A Third World Strategy' (2006) 27 *Third World Quarterly* 767.

—— 'International Law And Social Movement' (2003) 41 *Columbia Journal of Transnational Law* 397.

—— 'Locating The Third World In Cultural Geography' (1999) 15 *Third World Legal Studies* 1.

Randeria, S, 'Cunning States And Unaccountable International Institutions: Legal Plurality, Social Movements And Rights Of Local Communities To Common Property Resources' (2003) 44 *European Journal of Sociology* 27.

Rangnekar, D, 'Context And Ambiguity In The Making Of Law: A Comment On Amending India's Patent Act' (2007) 10 *The Journal of World Intellectual Property* 365.

—— 'No Pills For Poor People: Understanding Disembowelment Of India's Patent Regime' (2006) 41 *Economics and Political Weekly* 409.

—— 'The Supreme Court Judgment: Lawmaking In The South' (2013) 48 *Economic and Political Weekly* 39.

Reichman, J, 'Comment: Compulsory Licensing Of Patented Pharmaceutical Inventions: Evaluating The Options' (2009) 37 *The Journal of Law, Medicine & Ethics* 247.

Rodrigues Jr, E and Murphy, B, 'Brazil's Prior Consent Law: A Dialogue Between Brazil And The United States Over Where The TRIPS Agreement Currently Sets The Balance Between The Protection Of Pharmaceutical Patents And Access To Medicines' (2006) 16 *Albany Law Journal of Science and Technology* 423.

Roffe, P, 'Abuses Of Patent Monopoly: A Legal Appraisal' (1974) 2 *World Development* 15.

Sagar, R, 'Introduction Of Exclusive Privileges/Patents In Colonial India: Why And For Whose Benefit?' (2007) 2 *Intellectual Property Quarterly* 164.

Salama, B and Benoliel, D, 'Pharmaceutical Patent Bargains: The Brazilian Experience' (2010) 18 *Cardozo Journal of International and Comparative Law* 633.

Sampat, B and Shadlen, K, 'Patent Watch: Drug Patenting In India: Looking Back And Looking Forward' (2015) 14 *Nature Reviews Drug Discovery* 519.
—— 'TRIPS Implementation And Secondary Pharmaceutical Patenting In Brazil And India' (2015) 50 *Studies in Comparative International Development* 228.
Santos, A, 'Carving Out Policy Autonomy For Developing Countries In The World Trade Organization: The Experience Of Brazil & Mexico' (2012) 52 *Virginia Journal Of International Law* 551.
Sanyal, A, 'The Curious Case Of The Bombay Plan' (2010) 6 *Contemporary Issues and Ideas in Social Sciences* 1.
Scherer, F and Watal, J, 'Post-TRIPS Options For Access To Patented Medicines In Developing Nations' (2002) 5 *Journal of International Economic Law* 913.
Seckelmann, M, 'From The Paris Convention (1883) To The TRIPS Agreement (1994): The History Of The International Patent Agreements As A History Of Propertisation?' (2013) 14 *Journal der Juristischen Zeitgeschichte* [x].
Sell, S and Prakash, A, 'Using Ideas Strategically: The Contest Between Business And NGO Networks In Intellectual Property Rights' (2004) 48 *International Studies Quarterly* 143.
Sell, S and May, C, 'Moments In Law: Contestation And Settlement In The History Of Intellectual Property' (2001) 8 *Review of International Political Economy* 467.
Sell, S, 'Intellectual Property Protection And Antitrust In The Developing World: Crisis, Coercion, And Choice' (1995) 49 *International Organization* 315.
—— 'The Quest For Global Governance In Intellectual Property And Public Health: Structural, Discursive, And Institutional Dimensions' (2004) 77 *Temple Law Review* 363.
Sengupta, A, 'Two Decades Of Struggle' (2013) 48 *Economic and Political Weekly* 43.
Shadlen, K, 'The Politics Of Patents And Drugs In Brazil And Mexico: The Industrial Bases Of Health Policies' (2009) 42 *Comparative Politics* 41.
—— 'The Political Contradictions Of Incremental Innovation: Lessons From Pharmaceutical Patent Examination In Brazil' (2011) 39 *Politics & Society* 143.
Shaffer, G, Sanchez, M and Rosenberg, B, 'The Trials Of Winning At The WTO: What Lies Behind Brazil'S Success' (2008) 41 *Cornell International Law Journal* 383.
Shanker, D, 'India, The Pharmaceutical Industry And The Validity Of TRIPS' (2002) 5 *The Journal of World Intellectual Property* 315.
Shanker, D, 'Brazil, The Pharmaceutical Industry And The WTO' (2002) 5 *The Journal of World Intellectual Property* 53.
Shearing, C and Wood, J, 'Nodal Governance, Democracy, And The New 'Denizens' (2003) 30 *Journal of Law and Society* 400.
Slaughter, A and Burke-White, W, 'The Future Of International Law Is Domestic (Or The European Way Of Law)' (2006) 47 *Harvard Journal of International Law* 327.
Sreejith, S, 'An Auto-Critique Of TWAIL's Historical Fallacy: Sketching An Alternative Manifesto' (2016) 38 *Third World Quarterly* 1511.
Stiglitz, J, 'Economic Foundations Of Intellectual Property Rights' (2008) 57 *Duke Law Journal* 1693.
Sunter, A, 'TWAIL As Naturalized Epistemological Inquiry' (2007) 20 *Canadian Journal of Law and Jurisprudence* 475.
Trubek, D, Coutinho, D and Schapiro, M, 'Toward A New Law And Development: New State Activism In Brazil And The Challenge For Legal Institutions' (2012) *Legal Studies Research Paper Series Paper No 1207 World Bank Legal Review*.
Turner, T, 'Multinational Corporations And The Instability Of The Nigerian State' (1976) 3 *Review of African Political Economy* 63.
Tushnet, M, 'Critical Legal Studies: A Political History' (1991) 100 *The Yale Law Journal* 1515.
Tzouvala, N, 'TWAIL And The "Unwilling Or Unable" Doctrine: Continuities And Ruptures' (2016) 109 *AJIL Unbound* 266.
Unger, R, 'The Critical Legal Studies Movement' (1983) 96 *Harvard Law Review* 561.

Vaitsos, C, 'Patents Revisited: Their Function In Developing Countries' (1972) 9 *The Journal of Development Studies* 71.

Wade, R, 'Current Thinking About Global Trade Policy' (2014) 49 *Economic and Political Weekly* 18.

Walterscheid, E, 'The Early Evolution Of The United States Patent Law: Antecedents (Part 1)' (1994) 76 *Journal of the Patent and Trademark Office Society* 697.

Weyland, K, 'The Rise And Fall Of President Collor And Its Impact On Brazilian Democracy' (1993) 35 *Journal of Interamerican Studies and World Affairs* 1.

Williams, O, 'Access To Medicines, Market Failure And Market Intervention: A Tale Of Two Regimes' (2012) 7 *Global Public Health: An International Journal for Research, Policy and Practice* 127.

Wolfe, R, 'The WTO Single Undertaking As Negotiating Technique And Constitutive Metaphor' [2009] *Journal of International Economic Law* 835.

Xavier, S, Bhatia, A, Natarajan, U and Reynolds, J, 'Placing TWAIL Scholarship and Praxis' (2017) 33 *Windsor Yearbook of Access to Justice* v.

Xavier, S, Bhatia, A, Natarajan, U and Reynolds, J, 'Conspiring In Cairo & Canada: Placing TWAIL Scholarship And Praxis' (2017) 33 *Windsor Yearbook of Access to Justice* i.

Xavier, S, 'Learning From Below: Theorising Global Governance Through Ethnographies And Critical Reflections From The Global South' (2017) 33 *Windsor Yearbook of Access to Justice* 231.

Yauri, S, 'The Patent System In Nigeria' (2012) 34 *World Patent Information* 213.

Yu, P, 'A Tale Of Two Development Agendas' (2009) 35 *Ohio Northern University Law Review* 465.

Zoli, C, 'Islamic Contributions To International Humanitarian Law: Recalibrating TWAIL Approaches For Existing Contributions And Legacies' (2016) 109 *AJIL Unbound* 271.

MAGAZINE ARTICLES

Gahlot, M, 'High-Risk Behaviour: Government Apathy Leaves India's AIDS Programme In Crisis' in *The Caravan* (1 April 2015).

NEWSPAPER ARTICLES

Esdiake, B, 'Nigeria's HIV/AIDS Fight Gulps Billions Of Dollars, Yields Little' *Telegraph Newspaper* (28 October 2013)

Harris, G, 'Medicines Made In India Set Off Safety Worries' *New York Times* (14 February 2014).

Harris, G and Thomas, K, 'Low-Cost Drugs In Poor Nations Get A Lift In Indian Court' *New York Times* (1 August 2013).

Thakurta, P, 'Bombay Plan And Mixed-Up Economy' *The Hindu Businessline* (7 September 2004).

Timmons, H, 'India Expands Role As Drug Producer' *New York Times* (6 July 2010).

PRESENTATIONS OR LECTURES

Adewopo, A, 'According To Intellectual Property: A Pro-Development Vision Of The Law And The Nigerian Intellectual Property Law And Policy Reform In The Knowledge Era', Nigerian Institute of Advanced Legal Studies (Lagos): 5th Inaugural Lecture (2012).

Akunyili, D, 'Counterfeit And Substandard Drugs, Nigeria's Experience: Implications, Challenges, Actions And Recommendations' (Washington DC, World Bank, 2005).

Koskenmiemi, M, 'Histories Of International Law: Dealing With Eurocentrism' (Utrecht University, 2011).

Soludo, C, 'Can Nigeria's Manufacturing And Pharmaceutical Industry Compete?', National Conference of the Nigerian Association of Industrial Pharmacists, Lagos, Nigeria (2011).

Stiglitz, J, 'More Instruments And Broader Goals: Moving Toward The Post–Washington Consensus', WIDER Annual Lecture Helsinki, Finland (1998).

REPORTS

Centre for IPR Promotion and Management (CIPAM), 'Intellectual Property Rights Regime In India – An Overview' (The Centre for IPR Promotion and Management (CIPAM) at the Department of Industrial Policy and Promotion, 2018).

Chang, H, 'Kicking Away The Ladder: The "Real" History Of Free Trade' (Foreign Policy In Focus, 2003).

Chaturvedi, K, 'Policy And Technology Co-Evolution In The Indian Pharmaceutical Industry' (Open University, 2005).

Chaudhuri, S, 'TRIPS And Changes In Pharmaceutical Patent Regime In India' (World Health Organization, 2005).

Chete, L, Adeoti, J, Adeyinka, F and Ogundele, O, 'Industrial Development And Growth In Nigeria: Lessons And Challenges' (The Brookings Institute, 2012).

Deloitte, 'India: 2015 Health Outlook' (Deloitte, 2015).

Department of Trade and Industry, Republic of South Africa, 'Draft National Policy On Intellectual Property (IP) Of South Africa: A Policy Framework' (Department of Trade and Industry, Republic of South Africa, 2014).

Deutsche Bank, 'Indian Pharmaceutical Industry On Course For Globalization' (Deutsche Bank, 2008).

Drahos, P and Braithwaite, J, 'Who Owns The Knowledge Economy? Political Organising Behind TRIPS' (The Corner House, 2004).

Economic and Political Weekly, 'Intellectual Property Rights: The Geneva Surrender' (Economic and Political Weekly, 1989).

Ezell, S and Atkinson, R, 'The Indian Economy At A Crossroads' (Information Technology & Innovation Foundation, 2014).

Frost and Sullivan, 'Pharmaceutical Industry In Ghana And Nigeria' (Frost & Sullivan, 2011).

Grupo De Trabalho Sobre Propriedade Intelectual Opposition (GTPI), 'Opposition, Sofosbuvir, (Pi0410846 9 E Divisionais (Pi0419342 -3, Pi0419343 -1, Pi0419344 -0, Pi0419345 8) Wo2005003147)' (Patent Opposition Database 2015).

Gumel, F, 'Investment Opportunities In The Pharmaceutical Sector – Nigeria/Pakistan' (PwC, 2014).

Hoffmann, L and Nelly, P, 'Nigeria's Booming Borders: The Drivers And Consequences Unrecorded Trade?' (Chatham House, 2015).

International Chamber of Commerce Business Action to Stop Counterfeiting and Piracy (ICC BASCAP), 'Promoting And Protecting Intellectual Property In Nigeria' (International Chamber of Commerce Business Action to Stop Counterfeiting and Piracy (ICC BASCAP), 2015).

International Crisis Group, 'Nigeria: Want In The Midst Of Plenty' (International Crisis Group, 2006).

Mashelkar, R, Mehta, G, Datta, A, Menon, N and Sharma, M, 'Report Of The Technical Expert Group On Patent Law Issues' (Department of Industrial Policy and Promotion, Government of India, 2006).

Médecins Sans Frontières, 'The Impact Of Patents On Access To Medicines' (1997).

Multilateral Trade Negotiation: Uruguay Round (MTN/TNC/MIN(90)/ST/46), 'Statement By Dr. Subramanian Swamy, Union Minister Of Commerce, Law And Justice' (1990).

National Agency for the Control of AIDS (NACA), 'National HIV/AIDS Epidemiology And Impact Analysis (Nheia) Report' (National Agency for the Control of AIDS (NACA), 2014).

National Centre for Economic Management & Administration (NCEMA), 'Understanding Structural Adjustment Programme In Nigeria' (Global Development Network (GDN), 2004).

Office of the United States Trade Representative, 'The Special 301 Report' (2016).

Onoka, C, Onwujekwe, O, Hanson, K and Uzochukwu, B, 'Measuring Catastrophic Health Care Expenditures In Nigeria: Implications For Financial Risk Protection' (CREHS, 2010).

Organisation for Economic Co-operation and Development (OECD), 'OECD Health Statistics 2014' (OECD, 2014).

Organisation for Economic Co-operation and Development (OECD), 'Public Sector Integrity In Brazil' (OECD Secretariat, 2011).

Padmashree, G, 'Economic Aspects Of Access To Medicine After 2005: Product Patent Protection & Emerging Firm Strategies In The Indian Pharmaceutical Industry' (Commission on Intellectual Property Rights, Innovation and Public Health (CIPIH), 2005).

Peterson, K and Obileye, O, 'Access To Drugs For HIV/AIDS And Related Opportunistic Infections In Nigeria' (US Agency for International Development, 2002).

'Report Of The Patent Enquiry I' (1950).

Shri, Justice N Rajagopala Ayyangar, 'Report On The Revision Of The Patent Laws' (Government of India, 1959).

Statement by H E Mr Celso Amorim Minister of External Relations, 'General Agreement On Trade And Tariffs: Multilateral Trade Negotiations Group Frameworks (MTN.TNC/MIN(94)/ST/101)' (1995).

Statement by H E Mr Marcos Castrioto de Azambuia, Special Representative of the President of the Republic, General Secretary for Foreign Policy, 'General Agreement On Trade And Tariffs: Multilateral Trade Negotiations Group Frameworks (MTN.TNC/MIN(90)/ST/38' (1990).

Statement by the Representative of Brazil, Ambassador George Marciel, 'General Agreement On Trade And Tariffs: Multilateral Trade Negotiations Group Frameworks' (1977).

Templars Law Firm, 'Patentability Under The Nigerian Patents And Designs Act (PDA): An Introductory Analysis' (2012).

The National Institute for Health Care Management Research and Educational Foundation, 'Changing Patterns Of Pharmaceutical Innovation.' (NIHCM Foundation, 2002).

The Office of the United States Trade Representative (USTR), 'The Special 301 Report' (United States Government 2016).

Ukpanah, S, 'Statement At The Ministerial Level Meeting In Brussels (MTN.TNC/MIN (90)/ST/34, Multilateral Trade Negotiations, Uruguay Rounds)' (1990).

United Kingdom Department for International Development, 'DFID Nigeria: Operational Plan 2011–2015' (DFID, 2015).

United Nations Conference on Trade and Development, 'Report On The TRIPS Agreement And Developing Countries' (United Nations, 1996).

United Nations Development Program, 'The United Nations Secretary-General's High-Level Panel on Access to Medicines Report' (United Nations Development Program, 2016).

United Nations General Assembly, 'Declaration On The Establishment Of A New International Economic Order (3201 (S-VI)' (United Nations, 1974).

United Nations Programme on HIV/AIDS (UNAIDS), 'The Brazilian Response To HIV And AIDS' (UNAIDS, 2015).

United States Department of State, 'Nigeria Malaria Fact Sheet' (United States Embassy, Nigeria 2011).

Wambebe, C and Ochekpe, N, 'Pharmaceutical Sector Profile: Nigeria' (United Nations Industrial Development Organization (UNIDO), 2011).

World Intellectual Property Organization, 'World Intellectual Property Indicators 2017' (WIPO, 2017).

World Trade Organization, 'Trade Policy Review: Nigeria' (WTO, 2011).

—— 'Agreement On Trade-Related Aspects Of Intellectual Property Rights' (Geneva, World Trade Organization, 1990).

Yu, P, 'Are Developing Countries Playing A Better TRIPS Game?' (Social Science Research Network, 2013).

WORKING PAPERS

Baker, B and Avafia, T, 'The Evolution Of IPRS From Humble Beginnings To The Modern Day TRIPS-Plus Era: Implications For Treatment Access' (2011) Working Paper prepared for the Third Meeting of the Technical Advisory Group of the Global Commission on HIV and the Law, 7–9 July 2011, Global Commission on HIV and the Law.

Dreyfuss, R, 'The Role Of India, China, Brazil And Other Emerging Economies In Establishing Access Norms For Intellectual Property And Intellectual Property Lawmaking' (2009) Institute for International Law and Justice (IILJ) Working Paper.

Orford, A, 'The Past As Law Or History? The Relevance Of Imperialism For Modern International Law' (2012) 2 IILJ Working Paper.

Index